July 18th, 2018

Tai sweetly ripped
this page which
acknowledge his ole Nest!

Exploring Religion and Diversity in Canada

Catherine Holtmann
Editor

Exploring Religion and Diversity in Canada

People, Practice and Possibility

 Springer

Editor
Catherine Holtmann
Sociology Department
University of New Brunswick
Fredericton, New Brunswick, Canada

ISBN 978-3-319-78231-7   ISBN 978-3-319-78232-4   (eBook)
https://doi.org/10.1007/978-3-319-78232-4

Library of Congress Control Number: 2018942902

Printed on acid-free paper

This Springer imprint is published by the registered company Springer International Publishing AG part
of Springer Nature.
The registered company address is: Gewerbestrasse 11, 6330 Cham, Switzerland

Acknowledgments

The editor and contributors to this volume would like to acknowledge the extraordinary support they have received from Dr. Lori Beaman and the Religion and Diversity Project team members (www.religionanddiversity.ca). This support came in many forms including leadership, critical engagement, mentoring, professional development opportunities, access to funding for research and workshops, research collaborations, co-authored publications, and editorial experience. The words of contributor, Amélie Barras, who completed a postdoctoral fellowship with Lori Beaman, capture the how the opportunities provided by the Religion and Diversity Project impacted our scholarship:

> Religion and Diversity Project events were a fantastic opportunity to meet and develop relationships with scholars throughout Canada working on religion and diversity. It was also a way for me to have first-hand experience of how collaborative Canadian research projects are developed and carried out. As an assistant professor today, these experiences acted as an invaluable roadmap.

We also want to thank Emma Robinson, a graduate student at the University of New Brunswick, for her fine work on the organizational details of the manuscript, communication with the contributors, copy editing, and formatting.

We are grateful to the reviewers whose comments helped to improve the chapters in this publication. Finally, many thanks to the staff at Springer for their support in making this emerging scholarship on religious diversity in Canada affordably available to students.

February 2018   Catherine Holtmann

Contents

Introduction

Catherine Holtmann

Keywords Religious diversity · Social inequality · Homogenization · Learning resources · Critical reflection · Identities · Concepts · Politics · Complexity

I will never forget the email I got from Heather Shipley inviting me to create a Facebook page for the Religion and Diversity Project student caucus. It was no problem to create the page (https://www.facebook.com/RDPStudents/) but accepting the invitation from Heather, the Project's manager, was a big deal. It was my formal entry into the Religion and Diversity Project, a research program funded by the Social Sciences and Humanities Research Council of Canada on issues of religious diversity in Canada and abroad from a variety of perspectives including religion, law, communication, sociology, history, political science, education and philosophy, under the direction of Lori Beaman at the University of Ottawa. For seven years, scholars associated with the Project explored the questions:

1. How are religious identities socially constructed?
2. How is religious expression defined and delimited in law and public policy?
3. How and why do gender and sexuality act as flashpoints in debates on religious freedom?
4. What are alternative strategies for managing religious diversity?

Religion has become a prominent topic in public discourse, politics and international affairs, and for most of the contributors to this book the Religion and Diversity Project was a big deal because it provided a magnificent training milieu for our academic careers.

The Religion and Diversity Project consisted of a core team of thirty-seven established researchers of international repute, their graduate students, and staff. Through team meetings, workshops, public lectures, and conferences we got to know each other personally, learn about and share our research interests, take part in training opportunities, apply for research funding, expand our scholarly networks, engage in

C. Holtmann (✉)
Sociology Department, University of New Brunswick, Fredericton, New Brunswick, Canada
e-mail: cathy.holtmann@unb.ca

© Springer International Publishing AG, part of Springer Nature 2018
C. Holtmann (ed.), *Exploring Religion and Diversity in Canada*,
https://doi.org/10.1007/978-3-319-78232-4_1

critical conversations about key questions and controversies in the field, and collaborate on projects. Intense scholarly exchange was always evident as members of the Project wrestled with concepts that were either new to them or being considered in new ways. The fact that scholars were bringing perspectives from multiple national contexts—the issues that accompany religious diversity change depending on particular social, political and economic realities—made our academic exchanges themselves exercises in negotiating diversity. Much of the research that is the basis for the chapters in this book was funded by the Religion and Diversity Project. This edited collection provides a glimpse of some of the fruits of the Religion and Diversity Project largely from the perspectives of emerging scholars of religion in Canada.

Exploring Religion and Diversity in Canada: People, Practice and Possibility is organized according to themes and traditions related to religious diversity, from education to health care, from Christians to Muslims. Throughout the book, the contributors highlight concepts that are important in their fields of expertise. Although I will highlight a few of the concepts related to religion in this introduction, it is important to read and think about them in the chapters themselves in order to better understand how the concepts are used in relation to particular individuals and religious groups, or specific situations and contexts.

The category of religion has become problematic, given the mutually influencing and changing nature of religion and society. Many scholars of religion are asking critical questions about what should be the focus of our investigations. I interviewed James Spickard a few years ago as part of a series of short videos of scholars, religious leaders, and adherents speaking about religion that Nancy Nason-Clark and I created as teaching and learning resources <http://religionanddiversity.ca/en/projects-and-tools/projects/linking-classrooms/linking-classrooms-videos/>. Spickard suggests that there are at least six stories that indicate what is going on in the study of religion today: (1) religion is disappearing; (2) religion is becoming more conservative; (3) religion is increasingly congregational in form; (4) religion is more individualized than ever before; (5) the religious sphere is a marketplace offering different forms of religion to consumers; and (6) religion is globalized. At first glance, some of these stories appear to be contradictory—which is why coming to a critical understanding of religion in its contemporary manifestations is complex. In order to simplify things somewhat, I suggest that there are at least three trends in which elements of Spickard's six stories are embedded that contribute to the problematization of the category of religion. The advent of a global, networked, information society (Castells 2000) has contributed to two opposing trends, the process of homogenization of cultures and religion as well as the increasing heterogeneity of religious beliefs and practices. A third trend, related to the first two, is the rise of non-religion, as increasing proportions of people do not affiliate with any religious tradition or describe their beliefs and practices as religious or spiritual.

The homogenization of culture and religion means that in several ways religions are becoming more alike. Technological innovations enable people and information to travel rapidly around the globe. Using the internet, Canadians can easily access information about religion, particularly non-Christian religions. Our awareness of different religions is heightened as the religious diversity of our society increases due to immigration. For many students, the university is a much more multicultural and multi-faith space than was their local high school. Religious groups and individuals always adapt their practices to the social contexts of which they are a part. There is evidence that religious minority groups in Canada are reshaping aspects of their practices to conform to those of the Christian majority (Beyer and Ramji 2013). The adaptation of religious practices by minority groups can be understood as an effect of the pressure of Christian hegemony but it can also be viewed as strategic. Religious minorities seize opportunities to adapt to the congregational form which characterizes Christianity in order to position themselves favorably in relation to state policies on multiculturalism, religious freedom, and human rights as well as in relation to public opinion. Many Canadians associate Christians with regular attendance at churches and therefore expect that Hindus and Buddhists will worship in their temples and Muslims will visit their mosques on a weekly basis.

The homogenization of religion, however is not simply benign. Colonization is a violent project of cultural and religious homogenization through which Christianity and its values and practices are imposed on the colonized (Chidester 1996; Peterson and Walhof 2002). I write about the colonization process in the present tense, because it is ongoing and evident in the ways that public rhetoric and state interventions continue to distinguish between good and bad religions (Orsi 2005). Good religions are given state support such as the right to establish faith-based schools, but the state intervenes to curb bad religions such as banning certain religious symbols in the public sphere. Mainstream media sources reinforce the designation of good and bad religions when their reporting paints all members of a religious group with the same brush. News tends to focus on outliers within religious groups, usually the most conservative or radical, giving the impression that religions are essentially disruptive or destructive forces in society. If higher education has a role to play in the process of the homogenization of religions, this can be a constructive role in teaching that all religions have within them beliefs and practices that can be used for good or ill. Given my area of expertise is the intersection of religion and domestic violence, I think we can evaluate the social impact of religious practices and beliefs based on whether or not they are a source of harm or a source of liberation.

We have access to information on religion via the internet 24/7. This means that individuals and groups with the resources needed to spread information about religious teachings and practices are challenging the traditional authority of religious leaders. Individuals and groups can access information on religious teachings and practices with relative ease and are drawn to forms of religion that have widespread appeal. In this way, the religious marketplace caters to desires of the masses through their smart phones and iPads. To paraphrase McLuhan, the medium has become the message—religious seekers can surf the internet anywhere and anytime looking for forms of religion that fit with their lifestyle. This can contribute to the homogenization of religion, toning down its critical social function, especially those elements that critique consumerism, violence and environmental degradation.

Given the social pressures to conform, the rising heterogeneity of religious groups and the increasing diversity of religious beliefs and practices within religious traditions can be understood as forms of resistance to the global trend of cultural homogenization. Despite those that predict the disappearance of religion, religion continues to be a salient aspect of collective and individual identities. The internet and technological innovations have led to the proliferation of and widespread access to information about particular religious groups that would otherwise remain obscure. New religious movements are arising all the time. And although unmediated access to religious information can lead to the popular appropriation of religious messages and practices, it is also used to strengthen individual and collective commitment. Not only can religious people access sacred texts, commentaries, prayers, and music online but they can connect with other people in their religious group or with those who have similar spiritual goals through social media if they cannot do so face-to-face. In the face of seemingly unlimited choices, some people are choosing to limit their choices in order to follow strict forms of religious practice, such as Orthodox Jews or Salafi Muslims (Davidman 1991; Inge 2017). Individuals and groups choose to purposely foreground their religious identities in the face of social conditions in which the promises of science and democracy have not been fulfilled. Conservative or fundamentalist religious identities provide firm guidelines, stability and truth in an era of uncertainty and growing social inequality.

Religious groups can broadcast and podcast their services so that individuals can feel part of a congregation even if they cannot or choose not to physically participate. This is related to the phenomena called "believing without belonging" or "vicarious religion" (Davie 2007). Some people feel that religious groups have a role to play in society but they might only engage with religion periodically like when they want a religious wedding ceremony or funeral. Even leaders of secular states turn to religious language and practices in dealing with public tragedies such as terrorist attacks or mass shootings. Beyond congregational walls, home-centered faith sharing or spirituality groups can supplement or become the core of some people's religious practices. In these intimate gatherings, individual understandings of religious teachings can deepen and group members can hold one another accountable to maintain religious practices, especially if they are counter-cultural. This resistance to the homogenization of religion, especially in its institutional forms, is especially evident amongst women, whose religious beliefs and practices have historically been marginalized (Holtmann 2011) or take place under the radar of religious leaders (Gervais 2012). Some women who work for gender equality draw upon the resources of their faith traditions in order to address social problems such as domestic violence (Nason-Clark and Clark Kroeger 2010; Nason-Clark and Kroeger 2004).

Several chapters in this collection employ the concept of lived religion or everyday religion in order to capture the reality of day-to-day religious beliefs and practices of people in contrast to institutionally prescribed teachings and norms (Ammerman 2007; McGuire 2008). McGuire (2008) argues that this is not a new phenomenon—what constitutes authentic religious belief and practice has been contested throughout history. Questions of religious authenticity always involve power struggles. Lived religion is evidence of the healthy dialectic between individual and collective agency and religious and political institutional structures. That is why the subtitle of this book is *People, Practices and Possibility*—religion (and non-religion) as it is actually lived and practiced by Canadians is dynamic. Change is inevitable and exciting because it means that deep equality is possible (Beaman 2014). Widespread access to information about religion today has increased people's ability to craft their own approaches to religion without any necessary connection to or censure from religious institutions. Wise religious and political leaders who are aware of the power of the people, so to speak, are adapting accordingly.

This brings me to the concept of spirituality and its relationship with religion. During my Catholic theological studies, I learned that the relationship between religion and spirituality is like the relationship between bones and flesh— one needs both to be a healthy and whole person. Religion is associated with the structuring of religion—its rules, roles, texts and symbols—while spirituality is associated with the practicing of religion—one's body, emotions, thoughts, self-awareness, and sense of connection to others and the sacred. It makes sense that an institutionally grounded school of theology would promote this kind of understanding but sociological research concerning peoples' everyday religious practices indicates that the association between religion and spirituality is not so straightforward. Some people who describe themselves as deeply spiritual may or may not have a connection to a religious institution or group. Others who identify as members of a religious group may not engage in any kind of intentional spiritual practice. There are a range of possible combinations of religion and spirituality between these two examples.

The increasing number of people who do not identify with any particular religious tradition is the third trend in the contemporary study of religion. This group is of interest to scholars of religion because it is diverse and growing. Religious "nones" are comprised of atheists, non-theists, agnostics (those who have yet to decide where they stand about religion and the sacred), the spiritual but not religious, and those who do not attribute their beliefs and practices to religion yet whose lives resemble those of religious people. It is perhaps this group of people that are most impacted by the contemporary dynamics between religion and society—the opposing trends of homogenization and differentiation of religion. Perhaps they are even playing a role in driving these trends. In countries of the West, the domination of public discourse by the perspectives of politics, economics, and science (technology), has shoved religion to the side and many agree that is where it belongs. As consumers in a highly diverse religious marketplace, many people exercise their choice not to be religious. They reject, or at least choose not to use, religious or spiritual language to describe or give order to their everyday lives.

All of the chapters in this text will help you to further explore these complex trends within the academic study of religion. The structure of each chapter is similar in order to help facilitate your learning. The chapters include a real-life story based on empirical research. The stories we tell help us to make sense of our lives. In telling a story, religious and non-religious people assemble the different elements that arise from the relationships and situations that fill their days into a coherent whole. Stories are particularly appropriate when it comes to religion, because all religions are rooted in stories—meta-narratives and myths that have helped to explain some of the big questions in life such as: Why are we here? What should our relationship to others be like? What should I do with my life? And what happens after we die? Religious people understand their personal stories to be intertwined with larger religious narratives (Ammerman 2014).

In addition to highlighting key concepts, each author refers to statistical data in her/his chapter. These data, most often that collected by Statistics Canada, provide a snapshot of the population in relation to religion. Statistics help us to identify broad patterns of religion in society and are a good contrast to the rich details provided by individual and collective stories. The combination of qualitative and quantitative data in each chapter of this volume provide different perspectives on religious diversity. Differing perspectives on particular religious issues or traditions are important in understanding the complexity of religion. Each chapter addresses some of the current challenges and future opportunities in the author's field of inquiry.

All of the contributors are concerned about the dissemination of our research findings on religion and are aware of the multiple opportunities that people have for learning. Thus, this text has a focus on teaching and learning about religious diversity. Its electronic format is important so that it is widely accessible and affordable. The chapters include questions for critical reflection so that readers can begin to integrate the new information provided. It is hoped that these questions will assist in interrogating some of the assumptions or stereotypes that students have about religion. Students can also consult the online and print resources listed at the end of each chapter if they are interested in furthering their learning about a particular issue or religious/non-religious group. Some of the online resources are hosted on the Religion and Diversity Project website: <www.religionanddiversity.ca> and were created specifically for the study of religious diversity. The resources include short video clips of scholars, religious leaders, and adherents speaking about religion; photo essays; instructions on "how to" link classrooms using technology; a guide to organizing a religious leaders panel; and examples of assignments such as mapping the religious diversity of urban spaces.

The availability of print and multi-media learning tools recognizes that there are a variety of ways that learning takes place. It usually begins with tapping into what people already know—their personal experiences, opinions, and knowledge about religion and religious people. Many of the questions for critical review throughout this book are designed to encourage self-reflection. Online visual resources can also stimulate reflection through the juxtaposition of familiar images alongside the unfamiliar. For example, a photo essay on same sex marriage combines traditional symbols such as flowers and rings with feminist theory texts. Another example is the *Stained Glass Story of Abuse* on the RAVE Project website <www.theraveproject. org> which brings together the beauty of traditional stained glass with the ugliness of domestic violence. It is when personal knowledge and assumptions are made explicit that the starting point for further learning and change can be identified.

The chapters in this book cover a diverse range of religious traditions, themes, and issues concerning contemporary religious diversity in Canada. Four of the twelve chapters focus on a single religious group. Steve McMullin explores the changes taking place in evangelical Protestant congregations in Chap. 7. This is one group of Christians that is experiencing growth in the midst of widespread decline in mainstream Christian denominations. One of the denominations struggling with declining participation by its Canadian-born membership is the Catholic church. Chap. 8 features the findings of Paul Gareau's research on Catholic youth and their involvement in a program that is part of the church's attempts to revitalize a countercultural Catholic identity. This exploration of the identity formation of religious youth shines a light on the complex relationship between institutions and individuals. Jennifer Selby introduces readers to the lived religious practices of a young Muslim woman living in Newfoundland and Labrador in Chap. 10. This case study serves as a springboard for better understanding the unique challenges that Muslim Canadians face on a daily basis in a post 9/11 world. Selby's work highlights the ongoing social and political pressures of colonialism and their impacts on members of religious minorities. Although atheists are, strictly speaking, not a religious group, they are the exclusive focus of Steven Tomlins' research presented in Chap. 11. An increasing number of Canadians are identifying as religious "nones" on our national census. Tomlins helps to unpack this census category by means of examining historical legal cases and an ethnographic study of everyday atheists in Ottawa, Ontario.

The other chapters are organized according to themes and issues and position these in relationship to the diverse religious traditions being practiced throughout the country. In Chap. 2, I write about the role that religious social networks play in the lives of immigrant women who have recently settled in the Maritime provinces on Canada's east coast. The chapter highlights the role that formal and informal social networks play as Christian and Muslim women navigate life in a new society. Social networks assist them in dealing with the realities of becoming a visible minority and/or religious minority, experiencing discrimination, coping with shifting gender roles in their families, and living with religious diversity. Nancy Nason-Clark takes up the issue of domestic violence in families of faith in Chap. 3. She explains the unique vulnerabilities of religious women to victimization as well as the story of how violence and abuse become part of religious men's lives. The chapter highlights the important role that religious leaders can play both within their congregations and as part of a community-wide response to the problem of domestic violence. Nason-Clark's research addresses a gap in scholarship that has designated religion as part of the problem of domestic violence. She argues that religions have resources that can be harnessed to assist victims and perpetrators in the process of change, accountability and social justice.

In Chap. 4, Heather Shipley addresses the hot button issue of religion, gender and sexual diversity. Her chapter is based on the findings of the Religion, Gender and Sexuality among Youth in Canada project—research that reveals the complex diversity of young Canadian's identities. Youth identities are religiously diverse and involve a range of gendered identities as well as an array of choices concerning sexual relationships. Each of these identity categories are dynamic and mutually influencing as the young adults engage in a process of figuring out who they are. Van Arragon's work on religion and education is presented in Chap. 5. A longtime educator and administrator, he invites readers to ask critical questions about the regulation of religion by the state within educational systems in Canada. This chapter will be of particular interest to those training to be teachers as he skillfully reminds readers about the religious dynamics at play in and outside classrooms whether or not religion is the subject matter. Another significant location of religion in Canadian public life is its intersection with health care and this is the focus of Chap. 6 by Lisa Smith. Religious narratives become even more salient to individuals and groups during times of crises and this is certainly the case when people require medical care. Smith raises questions about the religious definitions of health and well-being and their implications for those who provide public health care in Canada. Again, this chapter could be helpful for those training to be health care workers.

The negotiation of religious diversity is the issue addressed by Amélie Barras in Chap. 9 in which she explores the concept of reasonable accommodation in case law and its movement into public discourse in Quebec. Using an example from her qualitative research with Muslims, Barras suggests an alternative framework for the negotiation of religious diversity.

It is fitting that Lori Beaman, the catalyst behind most of the research presented in this book and to whom all of the contributors are grateful, is the author of the concluding chapter. Beaman writes about the goals and design of the Religion and Diversity Project and how the work unfolded in ways that were unforeseen, as is often the case with collaboration and research. Beaman's assessment of the fruits of the Project over the past eight years incorporates the contributions of the authors of this text. She also describes research on religious diversity that is not included in the collection but which readers can learn more about by visiting the Project website. Finally, Beaman points to the future and describes emerging scholarship on the growth of non-religion, including her comparative research on religious and non-religious people involved in the protection of sea turtles—fascinating!

References

Ammerman, N. (2014). *Sacred stories, spiritual tribes: Finding religion in everyday life*. New York: Oxford University Press.

Ammerman, N. (Ed.). (2007). *Everyday religion: Observing modern religious lives*. New York: Oxford University Press.

Beaman, L. G. (2014). Deep equality as an alternative to accommodation and tolerance. Nordic. *Journal of Religion and Society, 27*(2), 89–111.

Beyer, P., & Ramji, R. (Eds.). (2013). *Growing up Canadian: Muslims, Hindus, Buddhists*. Montreal: McGill-Queen's University Press.

Castells, M. (2000). *The rise of the network society: The information age: Economy, society and culture* (Vol. 1, 2nd ed.). Oxford: Blackwell Publishers.

Chidester, D. (1996). *Savage systems: Colonialism and comparative religion in southern Africa*. Charlottesville: University Press of Virginia.

Davidman, L. (1991). *Tradition in a rootless world: Women turn to orthodox Judaism*. Berkeley: University of California Press.

Davie, G. (2007). Vicarious religion: A methodological challenge. In N. Ammerman (Ed.), *Everyday religion: Observing modern religious lives* (pp. 22–35). New York: Oxford University Press.

Gervais, C. L. M. (2012). Canadian women religious' negotiation of feminism and Catholicism. *Sociology of Religion, 73*(4), 384–410.

Holtmann, C. (2011). Workers in the vineyard: Catholic women and social action. In G. Giordan & W. Swatos (Eds.), *Religion, spirituality and everyday practice* (pp. 141–152). New York: Springer Publishing.

Inge, A. (2017). *The making of a Salafi woman: Paths to conversion*. New York: Oxford University Press.

McGuire, M. B. (2008). *Lived religion: Faith and practice in everday life*. New York: Oxford University Press.

Nason-Clark, N., & Clark Kroeger, C. (2010). *No place for abuse: Biblical and practical resources to counteract domestic violence* (2nd ed.). Downers Grove: InterVarsity Press.

Nason-Clark, N., & Kroeger, C. C. (2004). *Refuge from abuse: Healing and hope for abused Christian women*. Downer's Grove: Intervarsity Press.

Orsi, R. (2005). *Between heaven and earth: The religious worlds people make and the scholars who study them*. Princeton: Princeton University Press.

Peterson, D., & Walhof, D. (Eds.). (2002). *The invention of religion: Rethinking belief in politics and history*. New Brunswick: Rutgers University Press.

Immigrant Women and Religious Social Networks

Catherine Holtmann

Abstract Canada has one of the highest rates of immigration per capita in the world. This has led to a highly diverse population, particularly in large urban centres like Montreal, Toronto, and Vancouver. However other parts of the country, or what are referred to as non-traditional receiving societies, are working to attract more immigrants. Statistics Canada data reveal that the Maritimes is a region with low levels of ethnic and religious diversity, but that is beginning to change. Increasing levels of ethno-religious diversity in the population can be a challenge in terms of social cohesion. This chapter explores the role of immigrant women's social networks as they settle into Maritime society. Based on qualitative data, the analysis compares the roles that Christian and Muslim immigrant women's religious social networks play in the development of social capital. Social capital can contribute to immigrant women's self-confidence, well-being, and ability to fulfill their dreams for a better life. Ethno-religious social networks can also assist immigrant women as they individually and collectively negotiate their religious identities and practices, deciding which aspects to emphasize, reshape, and let go of in the Canadian context.

Keywords Social networks · Social capital · Christians · Muslims · Immigrant women · Maritimes · Gender · Ethno-religious diversity · Intersectional

1 Introduction

This chapter is based on sociological research conducted with Christian and Muslim immigrant women who live in the Canadian Maritime provinces of New Brunswick and Prince Edward Island (PEI)[1]. Using qualitative methods, the research explores the role of different social networks, including religious ones, in the lives of two groups of immigrant women during the settlement process. While considering the

---

[1] Funding for the fieldwork in this research was provided by the Religion and Diversity Project.

C. Holtmann (✉)
Sociology Department, University of New Brunswick, Fredericton, New Brunswick, Canada
e-mail: cathy.holtmann@unb.ca

multiple social networks that immigrant women access, the spotlight here will be on the role of religious social networks. Unlike the provinces of British Columbia and Ontario, the Maritimes are a non-traditional destination for immigrants and have relatively low levels of ethno-religious diversity. In the last decade however, this has begun to change as provincial governments in the region look to immigration as a strategy for population stability and economic growth. A myopic focus on the economic contributions of immigrants, however, has blinded public officials to the importance of considering other factors that contribute to social cohesion. Confronted with anti-immigrant political rhetoric and policies (Vitali 2017) as well as numerous media reports on acts of violence against Muslims (Globe and Mail 2017), education concerning the lived religious practices of immigrant women and their families is of heightened importance in Canada. Through the use of story, statistics, and online resources, this chapter will assist readers in learning about the important role that social networks play in the lives of Christian and Muslim immigrant women—particularly when facing challenges during the settlement process—and the individual and collective strengths drawn upon in overcoming these challenges.

2   A Real-Life Story from Qualitative Research

As you will learn in greater detail in the chapters by Barras and Selby that highlight Muslims (see Chaps. 9 and 10), regular weekly attendance at the mosque is not as an important religious practice for Muslim women as it is for men. Women do take part in public religious practices but for many, the heart of their religious activities takes place in the home. In Muslim majority contexts, women need not go to the mosque in order to be part of religious social networks. However, following migration to the Maritime region where Muslims make up less than one per cent of the population, they discover that mosques play a different social role than in their countries of origin. There is only one mosque in each of the large cities in New Brunswick and PEI, and they are meeting places for Muslims of different ethnic groups, economic classes, and theological perspectives. In recent years, women in the Maritime mosques have begun reaching out to new Muslim immigrants and families with young children. By paying attention to the needs of their faith community and reflecting on their own experiences as immigrants, Muslim women are aware that members of a religious minority group need to provide social support to one other.

One woman speaks about how her regular participation in the local mosque helps her to assist other Muslims. Through the mosque, she has become aware of the needs of Muslims in her city:

> If somebody in the community needed help with making food because they were sick, I would make food for them. I would take care, like go to their house and sit there for a while just to make them feel better. Or if I found out about someone that they're in the hospital, I would go visit them... There's always [an Auntie]... when I came here she was there for

me. So when I came here we found out about the mosque and we go directly to the mosque. So the whole community sort of helps the new immigrant. ... Our mosque is not just Pakistani. They're from Africa, people are from the Middle East and you know, the European Union – everywhere. So if the students need help, we would give money, we would give food, we would give clothes (Muslim #13).

A mother with a young daughter explains why she attends the same mosque regularly:

We have a mosque here and we do every Friday over there. Every Sunday we have Qur'an class. All the children start three years and four years [old] and people, like parents, volunteer work and read Qur'an and tell about our religion... I read the Qur'an in Arabic but I translate in my mother language, in Urdu... [During Ramadan] every Saturday we have a fasting dinner at the mosque. Every Saturday everybody goes there because we try to sit together. Yes, because it's hard [to break the fast with friends at home] – everybody's working and children go [to school] early in the morning (Muslim #19).

Through the religious social networks at their local mosque, these Muslim women have found ways to put into practice their religious values of care and charity. Mothers take care of the religious education of their children, and women have the opportunity to practice charity or the payment of *zakát* (Anderson and Dickey Young 2010, p. 209) to members of the Muslim community who are in financial need.

3   Key Concepts

Social networks consist of the interpersonal relationships people develop and maintain in the situations, organizations, and institutions of which they are a part through the course of daily life. Social networks usually begin in the family—the primary institution in which most individuals are socialized. Socialization includes the transmission of patterns of communication, belief systems, and actions from older to younger generations in families. Families are embedded in larger social networks in geographical locations such as neighbourhoods, villages, cities, and countries as well as through the institutional processes of education, the provision of public social services, employment practices, and political participation. Social networks are developed through regular face-to-face interactions and virtual connections using email and social media like Facebook. Interpersonal relationships within social networks differ in their quality. Some consist of strong emotional bonds such as those with friends, family, and co-workers. These are referred to as strong ties. Other social bonds or weak ties exist between acquaintances, members of a community organization, or employees in different divisions of a large company.

It is in social networks that individuals create *social capital*. The concept of social capital was developed by Pierre Bourdieu (1986). Similar to the way in which economic capital is exchanged by people for labour, goods, and services, social capital is the currency of interpersonal exchanges. In getting to know people and interacting with them, trust develops. Then when opportunities for further social interaction arise, people connect or reach out to people they know and trust. For example, many new immigrants get their first paid jobs through immigrant social networks. An established immigrant employer will hire a relatively unknown new-comer based on ethnic commonalities and word-of-mouth within ethnic social net-works. Let's say that there is a job opening as a cashier in an Asian grocery store in Charlottetown, PEI and a Korean immigrant woman successfully applies for it. She gets the job because of the social capital she has created within Asian social net-works. With this first Canadian job, she has the opportunity to start creating social capital beyond her ethnic networks as she interacts with coworkers, customers, and suppliers.

Bourdieu developed the concept of social capital in order to explain the social structuring of class and how class structures are reproduced. Social networks tend to be largely class-specific and homogeneous, since people tend to socialize with others who are similar to themselves. Robert Putnam (2007) further explains the concept of social capital by distinguishing between two types—bonding and bridg-ing. *Bonding social capital* is the emotional support that comes from strong inter-personal relationships and is critical for overall well-being. It is most likely to be developed through social networks that are homogeneous, such as those among immigrants who share the same ethnicity or country of origin. In contrast, *bridging social capital* develops in social networks that are diverse in terms of ethnic origins and class. Heterogeneous social networks can assist immigrants in social mobility, or in other words going from having nothing in the new society (no place to live, no job, no friends) to becoming settled and productive in their new home. Immigrants need to develop both bonding and bridging social capital in order to have a positive experience living in a new society.

In applying the concepts of bonding and bridging social capital to the rapid growth of ethno-religious diversity in the United States, Putnam suggests that the development of social networks for the creation of social capital in the early stages of immigrant settlement can result in increased tensions and divisions between native-born citizens and newcomers. This is because immigrants tend to support one another and native-born citizens are unfamiliar with and suspicious of minority cul-tures. However, over time, as bridging capital between the two groups is created, social cohesion will improve. Portes (2001) argues that the situation is more com-plex, depending on a variety of factors associated with immigrants from different ethnic and class backgrounds. His research highlights the process he calls *segmented assimilation*, in which second generation immigrant youth from some ethnic back-grounds integrate very well socially in the US while youth from other ethnic back-grounds drift towards the margins of society, unable to realize their immigrant parents' dreams for a better life in a new land. Portes asserts that social cohesion in an ethnically diverse society depends on effective social policies rather than on social capital. Strong social policies can mitigate ethnic segregation and ensure equality of opportunity (Portes and Vickstrom 2011).

Based on statistical data in Canada, Kazemipur has explored the social capital that immigrants develop through multiple dimensions of social life including par-ticipation in voluntary associations, political engagement, religious involvement, membership in labour or professional organizations, volunteering, informal associations, and subjective feelings of trust (2009, p. 13). In contrast to the situation in the US, he argues that Canadian immigrants are generally less socially segregated and have greater trust in their neighbours and in social institutions. In regards to the ability of immigrants to create social capital, Kazemipur finds that Canada's multicultural policies are working. Nevertheless, Muslims are struggling to create bridging social capital largely because of mistrust on the part of native-born citizens (Kazemipur 2014).

The *intersecting structures* of gender, class, and ethnicity contribute to complexity in a multicultural society (Walby 2009). Gender, class and ethnicity are social structures—creations of human society. The structures of gender, class and ethnicity exert directional pressure on individuals to act in particular ways. People can choose to resist or conform to these social pressures. In terms of gender, while biological differences lead to the assigning of male and female genders at birth, much of what we have come to expect of male and female behaviours depends on the society in which we live. In Canada and other Western societies, the problematizing of gender binaries has resulted in gender diversity (see Chap. 4) but in many parts of the world gender continues to be structured by patriarchy. Patriarchy is a hierarchical system in which males are assumed to be independent providers and women are expected to be dependent care givers. Class differences are based on the ownership of capital (natural resources and financial investments), the control of the physical means of production, and the control over the labour power of others (Satzewich and Liodakis 2013, p. 150). Regarding the structuring of ethnicity, there is no biological basis for distinguishing "race" yet ethnicity is often differentiated based on people's geographic origins. Ethnic majority and minority groups differ according to country or regional contexts.

Some social differences based on gender, class, and ethnicity are valued while others lead to inequality. Religious groups and the public perception of religion also influence the structuring of gender, ethnicity, and class relations, complicating things even further. This chapter will highlight the opportunities and challenges that the intersection of gender, class, and ethnicity present for Muslim and Christian immigrant women in the Maritimes. In what follows, the phrase *ethno-religious diversity* will frequently be used in reference to the intersection of ethnicity and religion. This is because they are often so closely intertwined in the lives of immigrant women as to be practically indistinguishable (Bramadat 2005).

In the process of migration and settlement, immigrants who come to Canada leave the social networks of which they were a part and enter into, or create, new social networks. The social capital that they relied on before immigration no longer has the same value in their new society. For some immigrants, the social capital that they had in their countries of origin was, to some extent, inadequate to meet their needs. That is why many people migrate internationally in search of better lives for their families. They seek opportunities and living conditions available to them as immigrants that they did not have in their home countries. Immigrants have to invest time and energy into the creation of new social capital in order to get emotional support and information, and to access opportunities for education and employment. In the initial days, months, and years of settlement, they are most likely to become part of social networks with those who share their language, ethno-religious background, or the experience of being a new immigrant. Because social interactions are often influenced by cultural norms, many immigrants also have to adjust some of the ways in which they socialize in order to create bridging social capital with Canadian-born people.

Research on social networks and social capital creation indicates that these are gendered processes (O'Neill and Gidengil 2005). Women find it easier than men to become a part of social networks and they use them differently. From a young age, women are socialized into emotionally close relationships, especially with other women (Chodorow 1999). This is quite evident for the immigrant women in my research. Many immigrant women come from societies with *collectivist values*—the individual's identity is secondary to the collective identity. Immigrant women understand their identities first and foremost in relationship with others. An emphasis on belonging to a community or considering the common good are also religious values for many of these women. This is in contrast to the values of individualism and autonomy promoted by Canadian society and liberal feminism. Collectivism and interdependence are values associated with what Mahmood (2001) refers to as non-liberal feminism or religious feminism (Fernandes 2003). This emphasis on the collective coupled with women's traditional role as care givers means that many religious immigrant women are adept at creating bonding social capital through *informal social networks*. They simply invite newcomers over for dinner or strike up conversations in the grocery store—telling other women where to shop for specific foods and housewares. When it comes to their engagement in *formal social networks*, research shows that women's use of social networks usually focuses on their care-giving responsibilities (Lowndes 2004). For example, immigrant women will become part of educational or extra-curricular social networks in order to take advantage of opportunities for their children. Or, as entrepreneurs, they will form a catering co-operative in order to promote and strengthen their ability to contribute to family incomes. Whether immigrant women are engaged with informal or formal social networks, the social capital that they create in these networks contributes to the collective well-being of their families and communities. This is an important consideration for the integration of immigrants and social cohesion—one often overlooked by governments and employers who focus only on economic factors (McLaren and Dyck 2004).

Social capital is an integral part of immigrant women's *agency* in the face of the dominant social *structures*. Every day social life is a continual encounter between the agency of individuals and groups and the pressures of social structures. In many instances, most people are not even aware of the pressures that social structures exert on individual thoughts and actions. However, with awareness comes the opportunity for individuals and groups to choose to resist these pressures or go with the flow. New immigrants encounter the pressures of the unfamiliar social structuring of gender, ethnicity, and class upon arrival in Canada, which often put them at a disadvantage compared to native-born citizens. Yet immigrant women are not without choices about how they will act, or exercise their agency, in the face of structural inequalities. This is why this research takes a *lived religion* approach. Rather than focusing on what Christian or Muslim teachings have to say about women, it focuses on how the women understand and live their religion on a daily basis. The remainder of this chapter will provide numerous examples of the kinds of social networks that immigrant women become part of in the initial years after arriving in Maritimes, and how they utilize them to take advantage of opportunities to create social capital and overcome the challenges that they face. But before turning to the research findings, it is important to understand some of the contextual factors of the Maritimes, in particular, the population's ethno-religious and immigrant diversity.

4 Statistical Data

Table 1 below provides data from the 2011 National Household Survey on the immigrant, ethnic origins, and religious diversity of the province of New Brunswick. At that time, immigrants only comprised four per cent of the provincial population. This is considerably lower than the national average which is approximately twenty per cent. Sixty-seven per cent of the New Brunswick population claim some form of European ethnic origins, followed by Aboriginal peoples at five percent, and those with any kind of Asian ethnic origins at only two per cent. Over eighty per cent of the provincial population identify as Christian, compared to sixty-seven per cent of

Table 1 Demographic profile of New Brunswick

Variable	Count	Percentage
Population		
Total	735,835	100
Non-Immigrants	704,235	96
Immigrants	28,465	4
Ethnic Origins		
Aboriginal	37,900	5
European	489,975	67
African	4435	0.6
Asian	14,535	2
Caribbean	1620	0.2
South, Central and Latin American	1650	0.2
Religion		
Buddhist	975	0.1
Christian	616,910	84
Hindu	820	0.1
Jewish	620	0.08
Muslim	2640	0.4
No religion	111,435	15

Source: Statistics Canada - 2011 National Household Survey. Catalogue Number 99–010-X2011032.

the national population. Less than one per cent of New Brunswickers identify with non-Christian religions, and fifteen per cent do not claim any religious affiliation.

Compared to the New Brunswick data, the province of PEI is even less ethno-religiously diverse. Data from Table 2 below indicates that in 2011 less than one per cent of the PEI population were immigrants. Seventy-seven per cent of the people in PEI claimed European ethnic origins and only three per cent were of Asian ethnic origins. Religiously speaking, the majority of Islanders identify with Christianity (84%), and fourteen per cent indicate that they have no religious affiliation. Even though Muslims are the largest non-Christian religious group, they comprise half of one per cent of the total population in the province. But keep in mind that overall, Muslims made up only a little more than three per cent of the entire Canadian population in 2011.

These statistics highlight the fact that new immigrants in the Maritimes encounter societies with very low levels of ethno-religious diversity. This situation changed somewhat in 2016 when the region accepted thousands of Syrian refugees. New Brunswick accepted more Syrians per capita than any other province in the country (Jones 2016). Syrian newcomers are religiously diverse, claiming Christian and Muslim religious affiliations.

Table 2 Demographic profile of PEI

Variable	Count	Percentage
Population		
Total	137,375	100
Non-Immigrants	129,390	99.05
Immigrants	7085	0.05
Ethnic Origins		
Aboriginal	4460	3
European	105,530	77
African	500	0.04
Asian	4360	3
Caribbean	310	0.2
South, Central and Latin American	445	0.3
Religion		
Buddhist	560	0.4
Christian	115,620	84
Hindu	205	0.1
Jewish	100	0.07
Muslim	655	0.5
No religion	19,815	14

Source: Statistics Canada - 2011 National Household Survey. Catalogue Number 99–010-X2011032.

5 Similarities and Differences Amongst Muslim and Christian Immigrant Women's Social Networks in the Maritimes

Eighty-nine women took part in my research on the role that social networks play in the settlement experiences of immigrant women in the Maritimes. Fifty-eight of the women identify as Christian, come from twelve different countries, and belong to five different ethnic origins groups, according to Statistic Canada's categories (2008). The Christians are Catholic, Orthodox, Protestant, and Mormon. On average, the Christian immigrant women had been living in the Maritimes for about two and a half years in 2012. Thirty-one of the women are Muslim, originating from fifteen different countries, and belonging to six different ethnic origins groups. The Muslim women are Sunni and Shiite. The Muslim immigrant women had been living, on average, a little over four years in either New Brunswick or PEI. More than half of the Muslim women (52%) and sixty per cent of the Christian immigrant women, are mothers.

Despite the tremendous ethno-religious diversity of the sample, analysis of the social networks of Muslim and Christian immigrant women shows that they share similarities. All of the women are impacted by globalization, there is heterogeneity within the women's ethnic origins groups, most are members of visible minority groups, and they've experienced shifts in the structuring of gender between their countries of origin and the Maritimes.

The women in this study are truly global citizens—some are social elites and some are doing what they need to do in order to survive—but all are seeking a better future. Their reasons for migrating to Canada can be categorized between those who migrate from stable social contexts because they have the economic resources to do so and those who have the means to migrate from countries of origin where there are situations of political turmoil and socio-economic instability. More people are on the move around the globe today than ever before. Globalization has had the dual effects of cultural homogenization as well as solidifying particular cultural identities (Meyer and Geschiere 2003). In terms of the homogenizing effects of globalization, the diverse Christian and Muslim immigrant women were all attracted to the Maritimes by governments seeking young workers. The Filipina Christians, for example, are part of well-developed, global social networks of Filipinos looking for work. Through the use of social media, the Filipinas, many of whom had been working in electronics factories in Taiwan, became aware of employment opportunities in New Brunswick, and procured temporary work permits through immigration brokers. Most of the women work in seafood and fish processing industries in coastal communities, while some are working as live-in caregivers. They stay in touch with family members in the Philippines, to whom they send regular remittances. Filipina workers stay connected to one another throughout the Maritimes to keep informed of further opportunities for work once their temporary permits expire. Their religious social networks are an important source of emotional support. As one Filipina said, "As long as we have a church service, a church where we belong, we feel very comfortable and we are really very fast to adjust ourselves, that we are very welcome to any kind of country.. . and we feel not alone, so we overcome the home-sickness. Especially because we are very far from our families" (Focus Group #3, Participant #3). Some of the Filipinas had not seen their children in years, but through faith they found the strength to keep on working abroad in order to provide them with a good education. The Filipinas are part of local Catholic and evangelical Protestant churches as well as a missionary church from the Philippines—*Iglesia Ni Christo*. The diversity of their Christian identities is secondary to their national identities as Filipinas. As Filipinas, they actively support one another in strategi-cally negotiating the local and global labour markets. They use bonding social capi-tal to help one another find work, housing, transportation, and social support.

This is not the case with the majority of immigrant women seeking high skilled jobs in the Maritimes. Many well-educated Christian and Muslim immigrant women are unable to find work commensurate with their professional expertise and feel forced to take low wage, service jobs in order to help support their families. Their inability to procure work for which they were assigned points in the immigration system and then admitted into Canada is an indication of the segmented assimilation of immigrant women into the Maritime labour market. This can be interpreted as either the result of their lack of bridging social capital or the need for provincial policies that address ethnic inequality in the workforce.

The ethnic origins groups of the Christian and Muslim immigrant women are heterogeneous. The Christians are East/Southeast Asian, East European, African, South American, and Western European. The Muslims are West Asian, Arab, South Asian, African, East/Southeast Asian, and South American. Most of the ethnic groups are comprised of women from different countries of origin. The largest Christian ethnic group is East/Southeast Asian women originally from the Philippines, South Korea, Vietnam, and China. West Asians are the largest ethnic group amongst the Muslims, with the majority coming from Iran. The Arabic Muslim immigrant women are highly diverse in terms of their home countries, orig-inating from Iraq, Saudi Arabia, Jordan, Egypt, Libya, and Morocco. Because there are relatively few immigrants in the Maritimes, the density of any particular ethno-religious group is low. Nevertheless, many Muslim and Christian immigrant women become part of or form social networks with others who share their ethno-religious backgrounds. A Muslim mother from Jordan, for example, knows the names and contact information for the only other two Jordanian families in the entire province of New Brunswick!

Heterogeneity is also present within religious groups. Some of the immigrant women share the same ethno-religious background, but have different religious practices. For example, one Muslim woman originally from Chad had been looking for work without success. Her husband suggested that she not wear her head scarf or *hijab* to the next interview. She took his advice and got a job at Tim Horton's. She went to her first day of work wearing a headscarf underneath her uniform cap. Her co-workers ask about her Muslim identity but her boss does not comment. She is happy with her job. This is in contrast to the perspective of a Muslim woman who came to PEI from Somalia. She also finds it difficult to find work because she refuses to work in a restaurant or store that sells pork or alcohol. The Muslim woman from Chad is willing to make compromises with her religious practice to get work while the Somali woman is not. This is not to say that one woman is more or less religious than the other, but it does highlight an aspect of heterogeneity or differences in the religious practices of women who share a common ethnic origin. These women do not live in the same city, but if they did, they could potentially be part of the only mosque or the African cultural association. Moving to the Maritimes sometimes leads to the first experiences of living with ethno-religious diversity for many Muslim and Christian immigrant women. In their countries of origin, they associated with people who shared their particular beliefs and practices. Immigration to the Maritimes gives them the opportunity to build bridging social capital with Christians and Muslims who have different class and ethnic backgrounds.

As part of its employment equity legislation (Government of Canada 1995), the federal government defines visible minorities as people who are not of Aboriginal origins, non-Caucasian in race, and non-white in colour. Almost forty-five per cent of immigrants living in Canada are members of visible minority groups (Statistics Canada 2013). With the exception of those with European ethnic origins, all of the Muslim and Christian immigrant women in this research transitioned from being part of the ethnic majority in their home countries to being members of visible minority groups upon their arrival in the Maritimes. As already mentioned, there are proportionately few immigrants in the Maritimes and only two to three per cent of the population are members of visible minority groups. Thus, visible minority women are highly visible in contrast to the rest of the local-born population. Their visible minority status makes social support networks even more important because the women and their children face subtle and not-so-subtle acts of discrimination on a regular basis. An example of this is shared by Yun,[2] a South Korean Christian woman from New Brunswick featured in Figs. 1, 2, 3, and 4 below, one of several

Fig. 1 On the Outside, photo credit: Denise Rowe

---

[2]Yun is a pseudonym.

photo essays developed as online teaching resources for the Religion and Diversity Project. In the creation of the photo essay, Yun chose the door as a symbol of the barriers she faces as a member of a visible minority group. When she encounters a doorway she never knows what awaits her on the other side. Will the people there be welcoming and helpful? Or will she experience misunderstanding and discrimination because of the way she looks, speaks English, her foreign education, or her lack of Canadian work experience?

During an interview, Yun shares this story:

> When I was driving one day, somebody yelled at me. A guy and his girlfriend—they were young people with a nice car—they were laughing and yelling. I didn't do anything wrong but they said, "Oh stupid Asian!" How do they know I'm stupid? They don't know that I have three degrees—maybe they don't even have one degree. That is inappropriate and

Fig. 3 On the Outside,
photo credit: Denise Rowe

those things are so discouraging. On that day I couldn't do anything. I have a strong person-ality—I like challenges to break through. On that day I couldn't do anything. I just returned back home and laid down on the sofa and until sunset I couldn't concentrate on anything and that made me so discouraged. Sometimes it leads to depression.

Yun is a devout Christian and like her, other Korean Christian women receive support from social networks in churches in the Maritime region. In particular, they use opportunities in Bible study or faith sharing groups to speak about their strug-gles against racism in light of the narratives of the Christian tradition—they under-stand their suffering as part of their journey with Jesus, who was also misunderstood and persecuted. They are comforted by their faith that suffering for the sake of their families' future is making them stronger in the present and that God is by their side. Like the hand on the other side of the door that Yun grasps in Fig. 4, members of visible minority groups, Christian or Muslim, tend to support one another because they share painful experiences of discrimination due to their visible minority status.

Fig. 4 On the Outside,
photo credit: Denise Rowe

In sharing their experiences of adversity, immigrant women create bonding social capital with one another.

Both Christian and Muslim women have experienced shifts in gender roles as a consequence of the immigration and settlement process. Practically without fail, immigrant women speak about becoming more independent after moving to Canada. This independence is the result of very pragmatic changes in their lifestyles. Many of the Christian women are living alone in the Maritimes, either as migrant workers like the Filipinas described above, or, like many of the Koreans, parenting their children while their husbands continue to work in South Korea. Korean women say that before immigration they relied upon their husbands for help with the day-to-day tasks of life, and their gender roles in the family were quite traditional. In the circumstances of their new home, they find themselves responsible for looking after all aspects of the household including repairs, car maintenance, yard work, and dealing with the ice and snow removal during the winter. Because of these very pragmatic concerns, they immerse themselves in their neighbourhoods and cities and become part of the religious and cultural social support networks. They learn English and develop stronger self-confidence and autonomy. If their husbands come to visit or decide to immigrate and join their families, the Korean men are sensitive to the change in their social status in Canada. They are unable to communicate in English in public with the ease that their wives or children possess. The social respect that the men gained amongst their peers from their careers in Korea is also absent. The men have lost their traditional gender role within the family as well as their higher social status outside of the family. This often results in conflicts in the family (Holtmann 2016). For those with access to social support networks, like the evangelical Christian immigrant women, they use relationships with other women in their social networks to process these changes and develop strategies for dealing with conflict. For those without access to social support networks, like some mothers with young children, they can feel isolated and lonely. This creates a situation of vulnerability for the women which can lead to mental health problems (Holtmann and Tramonte 2014) or exacerbate the problem of family violence. For more details on the unique vulnerabilities of women and faith in situations of family violence see Chap. 3.

Gender role shifts also occur in Muslim immigrant families, but in ways that differ from the Christians. Most Muslim women immigrate to the Maritimes with their whole family. Several of the Muslim research participants are graduate students, and their stories of gender involve their changing relationships with their fathers and brothers. In accordance with their ethno-religious backgrounds, these Muslim women were taught that they should not associate with non-relative males in public. As graduate students, it is novel for them to be in a co-ed atmosphere and their brothers tend to keep a close eye on them while at university. An engineering student finds the constant scrutiny of her behavior by her three brothers hard to take. She describes her brothers as controlling and insists that she is above reproach. She sought help from student counselling services because she was becoming depressed about the situation.

> I saw them once and then I just stopped, 'cause I didn't feel comfortable. Like ok, what's the point in going and telling them, and they can't do anything for me? Because I understand it's a cultural thing and in my point of view it's a very wrong culture, but I have to live with it because it's my culture right? Like either I can run away from the house and live my life independent but then I am going to lose my family, right?. .. but I wouldn't leave home for sure, like my parents are the most important thing in my life (Muslim #10).

Her brothers' control over her is lessening somewhat the longer the family is living in Canada, but she believes that ultimately, her independence as a Western-educated Muslim woman depends on her future husband. She wants to marry a Muslim man "who is really good, who is open and not controlling. .. but if I get a guy who is another version of my father and brothers then it's going to be terrible." This student became the president of the Muslim women's association on campus in order to provide opportunities for women to support one other as they deal with these conflicting gender expectations. The association organizes social gatherings, exclusively for Muslim women, and schedules regular access to the university pool. Although only a few women are taking advantage of these opportunities for supporting and creating bonding social capital with other Muslim women experiencing the pressures associated with shifting gender roles at this particular Maritime university, it is a start.

There are four important differences between immigrant women, depending on their ethno-religious origins, which have consequences for their participation in social networks and creation of social capital. The experience of migration between religious contexts differs for Christians and Muslims; the density of Christians from some ethnic origins groups in the region is higher than that of any Muslim group; Muslim women deal with a wider range of ethno-religious diversity than Christians; and the religious differences between Christian ethnic origins groups have structural support in the Maritime context while those between Muslims do not.

Canada is a Christian majority country and the proportion of the Maritime population who identify as Christians is even higher than the national average. People in Atlantic Canada are also more likely than Canadians elsewhere to indicate that they are religiously engaged (Clark and Schellenberg 2006). Thus, Christian immigrant women are moving from one Christian majority context into another. This contrasts with Muslim immigrant women who move from Muslim majority contexts to one in which they are a religious minority. Although there are many cultural differences to be negotiated, in a Christian majority context, even secular public social networks are sensitive to the religious beliefs and practices of Christians. For example, Christmas and Easter are religious as well as public holidays in Canada. Immigrant Christian workers and students get legislated time off to celebrate religious holidays with their families and friends. Even though many people must work on weekends, the regular work week runs from Monday to Friday, with Saturday and Sunday for leisure and voluntary activities—which is conducive for being part of Christian churches. In contrast, the Muslim day of public prayer is Friday, and it is practically impossible for a business owned and operated by Muslims to shut down on a Friday afternoon so that the owners and workers can attend the mosque—Maritime customers are at best unaware or at worst insensitive to this religious practice.

In addition to being part of the Christian majority in the Maritimes, Christian women also belong to immigrant groups that have a higher density than any single Muslim immigrant group. For example, there are relatively large numbers of Chinese, Korean, and Filipino immigrants living in New Brunswick. Once immigrant groups reach a critical mass, they begin to develop more formal social networks and institutions. Breton (1964) has theorized the process in which immigrant groups create businesses and services that support their cultural practices and are infused with their cultural values, the goal of which is what he refers to as institutional completeness. For example, a Chinese immigrant woman in the research, who came to Canada as an international student, became part of an evangelical Protestant church with a sizable Chinese population through the invitation of her friends. In addition to attending worship services, she is part of a Chinese-language Bible study group that meets weekly in the home of an elderly Chinese couple. For the regular church suppers, she joins other Chinese women for a day together to make hundreds of egg rolls with ingredients purchased from a local Chinese grocery store. The church is also home to the Chinese Cultural Association and hosts its annual New Year's celebrations. This woman is working in her first job in Canada as an administrative assistant for the Association, which not only organizes cultural events but supports networking amongst Chinese business owners. This example illustrates how it is possible for Chinese immigrants in this city to feel part of Maritime society while maintaining aspects of their cultural identity. The low density of Muslim ethnic groups in the Maritimes means that a degree of institutional completeness is not yet evident.

Even the fact that it is possible to identify Chinese evangelical Protestants as a sub-group of Christian immigrant women with their own cultural organization in this study is evidence of a major difference between Christians and Muslims in the Maritimes. Despite their ethnic and religious heterogeneity, Muslims are more likely than Christians to be perceived as a single group by the public. This is partly due to there being only one mosque in each Maritime city. Yet there is considerable ethno-religious diversity amongst the Muslim population. This diversity presents opportunities and challenges for Muslim women. For many, living in the Maritimes is the first opportunity in their lives to associate with Muslim women from other class and ethnic backgrounds. This was evident during an Eid al Fitr celebration which I attended at the end of Ramadan. A potluck dinner was held at a community centre in which the men and women gathered in separate rooms. The long buffet table in the women's room had a vast variety of foods—a colourful (and flavourful!) symbol reflecting the ethnic diversity of the participants united to share a collective religious feast. However, the women from different ethnic groups sat at separate tables. Differences were evident in the different ways that they dressed (the majority wore *hijabs* but some did not) as well as in their languages. Linguistic differences are a considerable challenge for Muslim women on several levels. At the Eid potluck, announcements to the group were made in a couple of different languages but it was apparent that not everyone present understood what was being said. This was not likely a problem, since there was not a lot at stake in terms of misunderstanding. But one research participant indicates that there are problems when it comes to decision-making in the mosque. There is no imam and the mosque leadership falls to the largest ethnic group by virtue of them sharing the same language. Public discussions are dominated by men of the Muslim ethnic majority and this puts those from ethnic minority groups at a disadvantage.

One issue over which there was misunderstanding amongst the women was that of veiling. Muslim women in the same city did not understand the reasons behind different choices concerning veiling practices. For example, because Iranian women had been forced by law to veil in their home country, some women from Iran had chosen not to veil in Canada. One woman is perplexed that in a context of religious freedom, some Muslim women choose to veil.

> It doesn't really matter what is your religion in Canada. No one asks you what is your religion or no one asks you why you have hijab or you don't have hijab. Even when I go to the mall and I see a woman with a burqa, I look at her more than people from Canada! No one cares that she covers her face or her hair (Focus Group #6, Participant #1).

This particular Iranian woman's perspective indicates that her understanding of religious freedom springs from her experiences of having been forced by the state to conform with a religious dress code. Religious freedom for her means not having to conform to standards set by the Iranian government and likely by any external authority. She is free to not be a practicing Muslim in Canada. But religious freedom can be exercised in different ways by other Muslim women, like those who choose to wear a burqa. Another research participant chose to wear the *hijab* after 9/11 to increase her visibility as a woman of faith and use people's questions as opportunities to promote Islam as a peaceful and tolerant religion. She believes that the *hijab* enables Muslim women and men to interact honourably with each other in public (Muslim #6). The lack of opportunities to discuss and understand the diversity of women's religious choices can become a problem amongst Muslim women when majority ethnic groups exert pressure on minorities to conform to particular norms for religious practices. Formal ethno-religious social networks might offer more opportunities for this kind of discussion and understanding to take place among Muslim women.

Gender segregated networks can play an important role in helping Muslim immigrant women negotiate their identities and practices in a new social context. With migration to a religiously pluralistic society like Canada comes the opportunity for Muslim women to choose which aspects of identity to maintain and/or heighten and which to let go (Bramadat 2005). Nason-Clark and Fisher-Townsend (2005) draw attention to a trend towards "gender inerrancy" in the rhetoric of contemporary conservative religious leaders, which influences the public perception of patriarchal religious groups. Through their rhetoric, some religious leaders give the impression that women's religious identities and practices are fixed. This puts pressure on religious women to conform to a narrow set of gender norms. Yet empirical studies highlight diversity in women's lived religious practices. In their study of Christian women in the US, Winter et al. (1995) found tremendous diversity of beliefs amongst theological conservatives and liberals accompanied by a consistent sense of discomfort with their tradition's gendered teachings. Gallagher (2003) has shown that despite professing a belief in gender traditionalism, many evangelical Protestant couples in fact practice gender egalitarianism in their families. The traditional social structuring of gender is being challenged collectively by women (and some men) in a variety of Christian denominations through organizations such as Christians for Biblical Equality and the Catholic Network for Women's Equality (Holtmann 2015). Differences in gendered religious practices and beliefs amongst individual Muslim women have been highlighted by empirical studies (Hoodfar 2012; PEW 2012; Zine 2012) and collective resistance is occurring through organizations such as the Canadian Council of Muslim Women and the Federation of Muslim Women. Problems arise when state attempts to assist Muslim women's emancipation actually curb their religious freedom and impose secular gender norms (Selby 2014).

Differences of practice and belief within religious groups are historically common. This is what led to the division between Sunni and Shia Islam, the schism between Roman and Orthodox Catholics, and the Protestant Reformation. Mosques may be few and far between, but Christian differences in practice and belief are supported structurally in the Maritimes. Cities and villages have multiple Christian churches and organizations. This is not the case, however, for Orthodox Catholic women. There are very few Orthodox churches in the region, making Orthodox immigrant women reliant on informal social support networks. As with all ethno-religious groups, difficulties in accessing social networks for the creation of bonding or bridging social capital with other Orthodox Christians means that Orthodox immigrant women may lack emotional support and information that can help them as they integrate into Maritime society.

6 Future Opportunities

Globalization has increased the flow of immigrants to non-traditional receiving societies like the Canadian Maritimes in recent years. The low density of all immigrant groups and the low levels of ethno-religious diversity in the region present challenges for immigrant women, especially when it comes to their involvement in social networks. Like the financial capital needed for housing, food, clothing, and transportation, the social capital that is created through social networks is an essential component in fulfilling immigrants' dreams for a better future in their new society. The substantial ethno-religious diversity amongst immigrants in the Maritimes means that for some, social networks are informal and this presents challenges in terms of immigrant women accessing support and information during the settlement process. Immigrant women must rely on word of mouth to find support from others who share their ethno-religious backgrounds. The local-born population lacks understanding of religious minority groups and this can be a problem amongst public service providers when social workers or public school teachers are insensitive to the ethno-religious practices of immigrant families (see Chap. 5). Racialization of members of visible minority groups, which can lead to acts of discrimination, has a negative impact on immigrant women's self-esteem.

Nevertheless, ethno-religious diversity presents opportunities for Christian and Muslim immigrant women and for the local-born population in the Maritimes. For the most part, evangelical Protestant churches in New Brunswick and PEI are welcoming of the new immigrants in their midst. Not only is immigration seen as an opportunity for the growth of congregations, but many churches have opened their doors to non-Christian and non-religious immigrants to participate in opportunities for language learning and fellowship. This contributes to social cohesion as Canadian-born Christians get to know and assist new immigrants. Other Christian churches have the opportunity to follow this example.

Christian and Muslim immigrant women have opportunities to create bridging social capital amongst the diverse immigrant population in the Maritimes, within the ethnic and class diversity of their religious groups, and with members of the local-born population. The language learning and employment counselling services offered by immigrant settlement agencies throughout the region are where many women start to become part of social networks of other immigrants who share common experiences. Women in the mosques in the Maritimes are beginning to reach out to newcomer Muslims and families with young children, encouraging them to become part of public religious social networks, even though this may not have been something they did in their countries of origin. Opportunities for creating bridging capital with non-immigrants in the region are the least available to immigrant women, according to those in this particular study. Many of them long to make more meaningful connections with their Canadian neighbours, coworkers, and classmates. Social policies that address ethnic and gender segregation in the labour market are needed. Social networking opportunities between Canadian-born citizens and immigrant women can help to break down barriers of misunderstanding and fear. Women from diverse backgrounds are potential allies in overcoming discrimination and social inequality. There is much that Maritimers can do in order to deepen appreciation of ethno-religious diversity and the values and practices that immigrant women hold dear.

7   Questions for Critical Thought

1. Which social networks (family and friends, education, employment, religious) are most important to you at this time of your life and why? What kind of social capital (bonding or bridging) are you creating and what return do you expect on this investment?
2. What is the difference between how you use virtual and face-to-face social networks in your life? Which of these are more important in terms of your education or your career plans?
3. Proposed state bans of full or partial veiling for public servants (teachers, day care workers) and in the courts in Canada and France are controversial. Do you think this is a violation of Muslim women's religious freedom or a move to ensure the equality of all women?
4. What are some of the advantages of studying women's lived religious practices as opposed to the teachings of religious institutions? What are some of the disadvantages?

8   Online Teaching and Learning Resources

There are several photo essays and accompanying materials (interviews, commentary, questions for students, and suggested readings) on the Religion and Diversity Project website, including the one used in this chapter called "On the Outside." For essays on the intergenerational transmission of ethno-religious identity see "Mother Daughter" and "Food and Family."

http://religionanddiversity.ca/en/projects-and-tools/projects/linking-classrooms/
photo-essays/

Several scholars speak about their research on religion and immigrants in short video clips including Peter Beyer, Helen Rose Ebaugh, Vivian Lee, and Michael Wilkinson:

http://religionanddiversity.ca/en/projects-and-tools/projects/linking-classrooms/
linking-classrooms-videos/

Moving People Changing Places is a website based on a major research program in the UK led by Dr. Kim Knott. It features information, stories, images and learning resources, with links and further reading to follow up.

http://www.movingpeoplechangingplaces.org/

The Religious Studies Project is a collection of podcasts from the leading scholars in the scientific study of religion:

http://www.religiousstudiesproject.com/

The Pluralism Project at Harvard University has a plethora of information on ethno-religious diversity in the United States. It includes a Case Study Initiative which shows how the case study method can be creatively applied to teaching and learning in the religious studies classroom. Topics range from inclusiveness in city-sponsored prayers to a controversy over bringing the kirpan to school.
http://pluralism.org/

9   Suggested Further Reading

Beyer, P. & Ramji, R. (Eds.). (2013). *Growing up Canadian: Muslims, Hindus and Buddhists*. Montreal: McGill/Queen's University Press.

This book is based on data from interviews conducted with hundreds of university students from three urban immigrant-receiving contexts—Toronto, Ottawa and Montreal. The research highlights the process of religious change in the lives of second generation and generation 1.5 non-Christian immigrants. It offers comparisons of the dynamics of young adult religiosity from the perspective of each of three minority religious groups. Several chapters have a focus on gender.

Breton, R. (2012). *Different gods: Integrating non-Christian minorities into a primarily Christian society*. Montreal: McGill-Queen's University Press.

Based on the results of smaller scale studies carried out by other researchers in Canada and the United States, this book investigates the place of religion in the lives of non-Christian ethno-religious minority communities and its role in their members' integration into a predominantly Christian mainstream society. Breton's analysis focuses on processes: the experience of individuals being uprooted from one social world and transplanted to another; changes to individual immigrant identities, beliefs, and practices; challenges to minority religious institutions; and the changes experienced by individuals and groups in mainstream society.

Kazemipur, A. (2014). *The Muslim question in Canada: A story of segmented integration*. Vancouver: UBC Press.

This is an empirical study using quantitative data from three surveys conducted by Statistics Canada as well as two surveys conducted by Environics. Qualitative data from interviews with 12 Muslims from the Prairie provinces are also analyzed. Kazemipur's work provides an overview of the situation of Canadian Muslims as a whole as well as a comparison with the non-Muslim population in Canada. He advocates for an increase in the levels of social interaction among people of different faiths in Canada at the level of neighbourhoods, schools, and workplaces and claims that improvement in social relationships between Muslims and non-Muslims could lead to improved economic experiences and a stronger sense of belonging for Muslims in Canada.

Lee, B. R., & Tak-ling Woo, T. (Eds.). (2014). *Canadian women shaping diasporic identities*. Waterloo: Wilfrid Laurier University Press.

This collection of essays explores how women from a variety of religious (Christian, Jewish, Mormon, Bahai, Hindu) and cultural backgrounds contribute to Canada's pluralistic society. The contributors show how religious women both conserve and transform their cultures and collective identities. A focus on women's informal and unofficial activities within their religious traditions provides new perspectives on religion, gender, and transnationalism.

O'Connor, P. (2014). *Immigrant faith: Patterns of immigrant religion in the United States, Canada and Western Europe*. New York: New York University Press.

This book is based on the statistical analysis of large data sets and offers an overview of general patterns concerning the role of religion in the immigration process. Without focusing on any particular religious group, O'Connor summarizes these patterns as the moving, changing, integrating and transferring of the religions of immigrants. The book offers a comparison of the contemporary dynamics of immigrant religions in the West.

Zine, J. (Ed.). (2012). *Islam in the Hinterlands: Muslim cultural politics in Canada*. Vancouver: UBC Press.

With this edited collection Zine convincingly shows that Muslim women are not a singular entity and should not be essentialized. Through critical essays and empirical studies of media content and educational settings, the researchers contributing to this book challenge some of the prevailing generalizations about Muslim women in Canada.

10 Researcher Background

Catherine Holtmann has spoken with over a hundred immigrant women from across Canada about their lived religious practices in the last decade. Her work highlights their stories of resiliency in the face of challenges. She co-produced the documentary, "Breaking Barriers Moving Forward" in 2017 to showcase some of these stories from immigrant women living in New Brunswick (https://youtu.be/I1ciRp-o9aA). She is currently working on a project using photovoice as a method to facilitate Muslim-Christian relationships. Catherine is Associate Professor in the Sociology Department and Director of the Muriel McQueen Fergusson Centre for Family Violence Research at the University of New Brunswick in Fredericton, New Brunswick.

References

Anderson, L. M., & Dickey Young, P. (Eds.). (2010). *Women and religious traditions* (2nd ed.). New York: Oxford University Press.

Bourdieu, P. (1986). The forms of capital. In J. G. Richardson (Ed.), *The handbook of theory and research for the sociology of education* (pp. 241–258). New York: Greenwood.

Bramadat, P. (2005). Beyond Christian in Canada: Religion and ethnicity in a multicultural society. In P. Bramadat & D. Seljak (Eds.), *Religion and ethnicity in Canada* (pp. 1–29). Toronto: Pearson Longman.

Breton, R. (1964). Institutional completeness of ethnic communities and the personal relations of immigrants. *American Journal of Sociology, 70*(2), 193–205.

Chodorow, N. J. (1999). *The reproduction of mothering: Psychoanalysis and the sociology of gender*. Berkeley: University of California Press.

Clark, W., & Schellenberg, G. (2006). Who's religious? *Canadian social trends*. Catalogue No.11-008, 2–9. Retrieved from http://www.statcan.gc.ca. Accessed 24 May 2012.

Fernandes, L. (2003). *Transforming feminist practice: Non-violence, social justice and the possibilities of a spiritualized feminism*. San Francisco: Aunt Lute Books.

Gallagher, S. K. (2003). *Evangelical identity and gendered family life*. New Jersey: Rutgers University Press.

Globe and Mail. (2017, February 10). The Quebec City mosque attack: What we know so far. *The Globe and Mail*. Retrieved from http://www.theglobeandmail.com/news/national/quebec-city-mosque-shooting-what-we-know-so-far/article33826078/. Accessed 12 Mar 2017.

Government of Canada. (1995). *Employment equity act*. Ottawa, ON. Retrieved from http://laws-lois.justice.gc.ca/eng/acts/E-5.401/. Accessed 5 Feb 2017.

Holtmann, C. (2015). Women, sex and the Catholic church: The implications of domestic violence on reproductive choice. In P. Dickey Young, T. Trothen, & H. Shipley (Eds.), *Religion and sexuality: Diversity and the limits of tolerance* (pp. 141–164). Vancouver: UBC Press.

Holtmann, C. (2016). Christian and Muslim immigrant women in the Canadian Maritimes. *Studies in Religion/Sciences Religieuses, 45*(3), 397–414.

Holtmann, C., & Tramonte, L. (2014). Tracking the emotional cost of immigration: Ethno-religious differences and women's mental health. *Journal of International Migration and Integration, 15*(4), 633–654. https://doi.org/10.1007/s12134-013-0302-8.

Hoodfar, H. (2012). More than clothing: Veiling as an adaptive strategy. In L. G. Beaman (Ed.), *Religion and Canadian society: Traditions, transitions and innovations* (2nd ed., pp. 187–216). Toronto: Canadian Scholars Press.

Jones, R. (2016, June 20). New Brunswick sets 3 populations records in first 3 months of 2016. *CBC News*. Retrieved from http://www.cbc.ca/news/canada/new-brunswick/new-brunswick-population-records-refugees-1.3643021. Accessed 5 Feb 2017.

Kazemipur, A. (2009). *Social capital and diversity: Some lessons from Canada*. Berlin: Peter Lang.

Kazemipur, A. (2014). *The Muslim question in Canada: A story of segmented integration*. Vancouver: UBC Press.

Lowndes, V. (2004). Getting on or getting by? Women, social capital and political participation. *British Journal of Politics and International Relations, 6*, 45–64.

Mahmood, S. (2001). Feminist theory, embodiment, and the docile agent: Some reflections on the Egyptian Islamic revival. *Cultural Anthropology, 16*(2), 202–236.

McLaren, A. T., & Dyck, I. (2004). Mothering, human capital, and the "ideal immigrant". *Women's Studies International Forum, 27*, 41–53.

Meyer, B., & Geschiere, P. (2003). Introduction. In B. Meyer & P. Geschiere (Eds.), *Globalization and identity: Dialectics of flow and closure* (pp. 1–15). Oxford: Blackwell Publishing.

Nason-Clark, N., & Fisher-Townsend, B. (2005). Gender. In H. R. Ebaugh (Ed.), *Handbook of religion and social institutions* (pp. 207–223). New York: Springer.

O'Neill, B., & Gidengil, E. (Eds.). (2005). *Gender and social capital*. New York: Routledge.

PEW. (2012). *The World's Muslims: Unity and diversity*. Retrieved from Washington, DC: http://www.pewforum.org/files/2012/08/the-worlds-muslims-full-report.pdf. Accessed 12 Mar 2017.

Portes, A. (2001). *Legacies: The story of the immigrant second generation*. Oakland: University of California Press.

Portes, A., & Vickstrom, E. (2011). Diversity, social capital and cohesion. *Annual Review of Sociology, 37*, 461–479.

Putnam, R. D. (2007). *E Pluribus Unum*: Diversity and community in the twenty-first century, the 2006 Johan Skytte prize lecture. *Scandinavian Political Studies, 30*(2), 137–174.

Satzewich, V., & Liodakis, N. (2013). *"Race" and ethnicity in Canada: A critical introduction* (3rd ed.). Don Mills: Oxford University Press.

Selby, J. A. (2014). Un/veiling women's bodies: Secularism and sexuality in full-face veil prohibitions in France and Quebec. *Studies in religion Sciences Religieuses, 43*(3), 437–466.

Statistics Canada. (2008). *Canada's ethnocultural mosaic, 2006* Census (Catalogue no. 97-562-X). Ottawa, ON. Retrieved from www.statcan.gc.ca. Accessed 4 Apr 2013.

Statistics Canada. (2013). *National household survey profile*. Retrieved from www.statcan.gc.ca. Accessed 14 Jan 2014.

Vitali, A. (2017, March 6). President Trump signs new immigration executive order. *NBC News*. Retrieved from http://www.nbcnews.com/politics/white-house/president-trump-signs-new-immigration-executive-order-n724276. Accessed 12 Mar 2017.

Walby, S. (2009). *Globalization and inequalities: Complexity and contested modernities*. London: SAGE.

Winter, M. T., Lumis, A., & Stokes, A. (1995). *Defecting in place: Women claiming responsibility for their own spiritual lives*. New York: Crossroads.

Zine, J. (Ed.). (2012). *Islam in the hinterlands: Muslim cultural politics in Canada*. Vancouver: UBC Press.

Religion, Domestic Violence and Congregational Life

Nancy Nason-Clark

Abstract The intersection between intimate partner violence and religion offers us an opportunity to explore ways in which religious beliefs and practices make a difference in the life of a woman or man when violence strikes at home. Within this chapter, we consider how faith communities are sometimes part of the problem surrounding abuse and sometimes part of the solution. When abuse is ignored, or minimized by congregational leadership, there is no attempt to be part of the journey towards healing and wholeness for a victim, or accountability and change for an offender. When abuse is condemned and its patterns understood by congregational leadership, there are practical, emotional, and spiritual resources available to assist all family members who are impacted by it. The development of faith-specific resources is still in its early days as are collaborative community efforts that include religious communities. As the chapter argues, intimate partner violence will never be eradicated until we offer best practices to those who suffer, including those who are religious, and challenge the structures of our society that privilege some people more than others. The chapter concludes with a challenge: we all have a role to play in making relationships and our communities a safe place for everyone!

Keywords Domestic violence · Intimate partner violence · Religious leaders · Victims · Abuse · Faith-specific resources · Christians · Safety · Abusers

1 Introduction

Intimate partner violence is always an ugly subject. It affects large numbers of women, though some men too are victims. It happens in all kinds of families—rich and poor, educated and uneducated, and in the broad spectrum of diversities represented by sexual orientation, ethnicity, race, culture, and religion. The emotional scars of intimate partner violence last a long time. Children within the family do

N. Nason-Clark (✉)
University of New Brunswick, Fredericton, NB, Canada
e-mail: nasoncla@unb.ca

© Springer International Publishing AG, part of Springer Nature 2018
C. Holtmann (ed.), *Exploring Religion and Diversity in Canada*,
https://doi.org/10.1007/978-3-319-78232-4_3

not escape unscathed: many learn to reproduce the patterns they observed, or experienced, in their childhood home and many too battle the impact of their families long after they have attained adulthood themselves. While abusive behaviour is certainly learned, it thrives most ferociously when it is misunderstood or minimized. Violence between intimates is a problem that impacts our society at so many levels and, as such, requires a coordinated community response in order that it might be reduced, and one day, eliminated.

In this chapter, we explore the interface between religion and intimate partner violence. We consider some of the ways that faith communities are part of the problem—augmenting, or ignoring, the abuse that abounds in their midst. And we focus, more particularly, on ways that faith communities are part of the solution—offering practical and emotional resources to assist victims as they heal and calling abusers to accountability and change.

Within our broader culture in Canada, but evidenced in other countries too, there is a prevailing view that religion has little to offer to the discourse on abuse, or violence between intimates. Such a position is misguided at best, and dangerous at worst, especially for religious victims, as it separates them from one of the few resources that might be able to be harnessed in the aftermath of abusive, controlling, or violent actions at home.

As the following story illustrates, there are many nuances to the way that religion and abuse co-mingle in the life of a victim, or a perpetrator, or their families. In some ways, the story of an explicitly religious woman who has been abused is similar to that of other women, but there are many unique features too, including how the abuse is understood and options in its aftermath. These are themes we will develop later in the chapter.

2   Mary's Story

After Mary waved good-bye to Sue and Pat, she unlocked her car door and slid into the driver's seat. She placed her purse, Bible, and cell phone on the console beside her and, as she did, she could feel her level of anxiety begin to increase. Why did she always feel this way after she got into the car on Tuesday morning at the completion of the Women's Bible Study? What was it about this small gathering of women that made her feel so loved while they were together and so very empty when the group disbanded? Tears began to form in her eyes and then stream down her cheeks. She wiped them away and quickly pressed the button to start her car. She did not want to draw attention to herself or risk the possibility that Brenda, always the last to leave, would come and see why she was still in the church parking lot.

As the car began to accelerate down the highway, so too did her tears. She took the first exit, in hopes that the "drive-thru coffee shop" with its expansive parking lot would be a place where she could grab a cup of java and sit alone in the car with her thoughts and her fears. Before she could sit and sip, she texted Angie, the neighbour who was minding her children, to say that she had a couple of things to do before she came home and asked if that was okay with her. She offered to bring back some fresh muffins from the bakery as a treat.

Snapshots of her life began to come to mind—the first night that Greg asked her out; the party where she introduced Greg to her friends; the first time they went to church together; his late night calls only to say he was missing her by his side; Greg's proposal; her beautiful wedding dress. These were pleasant pictures, and many brought a smile to her face as she continued to wipe the tears from her eyes. And then, like a roar of thunder, came the unwanted, but equally true to her life images: the first time he called her a slut; that Saturday morning when he pushed her with great force into the kitchen cupboards; the Sunday night when he back-handed her as they drove home from Jen's after-church snack. "*Imagine, Greg accusing me of flirting with the husbands of my friends!?*", she said aloud, although she was the only one in the car to hear her own voice.

In many ways, these snapshots were a vivid portrayal of the roller coaster ride of her life with Greg: the times that were ever so good, and the times that she felt like she was being swallowed up with the pain, the hurt, and the fear of what would happen next.

As she sipped coffee, alone in her car, she realized that it had been some time since she had allowed herself to prepare this kind of inventory of her relationship with Greg. Almost every time that she had been overcome with emotion about their relationship, or her failure to make Greg happy, she had focussed on what *she* could do to make things better. Like the time she went to see Krista, the leader of the Women's Bible Study. She told her that she wanted to be a better wife and mother: wanted to receive more practical help from her religious devotions; wanted to have more patience with the children; wanted to satisfy—no, more than satisfy—Greg's wants and needs. She neglected to disclose to Krista that she was frightened of Greg's anger, of the bruises he had put on her body, or the growing fear he had placed in her heart. Or, the time, that she and Greg together met with the pastor—oh, the tragedy of that time!

She drained the coffee cup and decided that, just this once, as a total indulgence, she would get another cup of coffee and sit for a few more minutes in the parking lot. For some reason, strange as it was, all this thinking was making her feel a little bit better, a little bit like perhaps she could take control of her own life—that she had some options.

Even though the young man at the window of the coffee shop drive-thru gave her an odd look, she picked up her order, this time the coffee being accompanied by a muffin. Then she steered the car to a back corner of the lot and backed into a parking spot, away from the view of most of the patrons. At this point, once she took a few bites of the muffin and a few sips of the brew, she let her mind return to the "visit with the pastor."

Mary tried to remember the date—best to get things straight in her mind, she thought to herself. It was spring, early spring, and the forsythia in her garden was just blooming. She remembered seeing it as she opened the door of Greg's truck and hopped into the seat beside him. Neither of them spoke as they drove to the church. Going to see the pastor was a mediated settlement for Greg: Mary had threatened to arrange to see a therapist or go home to spend some time with her parents, some 300 miles away, if Greg didn't agree to seek help for their ailing marriage. He certainly was not in favour of some "feminist" messing around with his wife's head, and he didn't like the idea that Mary's parents might "pry out of her," things that he felt should be kept private, "between the sheets," so to speak.

As they drove, Greg was thinking of all the things he had done *for* Mary over the years. He wanted to be sure that he could remember to drop into the conversation some of these stories as they spoke with Reverend Anthony Steel. Yes, Pastor Tony would love these. Greg knew that he needed to show what a caring, thoughtful husband he was, or else the "sharing" with the pastor could go badly, especially for the future of their marriage. He decided that he would take control of the interview, make it sound like he wanted to get help, and throw in a few Bible passages—something that he knew always impressed the pastor. He would never admit that it made him agitated when Mary went to services twice on Sunday, or that she insisted they give generously to the church, or that she wanted the children to remember to pray before they ate their meals. No, he would keep these frustrations to himself and instead focus on how, after supper, Mary got easily annoyed with the children when they did not want to go to bed, often did not have the supper ready for him when he got home from work later than her, or wanted to keep a part of her salary cheque "to herself."

As they drove, Mary was thinking of all the things *she* had done wrong over the years. She should not have allowed Greg to sleep with her before they were married, should have listened to her parents and have insisted on a longer engagement period, should have seen some of the signs of Greg's controlling behaviour, should have listened more carefully to what *he* wanted to do with *their* money, and should have sought help immediately the first time he hit her. She knew that she nagged him a bit about their church involvement, and she knew she nagged him a lot about helping with the children. But was this wrong? Surely it was her duty as a Christian wife and mother to ensure that they lived at home what was preached on Sunday. In fact, she had read in the Bible just this past week that sometimes we are called to suffer, that certain life experiences can be *our cross to bear.* Mary thought about that short devotional book for women: the one that she consulted almost every day. It said that Jesus was a suffering servant, and that there were times that as his followers we will be mistreated and have to suffer too! It also said that women should long to have a *servant's heart*—though she was not exactly sure what this meant. When she asked Greg, later in bed, he said that it was doing as your husband asked, and *not complaining.* She thought this was very self-serving of him to see it this way, though she kept her thoughts to herself.

Before long, Mary and Greg were sitting in two comfy chairs inside the pastor's study, a lovely office where the late afternoon sun was streaming in through the long, slender windows. Tony greeted them at the door, after having been called by the church receptionist to announce their arrival. Tony was a forty-something people-person who had served this growing congregation for almost 10 years. He was a trim man, who liked to keep fit, and was especially good at developing relationships with young families. He enjoyed his own family a great deal and was very enthusiastic about helping young people find "the right person" and to maximize living a "full life" in the family context.

As he had planned, Greg explained to Pastor Tony why he and Mary had come to seek help. He narrated their story in a way that so surprised Mary that she was almost unable to speak when the pastor turned to hear what she had to say. She admitted to some nagging. She admitted to some unhappiness. And she promised to do better. Greg admitted to nothing at all. He promised to be forgiving of Mary, just as the Scriptures taught. "Seventy-times-seven, isn't it, pastor?" he said at one point. Mary felt queasy and thought that she might throw up.

Mary did not disclose about the abuse. Mary did not say she was frightened of Greg and his anger. Mary did not tell Pastor T. that Greg took control of all of their spending, even refusing her a portion of her own pay cheque to "spend as she wished" on additional things for the children, or on lunches out with her friends, or on beauty treatments—things they could well afford.

At one point during the interview with Rev. Steel she sat up straight, took a deep breath, and was about to challenge one of Greg's accounts of their family life, but he threw her a look that so frightened her, that she exhaled, slumped back into her seat, and decided it was too risky to speak the truth.

Pastor Tony summed up their time together by suggesting that Mary focus on being thankful for all that Greg does for her, and the children, and that Greg continue with his forgiving spirit. "God will help to ease her out of her unhappiness," he said to Greg, with a pat on the back. Then he turned to them both and asked whether Greg would like to be more involved in helping with the Boy's Program on Saturday mornings.

In his prayer for them, before they left his office, Pastor Tony recited the verse "Unto whom much is given, much will be required," as a way to motivate Greg to take on an additional church responsibilities and to shake Mary out of her sadness—by reminding her of all their material blessings.

As they walked past the receptionist, she noticed that Mary looked downcast and Greg elated. "Great meeting," he said loudly to Mary, "I should have insisted on this earlier."

Her second coffee cup drained, Mary got out of the car and took both disposable cups and walked over to the large garbage can near the coffee shop. As she threw them in the trash, she felt a renewed sense that she needed to be making some plans for her future, and for her children. No longer was she going to wait for Greg to change, she was going to take steps to ensure that there would be peace and safety in her home. It was going to be up to her—that is what her parents told her the day they dropped her off at college and on the way to her wedding, as her mother kissed her for the last time as a single woman, and whispered: *With God's help, we will always be there for you. Please never forget how much we love you!*

Mary almost ran back to the car, buoyed by the contrast between her husband's abuse and her parent's offer of support. Why had she not realized this before? Mary told herself that each day for the next week, she would take at least one hour and focus on what her next steps might be. As an emergency room nurse, she worked a few days each week and then had a few days off. Maybe she could even ask Jill to look after the children for a few hours on one of her days off and use that opportunity to both call her parents and make a further appointment to see Pastor Tony. She dashed in to the bakery to pick up the treats for Jill and for her own family, and then went straight home to call the church for an appointment.

As we have learned from our ongoing program of research, what happens next depends in large measure on the pastor and their level of training and experience relating directly to abuse in the family. Will Reverend Steel be part of the problem, or part of the solution? Will he help or hinder Mary's journey towards healing and wholeness? Will he be prepared to hold Greg accountable for his actions? In essence, Mary will learn whether or not her church and the pastor's study are safe places for her to disclose that she is a victim of intimate partner abuse.

3 Understanding the Issues

Mary's story offers us a glimpse into some of the challenges faced by devoted Christian women when they are abused by their husbands. Mary's faith and her faith community can be harnessed as a resource at her point of deep personal need. But sometimes they become an obstacle when a pastor underestimates a woman's need for practical help, or the real danger to her physical or emotional health. Pastors often exaggerate the remorse of the abuser, or his ability or desire to change his way of thinking or behaving. Sometimes religious leaders overestimate the options of an abused wife and by so doing add to her guilt and resolve that she must try harder. Often ministers or other spiritual leaders do not know what to say or what to do when an abused woman of faith comes to them for help. Unaware of the dynamics of abuse and the community resources to assist, they attempt, but do not succeed, in helping her to take action that would increase her safety and longer term psychological well-being.

From our research program we have learned that less than 10% of Christian pastors report that they are well equipped to respond to the needs of abuse victims who seek their help (Nason-Clark 1997) and seminary students, as well, report a lack of preparedness for ministry in this area (McMullin and Nason-Clark 2011). As a result, it is not surprising that they underestimate the prevalence and severity of abuse and often fail to refer the women who seek their assistance to other experts in the community. In fact, referral rates are lowest amongst those pastors with the least knowledge of abuse—the very cases where a referral to an expert is so badly needed (Kroeger and Nason-Clark 2010). While there is no evidence from our research that pastors ignore the violence that is reported to them by women victims, they are often unaware of the impact it has on children, or the intergenerational patterns of abusive behaviour, or the temporary nature of remorse in the life of a violent man. Their lack of understanding places women and their children at risk.

Many religious women believe that if their abusive husbands receive help that they can, and will, change. This puts a lot of pressure on the pastoral counsellor or spiritual leader. Clergy too are often very optimistic that change will occur—even in the face of years of experience observing limited change in the lives of those abusive men (or women) they have attempted to help. Wise counsel from a religious leader must include an understanding that God's provision for victims of abuse is not limited to altered behaviour in the one who is causing their pain (Nason-Clark and Kroeger 2004).

One of the findings to emerge from our research is that many ministers are reluctant, unwilling, or perhaps even unable, to provide explicitly spiritual help to victims who come to them for help. We find this surprising, since for many women, the reason they go first to their religious leader is that they want help with the spiritual dimensions of their problem. Often women feel abandoned by God at their point of need, feel like they must keep on forgiving their abusive partner, or believe that divorce is never an option. Part of the counsel they need is related to their spiritual life and spiritual angst. This is something that normally cannot be offered at a community-based agency, from a worker who may or may not be familiar with their faith tradition.

We have learned that churches and religious leaders who are proactive when it comes to abuse encourage disclosures amongst those who attend their churches and assist victims and abusers alike to seek both help from a religious professional and as well as help from professionals based in the community. Not only do pastors have an important role to play in offering support and empowerment to Christian women who are abused, but they are vital in any community-based coordinated response (where workers from a variety of different agencies, including the police and the justice system, work together in an effort to coordinate their intervention and thereby increase its effectiveness) to work with those who act abusively. Challenging an abusive religious man, using the words of his faith tradition, is powerful. In so doing the religious leader helps to bring justice, accountability, and change.

3.1 Something to Think About and Something to Do

You have just read the story of Mary. Now I want you to picture in your mind how she might have felt as she approached the church building and the pastor's office after she made a phone call to see him alone.

If you have never attended a Christian church, or at least not for a long time, it would be a good idea to attend a service, or even two, just to remind yourself what happens there. There you will observe that a wide variety of people meet together to worship, sing, learn, and socialize.

When you do so, ask yourself this question: *Do I think that it would be safe for Mary to approach this pastor, in this church, with her story of intimate partner violence?* Are there any clues from the service that would either lead me to believe that this congregation would be a safe place to disclose violence or that this would be a place where her pain and her despair would be minimized or ignored?

Throughout this book, you are being presented with the richness of images, texts, and practices that come under the umbrella of *religious diversity*. Later in this chapter, you will be presented with the variety of behaviors that are included in any definition of abuse, or intimate partner violence. But, for the moment, I want you to reflect on the point about religious diversity and think about Mary's story from the perspective of a woman linked to a faith tradition other than conservative Christianity. To help you to do this, consult a variety of websites that focus on faith traditions other than Christianity. Google several shelters for battered women that are specifically for aboriginal women, or Muslim women, or Jewish women and read what is presented about these services online. You can also consult websites that are specifically designed to highlight a particular faith tradition and see if you can locate any information there that talks about intimate partner violence. And you can call a local shelter and ask if they have any information on hand about resources available for women of particular faith traditions. At this point, you should be ready to answer a few questions.

3.2 Religious Diversity and Mary's Story

1. In what ways do you think that Mary's story would unfold differently if Mary were practising a faith other than evangelical Christianity? What if she were Jewish? Or Muslim? Or Mormon? Choose two faith traditions to explore your answer. Listening to some of the scholars talk about their research on the Religion and Diversity Project website <http://religionand-diversity.ca/en/projects-and-tools/projects/linking-classrooms/#resources> might give you some ideas about the various world religions.
2. How might the story unfold differently if Mary had grown up as a Catholic, but drifted away from regular contact with her parish? Here it is important that you consider any additional challenges that a woman might have if she is no longer connected in a regular way with her faith community but its hold on her heart is still strong. To assist you with this, look at the photo essay of an older woman standing outside her church and looking in that has been placed on the Religion and Diversity Project website <http://reli-gionanddiversity.ca/en/projects-and-tools/projects/linking-classrooms/photo-essays/there-not-here/>.

4   Intimate Partner Violence: An Introduction to Key Concepts and Statistical Data

Around the globe, there is ample evidence of the prevalence and severity of violence against women and the girl child. The best way to become acquainted with the frequency of intimate partner violence is to consider the statistics that have been collected. At this point I invite you to go to the RAVE website, a website I developed together with other colleagues, based upon the results of our various research projects www.theraveproject.org.

For the remainder of this chapter, I will be asking you to consult regularly with the content that is presented there. Sometimes, you will be asked to read some text, other times to consider the visual representation of a concept, and sometimes to listen to an audio or watch a video clip.

4.1   How Common Is Violence Against Women?

Several years ago, a colleague and I worked with a number of student research assistants to compile a snapshot of the prevalence and severity of woman abuse around the world (Kroeger and Nason-Clark 2010). The amount of data collected in various countries leads to one overwhelming conclusion: violence against women is pervasive. And, most often, that violence is perpetrated by someone with whom women have shared intimacy and a common residence (United Nations 2013).

Working with other colleagues and student research assistants, that information has been updated and presented in a way that you can access now. So, to address the question we have posed at the beginning of this section, go to the Violence Around the World section on the RAVE website and click on a variety of different countries. When you click on the red markers, you will be taken to an in-depth look at data that has been collected by an organization like the World Bank, or the US Centers for Disease Control and Prevention (CDC), or the statistics department of the government of individual countries.

On our RAVE website, you will learn first-hand of the staggering rates of violence. Sometimes students want to know why there is such variations in the data that is presented from, and within, different countries. The answer to this question is that: well, it depends. Sometimes it depends on how the data were collected. Sometimes it depends on the precise way that the questions were composed, or asked. Sometimes it depends on how expansive the projects were, or the funding or time constraints under which the researchers were working. But, irrespective of these differences—and they are important—the conclusion is undeniable: violence against women is far too common, everywhere. Table 1 provides a snapshot of some of the data related to our country, Canada.

In their excellent and highly informative book, *Violence Against Women in Canada: Research and Policy Perspectives* (2011), Holly Johnson and Myrna Dawson document that violence against female partners is the most common form

Table 1 Fast facts concerning intimate partner violence in Canada

According to police-reported data, almost 88,000 people in Canada were victims of family violence in 2013 (Statistics Canada 2013);

Listed amongst the summary statements from the 2014 General Social Survey (GSS), the most commonly-reported type of spousal violence was being pushed, grabbed, shoved or slapped (35%), followed by sexually assaulted, beaten, choked, or threatened with a gun or a knife (25%), and kicked, hit, or hit with something (25%); women victims reported the most severe types of spousal violence;

Almost one in three (31%) victims of spousal violence reported physical injuries as a result of the abuse (Statistics Canada 2014);

According to the 2014 GSS, in the majority of cases of spouse violence, the police were never called or informed of the abuse (70%);

Canadian Aboriginal women are two times more likely to be a victim of spousal violence than are non-Aboriginal women (Statistics Canada 2014);

The highest one year rates of intimate partner abuse are reported by women between the age band of fifteen and twenty-four (Statistics Canada 2005);

The first transition houses in Canada opened in 1973—they were located in Vancouver, Calgary and Saskatoon (Tutty 2006);

By 2008, there were over 500 shelters for battered women in Canada, located in every region of the country (Johnson and Dawson 2011).

of family violence in our country. Like other researchers have found, Johnson and Dawson argue that women victims themselves often perceive *emotional abuse* to be more devastating than other forms of violence, including *physical abuse.* In my own research program, that has been ongoing for over twenty-five years, I have observed that women often claim that the persistent emotional put-downs and verbal abuse, like name calling, takes a greater toll on their mental health and well-being than other forms of abuse (Nason-Clark 1997; Nason-Clark and Kroeger 2004).

In Canada, and indeed around the world, we are becoming more aware of the various forms of violence against women and of the devastating consequences intimate partner violence brings to the lives of its victims (Asay et al. 2014; Black et al. 2010, 2011). While physical abuse refers to behaviours such as punching, grabbing, hitting, choking, or striking with an object, *financial abuse* refers to withholding access to money, or stealing resources that do not belong to you. *Spiritual abuse* includes denying, or limiting, the access of someone to their church or house of worship, or its faith leader.

There are many intersecting factors that create special vulnerabilities for designated groups of women when it comes to the issue of abuse, such as the elderly, the disabled, new immigrants, racialized minorities, the poor, and women connected to LBGTQI2SA communities. In more recent years, growing attention has been directed to the multiple ways that some groups of abused women are especially disadvantaged—both in terms of the experience of abuse and the strategies and resources available in its aftermath (cf. Crenshaw, 1994; Statistics Canada 2009; Nason-Clark et al. 2018).

4.2   How Can I Understand the Reason Why Violence Is So Common?

Violence against women happens because, as of yet, we do not have sufficient will or sufficient resources to stop it. You might be asking yourself, at this point, some very important questions, like:

- Why do men hurt the women that they claim to love?
- How are children impacted when violence hits home?
- What resources are available to women when violence occurs?
- What can be done to stop this awful behaviour?

I would invite you to again visit the RAVE website and click on the tab: FAQs—Frequently Asked Questions.

We developed the answers to these questions with content experts from Canada and the United States representing criminal justice, therapeutic, advocacy, and religious perspectives. As you read the variety of responses to each question, ask yourself to consider the many factors involved in understanding the *why, how, where,* and *when* of abuse.

Over the last forty years, there has been a growing interest in trying to understand the subject of abuse (Dobash et al. 2000). Initially conceptualized as the very private problem of one man treating one woman poorly within a marriage, or other intimate relationships, the social problem of violence against women is now understood to be rooted in the power imbalances between men and women in the broader culture as well as the social construction of masculinity and femininity. Feminists were central in highlighting early the need to make the personal issue of woman abuse a public issue and to work to provide both shelter and respite for victims (Timmins 1995).

While abuse is anything but new, talking about it in public settings is often not welcomed. Many of our great-grandmothers, and the women who have gone on before them, considered rough treatment at the hands of an intimate partner to be simply *life* and they believed that they had promised as part of their marital vows to stick it out in the good times as well as those times that brought pain and suffering.

Control is a key concept in understanding violent or abusive acts perpetrated by an intimate partner. While, in the last decade, there has been some suggestion of gender symmetry in abusive acts between partners, Walter DeKeseredy in his 2011 book, *Violence Against Women: Myths, Facts, Controversies*, argues that the notion of gender symmetry is erroneous, adding another level to the pain and suffering of woman abuse victims. Further, he claims that it has become a political excuse used by governments to deny, or reduce, funding to services for abused women. In defense of his position in opposition to gender symmetry, he cites data that document: (1) almost all requests for police assistance in terms of abuse are from, or in support of, women victims; (2) women are more likely to be injured in domestic violence cases than are men, and their injuries are more severe; (3) more medical assistance is sought by women than men in a hospital setting after domestic violence occurs; and (4) few men seek emergency shelter in the aftermath of abuse.

If you have never experienced abuse yourself, or known a close friend or family member who is suffering in this way, it might be difficult to understand why a woman would choose to keep silent what is happening behind closed doors. Almost all women who are victims of abuse feel alone, betrayed, and filled with fear (Martin 1981). Frequently they blame themselves for the abuse, believing if they had been a better wife, or mother, or girlfriend, that the abuse would have never taken place. They tend to minimize both the fear and the hurt they have experienced. And often they take so much energy trying to keep the abuse a secret that there is little energy left over for thinking through their next steps in the search for safety and a life free of the abuse. Safety, though, must always be the first priority in responding to any victim of intimate partner violence. Asking a woman directly whether or not it is safe for her to return back home after she has sought help, or disclosed violence, is extremely important.

4.3   Understanding Women's Narrative of Abuse

Over the years, through many different research projects, we have attempted to understand how women narrate their own story of being a victim, and then a survivor, of intimate partner violence. As you will have seen already, on our RAVE website, we have a variety of strategies to communicate the results of our research projects, and the implications of our findings. But, perhaps our most successful venture over the years in doing this has been the preparation of *The Stained Glass Story of Abuse.*

Return to the RAVE website and spend a few minutes looking at the various window panes that tell the story of abuse, as told to us by the women who experienced that abuse and those who walked alongside them, as friends, as advocates, or as religious leaders (Fig. 1).

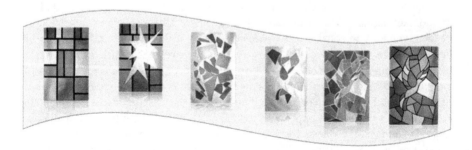

Fig. 1 The stained glass story of Abuse

What do you see when you look at this series of windows? What strikes you as the most important messages that are being conveyed by this visual representation of the lives of women who have been impacted by intimate partner violence? Perhaps, you are viewing the panes of glass through your own experience as a survivor. Perhaps, you are thinking of a loved one, or maybe a friend, as you look at the stained glass. Later in the chapter, we will be thinking about those who act abusively, but at this point, we want you to direct your attention to the way a victim tells her story.

Interestingly, almost all women begin their story when the intimate relationship was happy, peaceful, and loving. And it is to that time in the relationship that they long to return. But, as the second pane of glass reveals, the relationship never looks the same after violence strikes. Everything is transformed—the colours, the patterns, and the connections. There is no rewinding the tape as if the abuse could be erased from view. This does not mean that families cannot be reunited, or that separation always occurs. But it does mean that after violence there is a slow, and often painful, process of rebuilding until gradual renewal begins to occur. Abused women are very aware of those who have been helpful in their lives as they assembled the various jagged pieces—fragments from their past—and began a process of reshaping and reconfiguring them into a new life. Some of those who walked alongside them were friends and family, but sometimes it was a pastor, a woman's Bible Study leader, or an elder in the congregation who helped them to see that deep within them was courage, hope, talent, and endless possibilities. We all need help sometimes recognizing that we have strength and resiliency in the face of obstacles, but this is even more pronounced in the life of someone who has been told over and over that they can do nothing right.

4.4 Understanding Men's Narratives of Acting Abusively

In our 2015 book, *Men Who Batter*, Barbara Fisher-Townsend and I recount how men who have acted abusively tell their own story, a journey that often begins in childhood, ripens in their teenage years, and takes them down paths they were hoping to never travel. The men's accounts of their lives are told within a broader framework of the agency where they attended groups, and the regional coordinated community response to domestic violence, which includes the criminal justice workers (e.g., probation, parole, judges) and those who staff shelters and work in advocacy. Interwoven with this rich and colourful portrayal of the lives of the men, we interject reality checks from their own case files and those professionals who have worked within them. Women who have been victimized in intimate personal relationships hold out great hope that if their abusers are held accountable, brought to justice, and receive intervention, that peace and safety will be restored to their lives and to their homes. This is one of the many reasons we believe it is so important to understand how men themselves think about the abuse that they mete out on someone they claim to love.

Control is a central feature of abuse (Dobash and Dobash 1979; DeKeseredy 2011). Many men want to control every aspect of what happens in the life that they share with an intimate partner. Often they claim a sense of *entitlement*—to services, like house work, and to activities, like sex. When they believe that they are not receiving what they are entitled to, they use unkind words, demeaning gestures, and their fists to exert power and control over their partners (Bancroft 2002; Panchanadeswaran et al. 2010). Sometimes, an action that might appear loving, like texting a lot every day and every evening, can become a source of power and control in a dating relationship.

Theorists and domestic violence activists all agree that violence against women is multi-faceted, the result of a merger of interconnected factors including childhood experiences and present life circumstances. In an excellent article, Heise (1998) offers a model of explanation employing four concentric circles: personal history, microsystem factors, exosystem factors, and macrosystem factors. Personal history, as you might suspect, refers to witnessing or experiencing abuse in your childhood home. Microsystem factors refer to characteristics of your family of origin, including substance abuse, while poverty, or having close friends in trouble with the law are examples of the influence of the exosystem. Finally, the macrosystem refers to the influence of rigid gender roles, the social construction of masculinity, and the willingness to accept violence. Taken together, these concentric circles help us to begin to understand how a man might see violence as a way to get what he wants and believes he deserves.

In a similar fashion to the construction of *The Stained Glass Story of Abuse* as a way to share women's narratives of victimization and survivorship, we have collaborated again with stained glass artists to produce a window that highlights the stories of men who act abusively. You can view the window on the RAVE website, and it has been reproduced below so that you can look carefully at it even as you read the text to explain its various features (Fig. 2).

What do you see when you consider the tree as a representation of the life of a man who acts abusively with his intimate partner? Do you see that the tree is blown in one direction, responding to its environment, including the prevailing wind? Do you see the sun and the moon, reminding us that abuse occurs around the clock, when the sun is up and when we only see the moon? What do the blackened roots reveal? Or the prominent red line that snakes up and encircles the tree? Or the emerging streaks of red on the tender leaves? (If you are unable to see the colours displayed here, I invite you to go to the RAVE website at <www.theraveproject.org>).

This visual representation of the lives of men who batter helps us to understand that many men are repeating as adults what they experienced as children, watching their fathers harm their mothers, or as the victim of cruel aggression themselves (Nason-Clark and Fisher-Townsend 2015). Of course, not all men who experienced abuse in their childhood home repeat those acts of violence when they are adults, and some men who have been violent change their abusive ways and commit violent acts no longer. Many men also suffer from low self-esteem or struggle with addic-

Fig. 2 Stained glass portrait of men who batter

tions to alcohol or other substances (Gondolf 2002). Substance abuse and violence often co-mingle and it is very important that both of these significant problems are addressed in complementary, but not the same, intervention programs.

Intervention programs for men who batter are often part of a coordinated community response to domestic violence. Abusive men who have been processed by the criminal justice system and found to be guilty of domestic violence are sometimes mandated by a judge to attend such a group, while others go voluntarily, either at the request of their partner, or on their own. Irrespective of how they get there, men who attend batterer intervention programs are encouraged to develop *empathy* for the victim of their aggression, to take *responsibility* for their violent, abusive behaviour, and become *accountable* to others to live life differently than they have in the past, free from abuse. Sometimes religious leaders become part of a man's accountability structures.

4.5   Understanding the Impact of Religion in the Lives of the Abused and the Abusers

In our book, *Religion and Intimate Partner Violence: Understanding the Challenges and Proposing Solutions* (2018), my colleagues and I have explored the unique vulnerabilities facing abused *religious* women. When violence strikes the homes of deeply religious women, they are more likely to believe that their partners, can, and will, change. Many are reluctant to seek outside sources for help, believing that in some way that are compromising their faith or faith community in doing so. Many deeply religious women stay in a violent home, fearing that to leave, temporarily or forever, would be breaking a promise made to God during their marriage vows. Frequently, women of faith report disappointment, though, after they have sought the help of their religious leader—often because that leader does not really hear their cry for help or does not know what to suggest.

Unfortunately, many religious leaders are not at all well-equipped to respond with compassion and best practices to those who seek their help—abuser and abused alike. It is not that they are quick to ignore or minimize the suffering, but that they are reluctant to refer men and women to community-based agencies, or outside professionals that they neither know nor trust. As a result, sometimes abusers are able to manipulate their religious leader and, in so doing, compromise the safety and well-being of the entire family unit.

However, it is important to highlight that religious leaders and congregations can be part of the solution to domestic violence in families of faith. In fact, our research has revealed that they can be a very important part of the journey of a woman victim towards safety, security, and wellness for herself and for her children. Correspondingly, we have learned that when religious leaders call men to accountability and justice, their impact for good on the lives of abusive men and their families is profound.

Nevertheless, many workers in community-based agencies are skeptical of the added value of a religious leader, or a faith-based perspective, around the collaborative community table. In part, this is a reflection of prior negative experiences in working with religious people, or religious leaders. Shelter workers often hear abused women themselves report disappointment in the lack of support offered to them by a church or other house of worship. Notwithstanding these important impediments to collaborative efforts, when religious leaders are trained in the dynamics of abuse and when community-based workers understand the importance of faith to a highly religious person, the possibilities of working together can become a reality.

It is important to be clear: religious beliefs and practices can be harnessed by women and by men at their point of deepest need, including the experience of intimate partner violence. But whether those beliefs and practices contribute to the problem that is faced or help to overcome it will in large measure depend on how the experience of violence and the experience of their religion is framed by those from whom they seek help, religious and secular alike. If a woman's fear or her suffering is not well understood by a religious leader, she may be encouraged to return to an abusive home where her safety and health cannot be assured. If her fear that she will be abandoned by God and her faith community should she seek shelter for herself and her children in a transition house is not taken seriously by a worker there, she may go right back into the arms of the religious man who is abusive to her.

So, what are some practical things that a faith community can do to raise awareness about abuse and to make it a safe place for a woman to disclose that she is a victim of intimate partner violence? On our website, you will find a large number of suggestions, but some of my personal favourites include:

- Placing brochures in the stalls of the church washroom where it is safe to read the contents without anyone else seeing you;
- Ensuring that abuse is discussed when couples come for pre-marital counselling (months before the wedding takes place);
- Men offering their trucks to the local shelter on a Saturday for women who are moving into their first apartment after seeking refuge there;
- Taking school supplies to the local transition house for any children who are residing there.

5 Making Connections

At this point it is important to make some connections between what you are learning in this chapter and other chapters in this text and your broader educational experience. In an online course entitled Religion and Family Violence that Catherine Holtmann and I teach at the University of New Brunswick, we ask students to think through the implications of what they have read and seen (in the articles and the PowerPoint slides) in each of the 12 modules of the course. For many students this is a difficult undertaking—making connections between the material and what difference it makes, in their own lives, or within the society of which we are a part.

I would like to ask you at this point to make three sets of connections, one at the personal level, one at the level of your social network, and one at the broader community level, but we will start by thinking broadly first and then narrowing our response inward.

1. For the *community level connection*, I would like for you to visit Calgary's HomeFront website <http://homefrontcalgary.com/main/>. Read about their various initiatives and the data they have amassed to document their effectiveness (HomeFront Calgary, 2011). Look at some of their infomercials and consider the vast array of professionals with whom they collaborate. HomeFront is a coordinating body for over 50 community agencies, government departments, health care services, and legal advisers all working together to end abuse and to respond to women, men, and children impacted by it. You can read about their Specialized Domestic Violence Court, the Domestic Conflict Response Team, the High Risk Management Initiative, and Early Intervention and Outreach. This is a stellar example of one city in Canada deciding that it will take domestic violence seriously and work together in various sectors of government and non-

profits agencies to make a significant difference in the lives of abusers and the abused. They even work together with faith communities (Sevcik et al. 2015).

2. For your *social network connection* I would like you to think about the various songs you hear when you are out for an evening, the movies that you have watched recently, and the books or people that you discuss when you are hanging out with your friends. What would happen if you were to comment on the lyrics of a rap song? Or the violence amidst a sexual assault on the screen? Or share your worry about a friend that you thought was being stalked by a former partner? Think about whether or not it is safe, or comfortable, or commonplace for you to mention these kinds of observations to your friends. What does thinking about these matters say to you and about those with whom you share friendship?

3. For your *personal connection* I would like to ask you to think about the fairy tale, Beauty and the Beast, or Cinderella, or The Little Mermaid. If you have never been exposed to any of these fairy tales, you could probably read the storyline online, or browse a children's section of the library, or view the Disney version on the screen. What are some of the messages that these tales give to girls? To boys? What do they say about intimate relationships? In the case of Beauty and the Beast, what do they say about changing violent behaviour? And who is responsible for that change? If you have ever read the line, *And they lived happily ever after,* you will know only too well that our culture makes it very difficult for women (or men) to leave abusive relationships, temporarily, or forever.

The purpose of these three sets of connections is to help you to see that there are so many ways that we can begin to think about, and act upon, the subject of intimate partner violence. It is all around us, but often, we don't even see it. Now I am going to ask you to think about some critical questions that relate to the core of this chapter: religion and abuse.

6   Current Challenges and Future Opportunities/ Possibilities

In this chapter we have considered the intersection between intimate partner violence and religion. While there is little doubt that all religions need to respond to abuse in their own communities, the development of faith-specific resources is still in its early days. That brings both challenges and opportunities to the fore. There is ample room for the development of online and print resources that would assist in the healing journey of women, and for strategies and programs that would bring those who abuse to accountability and justice. Collaborative community efforts are an excellent way to coordinate agencies and resources and we have highlighted the initiative in Calgary, called HomeFront.

Intimate partner violence will never be eradicated until the structures of our society that privilege certain people over others are named and resisted. Of course, individual support for women victims should never be ignored, or sidelined, but we must continue to work to ensure that the political and structural dimensions of critical change are not forgotten (Profitt 2000). While safety must always be our top priority for victims, ensuring justice and accountability for offenders is also critically important. While it is true that we have resources in our communities today, like transition houses, that were not available 50 years ago, many attitudes towards the rights and responsibilities of women have not changed.

The challenges are for you, our students and future leaders, to call on our elected representatives to ensure that services for both those who are abused and those who are abusers are in place at the community level and across our nation. It is critical that all men and women who work as first responders, like police, emergency workers, and medical teams, understand how to recognize abuse when it is presented to them. Our institutions, like the educational system and the legal system, have important roles to play in raising our collective awareness about abuse and responding with justice and compassion to those impacted by it. But nothing can ever take the place of individual men and women speaking out against injustice whenever and wherever it occurs. Everyone, young and old alike, needs to be on guard to ensure that every house is a safe one and every relationship free from abuse. The next time you pass a church, or a synagogue, or a mosque, ask yourself: is this a safe place to talk about intimate partner violence?

7   Questions for Critical Thought

1. What do you consider to be some of the most progressive strategies that a religious congregation might adopt to make their house of worship a safe place for victims and survivors of abuse?
2. What do you believe to be the major advantages of a collaborative community response to domestic violence? Are there any disadvantages?
3. What do you see as some of the ways that religious professionals might contribute to the work of eliminating intimate partner violence in our society?

8   Canadian Website Resources (Partially Adapted from VAOnline.org and TheRAVEProject.org)

Canadian National Domestic Violence Hotline (1–800–363-9010).

Childhelp National Child Abuse Hotline (1–800-4-A-CHILD) where assistance is provided throughout North America in over 150 languages.

Alliance to End Violence is a resource centre in Calgary that offers excellent information and safety information for victims (www.endviolence.ca).

BC Association of Specialized Victim Service and Counselling Programs offers a provincial voice on the west coast of Canada and a plethora of community-based support services (www.endingviolence.org).

Canadian Forces Canadian/Family Resource Centres provide information and resource support for families connected to the Canadian Forces (https://www.cfmws.com/en/AboutUs/MFS/aboutus/Pages/AboutMilitaryFamilyResource Centres.aspx).

National Aboriginal Circle Against Family Violence acts as a national clearinghouse for information, training programs, and monitoring of family violence amongst Aboriginal peoples (http://nacafv.ca).

National Clearinghouse on Family Violence Canada is an excellent website that offers education and resources on various aspects of family violence including elder abuse, child abuse, and sexual abuse (www.phac-aspc.gc.ca/ncfv-cnivf/index-eng,php).

Ontario Network for the Prevention of Elder Abuse is a resource that offers training and advocacy related to the abuse in the lives of senior adults (www.onpea.org).

Ontario Women's Justice Network is an online legal resource for those attempting to understand more fully issues related to justice and the abuse of women and children (http://owjn.org).

The RAVE Project, standing for Religion and Violence e-Learning, is an extensive web-based resource related to violence in families associated with the Christian faith tradition. It offers a shelter map with contact information for every transition house in Canada and the United States. It provides information on safety plans and offers videos and on-line training modules (www.theraveproject.org).

9   Further Readings

Nason-Clark, N., Fisher-Townsend, B., Holtmann, C., & McMullin, S. (2018). *Religion and intimate partner violence: Understanding the challenges and proposing solutions.* New York: Oxford.

Based on research which spans a 25 year period, this book seeks to understand the trajectory of intimate partner violence in families of deep faith. Its focus on lived religion provides a powerful lens through which to investigate and assess ways in which religion contributes towards justice, accountability, healing, and wholeness for families experiencing abuse and violence.

Sevcik, I., Rothery, M., Nason-Clark, N., & Pynn, R. (2015). *Overcoming conflicting loyalties: Intimate partner violence, community resources, and faith.* Edmonton: University of Alberta Press.

This book focuses on the role of spirituality in the work that community-based agencies do to assist survivors of intimate partner violence by examining when and how religion and culture intersect in women's lives. It offers guidance for those who work with abused religious women in secular environments.

Williams, R. (Ed.). (2015). *Seeing religion: Toward a visual sociology of religion.* New York: Routledge.

In this edited collection, readers are presented with a wide scope and variety of religious practices that range from jewelry and articles of clothing to items found in people's homes and places of employment. *Seeing Religion* offers myriad examples of the application of visual methods to the scientific study of spirituality and religion.

Beyer, P., & Ramji, R. (Eds.). (2013). *Growing up Canadian: Muslims, Hindus, Buddhists.* Kingston: McGill-Queens University Press.

Contributors to this volume explore religion and religious diversity amongst a generation of young Canadians who have immigrated to Canada in the post-1970 era. It is a comparative look at spirituality amongst young adults connected to immigrant families. Through the voices of these young men and women, the reader is able to appreciate more fully religious diversity and multiculturalism in Canada today.

10   Researcher Background

Nancy Nason-Clark is a professor of Sociology at the University of New Brunswick (in Canada) and the director of the RAVE Project, a research initiative that was funded by the Lilly Endowment <www.theraveproject.org>. She is the author of numerous books, including *Religion and Intimate Partner Violence* (with Fisher-Townsend, Holtmann, and McMullin; Oxford University Press, 2018), *Men Who Batter* (with Fisher-Townsend; Oxford University Press, 2015), *Overcoming Conflicting Loyalties* (with Sevcik, Rothery, and Pynn; University of Alberta Press, 2015) and *No Place for Abuse* (with Kroeger, IVP, 2nd ed., 2010). She has served as President of the Society for the Scientific Study of Religion, the Association for the Sociology of Religion, and the Religious Research Association, and two terms as editor of *Sociology of Religion: A Quarterly Review.*

References

Asay, S. M., DeFrain, J., Metzger, M., & Moyer, B. (2014). *Family violence from a global perspective.* Los Angeles: Sage.

Bancroft, L. (2002). *Why does he do that? Inside the minds of angry and controlling men.* New York: Penguin.

Black, D. S., Sussman, S., & Unger, J. B. (2010). A further look at the intergenerational transmission of violence: Witnessing interparental violence in emerging adulthood. *Journal of Interpersonal Violence, 25*(6), 1022–1042.

Black, M. C., Basile, K. C., Breiding, M. J., Smith, S. G., Walters, M. L., Merrick, M. T., et al. (2011). *Intimate partner and sexual violence survey (NISVS): 2010 summary report.* Atlanta: National Center for Injury Prevention and Control of the Centers for Disease Control and Prevention.

Crenshaw, K. W. (1994). Mapping the margins: Intersectionality, identity politics, and violence against women of color. In M. Fineman & R. Mykitiuk (Eds.), *The public nature of private violence: The discovery of domestic abuse* (pp. 93–118). New York: Routledge.

DeKeseredy, W. S. (2011). *Violence against women: Myths, facts, controversies.* Toronto: University of Toronto Press.

Dobash, R. P., & Dobash, R. E. (1979). *Violence against wives: A case against the patriarchy.* New York: Free Press.

Dobash, R. P., Dobash, R. E., Cavangh, K., & Lewis, R. (2000). *Changing violent men.* Thousand Oaks: Sage.

Gondolf, E. W. (2002). *Batterer intervention systems: Issues, outcomes and recommendations.* Thousand Oaks: Sage Publications.

Heise, L. (1998). Violence against women: An integrated ecological framework. *Violence Against Women, 4*(3), 262–290.

HomeFront Calgary. (2011). *HomeFront's 2011 report to the community: United in breaking the cycle of domestic violence.* www.navigatormm.com/HFReport. Accessed 1 Sept 2016.

Johnson, H., & Dawson, M. (2011). *Violence against women in Canada: Research and policy perspectives.* Toronto: Oxford University Press.

Kroeger, C. C., & Nason-Clark, N. (2010). *No place for abuse.* Downers Grove: InterVarsity Press.

Martin, D. (1981). *Battered wives.* San Francisco: New Glide.

McMullin, S., & Nason-Clark, N. (2011). Seminary students and domestic violence: Applying sociological research. In N. Nason-Clark, C. C. Kroeger, & B. Fisher-Townsend (Eds.), *Responding to abuse in Christian homes* (pp. 231–246). Eugene: Wipf and Stock.

Nason-Clark, N. (1997). *The battered wife: How Christians confront family violence.* Louisville: Westminster/John Knox Press.

Nason-Clark, N., & Fisher-Townsend, B. (2015). *Men who batter.* New York: Oxford University Press.

Nason-Clark, N., & Kroeger, C. (2004). *Refuge from abuse: Hope and healing for abused Christian women.* Downers Grove: InterVarsity Press.

Nason-Clark, N., Holtmann, C., McMullin, S., & Fisher-Townsend, B. (2018). *Religion and intimate partner violence: Understanding the challenges and proposing solutions.* In press. New York: Oxford University Press.

Panchanadeswaran, S., Ting, L., Burke, J., O'Campo, P., McDonnell, K., & Gielen, A. C. (2010). Profiling abusive men based on women's self-reports: Findings from a sample of urban low-income minority women. *Violence Against Women, 16*(3), 313–327.

Profitt, N. J. (2000). *Women survivors, psychological trauma, and the politics of resistance.* NewYork: The Haworth Press.

Sevcik, I., Rothery, M., Nason-Clark, N., & Pynn, R. (2015). *Overcoming conflicting loyalties: Intimate partner violence, community resources, and faith.* Edmonton: University of Alberta Press.

Statistics Canada. (2005). *Family violence in Canada: A statistical profile.* Ottawa: Canadian Centre for Justice Statistics.

Statistics Canada. (2009). *Family violence in Canada: A statistical profile.* Ottawa: Canadian Centre for Justice Statistics.

Statistics Canada. (2013). *Family violence in Canada: A statistical profile.* Ottawa: Canadian Centre for Justice Statistics.

Statistics Canada. (2014). *Family violence in Canada: A statistical profile.* Ottawa: Canadian Centre for Justice Statistics.

Timmins, L. (1995). *Listening to the thunder: Advocates talk about the battered women's movement.* Vancouver: Women's Research Centre.

Tutty, L. (2006). *Effective practices in sheltering women: Leaving violence in intimate relationships.* Toronto: YMCA Canada.

United Nations. (2013). *UNite to end violence against women.* Retrieved from http://endviolence.un.org/ Accessed 22 Oct 2013.

Religious and Sexual Identities in Motion: Challenging Stereotypes, Exploring Nuance

Heather Shipley

Abstract The relationship of religion, gender and sexuality is frequently the subject of controversy and debate within media, public discourse, and policy modifications. However, the debates about these categories and their relationship often essentialize the topics as incompatible markers, requiring mediation in order to produce policies that do not offend one over and above the other. These essentializations ignore the lived intersectional identities of individuals who are religiously, gendered or sexually diverse and who exist across these identity possibilities. Drawing on data from the Religion, Gender and Sexuality Among Youth in Canada project (RGSY) this chapter will explore the ways young people in Canada are developing, negotiating, and understanding the dynamics of religion and sexuality. The RGSY project is led by Pamela Dickey Young (Queen's University) and is a mixed methods study of 18 to 25-year-olds in Canada, comprised of an online survey, semi-structured interviews, and video diaries. While legal challenges, and the media coverage of these challenges, often represent both religion and sexuality within narrow parameters, on-the-ground research continues to debunk stereotypes about both categories of identity.

Keywords Religious identity · Sexual identity · Religious practices · Sexual practices · Gender · Public policy · LGBTQI+ · Stereotypes · Nonreligious

1 Introduction

Notions about religion and sexuality, and their relationship to one another, are frequently drawn from public debates and controversies as they are portrayed in media and played out in legal disputes. These public debates and their representation in media and legal decisions, however, narrowly construe both categories of identity and continue to perpetuate misunderstanding about the complicated relationship of

H. Shipley (✉)
York University, Toronto, ON, Canada
e-mail: hshipley@yorku.ca

© Springer International Publishing AG, part of Springer Nature 2018
C. Holtmann (ed.), *Exploring Religion and Diversity in Canada*,
https://doi.org/10.1007/978-3-319-78232-4_4

(non)religiosity and sexuality, historically and in contemporary society. Sexuality is a topic of frequent consternation within religious doctrine and teaching, however, it recently has also become a core area of analysis within the study of religion, with a trend towards considering how both religious and sexual identities are framed and regulated in relation to one another (Hunt and Yip 2012; Jakobsen and Pellegrini 2003; Pellegrini and Jakobsen 2008; Wilcox 2009). Increasing research attention on these categories as tied to one another has developed out of these public debates and anxieties about religion within public spaces, and the tensions that are witnessed as religious voices are heard contesting space for gender and sexual diversity (Boisvert 2013; Pellegrini and Jakobsen 2008; Young 2015).

Normative attitudes towards gender and sexuality continue to permeate policy and discourse and are the subject of ongoing critique and analysis. Religious normativity is an increasing area of research which sheds light on the ways the relationship between religion and sexuality is perceived and, as more research on intersectionality is conducted, how religious and sexually diverse identities are experienced on the ground (see for example Lefebvre and Beaman 2014).

Both religion and secularism are categories embedded with ideological assumptions and frequently contested as to the genealogy of their meanings (Beckford 2012; Pellegrini and Jakobsen 2008; Woodhead 2013). Strategic deployment of the category of religion and the category of secularism offers important insights on perspectives about religion and its relationship to gender and sexual diversity. Religion is frequently assumed to be irrational, exclusive, and inherently opposed to rights based on gender identity or sexual diversity; secularism, on the other hand, is portrayed as the "bastion" of inclusivity, rationalism, and openness towards minorities, especially gender, racial, and sexual minorities (Aune 2015; Shipley 2016; Young 2014). The deployment of these pervasive norms regarding both religion and secularism in national and international politics and policies is connected to larger debates about religious identity, religious freedom, and "acceptable" religiosity. Nations that consider themselves "secular" frame themselves as inclusive and welcoming, while simultaneously portraying "religious" nations as intolerant and exclusive. There are numerous examples of exclusive policies, including state-sanctioned violence towards gender or sexual difference, that can be used to support these dichotomous categorizations (see for example Chan and Huang 2014; Chinwuba 2014), but what ought not be lost in those examples is the reality that pervasive forms of discrimination exist towards minority identities in "secular" or nonreligious nations and spaces (Aune et al. 2008; Shipley 2016).

This chapter will consider the ways two participants in the Religion, Gender and Sexuality among Youth in Canada project (led by Pamela Dickey Young, Queen's University; funded by the *Religion and Diversity Project*, University of Ottawa) construct and negotiate their (non)religious, gendered and sexually diverse identities as intersectional, fluid and evolving. Challenging the assumption that the secular sphere is inherently inclusive, Colin's experiences at a public high school continues to impact his perceptions and acceptance of his sexual identity. Michelle's conversion to Islam is complicated by her queer, trans, and polyamorous identity; her current practice and engagement with Islam is subsequently shaped by her identity as a combination of markers. These two stories are just part of the larger picture of young people's negotiation and construction of (non)religious, gendered and sexual identities in contrast to prevailing norms and assumptions about these categories.

The RGSY project is a mixed methods study of 18–25-year-olds in Canada, comprised of an online survey, semi-structured interviews, and video diaries. Drawing on results from that project, highlighting Colin and Michelle's narratives, I will challenge common perceptions about religion and sexuality, exploring the ways nonreligious spaces (such as a public high school) can be seen as disciplining spaces for gender and sexuality. I will also explore the narrative of conversion to Islam for Michelle, to reflect on the ways religious, gendered, and sexually diverse identities develop together. While legal challenges, and the media coverage of these challenges, often represent both religion and sexuality within narrow parameters, on-the-ground research continues to debunk stereotypes about both categories of identity.

There is still much to be studied in this rapidly expanding field that connects religion and sexual diversity. The preponderance of literature on young people and religion has been developed out of U.S. research projects, although research initiatives in Canada, the U.K., and Europe have increasingly examined subjects within their own national contexts (Lövheim 2008; Taylor and Snowdon 2014; Yip and Page 2013). Generating geographically specific research serves to broaden analytic discussions for a more robust international dialogue.

1.1   Canadian Identities: Religion and Sexuality, Past and Present

The relationship of religion and sexuality in Canada, as with elsewhere, is one of tensions and conflicts, as well as one of intersections and complex nuance. Religion is most often seen as the primary source of constraint when it comes to gender norms and sexuality, both publicly and privately. The role of religion in setting boundaries for normative expressions of both gender and sexuality has been evident since the earliest settlers arrived from Europe in the seventeenth century (Wilson 2015). Public attitudes and public policy towards gendered and sexual stereotypes have shifted in the last several decades in response to grassroots feminist activism and movements, most vocally in the 1960s and 1970s. Recognition of women as persons (1929), the right to vote (1916–1940, though for First Nations women it wasn't until 1960), and wartime labour needs during both the First and Second World Wars that saw women in the workforce in new and unexpected ways, spearheaded subsequent movements that actively challenged policies, ideologies, and restrictions placed on women based on gender.

Lesbian and gay rights movements found a home under the umbrella of women's movements in the 1970s (Smith 1999). While neither feminist nor lesbian, gay, bisexual, trans, queer, intersex (LGBTQI+) movements are monolithic, the mission to challenge negative and discriminatory treatment and policies based on gender and sexuality has been a foundation of both LGBTQI+ and feminist movements. Pay inequality, the inability of same-sex couples to marry or adopt children, restrictions regarding access to abortion, and discriminatory hiring policies are just some of the systemic disadvantages that have been imposed on women and LGBTQI+ individuals, rooted in ideological presumptions about normative gender and normative sexuality. In the last decades of the twentieth century, activists and scholars began insisting on the consideration of intersectional disadvantages (Crenshaw 1991): that many individuals experience these systemic forms of discrimination across more than one minority identity. Within intersectional studies, the spaces for individuals who identify across religious, gendered, and sexually diverse identities have not yet received a great deal of attention, though the voices within these spaces have increased (Taylor and Snowdon 2014; see for example Native Youth Sexual Health, <http://nativeyouthsexualhealth.com/>).

Beginning in the 1960s, the Quiet Revolution in Québec was a time which saw intense challenges to the dominance of the Roman Catholic Church in state and social policy; state policies regarding abortion, education, and the treatment of minorities were directly challenged and overturned. Similarly, in other parts of Canada, the primacy that had been accorded to Christian ideologies within education and public policy was being challenged in public and legal spaces (*Big M* 1985; *Zylberberg* 1988). The movement for marriage equality, which began in the 1970s, is often equated with a movement to remove overt forms of religiosity from public policy (Farrow 2007; MacDougall and Short 2010). Although this ignores engagement by religious groups in support of marriage equality, the push to redefine marriage to include same-sex couples was a challenge to what many religious groups felt had been a religiously preordained definition, intended for procreation and based on gender "complementarity" (Interfaith Coalition on Marriage and Family 2003). In addition to marriage equality, adoption rights, family benefits, and the right to be protected from discrimination are all areas in which rights based on sexual orientation have been successfully challenged (Hurley 2007; Shipley 2016). However, the reality is that these rights predominantly benefit particular subsets of the LGBTQI+ communities—i.e. monogamous, lesbian and gay couples who wish to get married and/or wish to have children—and do not encompass all challenges faced by members of the LGBTQI+ communities (Shipley 2016).

Today in Canada, shifting statistics regarding Canada's religious makeup are the subject of much recent research about religious identity, how it is understood, and what has transpired to cause these shifts in Canadian religiosity. In the most recently released statistics (National Household Survey 2011) regarding religious identity, Canadians selected Christianity as the majority religion, which is not surprising given Canada's migration patterns, however the figure of 67.3% for 2011 is down from the 2006 census which held 77% of Canadians identifying as Christian. The most noticeable surge in these changing demographics was in the nonreligious category, with 23.9% of census participants identifying as nonreligious—up from 16.5% in 2006. While there are, of course, cautionary notes about the numbers and their meaning, there is clearly something changing within the Canadian religious landscape regarding self-selected affiliation and how contemporary Canada is identifying regarding the religion question. Unfortunately, the census does not provide the same set of figures for reporting sexuality or sexually diverse relationships—both because of the design of the questionnaire (the census does not ask such detailed questions) and also as a result of a flaw in the census (an assumption in the matrix which presumed that two people of the same-sex living together were in a relationship).

While the involvement of particular religious groups and ideologies are present, both in history and in contemporary debates, the picture of religion and sexuality in Canada is much more complex. Restrictions imposed on access to services for sexual minorities are not simply relegated to religious contexts. Shifting perceptions about both religious identity and sexual diversity make the perceived relationship between these two categories ever more nuanced.

2 Project

The *Religion, Gender and Sexuality Among Youth in Canada* research team consists of Pamela Dickey Young (Principal Investigator, Queen's University), myself (Collaborator, University of Ottawa) and Ian Cuthbertson (Research Assistant, Queen's University). It is funded by the *Religion and Diversity Project*, a Social Sciences and Humanities Research Council of Canada Major Collaborative Research Initiative (SSHRC MCRI) hosted at the University of Ottawa and led by Lori Beaman. RGSY is a mixed methods project, which involves an online survey (open from July 2012–July 2013), semi-structured one-on-one interviews, and video diaries. The project was developed with the support of the *Religion, Youth and Sexuality: A Multi-Faith Exploration* project, led by Andrew Kam-Tuck Yip and funded by the Religion and Society Programme (U.K.). The Canadian project was developed as a way to connect everyday religion and everyday sexuality, exploring youth identities as they connect with lived religion and lived sexuality.

The RGSY project has four primary aims:

- To explore the construction and management strategies undertaken by young adults (aged 18–25) concerning their religious and sexual identities, values, and choices;
- To examine the significant social, cultural, and political factors that inform the above-mentioned processes;
- To study how these young adults manage their religious, sexual, and gender identities;
- To generate rich qualitative and quantitative data that will contribute new knowledge to academic and policy debates on religion, youth, sexuality, and gender.

The project was open to youth of all faith or nonfaith backgrounds and identities to share their thoughts and opinions on religion, gender, and sexuality as youth living in Canada. The majority of our respondents self-identified as Christian 61% ($n = 252$; various denominations, and in some instances paired with non-Christian identities). Our next largest grouping was in the nonreligious, spiritual-but-not-religious (SBNR) and "other" categories (43.7%, $n = 181$). This number correlates with recent statistical data on the religious makeup of Canada which I have mentioned already (NHS 2011) and offered us the ability to consider more fully the relationship of religion, nonreligion, and secularism in relation to gender and sexuality as experienced and reflected on by our participants.

The survey was designed with sets of questions organized in categories: religious views, attitudes towards sexuality, values and practices, behavioural influences, and attitudes and experiences related to gender. In the one-on-one interviews we were able to expand on topics from the survey, as well as explore questions and issues that had been raised in the survey responses that we had not intentionally asked about (i.e. media and education). The video diaries were daily 10–15 minute entries made by participants and submitted to us through secure servers. We created a general set of guidelines for the video diaries, however we let the participants themselves decide which topic(s) to address during the daily video diary entries.

Two main thematic observations that emerge from this data is that young people's identities are very much under construction; they are negotiating, developing, challenging and constituting their identities in real time – their (non)religious, gendered and sexual identities are shaped by multiple influences and sources, and ultimately they see themselves as the primary authors of these identity constructions. The research has also shown to us the need for a new grammar of identity (Shipley 2016). Participants in our study are well versed in contemporary language and nuance about gender and sexuality, they discuss their own identities on continuums and with reference to feminist and queer theoretical analysis and debates. But the language of (non)religion serves as a barrier when they seek to describe and explicate the same nuance for their ideological, ethical and value-driven characteristics.

In the following section, I will explore the narratives of two of our participants as described in their interviews, Michelle and Colin. Michelle and Colin's identities both challenge common assumptions about the relationship between (non)religion, gender, and sexual diversity. Their narratives also demonstrate the two core themes that have emerged through our project—their identities are under construction and the language available to discuss core components of their identities is limited. These two narratives offer a pathway for teasing out complex negotiations of identity norms as religious and sexually diverse youth, as well as the real, lived process of complex identity development.

3   Real-Life Narratives: Religion, Secularism, Sexuality

3.1   Conversion and the Development of Identities in Tandem: Michelle

Michelle is a 22-year-old convert to Islam who arrived at the interview in a burqa, escorted by a male partner. Once she determined that there were no males present and that none would be looking in the window, she took off the burqa for the interview (her male companion waited outside for her). She self-identifies as trans, is currently in a polyamorous relationship with two men, of differing religious and nonreligious identities, and describes herself mostly as an "online Muslim."

Michelle was raised Catholic, describing her family as pretty strict Irish-Catholics who attended mass every week, fasted at Lent, and attended Catholic school. She moved away from religion in her teen years, feeling that religion "was something only old people did", but reconnected with various religious practices after high school. Her paternal grandmother had become Buddhist, a few Muslim kids had moved in to her neighbourhood, and she started to read up on differing Christian traditions to get a better understanding of Christianity beyond Catholic teaching. In college her boyfriend and close friends were all atheist and, feeling that being "without a religion" meant she was an atheist too, Michelle says she regularly argued with all her religious friends, telling them their beliefs were stupid. When she began reading about religion again what she discovered was a personal connection to the teachings she uncovered within Islam. Describing herself as being in a crisis during this time, it was her atheist boyfriend who finally said to her "Well, if you're going to do all this weird Muslim stuff, why aren't you just a Muslim then?"

Michelle's process of experiencing, rejecting, and redefining her personal religious identity is particular to her, but it is also a process that many young people in Canada describe. Participants in the RGSY project frequently describe childhood encounters with religious traditions and beliefs as connected to their families and the process of negotiating their identities in relation to early encounters and experiences. For some, this means moving away from parental religious influence. For others, it can involve moving away and returning. And still others do not move away but describe themselves as redefining these early religious teachings in light of their own perspectives and experiences.

While Michelle's narrative is unique, it connects with sentiments expressed by many religious and nonreligious young people: the sense of exploring and "becoming" religious or nonreligious as a process, frequently positioned in relation to family practices in childhood and also expressed as something that can change later in life. Many participants who do not currently engage in any religious practices, and do not define themselves as religious, also express the possibility of re-engaging with religion later in life—in order to be married in a religious institution, to raise their children within a religious tradition, and so on. These "imagined futures" (Page et al. 2012) involve their consideration of the role religion might play in later life, which is not felt or seen as required—yet.

Michelle's narrative involves multiple aspects of identity negotiation and development—religious, gendered, and sexual. These aspects of who she is developed in relation to one another and in relation to her family, her community, and her friends. This sense of identity exploration as something unfolding throughout her life is prevalent in Michelle's exploration of her identity history, as is her sense that, while she considers the mosque to be inhospitable—to herself and many others—she hopes that this will change so that she can find a physical space to engage with Islam.

The intersections of multiple marginalized identities in Michelle's narrative challenge assumptions about the relationship between religion, sexuality, and sexual behaviours—in this case, specifically Islam and queer sexualities. Michelle's behaviour, both conservative (arriving in a burqa with a male chaperone) and progressive (identifying as trans and polyamorous) undoes rigid notions about the "facts" of the relationship of these categories in lived experiences. Michelle is aware that her current affiliations are not the norm—for religion or for queerness—but they are identities that have developed together for her. Her hope for a more open mosque experience is the result of her belief that it's not the religion that is restrictive but rather the people interpreting the religion.

3.2 Secular Sexuality Disciplining: Colin

Describing himself as being back and forth between nonreligious and spiritual-but-not-religious identities, Colin (26) explains that while his paternal grandparents were devoutly Irish Catholic, his own parents were much more relaxed about religion—at home and in terms of family attendance at church. He began "dabbling" in Buddhism as a teenager, eventually saying he settled into the SBNR or nonreligious category in his early twenties. Colin attends mass at a Catholic church near where he lives on occasion for the sense of community, and otherwise infrequently attends church with his mother at Christmas. Although his early encounters sexually were "strictly heterosexual" (although difficult), Colin describes himself as having a "major break" in his early twenties when he became polyamorous and embraced bisexuality. He states that this shift in his identity came as a result of two processes; the first was his realization that there were parts of monogamous relationships that didn't make sense to him (sexual exclusivity during a relationship but not before or after). The second part of Colin's process was realizing in conversation with another male friend, who suggested he had wanted to have sex with Colin's girlfriend at the time, that the idea of his girlfriend having sex with someone else did not bother him "in the slightest", and he began to examine why relationships were so closed in the first place.

Although the process of opening his relationships to polyamory is one that Colin found felt natural to him, what he had a more difficult time with was the reconfiguration of his own sexual identity narrative. He had always identified strongly as being straight and accepting this new sexually fluid identity proved more difficult for him than opening his relationship to other sexual partners. One of the messages Colin felt strongly growing up was the negative associations with, and treatment of, gay men. He traces these influences and notions about sexual normativity to the homophobic environment that was prevalent in his high school.

> Well the first influence that my peer group had on me sexually was in high school growing up in public school you really didn't want to be gay and I still kind of struggle with this whole bisexual thing, like I mean I don't, I don't identify as gay, I identify as MSM, if you'd like, man who has sex with men, or bisexual, and I think that, and I still have a lot of

discomfort, it takes a long time for me to warm up to a sexual partner who is male and I do really strongly associate that with... the sort of homophobic environment that maybe still exists in high school but it certainly did when I was going through, especially for men.

Colin's experience of negative attitudes towards homosexuality, especially towards gay men, is not connected to particular religious teachings or ideologies; he attended a public school and the negative attitudes in high school were not declared from religious or ideological standpoints. For Colin, this continues to impact his personal identity as bisexual, being clear that his self-selected terminology of MSM or bisexual is a response to his wish not to be identified as gay. Although homosexuality was introduced into the sex education curriculum towards the end of his high school career, the atmosphere in his high school was "reductive" when it came to notions about gender and sexual identities, requiring a certain normative performance of masculinity "in order to avoid censure." It was in university that Colin's views on sexuality were broadened, influenced by a course in women's studies and by speaking with faculty in the women's studies program.

Colin's notions about acceptable sexuality in high school, and acceptable performances of gender and sexual normativity, mirror other participants' comments about the environment in high school regarding diversity contrasted to the feeling of openness they experience in university. Colin's comments about censure for non-normativity also connect with data on homophobic, transphobic, biphobic, and gender-negative experiences in public high schools in Canada (Naugler 2010; Taylor and Peter 2011a, b). His fluid, nonreligious identity, attendance and connection to Catholic mass on occasion, and further his identification in the nonreligious/SBNR categories, is not a source of contention for his own sexual identity or in his relationships. But the rigid heteronormative prescriptions learned in high school, and the impact of homophobic attitudes in the secular sphere, continue to influence his own personal notions about his sexual identity.

These two narratives are illustrative of the dynamic process that is identity development and negotiation in relation to childhood experiences and teaching, and in adulthood—be it through personal or formal education, peer networks, and identity formation. Colin and Michelle demonstrate the complex reality that is living across multiple identity categories, categories that are formally thought to be inherently oppositional.

4   Key Theoretical Concepts

The meta-narrative of *heteronormativity* developed out of challenges to rigid notions about the "biological complementarity" of males and females, which has been used to justify normative sexual relations as those which are procreative (Rich 1976; Rubin 1994; Warner 1991). Constructions of acceptable sexuality were tied to heteronormative prescriptions regarding the "acceptable" family, which was further enforced in policies where family and marriage were intertwined and seen as "natural" expressions of gender and sexuality (Butler 1993; Cossman and Ryder 2001; Halberstam 1998). Early feminist critiques of heteronormativity challenged assumptions about normative gender identity and normative gender roles (Irigaray 1984; Rubin 1994). Adrienne Rich's (1980) critique of the ways that heterosexuality, as an institution, restricted women, was encapsulated by her articulation of *compulsory heterosexuality*; a framing which demonstrated the ways women were expected to orient their sexual desire to men, and formalized them through idealized notions such as the "big, white wedding" depicted in popular culture. Compulsory heterosexuality is designed and structured to meet the needs of heterosexual men and sex is defined and contoured to fit male eroticism and male pleasure, further institutionalized through such cultural norms as the association between sex and heterosexual vaginal sex (see Lewis et al. 2013).

All other forms of sex, be it lesbian or gay sex, bisexual sexual desire, or polygamous relationships, are therefore constructed as "deviant" and marked as problems to be corrected or punished (or both) (see Anapol 2010; Calder and Beaman 2014; Califia 2001). The taken-for-granted expectations that heterosexuality is the norm and all other forms of sexuality are deviations has resulted in constraints on non-heterosexual identities based on social expectations and stigmas (Jagose 1996; Warner 1991; Weeks 2011). Constraints run from gender and identity disciplining such as taunting and casual homophobia, often witnessed in schools (Seitz 2014; Taylor and Peter 2011a, b) but also in other social environments, including social media (Ringrose 2015). Further disadvantages include lack of access to health care benefits because of normative definitions of what constitutes "family status" (Cossman and Ryder 2001), and restrictions on adoption and fostering eligibility for same-sex couples—in some cases not as a result of direct discrimination but rather by covert discrimination, such as the limitation that adoptive parents must be married (Denike 2007).

Normative expectations and standards regarding *religious identity* also permeate the landscape, where non-normative expressions of religiosity are similarly disciplined and constrained (Bakht 2012; Barras 2014; Beaman 2013). The growing body of literature on *lived religion* in relationship with doctrinal religion seeks to expand on the restrictive assumptions about religious identity as experienced by individuals, beyond formal teaching (Davie 2014; Day 2011; McGuire 2008; Ammerman 2014). Acceptable and unacceptable forms of religious expression continue to be central topics of debate across numerous national contexts. In Canada, this includes restrictions on religious clothing and jewelry in public spaces—be it to access public services or for those who work in the public service (Montpetit 2016). There is both implicit and explicit reference to *national values* when debates about public religiosity are connected to debates about national security; when the Hutterian Brethren lost the right to have driver's licenses without photographs (*Hutterian Brethren* 2009) the decision was supported by reference to concerns about identity and national security (*Hutterian Brethren* 2009, at para 4). Statements within legal and public discourses about *religion* and *secularism* often posit that "secularism" is an inclusive space for gender and sexual diversity, but that the "secular" sphere is one without preference for any particular religiosity (Alcoff and Caputo 2011)—thus justifying the restrictions on *non-normative* religious practices (Beaman 2013). In reality, certain expressions of normative religion continue to permeate the so-called secular sphere, having been reclassified as secular, nonreligious, or Canadian "heritage" (Beaman 2013).

Exploring the challenges for individuals at the intersections of multiple minority identities, Kimberlé Crenshaw's (1991) pioneering work on *intersectionality* as the experience of systemic discrimination on multiple levels also offers key insights when considering normative and non-normative identity constructions, and the relationship of identities imbued with these normative assertions. Considering the ways young people negotiate their identities across religious, secular, gender, and sexually non-conforming identities is critical to developing a more nuanced framework for identity research and, further, to combat problematic misrepresentations of these categories. We have all been witness to the ongoing debates, nationally and internationally, regarding the relationship between religion and gender equality and religion and sexual diversity. These debates and controversies are not new. However, they have been cementing certain notions about the relationship of these categories to one another (Allen 2005; Fetner et al. 2012; Freitas 2008; Shipley and Young 2016) and, particularly in a contemporary context, have been fueled by supplementary debates about religion and secularism, sometimes in the form of considerations of the separation of church and state, for example.

These key concepts require systematic analysis and interrogation; their role in directing both academic and public lenses is frequently challenged, and yet normative mainstays regarding sexual relationships, acceptable religiosity, and the presumption of secularism's inclusivity continue to be reaffirmed through discourse, media, and popular culture. In order to develop a more sound understanding of these complex notions, it is necessary to begin from the ground up by challenging assumptions and stereotypes and integrating empirical and theoretical analysis.

5 General Findings

The RGSY project has found that our respondents are quite comfortable bringing together religious, nonreligious, spiritual, and secular principles in order to develop their own unique views of ethics and morals. These bridging exercises combine family influence, peer networks, online information, and formal education. Even participants who align themselves within a particularly doctrinal aspect of a religious tradition demonstrate negotiated understandings about the teachings.

Survey respondents were overwhelmingly female, as demonstrated in Fig. 1 ($n = 476$):

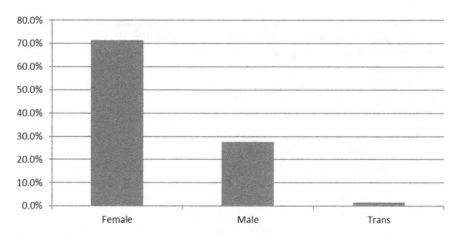

Fig. 1 What is your sex?

The majority of our survey respondents identified as Christian, though some paired this identity with other non-Christian religious identities, and others complicated their religiosity by explaining that they were baptized Christian, though largely only participated during the holidays with their family.

The breakdown of religious identity from the survey is as follows:

- Buddhism 1.9% (*n* = 8)
- Christianity 61.0% (*n* = 252)
- Hinduism 0.9% (*n* = 4)
- Islam 4.3% (*n* = 18)
- Judaism 3.3% (*n* = 14)
- Non-Religious 20.3% (*n* = 84)
- Sikhism 0.2% (*n* = 1)
- Spiritual but not religious 14.2% (*n* = 59)
- Other 9.2% (includes theist, agnostic, wiccan, combination of religions, etc.) (*n* = 38)

The next largest grouping in the religion question from our survey was the nonreligious, spiritual-but-not-religious and "other" category (which included theist, agnostic, wiccan, and combinations of religious identities). Between these three categories, there is overlap from our respondents to the survey. Of the total number of individuals who checked these boxes (181), 159 of those responses are unique. That is, if we were to look at each of the three categories individually, the numbers would be:

- Non-Religious: 84
- SBNR: 59
- Other: 38

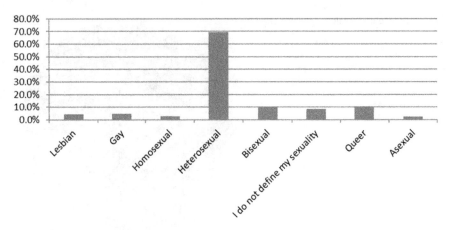

Fig. 2 How would you define your sexuality?

Some of the qualitative descriptors provided by the respondents for these identities included:

- Non-religious: atheist, agnostic, "it's complicated"
- SBNR: Baptized/Raised Catholic (i.e.) but non-practicing, Mohawk/Aboriginal beliefs, "I was born Muslim but I am spiritual and not religious"
- Other: self-defined, agnostic, unsure, and Unitarian Universalist

Religious identities as defined by our interviewees are as follows:

- Christianity: 56%
- Judaism: 6.3%
- Islam: 3%
- Nonreligious, SBNR, other: 47%
- Identity qualifiers: non-practicing, baptized within particular tradition, raised Christian (attends some services with family), "dabbles" in other religions, "currently Catholic", "agnostic Catholic"

In terms of sexuality, our survey respondents identified as such ($n = 401$) (Fig. 2):

Our participants were very savvy to current academic discourses about gender and sexuality, using queer feminist theoretical analysis to discuss their own gendered and sexual identities but also to discuss the ways that gender and sexuality are regulated and restricted, by both religion and by society more broadly. Respondents were predominantly inclusive towards a broad range of sexual behaviours for others, though exhibited much more conservative attitudes towards their own sexual practices.

When asked about gender roles and gendered norms, participants generally addressed male and female gender identities and expectations concerning straight and queer sexualities. Bisexuality and trans identities were less frequently discussed,

Fig. 3 Do you engage in casual sex?

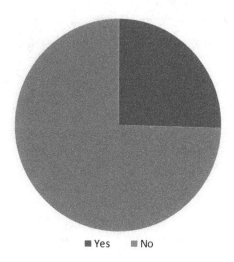

Yes   No

though a number of participants acknowledged that there is a lack of understanding about sexual diversity. Parents were seen as having the strongest influence on gender identity, although they were less influential when it came to sexual practices. The influence of parental gender performances was quite strong, although some respondents contested gender modeling by parents and others admired it (and aspired to mirror it). In our interviews, we asked participants how important gender was to their overall identity. Interview participants were quite varied as to how they saw their own gender identity and as to how important they felt it was in their day-to-day lives. Although many acknowledged the pressures to conform to stereo-typical gender roles, they did not personally feel the need to follow rigid ideas about gendered presentations of self.

Participants did not typically feel their parents had a strong influence on their sexual behaviours. Rather, peers and the internet offered more guidance for their own sense of sexual activity. The majority of our respondents identified on the liberal to very liberal side of the liberal-conservative scale (65.6%, $n = 261$), though we have noted that liberal attitudes towards other people's sexual behaviours are evidenced much more than with their own sexual behaviours. Respondents were quite open-minded towards the sexual behaviours of others, as long as it was consensual, however they placed more boundaries around what they considered acceptable for themselves. While they were quick to state that they had no issue with their friends or peers engaging in casual sex, very few actually indicated it was something they themselves engaged in (Yes 25.4%; No 74.6%) (Fig. 3).

Further, when we asked them about a list of sexual practices and whether they considered these practices to be acceptable outside the context of marriage or within the context of marriage, it was interesting to note that group sex and virtual sex both were seen as somewhat problematic outside and within marriage (Figs. 4 and 5).

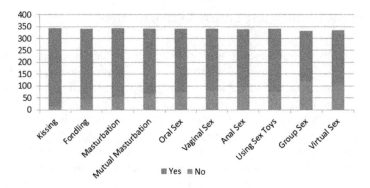

Fig. 4 Do you think the following practices are acceptable outside marriage?

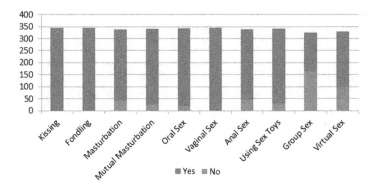

Fig. 5 Do you think the following practices are acceptable within marriage?

Continued consternation regarding non-monogamous sexual relationships is demonstrated in young people's attitudes towards group sex, especially within marriage. The challenges faced by polyamorous, non-monogamous relationships and sexual pairings are evidence of negative assumptions associated with non-monogamy, regardless of the lack of empirical evidence to support those associations (Johnson 2014). Furthermore, the variation between young people's attitudes towards other people's sexual behaviours and the scripts they follow themselves offers another pathway to dispel common assumptions about casual sex as a rapidly increasing "fact" among young people.

6   Current Challenges; Future Opportunities

As evidenced by the responses to questions regarding acceptable practices within and outside marriage, group sex continues to be cast as problematic, regardless of consent. The dominance of monogamy as the "acceptable" relationship standard is a long way from being fully explored; associations of polyamorous or polygamous relationships with being "unfaithful" are prevalent enough that it continues to be treated as a deviant sexuality. Monogamy is strongly endorsed, particularly in Western contexts, and current national debates about polyamorous relationships are frequently tied to assumptions about gender inequality and forced marriage. The common perception about polygamous relationships is primarily associated with notorious Mormon groups, in the U.S. those associated with Warren Jeffs and in Canada, Winston Blackmore. Polygamy is seen as patriarchal, abusive to women and children, and these negative associations are taken as a given (Calder and Beaman 2014). However, closer examination of the similarities between monogamous and polygamous relationships—as it pertains to harm towards women and children via domestic violence—reveals that polygamy is not more inherently harmful than monogamy (Calder and Beaman 2014). While there are clear examples of the ways polyamory can be exploitative and problematic, these examples are also evident across monogamous contexts (Johnson 2014).

Both of the narratives included earlier in this chapter are from young people who engage in polyamorous relationships, both in very different religious and social contexts. Survey respondents point to group sex (or sex outside monogamous relationships) as continually problematic, and this is affirmed by the experiences of both Michelle and Colin, whose experiences and choices are not always accepted by their family and friends. Although both Michelle and Colin engage in these relationships as consenting adults, with partners who are also consenting adults, the script about polygamy as inherently harmful is still strongly evidenced in their experiences and in public responses to media coverage of polygamous groups.

As noted earlier, although I am using the acronym LGBTQI+, it is clear that the progress that has been made regarding inclusivity, socially and in public policy, has primarily been progress made for some members of LGBTQI+ communities—bisexuality and trans identities are far from having the same levels of understanding or inclusion that (monogamous) same-sex couples have obtained (Califia 2001; Kinsman 1996; Irving 2008; Toft 2012). Toft (2012) exposes the false assumption that bisexual Christians face the "same" issues as lesbian and gay Christians, an assumption which continues to delegitimize bisexual identities and render their struggles invisible. Trans communities also face widespread challenges, which are often misunderstood and underrepresented (Irving 2008). Although these areas of research are beginning to grow, much is yet to be uncovered from exploring the challenges faced by bisexual, trans, and intersex identities, and even further when linked to other marginalized identities.

Cragun and Sumerau's (2017) examination of attitudes towards intersectional identities, considering five nonreligious identities and four gender/sexual identities, exposes the ways sexual and gender identities are seen to "pollute" religious identities. Considering attitudes towards religious and nonreligious identities as connected to sexual and gender identities, Cragun and Sumerau's study demonstrates preconceived negative attitudes towards atheism and nonreligion as connected to sexual and gender minorities: nonreligious sexual and gender minorities were more likely to be seen as acceptable than religious sexual and gender minorities (2017).

Attitudes towards atheism, nonreligion, and SBNR identities as connected to attitudes toward gender and sexual diversity are areas of research that are critical for future study. Understanding the nuance of religious and secular attitudes, the negative associations about nonreligion, atheism, and SBNR attitudes, and their relationship to sexual and gender diversity is necessary to explore the reality of intersectional identities but also the reality of the nonreligious and sexually diverse landscape, in Canada and elsewhere.

7   Conclusion

In line with other similar studies, RGSY respondents are articulate and possess a broad knowledge base when it comes to thinking through gender and sexuality as identity categories—they are comfortable discussing "my" gender and "my" sexuality as something they experience, seeing it as personal and political, but very much a continuing part of who they are (whether it's the most prominent part of their identity or not). Analysis of religion as a category remains bifurcated. "My" religion versus "religion" in general are very much separate categories for RGSY respondents.

Our participants have clearly indicated that they think religion can and should adapt to contemporary society; many of our respondents do not think it has yet (or has enough) but think that the shift can occur (Young and Shipley 2015). They are comfortable pulling together teachings, beliefs, and practices from different sources to construct their own sense of religiosity/spirituality as they define it. In light of the shifting self-identification regarding religious/spiritual/ethical categories, it is clear that our respondents are comfortable "picking and choosing" (or mixing and matching) from multiple influences to create a personal set of values, beliefs, and attitudes.

Many of our respondents do not currently engage in any regular religious practices (i.e. attending religious services), however most see themselves as having a future relationship with religion—whether it's being married in a religious ceremony, or in a religious institution, or bringing their children to religious services. This is what Page et al. (2012) describe as part of young people's "imagined futures"; while they might not participate in overtly religious activities now, they do not rule it out for their future lives. This is not how they would describe their gendered or sexual lives. There is not a separate, external engagement related to gender or sexuality that is "on hold" until they engage with it again in the future; these aspects of their identity are very much a part of who they are in day to day life—even those who are not currently in sexual relationships, who are abstaining, and so on.

Unlike gender or sexuality, our respondents do not ascribe an inherency to religious identity for the most part. The challenges of the language of the study of religion are very much evidenced in the ways our respondents wrestle with the category—particularly given the high numbers of nonreligious/SBNR/other participants. Religion (qualified also as nonreligion, spirituality, and so on) is still a much more complex category than gender or sexuality, at least at this particular moment in time with these respondents (although as I suspect this is shifting)—one that is often framed as an external force that they do or do not engage with at different points in their lives, and one whose conceptualization often hits a hard wall when delineating the nuances between "religion" and "my religion."

8   Questions for Critical Thought

1. What are the historical influences on our notions about both religion and sexuality?
2. What contemporary social changes have occurred to shift perceptions about religious identity and sexual identity?
3. What is the relationship between feminist and LGBTQI+ movements in North America?
4. What has influenced your own attitude towards sexuality and religion?
5. What should scholars be considering in order to develop more nuanced perspectives on the relationship between religion, secularism, sexuality and gender?

9   Online Resources

The Institute for Sexual Minority Studies and Services at the University of Alberta, directed by Kristopher Wells, has produced numerous online resources including fact sheets, recommended readings, and teacher guides for supporting students.

The United Church of Canada has produced a list of resources, online and hard copy, as well as scriptural interpretation in support of sexual diversity.

OPHEA has created teaching tools and recommendations for teachers to facilitate the implementation of sexual health curriculum changes.

Trans Student Educational Resources have created "The Gender Unicorn" as a tool for discussing gender identity, expression and presentation as well as sexual attraction and relationships.

10   References for Further Reading

Aune, K., Sharma, S., & Vincett, G. (2008). *Women and religion in the west: challenging secularization.* Farnham: Ashgate.

This book offers unique insight into the relationship of women, religion and secularism. Examining women's roles in and out of religion, the volume also considers questions of secularization specific to women's rights and inclusivity.

Brown, C. G. (2012). *Religion and the demographic revolution.* Woodbridge: The Boydell Press.

Brown examines the changing demographics of religion in Europe, Canada and Australasia in relationship to rapidly changing social and cultural changes – secularization, changing family structures and expectations, and in response to feminist activism and women's rights campaigns.

Hunt, S. J., & Yip, A. K. T. (2012). *The Ashgate research companion to contemporary religion and sexuality.* Farnham: Ashgate.

Hunt and Yip bring together a range of topics, geographies and methodologies in an innovative and complex text that considers religion and sexuality as subjects of research. This text offers critical theoretical and methodological guidance in the study of religion and sexuality, as well as providing much needed comparative data, helpful for students and scholars alike.

McGuire, M. (2008). *Lived religion: Faith and practice in everyday life.* Oxford: Oxford University Press.

McGuire's articulation of lived religion brought into focus language about the ways religion is practiced, expressed and felt by participants in contrast to the tendency toward doctrinal representation as to what 'counts' as religion.

Rasumussen, M. L., & Allen, L. (2016). *Handbook of sexuality education.* London: Palgrave.

The role of religion in relation to other categories, such as gender and sexuality, is considered and challenged in this text which examines sexuality education – education which is frequently the source of consternation, whereby religion (i.e. 'morality') finds itself placed as the counter point to teaching sexuality.

Wyn, J., & Cahill, H. (2014). *Handbook on child and youth studies*. Cham: Springer.

The most comprehensive text available on child and youth studies at an international level, this volume includes chapters on 13 separate themes, challenging the notion that analysis of children and youth should only focus on problems.

Yamane, D. (2016). *Handbook of religion and societ*. Cham: Springer.

The 2016 edition of this volume offers updated content to consider the relationship between religion and society in a contemporary framework, including a chapter on sexuality for the first time. This volume is comprehensive and wide ranging in topics as well as the application and analysis of theories and methods.

11 Researcher Background

Heather Shipley is an Education and Communications Advisor at the Centre for Human Rights, Equity and Inclusion at York University and has been Project Manager for the *Religion and Diversity Project*, (SSHRC funded initiative, University of Ottawa, led by Lori Beaman) since 2010. Her research focuses the construction, management and regulation of religion, gender, sexuality, and sexual orientation as identity categories in media, legal, and public discourse. Publications include: (2015) "Religious Freedom and Sexual Orientation: Equality Jurisprudence and Intersecting Identities," *Canadian Journal of Women and Law*, 27(2): 92–127; *Globalized Religion and Sexual Identity: Contexts, Contestations, Voices*, (2014, editor) Brill Academic Press.

References

Alcoff, L. M., & Caputo, J. D. (2011). *Feminism, sexuality, and the return of religion*. Bloomington: Indiana University Press.
Allen, L. (2005). *Sexual subjects: Young people, sexuality and education*. Basingstoke: Palgrave Macmillan.
Ammerman, N. T. (2014). *Sacred stories, spiritual tribes: Finding religion in everyday life*. Oxford: Oxford University Press.
Anapol, D. (2010). *Polyamory in the 21st century*. Lanham: Rowman and Littlefield Publishers.
Aune, K. (2015). Is secularism bad for women? Transformation: *Where love meets social justice. OpenDemocracy*. Retrieved from https://www.opendemocracy.net/transformation/kristin-aune/is-secularism-bad-for-women. Accessed 7 Aug 2015.
Aune, K., Sharma, S., & Vincett, G. (2008). *Women and religion in the west: Challenging secularization*. Farnham: Ashgate.
Bakht, N. (2012). Veiled objections: Facing public opposition to the niqab. In L. G. Beaman (Ed.), *Reasonable accommodation: Managing religious diversity* (pp. 70–108). Vancouver: UBC Press.
Barras, A. (2014). *Refashioning secularisms in France and Turkey: The case of the headscarf ban*. London: Routledge.

Beaman, L. G. (2013). Battles over symbols: The 'religion' of the minority versus the 'culture' of the majority. *Journal of Law and Religion, 28*(1), 67–104.

Beckford, J. A. (2012). Public religions and the postsecular: Critical reflections. *Journal for the Scientific Study of Religion, 51*(1), 1–19.

Boisvert, D. (2013). What kind of man are you: Same-sex relations, masculinity and Anglican queer malaise. *Studies in Religion., 42*(2), 226–236.

Butler, J. (1993). *Bodies that matter: on the discursive limits of 'sex'.* New York: Routledge.

Calder, G., & Beaman, L. G. (2014). *Polygamy's rights and wrongs.* Vancouver: UBC Press.

Califia, P. (2001). *Speaking sex to power: The politics of queer sex.* Berkeley: Cleis Press.

Chan, S. H., & Huang, P. (2014). Religion and homosexuality in contemporary China: Debates, identity and voices. In H. Shipley (Ed.), *Globalized religion and sexual identity: Contexts, contestations, voices* (pp. 170–192). Leiden: Brill Academic Press.

Charter of Rights and Freedoms (Constitution Act 1982). http://laws-lois.justice.gc.ca/eng/const/page-15.html

Chinwuba, N. (2014). 'They Go Burn in Hell!': Exploring how African MSM negotiate religion and sexuality in Canada. In H. Shipley (Ed.), *Globalized religion and sexual identity: Contexts, contestations, voices* (pp. 256–275). Leiden: Brill Academic Press.

Cossman, B., & Ryder, B. (2001). What is marriage-like like? The irrelevance of conjugality. *Journal of Family Law, 18*(2), 269–326.

Cragun, R., & Sumerau, J. E. (2017). No one expects a transgender Jew: Religious, sexual and gendered intersections in the evaluation of religious and nonreligious others. *Secularism and Nonreligion, 6*, 1. https://doi.org/10.5334/snr.82.

Crenshaw, K. (1991). Mapping the margins: Intersectionality, identity politics, and violence against women of color. *Stanford Law Review, 43*(6), 1241–1299.

Davie, G. (2014). *Religion in Britain: A persistent paradox* (2nd ed.). London: Wiley.

Day, A. (2011). *Believing in belonging: Belief and social identity in the modern world.* Oxford: Oxford University Press.

Denike, M. (2007). Religion, rights and relationships: The dream of relational equality. *Hypatia: A Journal of Feminist Philosophy, 22*(1), 71–91.

Farrow, D. (2007). *A nation of bastards: Essays on the end of marriage.* Toronto: BPS Books.

Fetner, T., Elafros, A., Bortolin, S., & Dreschsler, C. (2012). Safe spaces: Gay-straight alliances in high schools. *Canadian Review of Sociology, 49*(2), 188–207.

Freitas, D. (2008). *Sex and the soul: Juggling sexuality, spirituality, romance and religion on America's college campuses.* Oxford: Oxford University Press.

Halberstam, J. (1998). *Female masculinity.* Durham: Duke University Press.

Hunt, S. J., & Yip, A. K. T. (2012). *The Ashgate research companion to contemporary religion and sexuality.* Farnham: Ashgate.

Hurley, M. (2007). *Charter equality rights: Interpretation of section 15 in Supreme Court of Canada decisions.* Ottawa: Parliamentary Information and Research Service.

Interfaith Coalition on Marriage and Family. (2003). Factum of the Interverner. Halpern et al. https://www.samesexmarriage.ca/legal/ontario_case/appeal/Interfaithcoalition.pdf.

Irigaray, L. (1984). *An ethics of sexual difference.* Ithaca: Cornell University Press.

Irving, D. (2008). Normalized transgressions: Legitimizing the transsexual body as productive. *Radical History Review, 100*, 38–60.

Jagose, A. (1996). Queer theory. *Australian Humanities Review* [online]. Retrieved from http://www.australianhumanitiesreview.org/archive/Issue-Dec-1996/jagose.html. Accessed 5 Dec 2007.

Jakobsen, J., & Pellegrini, A. (2003). *Love the sin: Sexual regulation and the limits of religious tolerance.* New York: Beacon Press.

Johnson, R. (2014). Reflecting on polygamy: What's the harm? In G. Calder & L. Beaman (Eds.), *Polygamy's rights and wrongs: Perspectives on harm, family, and law* (pp. 97–119). Vancouver: UBC Press.

Kinsman, G. W. (1996). *The regulation of desire: Homo and hetero sexualities.* Montréal: Black Rose Books.

Lefebvre, S., & Beaman, L. G. (2014). *Religion in the public sphere: Canadian case studies*. Toronto: University of Toronto Press.

Lewis, R., Marston, C., & Wellings, K. (2013). Bases, stages and 'working your way up': Young people talk about non-coital practices and 'normal' sexual trajectories. *Sociological Research Online, 18*(1). https://doi.org/10.5153/sro.2842.

Lövheim, M. (2008). Rethinking cyberreligion? Teens, religion and the internet in Sweden. *Nordicom Review, 29*(2), 205–217.

MacDougall, B., & Short, D. (2010). Religion-based claims for impinging on queer citizenship. *Dalhousie Law Journal, 33*(2), 133.

McGuire, M. (2008). *Lived religion: Faith and practice in everyday life*. Oxford: Oxford University Press.

Ministry of Ontario. Bill 13: Accepting Schools Act (2012). http://ontla.on.ca/web/bills/bills_detail.do?locale=en&BillID=2549

Montpetit, J. (2016, September 5). Quebec's charter of values, revisited. *CBC News*. Retrieved from: http://www.cbc.ca/news/canada/montreal/caq-quebec-charter-of-values-identity-politics-1.3748084

National Household Survey. (2011). *Census profile*. https://www.google.ca/search?q=national+household+survey+2011&ie=utf-8&oe=utf-8&gws_rd=cr&ei=B4W4WILNN-rajwTa-LigCQ

Native Youth Sexual Health Network. http://nativeyouthsexualhealth.com/

Naugler, D. (2010). Wearing pink as a stand against bullying: Why we need to say more. *Journal of Homosexuality, 57*(3), 347–363.

Page, S.-J., Yip, A. K.-T., & Keenan, M. (2012). Risk and the imagined future: Young adults negotiating religious and sexual identities. In S. Hunt & A. K.-T. Yip (Eds.), *The Ashgate research companion to contemporary religion and sexuality* (pp. 255–270). Farnham: Ashgate.

Pellegrini, A., & Jakobsen, J. (2008). *Secularisms*. Durham: Duke University Press.

Rich, A. (1976). *Of woman born: Motherhood as experience and institution*. New York: New York University Press.

Rich, A. (1980). Compulsory heterosexuality and lesbian existence. *Signs, 5*(4), 631–660.

Ringrose, J. (2015). "BBM is like match.com": social networking and the digital mediation of teen's sexual cultures. In J. Baily & V. Steeves (Eds.), *Egirls, Ecitizens: Putting technology, theory and policy into dialogue with girls' and young women's voices*. Ottawa: University of Ottawa Press.

Rubin, G. (1994). Thinking sex: Notes for a radical theory of the politics of sexuality. In C. S. Vance (Ed.), *Pleasure and danger: Exploring female sexuality* (pp. 267–319). Boston: Routledge and Kegan Paul.

Seitz, D. K. (2014). Unpacking queer secularity: Queer kids, schools and secularism in Toronto, Ontario, Canada. In Y. Taylor & R. Snowdon (Eds.), *Queering religion, religious queers* (pp. 85–100). London: Routledge.

Shipley, H. (2016). Religious freedom and sexual orientation: Equality jurisprudence and intersecting identities. *Canadian Journal of Women and Law, 27*(2), 92–127.

Shipley, H., & Young, P. D. (2016). Religion, youth and queer identities in Canada. In M. Jaime (Ed.), *Sexual diversity and religions* (pp. 219–234). Lima: PEG/Diversities Publishing.

Smith, M. (1999). *Lesbian and gay rights in Canada: Social movements and equality-seeking, 1971–1995*. Toronto: University of Toronto Press.

Taylor, C., & Peter, T. (2011a). Every class in every school: Final report on the first national climate survey on homophobia, biphobia, and transphobia in Canadian schools. *EGALE Canada*. Retrieved from http://archive.egale.ca/EgaleFinalReport-web.pdf. Accessed 18 Dec 2011.

Taylor, C., & Peter, T. (2011b). 'We are not aliens, we're people, and we have rights': Canadian human rights discourse and high school climate for LGBTQ students. *Canadian Review of Sociology, 48*(3), 275–313.

Taylor, Y., & Snowdon, R. (2014). *Queering religion, religious queers*. London: Routledge.

Toft, A. (2012). Bisexuality and Christianity: Negotiating disparate identities in church life. In S. J. Hunt & A. K. T. Yip (Eds.), *The Ashgate research companion to contemporary religion and sexuality* (pp. 189–203). Farnham: Ashgate.

Warner, M. (1991). Introduction: Fear of a queer planet. *Social Text, 29*, 3–17.

Weeks, J. (2011). *The languages of sexuality*. New York: Routledge.

Wilcox, M. (2009). *Queer women and religious individualism*. Indianapolis: Indiana University Press.

Wilson, A. (2015). Our coming in stories: Cree identity, body sovereignty and gender self-determination. *Journal of Global Indigeneity, 1*(1), 1–5.

Woodhead, L. (2013). Liberal religion and illiberal secularism. In G. D'Costa, M. Evans, T. Modood, & J. Rivers (Eds.), *Religion in a liberal state* (pp. 93–116). Cambridge: Cambridge University Press.

Yip, A. K. T., & Page, S. (2013). *Religious and sexual identities: A multi-faith exploration of young adults*. Farnham: Ashgate.

Young, P. D. (2014). 'Severely normal': Sexuality and religion in Alberta's Bill 44. In P. D. Young, H. Shipley, & T. Trothen (Eds.), *Religion and sexuality: diversity and the limits of tolerance* (pp. 45–66). Vancouver: UBC Press.

Young, P. D. (2015). Who speaks for religion? In L. G. Beaman & L. Van Arragon (Eds.), *Issues in religion and education: Whose religion?* (pp. 307–320). Leiden: Brill Academic Press.

Young, P. D., & Shipley, H. (2015). Belief, not religion: Youth negotiations of religious identity in Canada. In J. Wyn & H. Cahill (Eds.), *Handbook of child and youth studies* (pp. 861–873). New York: Springer.

Case List

Alberta v. Hutterian Brethren of Wilson Colony, 2009. SCC 37, [2009] 2 S.C.R. 567.

R. v. Big M Drug Mart Ltd., [1985] 1 S.C.R. 295.

Reference re Same-Sex Marriage, [2004] 3 S.C.R. 698, 2004 SCC 79.

Zylberberg v. Sudbury Board of Education, 1988 CanLII 189 (ON CA).

Religion and Education: The Story of a Conflicted Canadian Partnership

Leo Van Arragon

Abstract In Canada, education is a matter of provincial and territorial jurisdiction so that, while there is a federal constitutional framework, there is not a national system of education. This has had implications for regulation and protection of religion and religious diversity in and by education systems. This chapter examines the resulting regulatory variety but does so in the context of some of the conceptual ambiguities and creative social tensions inherent in the intersection of religion and education. Readers are encouraged to become critically aware of their own positionality in relationship with issues related to this dynamic and complex area of social engagement. This is an important topic because both education and religion are areas of social practice about which most people have strong opinions and feelings. Education represents huge investments of social and financial capital and regularly appears on political platforms during elections as an important measure of commitment to social equality. Education, in other words, carries a lot of freight and debates about education seem to generate a great deal of energy. This chapter is a contribution to an ongoing social conversation, encouraging readers to reconsider issues about which there is considerable accepted but often unexamined common sense.

Keywords Education · Religious freedom · Citizenship · Canadian values · Regulatory frameworks · Indoctrination · Government · Secularization

1 General Introduction and Synopsis of the Theme

The primary purpose of this chapter is to encourage students of education to become more critically aware of the constitutional, legal, political and social contexts in which religious diversity is regulated in and by the jurisdictions in which they work. This is important for three reasons. The first is that teachers' professional practice is

L. Van Arragon (✉)
University of Ottawa, Ottawa, Ontario, Canada

© Springer International Publishing AG, part of Springer Nature 2018
C. Holtmann (ed.), *Exploring Religion and Diversity in Canada*,
https://doi.org/10.1007/978-3-319-78232-4_5

shaped by the boundaries of what is considered appropriate and inappropriate in their schools, some of which are explicit but many of which are implicit commonly accepted sense.

The second is that it is in their professional interest to better understand the religious diversity they will encounter in their practice. Usually they will experience religious diversity as enriching and stimulating, creating opportunity for mutual learning. Sometimes they will experience diversity in conflicts over a wide range of issues, some of which may seem to have little to do with religion. In either case, it is important for teachers to be critically aware of the ways in which religious diversity is conceptualized and managed in their professional contexts.

The third reason is one of positionality. Teachers need to be aware of their own predispositions and opinions in relation to the religious diversity they encounter within their classrooms, their schools and the jurisdictions within which they practice. What they commonly accept as universally true may be open for reconsideration when compared with other possibilities. This chapter invites students of education to hear voices from the wider context of religious diversity in education in Canada.

However, while its primary audience is students of education, the issues raised in this chapter have implications beyond the world of professional education because of three things. The first is that the outcomes of education have obvious implications for civil society by being more or less effective in preparing students for success in a modern society. In addition, education and its delivery represents a site in which "Canadian values" are formulated and debated. Foremost of these is equal access to an essential social practice designed to deliver tolerance and other attitudes necessary in a diverse society. Furthermore, education is an important industry, generating jobs and other benefits, and funded by either private or public resources so that debates over education are often among stakeholders trying to protect their interests.

Therefore, education and the boundaries constructed around its delivery are often topics of vigorous debate throughout Canada and this chapter is intended for students in all disciplines. Most obviously, this is because their lives as students are all about education but also because they are citizens who will be called on to offer informed participation in debates in the future in their roles as parents, members of school communities and school board members.

1.1 Getting Started

Let's get started by thinking about religion and education as a social and conceptual conundrum in which teachers are front line workers. Religion and education are hot topics, particularly in the current global context of heightened security concerns and population movement. While these topics are debated on multiple levels by a wide array of interested parties, teachers and schools are on the front line of responding to real students coming to their classrooms with an astonishing range of vocabularies, sensitivities and experiences shaping their imaginations and understanding of how the world works. Teachers filter that complexity through their own imaginations so they are constantly alert to the reality of their classrooms being places where a world of imaginations meet, to shape and be shaped by and in that meeting. Usually the meeting of different imaginaries is interesting and stimulating but sometimes it is shocking and offensive, to teachers, students and their parents.

Teachers are aware of a number of things regarding religion, among them their position of power and their own positionality in relation to their students. Being gatekeepers in their classrooms, they give and withhold permission, often in incidental interactions and sometimes in intentionally structured lessons. What makes this work on their students' behalf is their professional commitment to a classroom environment which encourages respectful engagement and re-examination of their own and their students understanding of the world (Sergiovanni 1999).

However, teachers must also be critically aware of how the political and regulatory context in which they work shapes their professional practice (Glenn and de Groof 2005). There are two parts to critical awareness. The first is *critical* awareness which is the humble recognition that their context is socially constructed in a particular historical, social and political situation rather than being universally normative. The second is critical *awareness* or *attentiveness* to the power issues inherent in the ways their context emerged and is maintained so that their sense of what is "normal" is somewhat destabilized. This is true in all educational contexts, including homeschools, privately-funded and state funded schools.

1.2   Questions for Critical Thought

Careful listening to dissonant voices is key to the development of critical awareness raising a number of questions for your consideration. Think about the following concepts and reflect on what you think is normal or what "feels right". Then see if you can talk with someone who has a different sense of what is normal.[1]

1. What is "religion"? What is its role in education? In society? In the life of an individual?
2. In a number of provinces, faith-based schools[2] are either fully or partially funded by governments. What is your reaction? Talk to someone who participates in a faith-based school or in a homeschool. What is the logic behind those choices? Or, talk to someone working in a state funded school identifying itself as "secular". How does she navigate the space for religion in her environment?

---

[1]You can also go to the Religion and Diversity website (http://religionanddiversity.ca/) for links to more detailed discussions and debates on issues relating to religion in society and, more specifically, religion and education.

[2]"Faith-based schools" refers to those schools for whom religion, such as Islam, Christianity, Judaism, Sikhism, etc., forms the central tenet of their identity. However, this term is somewhat arbitrary since all schools are "faith-based" in two ways. First, the actual outcomes of any

2   A Real-Life Story Based on Qualitative Research: "Navigating Regulatory Space"

While the regulatory context within which teachers work is established at various levels of government, what actually happens in teacher-student interactions can nuance the distinctions between private and public, religious and secular and other ways in which schools and education are often portrayed. This section provides insight into the working lives of teachers based on interviews with two participants, both identifying themselves as Christians in an Ontario public high school. The purpose of the interviews was to hear how teachers navigated the space created for religion in their professional interactions with students. This is by no means exhaustive but does give a snapshot into the nuanced complexity of how teachers interpret and practice the regulatory frameworks within which they work.

The teachers were active in their religious practice (weekly attendance at church services, prayers), saying that religion for them was a lived relationship with Jesus, describing themselves as "followers of Jesus".[3] One described himself as being a "religious skeptic" and "agnostic" about most institutional religion. Their primary and secondary education had occurred mainly in public schools and religion played a somewhat vague role in their schooling, although one of them said that public schools, before 1990, were "Christian", recalling that he had memorized Bible passages as a poetry memorization exercise. The current school opening exercises consisted of the national anthem and a moment of silence, during which both teachers prayed for their students and for the day's activities.

They described the relationship between religion and education in terms of finding and taking opportunities for students to engage important questions about the meaning of life, human destiny, origins etc. in a safe space. In their view, all people are on a spiritual quest, searching for meaning and purpose, but their students tended to be cautious about discussing that aspect of their lives. Their role as teachers was to "open a door" through which students could go if they needed to do so, both in informal interactions and in formal classroom activities. Their responses to students were both opportunistic and strategic. For example, one of the participants described his classes as preparation for "the final examination of life", encouraging his students to think beyond jobs to consider the bigger questions of what kind of life they envision for themselves. Both agreed that education must transcend any reductionist

---

educational process are impossible to predict with certainty, so all schools operate on the basis of "faith" that their educational process will lead to a preferred outcome in terms of a graduate profile. Second, all educational endeavours operate on the basis of a more or less clearly defined set of "first principles" forming the imaginative screen for the social and educational activities that occur within them. There are two further complicating factors. The first is that, although in most jurisdictions, they are an important component in the delivery of education, there is a great deal of regulatory diversity in Canada and around the world for faith-based schools. Second, there is a great deal of diversity among faith-based schools, including within particular categories, so that there are many different kinds of Islamic, Christian, Jewish, Sikh etc. schools. In this chapter, the use of the term "faith-based" is a provisional matter of convenience.

[3] See McGuire, M. (2008) on a more detailed examination of "lived religion". It was interesting to see the teachers use the term without reference to McGuire's ground-breaking work.

view which denies students the opportunity to consider questions of ultimate importance. They agreed that a teacher is a "whole person" and that the idea of separating one's spiritual self from one's professional self is futile, leading to a lack of authenticity about which students are very perceptive. They described their school as hospitable to religious diversity and their student population as very diverse, with, among other things, a Jewish Cultural Club, Muslim prayer space and a Christian club. The teaching staff were primarily from a variety of Christian traditions, many of whom described themselves as such, while others would describe themselves as "secular". They experienced limitations on their religious expression in a number of ways. Many of the Christian teachers, like their students, were sensitive about expressing their religious selves. While a code of silence might be too strong a description, they described a "code of caution" around religion. Sometimes the restrictions were explicit, one teacher recalling an incident in which he was unofficially reprimanded for referring the amazing "design" of the human body, "design" suggesting a commitment to an "intelligent design" model of the world which was interpreted as being too close to an explicitly religious concept. In the words of one participant, a teacher whose imagination is shaped by religion and spirituality must, therefore, be "as wise as a serpent and as gentle as a dove", a reference to the gospel of Matthew 10:16. In summary, both were committed to "walking the talk" described in Philippians 4:8 which says "Finally, brothers and sisters, whatever is true, whatever is noble, whatever is right, whatever is pure, whatever is lovely, whatever is admirable—if anything is excellent or praiseworthy—think about such things." Thinking was seen to include action or praxis which, in turn, was understood as a natural and positive link with character education.

3   Key Terms and Concepts

The chapter is organized around three clusters of concepts, examining the implications of defining key terms in rhetorical binaries as they often are in public debate. They are *religion*, *education* and *citizenship*.

> *Religion*: a mode of human thought, a social practice and a conceptual problem often defined by opposing harmful and benign forms of religion, religion and secular, religion and modernity.
>
> *Education:* defined by opposing critical thought and indoctrination, education about religion and religious education, public, sectarian and private education and religion and science.
>
> *Citizenship*: often debated by opposing what is included and not included in "Canadian values", the challenges of integration, social cohesion versus assimilation, and the threats posed by fundamentalism, radicalization and sectarianism.

This chapter does not offer a definitive resolution to the lively academic debate about the precise definition of religion. Rather, the purpose here is to encourage readers to reflect on their own working definitions of religion to understand how they may interpret and understand their experience of religious diversity. Working definitions are important because they animate debates over the educational resources, time and space which should be allocated to religion. However, they are usually unexamined in debates over prayer space in schools, gender diversity, course content, textbooks and school funding (among others). Students and teachers may have opinions about things, for example, gender equality, which when first expressed, may seem to have little to do with religion.

Careful examination and listening may open up consideration of deeply held convictions which the teacher must engage with professional detachment and respect. Parents and students who worry about sex education curriculum or presentations of gender diversity will do so for a variety of reasons but religious sensitivities may well be an important part of their thought process. Students have the developmental task of navigating the intersection between the intimate worlds in which they grow up and their school world which can open up new ways of thinking. However, in the absence of careful respect, that process can also create turmoil which can be more destructive to their sense of who they are. Living in a diverse society can be challenging for minority groups but is equally so for members of a dominant group who may not have had to examine their own biases and conceptual predispositions. Definitions of religions are more often a subtext in educational encounters rather than the explicit text and are therefore masked while, nevertheless, being powerful in their effects.

Readers are invited to become more critically aware of their own understanding of religion and of the often unexamined assumptions about religion in their working environment while recognizing that they will encounter counter discourses in their work with students, parents and colleagues. In fact, for students with cultural backgrounds other than Abrahamic traditions[4] and for the growing population of religious "nones", religion as a category may not make sense or may not be important. Nevertheless, education systems in Canada have their roots in Christianity and debates about the intersection of religion, education and citizenship take a particular shape within which this chapter works.

In the world of education, religion and religious diversity are usually non-issues, people living in respectful harmony or at least tolerance, negotiating differences in ways that do not attract attention. Sometimes debates involving religion can be vigorous and, at times acrimonious. However, the main fault lines are not, in the first place, between religion and non-religion, nor are they driven primarily by an impulse to eliminate religion from society. Canada, along with many other countries, is a signatory to United Nations declarations affirming the rights of people to religious freedom of choice and to anti-discrimination legislation. Rather, the more

---

[4]Abrahamic traditions include Muslim, Jewish and Christian religions, each of which has its own fascinating diversity.

pressing issue is the distinction between harmful and benign forms of religion or between bad and good forms of religion. Those boundaries are interpreted in different ways in different contexts but in western states the issues of "radicalization", religious "fundamentalism" and the links between religion and political violence provide insight into how the distinction between good and bad forms of religion are constructed.

In the Canadian context, shaped as it is by its Christian ideological past, the definition of religion and its role in the world is an important matter with implications for education and citizenship. There are two broad clusters of definitions which, although they are presented here as opposites, exist in the real world along a nuanced continuum. The first is that religion provides a comprehensive platform for truth and morality, essential to social moral order and a personal sense of meaning and purpose. On the other extreme, religion is seen as a social and epistemological barrier to social and personal development in conflict with modernity. It is important to reiterate that no person lives completely and consistently on one or the other extreme although sometimes in the heat of political debate one might think otherwise. Getting to know people who live religion in a variety of ways is a good way to nuance the picture (and complicate your life!!). This chapter proceeds on the principle that religion is an important mode of human knowing and experience, shaping both the individual and communal lives of students but it has also been an important factor in Canada's social diversity (Beckford 2003).

3.1 Questions for Critical Thought

1. Religion actually does not do anything, just as science or art do not. Rather, people do things, narrating, explaining and justifying what they do in a variety of languages, among them religion. How might religion be deployed in ways that are harmful? How might it provide a language for positive contributions to society and personal development? Where do you find yourself in this discussion?
2. How would you define *fundamentalism*? What about *radicalization*? Consider the idea that fundamentalism and radicalization can have sources other than religion.
3. What is secularism? What are the boundaries between the religious and the secular?

3.2 Education: Beyond the "3 R's"

Next, let's think about education in order to get beyond a "common sense" but limited understanding of education as a transmission of the "3R's", which very few teachers really believe anyway (Palmer 1993). Broadly speaking, education is a social practice with a number of goals, some existing in a state of creative tension with one another. It can be organized in a wide variety of ways which include different ways of understanding the relative roles of various stakeholders in the educational process. Readers are invited to consider three issues in educational politics.

The first of these is the goal of education, or what education is designed to do both for individuals and/or for the society in which it is practiced. Education in any context lives on a kind of razor's edge between its conservative and its innovative impulses and purposes. On the one hand, education is an initiation process into a tradition and a community. On the other hand, education equips students for successful adaptation to an ever-changing world (Schiffauer et al. 2004).

The second issue, related to the first, is educational practice, in which the reader is invited to consider the distinction between education and indoctrination.[5] Because the tension between its innovative and conservative roles is inherent in education, the distinction between education and indoctrination is not always clear (Richardson 1991, 1996; Richardson and Introvigne 2001; Van Arragon 2015). This is an important point to make in a chapter on religion and education because of the tendency to link religion with indoctrination and the secular with education. While these linkages serve a rhetorical purpose in case law and in political debate, there is less evidence that they serve a useful purpose in describing what actually happens in classrooms across Canada. In addition, they can be a hindrance to productive discussion about the role of religion in education (Beaman and Van Arragon 2015).

The third and related issue involves the question of who "owns" the educational enterprise, often framed as a problem of the distinction between "public" and "private" education. Education lives at the nexus of actors highly invested in the outcomes of an educational process. What students will retain and value, even as they expand their knowledge base, their critical thinking skills and their perspectives is the subject of intense interest of parents, religious communities, education professionals, state regulators and, of course, the students themselves (Bader 2007). In the western world, parents, religious organizations, students, the state and state actors are most often seen as the stakeholders. However, there are important differences in understanding who, among those, is the primary stakeholder. During the nineteenth century the nation-state emerged as the dominant institution in the organization of public space, including public education delivered in public schools. However, counter-discourses are expressed by other stakeholders including religious

---

[5] "Indoctrination" in its popular usage is associated with "brainwashing" and the practice of depriving learners of access to information and opinions which challenge the achievement of a particular outcome. It is often associated with religion, as in "religious indoctrination" or with the practices of non-liberal state educational strategies designed to produce unthinking adherents. It is often contrasted with education, identified with the free and critical thought delivered by liberal and secular educational jurisdictions. However, there is a body of literature suggesting that these are constructions for the purposes of privileging some forms of education while marginalizing others.

organizations, parents, business interests and professional organizations in a wide array of schooling options. Conflicts over school funding, academic programs and school culture often reveal fault lines over assumptions about what schooling is for and who should, in the end, decide what is best and what is harmful to children and society.

The reader is asked to reconsider the rhetorical binary between "public" and "private" in education for two reasons. The first is that "public" is a malleable term used in various ways but in the context of education, it is most often linked to the state and state actors. The conclusion is that "public schooling" is schooling in which the state and state actors are the primary stakeholders while "private" and "sectarian" schooling is delivered by non-state actors. Religion is usually linked to private interests, along with family and other social activities.

However, linking "public" to the more general idea of the "common good" and the generation of *social capital*[6] opens other conceptual possibilities, one of which is that all social activities and the organizations and institutions in which they occur are both "private" and "public". For example, churches, usually thought of as "private" institutions, make contributions to public welfare or the common good when they engage in refugee resettlement or providing support services for homeless people. States and state actors, usually thought of as serving the public good, intervene in family matters which are usually thought of as "private". So, reconsideration of the "public" and "private" categories can be a useful exercise, opening up possibilities that state and non-state actors live in partnership to deliver the common good by generating social capital.

The second reason is more specific to the delivery of education when considered as a social practice with both private and public implications. The choice to provide education in a homeschool setting, a faith-based school or a school identifying itself as "secular" is made for reasons unique to the families making those decisions and, in that sense, is highly personal or private (Arai 2000; Van Pelt et al. 2007). However, the education provided in each of those settings is a public service in the sense that they each equip students to enter society along with students educated in other situations. In Canada, students can enter universities based on the education they receive in a wide variety of settings and there is no evidence that students are handicapped by their pathway choices. Regulatory frameworks across the country incorporate educational diversity in a variety of ways but all Canadian jurisdictions recognize the rights of parents and students to make choices about the schooling that they feel best serves their needs. The point is that the distinction between "public" and "private" education is less clear and more fluid than it is often represented to be.

---

[6] Social capital does not have one definition but refers to social relationships and networks based on trust as an important factor in society. For a quick introduction see "Definitions of Social Capital" by *Social Capital Research* <http://www.socialcapitalresearch.com/literature/definition.html>

3.3   Questions for Critical Thought

1. What is education "for" in your opinion? Who should be the primary
   stakeholder in making key decisions in education? In your educational
   world, who is the primary stakeholder or where are the key decisions
   made? What are the implications of that choice?
2. The current use of indoctrination has often had negative connotations and
   has been associated with religion. What is indoctrination? How is it different from education? What happens if you separate religion and indoctrination? Can indoctrination occur in a non-religious environment?
3. Is there such a thing as "bad education"? What might that look like? What
   about good education? What makes education good or bad?

4   Current Challenges and Opportunities in the Nexus of Religion, Education and Citizenship: A Mapping Exercise in Three Parts

The intersection of religion and education in modern Western states is shaped by the
question of what it means to be an educated citizen and who has the mandate to
deliver her. In the Canadian context, the educated citizen is one who, among other
things, can distinguish between good and bad forms of religion, the standard for the
distinction being "Canadian values" and the skill in applying it being critical thought.
The distinction between good and bad forms of religion involves two things. The
first concerns religious practices and values themselves and the second is the location of religious practices. For example, some religious modes of thought are considered inherently bad or good (for example, their implications for attitudes about
gender) but might be tolerable if they are practiced or expressed in private. Still other
forms of religious practice are acceptable in public, an example being religious
engagement in interfaith dialogue or participation in food banks. The distinction
between what is and what is not acceptable religious practice is further complicated
by the jurisdiction in which they occur and which religious groups practice them. In
Quebec, for example, religious symbols in public spaces or worn by state employees
(or public servants) are a topic of considerable debate although no one seems to be
advocating for the banning of such symbols in homes or places of worship. However,
the issue of religious symbols has less social urgency in other Canadian jurisdictions. Another example can be found in education. In Ontario, education delivered in
Roman Catholic separate schools is fully funded by the government while for other
religious groups, the alternatives open to them other than public or Roman Catholic
schools are privately funded schools or home schools. However, other provinces
have developed mechanisms to fund a greater variety of faith-based schools.

 While there are a number of different ways in which jurisdictions have responded
to religious diversity, there are two common features or themes. The first is that all

governments express interest in the limits of religious diversity based on an assessment of what practices and modes of thought represent sources of harm to social order (Beaman 2008). The second is that education is universally seen as one of the key practices to deliver citizens who embrace common civic values and have the skills to identify and resist harmful modes of thought and practices. There are a number of conundrums inherent in the intersection of religion, education and citizenship with educators being on the front line of managing the resulting creative tensions in their schools and classrooms.

You are asked to consider the nexus of religion, education and citizenship from three perspectives. They are the distinction between public and private educational practices, the relationship between religion and science and the role of religion and education in the delivery of citizenship in a modern society. The purpose of the following paragraphs is to stimulate reconsideration of your assumptions about each of these perspectives.

In some contexts, religion is seen as a private matter, tangential to and even hostile to education. In contexts in which modernity and religion are opposed, religion and education are seen as existing in two parallel worlds. This binary crosses religious lines so that some religious groups agree that religion and education exist in two parallel worlds divided by "religious – secular" and "private – public" boundaries. In contexts where religion is seen as important in the private lives of students and parents, schools may respond by creating extra-curricular space for prayer and other religious activities. Academic programs may include references to religious groups and their activities as part of the Canadian multicultural mosaic or in courses such as World Religions. The point is that the academic program includes religion, not so much to achieve an intimate knowledge of religion but rather to enhance attitudes of tolerance of religious diversity. In this context, religion may or may not be considered important in the formation of a fully realized human being but may be seen as an important facet of social life which students must learn to navigate in order to achieve harmonious social diversity protected by a reasonable level of social tolerance.

However, where it provides a comprehensive framework fundamental to the fully developed life, religion occupies a central role in the educational process. Education is a form of religious practice designed to strengthen social bonds and an imaginary which rejects the religious-secular boundaries. Religion provides an apex of a conceptual hierarchy (Rappaport 1999), the foundation for a "chain of memory" (Hervieu-Léger 2000), a framework for "wisdom" (Blomberg 2007) or a platform to engage the world (Zine 2008). Faith-based schools and many home schooling movements are expressions of religion as a more comprehensive category which tends to be viewed with suspicion in Western societies (Sullivan 2005).[7]

---

[7]Winnifred Sullivan describes "protestantism" in this secularized sense, saying, "Religion –'true' religion some would say on this modern protestant reading, came to be understood as being private, voluntary, individual, textual and believed". In contrast, 'public, coercive, communal, oral

The different ways of understanding religion and its role in education are expressed in a wide variety of forms and contexts, mostly in harmonious coexistence. However, there are important differences among them, sometimes expressed in vigorous public debates. One of these is over the roles of science and religion in education. One way of thinking about science and religion is that they exist in parallel universes, science being a source of public discourse while religion is restricted to private areas of social and personal life. One conclusion is that the fully realized citizen is one whose public discourse is, in the first place, informed by science or scientific reasoning (Mackay 1969; Spinner-Halev 2000). Religion is often associated with non-rational or even irrational emotion while science, in contrast, is often associated rational and critical thought. Science is considered secular and modern while religion is considered, well, religious and traditional.

However, there are a number of things to consider here. The first is that a survey of the history of science reveals an intimate link between science and religion and that science, while it proceeds on the basis of "scientific method", is triggered as much by intuition, prejudice and self-interest in particular political contexts as it is by a commitment to a form of truth based on observable data. In the same way, a survey of religions reveals that they have their own rational systems of thought which satisfy particular human needs and have done so throughout history. The idea that Western societies, leading with scientific rationality, have achieved the pinnacle of human achievement, is a modern conceit with disturbing implications. Conversely, forms of religion which deny scientific evidence in favour of particular readings of religious texts about, for example, the age of the earth, have contributed to misunderstanding between science and religion (Numbers 1992).[8]

Consideration of the relationship between science and religion becomes more complicated by the association between science and modernity narrated in terms of a "secularization thesis" which assumed that religion would disappear as societies "modernized". At the same time, a secularization narrative adopted by religious communities can result in a kind of defensiveness which leads to other conclusions about the evils of modernity and the threat represented by modern science. A simplistic secularization narrative has contributed to misunderstanding of both religion and modernity, contributing to suspicion of science and marginalization of religious voices in public discourse, including education.

There are a number of flaws in a secularization narrative and, in fact, academic literature on secularization has become much more nuanced since the mid-twentieth

---

and enacted religion ... was seen to be 'false' ... iconically represented historically in the United States, for the most part by the Roman Catholic Church (and by Islam today) was and perhaps still is, the religion of most of the world" (2005, p.8).

[8] The 1925 Scopes Monkey Trial in Tennessee is an iconic example of a conflict which probably did not need to happen. "The Creationists" by R.L. Numbers traces the hardening ideological binary between religion and science, providing evidence that creationism, in an ideological sense, is contested within religious communities. Creationism in the twenty-first century continues to be associated with a kind of "culture war" in which science has become a battleground obscuring more nuanced and productive engagement.

century (Asad 2003; Beckford 2003; Beyer 2006; Cavanaugh 2009; Hurd 2008; Martin 2005; Nisbet 1976). One flaw is that a secularization thesis assumes that "modernity" was one linear process modelled on Western liberal social developments. However, "modernity", like so many terms, is malleable meaning different things in different contexts and has been subjected to critical scrutiny by feminist and non-Western scholars who point to the fact that religion, rather than disappearing, has continued to flourish in modern societies.

Rather than placing science and religion in opposition, readers are asked to consider the idea that both religion and science are profoundly human modes of thought addressing different and complementary ways of knowing the world. Seen this way, education can provide a context which does not have to exclude either religion or science but rather, can draw on both to address the needs of students to know the world and themselves as actors in the world.[9]

This leads to the third perspective on the nexus of religion, education and citizenship in Canada which is the role of education in delivering graduates committed to "Canadian values". Like many other terms in discussions about religion, education and citizenship, "Canadian values" is variously defined, but intended to create a comprehensive imagination leading to harmonious social diversity in which religion plays an ambiguous role. For some, religion is seen as a source of sectarian division best restricted to private life with education serving to teach students how to adopt Canadian values which transcend religious particularities. However, there are citizens for whom Canada and Canadian values are not the highest point of their values hierarchy and loyalty. As a result, their citizenship loyalties are often called into question, an assessment which may have little to do with their actual behaviour and more to do with their ways of engaging public discourse. For some, engagement includes challenging aspects of the educational and social programs within public schools while for others it has meant opting out of a public education process considered by most Canadians to be essential to the development of fully realized citizenship. In either case, dissenting voices are often associated with unacceptable modes of thought and questionable values relating to, among other things, gender equality and biological diversity and origins.

Much of the conflict is over the intersecting roles of the state, religious communities, parents and professional organizations in delivering citizenship. The question here is about which of the stakeholders is the primary one and which ones play various supportive roles in the educational process designed to achieve the educated graduate. Very few of these constructions view the others as having no constructive role but there can be intense disagreement about their relative importance in delivering education (Bader 2007; Glenn 2000, 2011).

---

[9] Readers could consult a number of sources starting with *Science and Religion: Reconcilable Differences* <http://undsci.berkeley.edu/article/science_religion>; *Science and Religion* by Albert Einstein <http://www.westminster.edu/staff/nak/courses/Einstein%20Sci%20%26%20Rel.pdf>; *What is the Relation between Science and Religion?* by William Lane Craig <http://www.reasonablefaith.org/what-is-the-relation-between-science-and-religion>. Each article has further references. These are included in Sect. 7 to give the reader a sense of the diversity of the debates and not because they reflect the opinion of the author.

The relationship between education, religion and citizenship is uneasy because education, at its best, opens up new ways of seeing, helps students find their own intellectual and moral voices and gives them the skills to critically assess information. Freedom to think and choose is inherently disruptive so education lives on a kind of razor's edge between its conservative and its innovative functions. Its conservative function is to inculcate students into an existing belief and value system, for example, Canadian values (Ontario Ministry of Education 2008) or an Islamic "straight path" (Zine 2008). In contrast, the innovative function of education is to have students become adept at applying existing values to new developments. This is obvious for immigrants whose sense of social organization, values and behaviours are subjected to critical scrutiny by the next generation who must figure out how to live in their new country. However, it is equally true for those who are more established, seeing their children embrace new technologies and new social conventions. Education lives in a dynamic liminal space, having disruptive potential to any value system associated with socialization and is one of the reasons that education is the topic of intense social discourse and contestation. The regulatory framework adopted by provinces, school districts and schools include commitments to what forms of religion are identified as an important part of achieving educational outcomes and which ones are seen as harmful.

4.1 Questions for Critical Thought

1. What is your answer to the conundrums inherent in the nexus of religion, education and citizenship? Where do you see those tensions at play in your education and professional practice?
2. Why do people choose a particular educational pathway for their children? Why might people choose a state school over a private option? Why might they choose a privately funded option? How does religion figure into decisions about educational pathways?

5 Religion, Education and Citizenship in Canada

Having outlined the conceptual issues in the intersection of religion, education and citizenship, we now turn our attention to the ways in which the issues of religion, education and citizenship are problematized and resolved in Canada.[10]

Religion is present in education systems in many ways of which three are the focus of this chapter. First, religion can be seen as a comprehensive category driving

---

[10] For a more comprehensive and detailed analysis of this topic, see Van Arragon, L. (2015) and Beaman, L. and Van Arragon, L. (2015).

the entire ethos of an educational endeavour. These include faith-based or faith schools but also the homeschool movement much of which is religiously inspired. In such settings, religion is more or less evident in all areas of school social and academic life and it is also evident in religious instruction designed to inculcate religious information, and encourage commitment to the tradition in which the school finds itself. People participating in these endeavours insist that they are not anti-social and that they are good citizens who embody Canadian values, even though they are choosing an alternative path to educated citizenship.

Second, religion can be seen as a discrete area of scholarly investigation, much like other academic disciplines expressed in the phrases "education about religion" or "religion education". As such the study of religion must work within the usual rules of scholarly work involving the stance of academic detachment and awareness of one's own biases with investigation disciplined by critical thinking and other academic skills. This is not unique to the study of religion and, in that sense, education about religion has a legitimate place in the academic program along with other social sciences and humanities. Aside from being a discrete academic subject, consideration of religion can also be included as a factor in analyzing human motivation, historical events, varieties of human knowing and experience, social diversity and alternative models for thinking about biological origins and diversity.

Third, religion is a fact of social life in a school, represented by the religious diversity among students and their families. Schools develop strategies for addressing religious diversity in a variety of ways, including more or less formally organized activities to acknowledge and even celebrate religious practices important to the student population. In addition, reflecting the constitutional protections of freedom of religion school boards across Canada have adopted anti-bullying, discrimination and inclusion policies which identify religion as an identity category to create safe space for students.

In summary, religion can be seen as an identity category which must be protected, a mode of human knowing and/or a subject of scholarly investigation. Professional educators have choices about the role of religion in their practice but their practice occurs within a regulatory framework that encourages some ways of seeing religion while discouraging others.

5.1 Regulatory Frameworks for Education in Canada

Education in Canada is regulated within a framework outlined in the *Constitution Acts of 1867* and *1982*. Canada's system of government divides powers between the federal and provincial governments and *Section 93* of the *Constitution Act of 1867* designates education as a matter of provincial jurisdiction. In addition, it creates a framework for "separate schools" designed to protect minorities from the majority. In the 1860's the identified minorities in Quebec were English, Protestant and First Nations while the majority was French and Roman Catholic, in contrast with Ontario where the minorities were Roman Catholic, French and First Nations and the majority was English and Protestant. Educational spaces for minorities in Quebec and Ontario were created in "separate" and "residential schools" as strategies to manage a political impasse or to assimilate a minority into a majority culture. Non-identified minorities were enrolled in common (later "public") schools. In addition, non-identified minorities have used the services of "private" schools from before Confederation. As other provinces joined the Canadian federation, they interpreted *Section 93* in their own ways, regulating the role of religion in education in ways that reflected the social and political dynamics of the day. Those initial resolutions to the challenges of religious diversity in education have continued to evolve reflecting changing demographics and trends in educational theory and practice in the context of dynamic political realities.

The *Constitution Act of 1982* includes a number of sections relevant to how religion intersects with education. *Sections 2* and *15* identify the protection of religious freedom and equality which have been used in attempts by various religious minorities to advance their interests in education. *Section 1* is relevant, giving governments the power to override *Sections 2* and *15* claims.

In addition, Canada adopted a Bill of Rights in 1960 which includes protection of religious freedom (among other rights) and is a signatory to the United Nations Universal Declaration of Human Rights. The provinces have adopted human rights codes modelled on the Canadian and United Nations declarations.

In summary, religion has been identified as a category deserving protection at various levels of government in Canada, placing Canadian governments in company with other liberal Christian jurisdictions around the world. In fact, religious freedom has become an important theme in foreign policies and a feature distinguishing liberal from non-liberal states. However, just what that means is contested and there is a body of critical literature suggesting that religious freedom is less about religion and freedom and more about the achievement of domestic and foreign policy objectives (Bosco 2014; Hurd 2008).

In Canada, provinces have interpreted the two constitution acts and protection of religious freedom in their own ways so that the Canadian education scene is characterized by a wide variety of regulatory systems and funding mechanisms reflected in provincial education acts within which education is delivered. There are similar legal and regulatory structures which include ministries of education, education acts and regulations administered by regional school boards with educational services delivered by professional teachers.

Ministries of education consistently express a commitment to diversity and protection from discrimination and bullying but beyond that, provinces have made a range of choices in the management of religious diversity in the *social life* of schools and the management of religious diversity in the *academic programs*. These are discrete areas with their own regulatory frameworks, legal and social histories but they also intersect in important ways to produce a particular outcome or graduate profile. In addition, each area is contested by a variety of groups promoting their interests in the dynamic regulatory world of education.

5.2   Religion in the Social Life of Schools

There are two aspects to the issue of religious diversity in the social life of education systems across Canada. The first is that all provinces and territories express respect for the religious diversity of students and families served in their school systems, expressed by the concept of "inclusivity". The second is that there are conflict zones over the role of religion and the limits to the expression of religious diversity in schools. These include responses to gender diversity with potential friction between guidelines for protection of gender diversity issued by ministries and departments of education and religious groups. Other points of friction can include choices of literature, the distribution of religious literature, prayer space in schools and religious symbols. Table 1 below gives a snapshot of ways in which Canadian jurisdictions are managing religious diversity in the social life of schools.

The focus on inclusivity as a concept for embracing religious diversity can be experienced as suppression of diversity in disputes over issues often not directly related to religion. Dissident voices in debates over gender diversity and bullying often arise from religious groups both within and outside public schools who have divergent ways of seeing human development and human interactions. Teachers need to be aware of these debates and their own positionality so that they can treat their students, parents, colleagues in other school systems with respect and listening, sometimes with "agonistic respect" (Connolly 2002, 2005) on the basis of "deep equality" (Beaman 2014, 2017) which includes a willingness to learn and adapt.

There are any number of ways in which space for religion in the social life of public schools is contested. They can include clothing as in the case of a student in

Table 1   Religion and social life in schools

British Columbia has a publication titled "Diversity in BC Schools: A framework" https://www.bced.gov.bc.ca/diversity/diversity_framework.pdf. British Columbia works with the theme titled "Safe, Caring and Orderly Schools" with access to resources https://www.bced.gov.bc.ca/sco/resources.htm and a guidebook http://www.bced.gov.bc.ca/sco/guide/scoguide.pdf.
The Alberta School Board Association has issued a statement on "Welcoming, caring, respectful and safe learning environments" http://www.asba.ab.ca/services/resources/policy-advice/welcoming-caring-respectful-and-safe-learning-and-working-environments/
Manitoba has an extensive section on religious diversity in schools, drawing on the work of Lori Beaman and the Religion and Diversity Project. Publication "Responding to Religious Diversity in Manitoba's Schools" http://www.edu.gov.mb.ca/k12/docs/support/religious_diversity/full_doc.pdf
The Government of Ontario has a great deal of literature on the accommodation of religious diversity in its school system ranging from publications by the Ministry of Education http://www.edu.gov.on.ca/eng/policyfunding/equity.pdf, www.edu.gov.on.ca/eng/policyfunding/inclusiveguide.pdf, the Ontario Education Services Corporation equity.oesc-seo.org/Download.aspx?rid=9966 and by regional school boards tldsb.ca/wp-content/uploads/2013/.../BD-2038-Religious-Accomodation-Procedure.pdf and www.peelschools.org/aboutus/.../FINALReligiousAccommodationCOMS8.pdf

Nova Scotia insisting that he has the right to wear a T-shirt with a "pro-Jesus message" (Boesveld 2012) and other religious symbols in public spaces as in Quebec (Globe and Mail 2010). It can also include debates over other religiously oriented activities in schools during non-instructional times including prayer space for Muslim students, sometimes from groups who contest the idea in principle but also from other religious groups who claim that Muslims are being given preferential treatment (Browne 2015; CBC News 2011).

Many of the debates over the space for religion in public schools occur in the language of "reasonable accommodation" and "tolerance" in "secular" spaces. However, both reasonable accommodation and tolerance have been critically examined by Wendy Brown (2006) and Lori Beaman (2014), the key issue being the one of power. Who decides what can and cannot be "reasonably accommodated" is a matter of great interest for religious minorities who experience their minority status in being granted space which can as easily be withdrawn. In addition, faith-based schools experience their own debates over the limits of diversity, including issues of gender, dress and theology. There is a great deal of variety in the admissions policies and practices of faith-based schools, many of which accept students with religious traditions other than the one on which the school is based. One example is the Roman Catholic separate school system in Ontario which serves students from many different religions but the same thing can be observed in privately funded schools. The point is that all schools have their own ways of accommodating religious diversity and the boundaries of accommodation provides rich opportunity for energetic debate.

5.3   Questions for Critical Thought

1. How should religious diversity be accommodated in the social life of schools?
2. Who should provide the leading voice in determining the boundaries of religious accommodation?
3. What should be the ultimate criteria is decisions about limits to diversity?

5.4   Religion in Academic Program Design and Content

The focus of this section is the diversity of approaches in how religion is incorporated into academic programs. The specific references are just illustrative since course outlines and program requirements are regularly (more or less) updated, making any specific information time sensitive. Generally, one gains access to the information through ministries and departments of education finding links to academic programs and courses. Sometimes more specific information is available on school board and school websites, sometimes but not always facilitated through the use of a "search" function. The most productive search words are "religion" and "world religions" on ministry of education websites.

All ministries of education express commitments to social diversity and have extensive documents regarding protection of students from discrimination and bullying arising from their being members of religious minorities. However, the issue of the role of religion in academic programs is more complicated for a variety of reasons. First, provincial guidelines allow varying degrees of interpretive latitude for school boards and individual schools. Second, schools and school boards have different ways in which they monitor teacher interpretation of and compliance with guidelines and policy documents (Gravel 2015). Third, there is little consistency in web design and access of information regarding the academic programs offered in provinces, school boards and schools. Some schools have detailed information about programs and courses on their websites while on others academic programs are less accessible. Further, there is no clear connection between the information available on websites and the quality of program and program delivery in schools. However, there is considerable evidence that education in Canada is both centralized in provincial and territorial governments (all of which have a ministry or department of education) and increasingly decentralized the closer one gets to the actual classroom. Tables 2 and 3 give a snapshot of the ways in which Canadian jurisdictions are managing religious diversity in academic programs.

There are a number of issues that provide an entry point into the ways religion in academic programs is contested, two of which are examined here. The first is over the role of religion in academics and the second is over the role of "opting out" as a strategy deployed by parents to address their discomfort with elements in the academic program. The role of religion in public schools has always been controversial and the current resolution is to identify public schools as "secular", meaning that engaging in religious practices and religious instruction should be kept out of public school classrooms. However, the line between "secular instruction" and "religious practice" is not always clear, illustrated by the National post describing a reaction to an Aboriginal cleansing ceremony in a school in British Columbia (Humphries 2016). The concern expressed by one parent was that the cleansing ceremony was a spiritual practice and therefore violated provincial legislation protecting the secular nature of public education. The school board in this case has argued that the smudging ceremony is a cultural practice with educational and social value by introducing students to Aboriginal cultural practices in a respectful context.

The distinction between religion and culture is not fixed and clear, nor is the identification of harm to children. So, what is a parent to do when her child is in a classroom where activities are taking place which are offensive in some way? One way is to exercise the right to "opt out", either out of specific programs and lessons or out of a school system entirely and to join another school option or to engage in home schooling.

Table 2 Religious diversity in Canadian Academic Programs

Manitoba – note the links to Lori Beaman's work and to the RDP, and to the global discussions about religious diversity and interfaith interactions Section Seven Interfaith Education Resources
http://www.edu.gov.mb.ca/k12/docs/support/religious_diversity/section7.pdf

Quebec has the most comprehensive set of documents relating to religion, tracing the genealogy of the current Ethics and Religious Culture Program (ERC)
http://www.education.gouv.qc.ca/en/search-engine/search-the-site/?94404E2F=8487491C81A0
FF3A5E7D78210EA972E0&tx_solr%5Bq%5D=&submit-search=Search&id=30735&L=1

Newfoundland has an extensive K – 12 program of "Religious Education"
http://www.ed.gov.nl.ca/edu/k12/curriculum/POS/Program_of_Studies_2016-2017.pdf
which "enables and encourages students to grow religiously, spiritually and morally". It identifies religion as an important aspect of social and moral development and as an important factor in Newfoundland history.

Northwest Territories draws selectively on Alberta and Saskatchewan provincial curricula for some of its academic program but has developed its own curricula in Aboriginal Languages, French, Health Studies, Northern Studies, Social Studies (K – 9).
https://www.ece.gov.nt.ca/en/services/k-12-education-and-curriculum

In parts of the program developed in and for the Northwest Territories, there is widespread reference to spirituality as an integral element in aboriginal identities and perspectives. An example is Dene Kede under the Aboriginal Languages file https://www.ece.gov.nt.ca/sites/www.ece.gov.nt.ca/files/resources/dene_kede_grade-9_curriculum.pdf

The Yukon Department of Education website under the "curriculum" file directs people to the British Columbia website for information on "what your child learns in school". http://www.education.gov.yk.ca/curriculum.html#Yukons_current_curriculum

However, there is a parallel file titled "First Nations education" referring extensively on aboriginal spirituality. http://www.yesnet.yk.ca/firstnations/unit.html. It would be difficult and inappropriate to isolate "spirituality" from other modes of human experience, including language, social relationships, relationship to the land, law and history. Doing so would impose a particularly European protestant framework of religion on a very different way of seeing spirituality. This file includes a "Handbook of Yukon First Nations Education Resources for Public Schools (2013/2014) http://www.yesnet.yk.ca/firstnations/pdf/13-14/handbook_13_14.pdf with, among other things, a review of residential schools with references to the Truth and Reconciliation Commission.

Table 3 Statistical data on education in Canada

For information about student numbers in the context of a discussion about academic outcomes in private and public schools see "Academic Outcomes of Public and Private High School Students: What Lies Behind the Differences?" by Marc Frenette and Ping Ching Winnie Chan. It includes comparative work with other countries, a literature review, research methodology and data. http://www.statcan.gc.ca/pub/11f0019m/11f0019m2015367-eng.htm).

Statistics about education funding are available from a number of sources. For a 2015 Fraser Institute study see "Enrolments and Education Spending in Public Schools in Canada" by Clemens, Van Pelt and Emes (https://www.fraserinstitute.org/sites/default/files/enrolments-and-education-spending-in-public-schools-in-canada.pdf). For a Statistics Canada report see (http://www.statcan.gc.ca/pub/81-595-m/2010083/c-g/c-g008-eng.htm).

Opting out has long been protected in education acts across the country as a way of protecting minorities from the majority and people exercise their right to do so for a wide variety of reasons.[11] However, opting out has been and continues to be controversial, one reason being that opting out creates the potential for social pressure and anxiety for those exercising that option.[12] In addition, the decision to opt out of a state funded system in favour of a privately funded school or home schooling can have significant financial implications. However, arguments against opting out include the idea that parents may not have all the information with which to make good decisions and may not have a sufficiently broad perspective resulting in harm to their children by depriving them of valuable exposure to a variety of experiences.

In Canada the state has the power to limit parental rights of opting out as indicated in a 2012 Supreme Court ruling in a case testing the rights of parents to opt out of Quebec's Religion and Education Culture course (ERC) (McGarry 2012).

5.5   Questions for Critical Thought

1. While the link has often been made between religion and opting out, what other reasons might people have for opting out of particular classroom activities? You might think in terms of online and visual information which parents consider developmentally inappropriate, physical limitations and learning challenges as a way of getting started.
2. Should the right to opt out be protected and, if so, under what circumstances?
3. What are the implications of removing the right to opt out or of constructing barriers that make opting out a theoretical possibility but a practical impossibility?

---

[11] Cardus, a Christian research think tank, has done extensive research on issues relating to choice in education. It does not use the term "opting out" but their research sheds light on why people choose educational alternatives and on learning outcomes in an array of educational environments (https://www.cardus.ca/research/education/). See also Arai, B. (2000).

[12] "Opting out" as a way of dealing with offensive classroom practices was rejected by courts in *Zylberberg (1988)* and *Elgin County (1990)* in decisions which declared school prayers and religious instruction in Ontario public schools to be a violation of students ss 2 and 15 rights and a source of social and psychological harm. However, opting out has continued to be protected in Ontario and in other provinces. The right to opt out has been a theme in challenges to Quebec's implementation of the ERC.

6   Conclusions

The dynamic nexus of religion and education is not unique to Canada or to the twenty-first Century. There are a number of reasons for the intense interest becomes especially animated when issues of citizenship become part of the debates in diverse societies trying to resolve the conundrums inherent in finding the balances between individual freedoms and social cohesion. Teachers live these conundrums and this chapter respects the challenges inherent in their professional lives. At the same time, it encourages teachers to practice critical attentiveness to their own biases and those inherent in the jurisdictions in which they work, re-examining rhetorical binaries which create a world of multiple solitudes. It does so in two ways. First, it examines the binaries themselves and second, it invites teachers to become aware of the many ways the role of religion in education can be conceptualized and structured. By doing so, it engages teachers in a conversation which will benefit their students and parents in a diverse, complicated and exciting society.

7   Further Reading

This section includes resources which expand some of the themes of the chapter. They nuance and complicate the world of education by offering different perspectives on the intersection of religion and education. The chapter invites readers to reconsider the categories and distinctions which are often presented as common-sense in a modern, secular and diverse society. The authors of the resources included here take readers into more specific issues in the world of religion and education. The resources also provide evidence of the rich variety in the world of religion and education.

Asad, T. et al. (2009). *Is critique secular? Blasphemy, injury and free speech.* Berkeley: The Townsend Center for the Humanities, University of California.

This is a volume with contributions by four scholars who examine the Danish cartoon debates from a variety of perspectives. It questions the link between secular and critical thought, suggesting ways in which "secular" thought is embedded in particular worldviews with its own limitations.

Bolt, J. (1993). *The Christian story and the Christian school.* Grand Rapids: Christian Schools International. Bolt develops a philosophy of Christian education based on a narrative approach, arguing that Christian schools are carriers of a story into which students are drawn, giving them a memory, a vision and, in this way, a mission. The book is a contribution to wider conversations about the role of education in modern societies, raising questions about what gives education its meaning and purpose.

Chamberlin, J. E. (2003). *If this is your land, where are your stories? Reimagining home and sacred space.* Cleveland: Pilgrim Press.

Story has a way of transcending the categories of the religious and secular. Chamberlin comes at story from a First Nations perspective while Bolt does so from a Christian tradition. The reader is invited to take seriously the idea that education and story-telling from multiple perspectives enrich the delivery of education in a diverse society.

Puett, T. (2014). *The political discourse of religious pluralism: World religions textbooks, liberalism and civic identities.* (Doctoral dissertation). Waterloo: University of Waterloo.

Puett engages the perspectives embedded in world religions textbooks, allowing readers to see more clearly ways in which texts tell a story from a particular point of view for a particular purpose.

Zine, J. (2007). Safe havens or 'religious ghettos'? Narratives of Islamic schooling in Canada. *Race, Ethnicity and Education, 10*(1), 71–92.

Zine looks at the role of Islamic schooling in providing a safe platform from which minority students can navigate the space between their traditions and the social world to which they have moved.

8   Researcher Background and Connection to the Topic

Leo Van Arragon was a professional educator, working as a teacher, school principal and educational consultant in privately funded Christian schools organized under the Ontario Alliance of Christian Schools,[13] Christian Schools Canada[14] and Christian Schools International[15] from 1973 to 2010. He also worked in curriculum, leadership and school development and, occasionally in political advocacy during that period. He earned an undergraduate degree in psychology and philosophy at Trinity Christian College in Palos Heights, Illinois (1973) and a Master's degree in education (Social Studies and History) from Calvin College, Grand Rapids, Michigan (1996), both Christian liberal arts colleges and a PhD through the Religious Studies Department at the University of Ottawa (2015). His doctoral research area was the regulation of religion in Ontario public education.

---

[13] http://www.oacs.org/

[14] http://christianschoolscanada.com/

[15] http://www.csionline.org/home

References

Arai, B. (2000). Reasons for home schooling in Canada. *Canadian Journal of Education, 25*(3), 204–217.

Asad, T. (2003). *Formations of the secular*. Stanford: Stanford University Press.

Bader, V. (2007). *Secularism or democracy? Associational governance of religious diversity*. Amsterdam: Amsterdam University Press.

Beaman, L. (2008). *Defining harm: Religious freedom and the limits of the law*. Vancouver: University of British Columbia Press.

Beaman, L. (2014). Deep equality as an alternative to accommodation and tolerance. Nordic. *Journal of Religion and Society, 27*(2), 89–111.

Beaman, L. (2017). *Deep equality in an era of religious diversity*. Oxford: Oxford University Press.

Beaman, L., & Van Arragon, L. (Eds.). (2015). *Issues in religion and education: Whose religion?* Leiden: Brill.

Beckford, J. (2003). *Social theory and religion*. Cambridge: Cambridge University Press.

Beyer, P. (2006). *Religions in a global society*. London: Routledge.

Blomberg, D. (2007). *Wisdom and curriculum*. Sioux Center: Dordt College Press.

Boesveld, S. (2012, May 3). Suspended Nova Scotia student defiantly wears t-shirt with pro-Jesus message. *National Post*. Retrieved from http://news.nation alpost.com/holy-post/suspended-nova-scotia-student-defiantly-wears-t-shirt-with-pro-jesus-message

Bosco, R. M. (2014). *Securing the sacred: Religion, national security and the western state*. Ann Arbor: University of Michigan Press.

Brown, W. (2006). *Regulating aversion: Tolerance in the age of identity and empire*. Princeton: Princeton University Press.

Browne, R. (2015). Space for faith: Accommodating religion on campus. *Macleans*. Retrieved from http://www.macleans.ca/education/university/space-for-faith-accomodating-religion-on-campus/

Cavanaugh, W. (2009). *The myth of religious violence: Secular ideology and the roots of modern conflicts*. Oxford: University of Oxford Press.

CBC News. (2011, September 18). Tempers flare over prayer space in schools. *CBC News*. Retrieved from http://www.cbc.ca/news/canada/toronto/tempers-flare-over-prayer-in-schools-1.1104775

Connolly, W. (2002). *Theory out of bounds*. Minneapolis: University of Minnesota Press.

Connolly, W. (2005). *Pluralism*. Durham: Duke University Press.

Glenn, C. L. (2000). *The ambiguous embrace: Government and faith-based schools and social agencies*. Princeton: Princeton University Press.

Glenn, C. L. (2011). *Contrasting models of state and school: A comparative historical study of parental choice and state control*. New York: The Continuum International Publishing Group.

Glenn, C. L., & de Groof, J. (2005). *Balancing freedom, autonomy and accountability in education*. Nijmegen: Wolf Legal Publishers.

Globe and Mail. (2010, March 9). Niqab-wearing woman kicked out of Quebec class again. *Globe and Mail*. Retrieved from http://www.theglobe andmail.com/news/national/niqab-wearing-woman-kicked-out-of-quebec-class-again/article1209384/

Gravel, S. (2015). Le programme québécois éthique et culture réligieuse : Enseignants et impartialité? In L. Beaman & L. Van Arragon (Eds.), *Issues in religion and education: Whose religion*. Leiden: Brill.

Hervieu-Leger, D. (2000). *Religion as a chain of memory*. New Brunswick: Rutgers University Press.

Humphries, A. (2016, November 15). B.C. mother asks court to keep aboriginal 'cleansing' ceremony out of public schools. *National Post*. Retrieved from http://news.nationalpost.com/news/canada/b-c-mother-asks-court-to-keep-aboriginal-cleansing-ceremony-out-of-public-schools

Hurd, E. S. (2008). *The politics of secularism in international relations*. Princeton: Princeton University Press.

Mackay, K. (1969). *Religious information and moral development: The report of the committee on religious education in the public schools of the province of Ontario.* Toronto: Ontario Department of Education.

Martin, D. (2005). *On secularization: Towards a revised general theory.* Aldershot: Ashgate.

McGarry, J. (2012, February 21). Supreme Court ruling on Quebec religion classes puts limit on parental rights. *National Post.* Retrieved from http://news.nationalpost.com/holy-post/opinion-supreme-court-ruling-on-quebec-religion-classes-puts-limit-on-parental-rights

McGuire, M. B. (2008). *Lived religion: Faith and practice in everyday life.* Oxford: University of Oxford Press.

Nisbet, R. (1976). *The quest for community.* London: Oxford University Press.

Numbers, R. L. (1992). *The creationists: The evolution of scientific creationism.* New York: Alfred A. Knopf.

Ontario Ministry of Education. (2008). *Finding common ground: Character development in Ontario schools, K – 1 2.* Retrieved from http://www.edu.gov.on.ca/eng/policyfunding/memos/june2008/FindingCommonGroundEng.pdf

Palmer, P. (1993). *To know as we are known: Education as a spiritual journey.* San Fransisco: HarperCollins.

Rappaport, R. (1999). *Ritual and religion in the making of humanity.* Cambridge: Cambridge University Press.

Richardson, J. T. (1991). Cult/Brainwashing cases and freedom of religion. *Journal of Church and State, 33*(1), 55–75.

Richardson, J. T. (1996). "Brainwashing" claims and minority religions outside the United States: Cultural diffusion of a questionable concept in the legal arena. *Brigham Young University Law, 4*, 873–904.

Richardson, J. T., & Introvigne, M. (2001). "Brainwashing" theories in European parliamentary and administrative reports on "cults" and "sects". *Journal for the Scientific Study of Religion, 40*(2), 143–168.

Schiffauer, W., et al. (Eds.). (2004). *Civil enculturation: Nation-state, school and ethnic difference in The Netherlands, Britain, Germany and France.* New York: Berghahn Books.

Sergiovanni, T. J. (1999). *Building community in schools.* San Francisco: Jossey-Bass.

Spinner-Halev, J. (2000). *Surviving diversity: Religion and democratic citizenship.* Baltimore: Johns Hopkins University Press.

Sullivan, W. (2005). *The impossibility of religious freedom.* Princeton: Princeton University Press.

Van Arragon, L. (2015*). We educate, they indoctrinate: Religion and the politics of togetherness in Ontario public education* (Doctoral dissertation). Ottawa: University of Ottawa.

Van Pelt, D. A., Allison, P. A., & Allison, D. J. (2007). Ontario's private schools: Who chooses them and why? *A Fraser Institute Occasional Paper.* Retrieved from https://www.fraserinstitute.org/sites/default/files/OntariosPrivateSchools.pdf

Zine, J. (2008). *Canadian Islamic schools: Unravelling the politics of faith, gender, knowledge and identity.* Toronto: University of Toronto Press.

Religious Diversity, Health and Healthcare in Canada

Lisa Smith

Abstract *Is religion still a factor in how Canadians understand and experience health? And if yes, how?* This chapter will examine religious diversity as it relates to health and healthcare, and will include a consideration of individual experiences of health and well-being, healthcare workers and institutions, and population health. Particular attention will be paid to the ways that religious groups and individuals have played a formative role in building the Canadian healthcare system, as well as hospitals and medical schools. I will document the ways that recent shifts in immigration have raised new issues for healthcare institutions and workers by opening up new debates around the meaning of health, and in particular raising questions around religious healthcare considerations for patients. The chapter concludes with an exploration of current pressing public health issues in Canada as tied to religious diversity and suggestions for further study and research.

Keywords Healthcare system · Public health · Social determinants of health · Biomedicine · Religious diversity · Relations of ruling · Spiritual caregiving

1 Introduction: Religion and Health in Question

The focus of this chapter is religious diversity, religion, and health. I begin with a somewhat simple question: *Is religion still a factor in how Canadians understand and experience health?* The short answer to this question would be, no. Popular wisdom suggests that Canada is a secular state entering a "post-Christian era" (see Grossman 2010), and as such, is increasingly defined by religious pluralism (Smith 2007). Indeed, the most recent data from Statistics Canada in 2001 and the National Household Survey in 2011 confirm that overall, religion and religious believers are on the decline, when compared to the past. However, as Seljak et al. (2007) observe,

Since the 1970s, Canada has become both more secular as well as more religiously diverse. At the same time, historical forms of prejudice and discrimination have been left unaddressed and new forms are emerging because of the increased religious diversity of Canadian soci-

L. Smith (✉)
Douglas College, New Westminster, BC, Canada

© Springer International Publishing AG, part of Springer Nature 2018   107
C. Holtmann (ed.), *Exploring Religion and Diversity in Canada*,
https://doi.org/10.1007/978-3-319-78232-4_6

ety as well as international conflicts between religious communities that play themselves
out on Canadian soil. In the 1980s and 1990s, Canadian Sikhs, Muslims, Hindus, Buddhists,
Chinese and Jews struggled to be integrated into structures that had been defined first by
Christianity and then by Canadian-style secularism (p. 1).

Speaking more specifically about health and healthcare, it is widely acknowledged that Canadian hospitals, healthcare systems, and medical schools, have long-
standing ties with religious groups, most notably, Christian and Jewish. Today, it
would seem that these institutions function independent of religious influence.
However, scholars of health and religion tend to adopt a broader understanding of
these terms. For example, the World Health Organization, defines *health* as "… a
state of complete physical, mental and social well-being and not merely the absence
of disease or infirmity (World Health Organization 2018). Speaking of *religion* as
"lived religion", Orsi (2002) states, "Religion is always religion-in-action, religion-
in-relationships between people, between the ways the world is and the way people
imagine or want it to be" (p. 172). If we follow the guidance of the WHO and Orsi,
we can begin to see that the answer to the above question is not so simple. In a report
entitled, *Standards of Spiritual and Religious Care for Health Services in Canada*,
the Catholic Health Association of Canada (2000) observed that interfaith negotiations are increasingly central to the work of health in a multicultural context. When
confronted with questions of life and death, pain and suffering, Canadians continue
to draw on religion, albeit in a combination of old and new ways, ultimately raising
new and at times perplexing questions for discussion and debate within health and
healthcare.

The continued importance of religion to health is perhaps not surprising.
Questions of life and death have always been part of religion and, as such, most
religious traditions have something to say about the body and, by extension, health
and well-being. As Stephenson (2004) has observed,

The transformations of pregnancy, and birth (new bodies) and death (the culmination of
bodies) ramify throughout both religious practices and beliefs about medicine. Thus, the
body is a kind of contested arena where life processes meet with both religion and medicine
(p. 202).

For example, Tibetan Buddhists practice meditation to move beyond suffering
(both physical and mental); the ailments of the body are something to move beyond
to attain enlightenment. Within Christian Science, "Sickness is part of error which
truth casts out. … We classify disease as error, which nothing but truth can heal, and
this mind must be divine not human" (Eddy 1934, cited in Nancarrow Clarke 2016,
p. 340). Brown (2001) observes that Australian Indigenous spiritual traditions tend
to express a more holistic view of health that extends beyond one individual. For
example, for many Australian Indigenous peoples, health cannot be separated from
one's spiritual well-being. Further, health refers to the physical and mental well-
being of an individual, as well as the overall condition of the community. These are
just a few examples of how different groups understand the connection between
religion / spirituality and health.

I come to the study of health and religion as a sociologist. Central to the practice of sociology is applying the sociological imagination. This means gaining a deeper understanding of the intersection between two key forces: individual biography and social / historical conditions. As Mills (1959) observes, "Neither the life of an individual nor the history of a society can be understood without understanding both" (p. 3). Health and religion offer up a considerable and wide-ranging set of issues to explore and provide excellent terrain for employing the sociological imagination. Below I have outlined three dimensions that inform this chapter and help further elucidate a sociological analysis of religion and health.

1. The human dimension: Religion and spirituality, like health, are experienced by people within day-to-day life. The human dimension draws our attention towards individual experience and subjectivity. For many individuals, religion and spirituality play pivotal roles in how they understand who they are, as well as their place within the wider community and society they inhabit. As a result, health, and health treatment choices, engage with an individual's sense of self and belonging. From a practical standpoint, those working in healthcare fields often need to take religion and spirituality into consideration when interacting with patients and delivering services. Take the time to consider this: As a nurse, how might you respond if a patient requested religious or spiritual care as part of their treatment?

2. The structural dimension: A variety of institutions, systems, and social structures manage, administer, and organize both health and religion. In Canada, the *healthcare system* exists to improve, but equally maintain, the health of Canadians. Healthcare policies and institutions are further supported by both formal and informal social systems and processes. As we will explore in this chapter, the delivery of healthcare raises ethical questions about life and death, as well as the right of individuals to make choices in line with religious belief systems. Religion and spirituality continue to inform how individuals understand health and wellness, and as such, religious groups and individuals often seek to shape the form and content of healthcare. Take the time to consider this: As a doctor, how might you respond if someone refused treatment on religious grounds?

3. The population dimension. Modern societies are characterized by a concern for the overall well-being of the population, as characterized by the rise of *public health* initiatives and increased knowledge about *social determinants of health*. Social *epidemiology* refers to the notion "that not only are health disparities socially produced, leading to the perpetuation of social inequality, but also that the conditions that make people healthy are socially produced" (Segall and Fries 2011, p. 207). Increasingly, healthcare systems and structures are challenged to deliver health services to a diverse population and take into consideration factors that can contribute to the experience of inequalities in health. In line with this, recent studies have examined religion as a social determinant of health (Wolpe et al. 2014). Others have considered the benefits of religion and spirituality for overall health and well-being (see Larimore et al. 2002; Masters 2005; Masters and Spielmans 2007; McCullough 1995). Religion is also often understood as an

intervening variable that can lead to differential health outcomes, in combination with other factors, such as race, social class, and ethnicity (Brotman et al. 2010). Take time to consider this: As a healthcare administrator, how might you respond if you noticed poor health outcomes within a particular minority religious group?

These dimensions are not meant to be exhaustive or mutually exclusive. They are inter-related and inform one another. Further, they involve and are shaped by power and power relations. The aim here is to gain a deeper understanding of health, healthcare, and religion as social phenomena by activating our sociological imagination. Doing so helps us to see that religion and health, like all parts of society, are shaped by people, within the communities, cultures, and societies that they are a part of.

This chapter begins by introducing the social study of health, religion, and religious diversity. The chapter then turns to a consideration of the broader history played by religion and religious groups in forming the structures of healthcare, and assesses recent demographic shifts in Canada. This chapter explores several significant sites of contention, as well as more recent shifts around the place of religion and spirituality within health and healthcare in Canadian society. Following this, I present results from a qualitative research study examining the controversy around the Quebec Charter of Values. A central focus of these debates related to the presence of religion in public institutions, like hospitals, and the wearing of "ostentatious" religious symbols by hospital employees. The chapter concludes with a consideration of current challenges and future opportunities within the field of health and religion. Many of the cases discussed in this chapter emerge out of conflicts over values and power struggles that often serve to reinforce the dominance of the majority group. However, attention will be drawn towards the ways that these conflicts are also active in shaping the meaning of health as it relates to spirituality, religion, and religious belief, for an increasingly diverse Canadian population.

2 Health, Religion, and Religious Diversity

All Church members typically sign an "Advance Decision to Refuse Specified Medical Treatment," outlining their wish to refuse blood transfusions. As well, the Church carefully follows expectant mothers in its flock to ensure its prohibition of blood transfusions is enforced. According to one document obtained by *Maclean's*, on Sept. 3 the Church reminded its "brothers" that the Church's "Care Plan for Women in Labour Refusing Blood Transfusion" was to be given to expectant mothers (Patriquin 2016).

Health, and decisions about health, are things that can easily be taken for granted. A recent article in Macleans tells the story of Éloïse Dupuis, a young mother who died due to complications after giving birth. The journalist questions whether she could have been saved by a blood transfusion and indicates that there may be further investigations into whether her health was put at risk by her religious community. Dupuis was a member of the Jehovah's Witnesses. As indicated by the excerpt from the article, blood transfusions are strictly forbidden for Jehovah's Witnesses. The story features the photo below, Fig. 1, of Éloïse as an expectant mother, glowing with health. This image stands in stark contrast to the title of the article: "A Jehovah's Witness and her deadly devotion". According to the journalist, the question of health is straightforward, and religion should play no role in a person's decision. Indeed, who would not do anything they could to save the life of a new mother? However, as already mentioned, this chapter aims to move beyond taken-for-granted assumptions about where religion fits within decisions about health, by adopting a sociological perspective. In this section I introduce the reader to the social study of health and religion, and provide an introductory consideration of the place of religious diversity within these broader fields of study.

2.1   Defining Health, Religion, and Religious Diversity

Within *biomedicine* or a biomedical understanding of the body, health is typically understood in relation to the presence or absence of disease (see Germov and Hornosty 2017; Nancarrow Clarke 2016; Segall and Fries 2011). The presence of disease indicates illness, while the absence of disease indicates health. Healthcare and medical interventions are delivered with the intention to treat illness and

Fig. 1 Éloïse Dupuis

preserve life, and the prevention of death is seen as natural and normal. In line with this, a doctor is trained to identify conditions in the physical body—loss of blood—and offer treatment—blood transfusions. However, as mentioned at the outset of this chapter, sociologists seek to embrace a more holistic understanding of health that would take into account, among other things, differing belief systems about life and death. For some individuals, life should not be preserved at all costs, and further, intervening may run contrary to sincerely held religious beliefs.

Sociologists of health seek to understand health, illness, and well-being as *social constructions*, meaning they are shaped by social relations and the society we live in. According to Segall and Fries (2011), "...both the health and illness of our bodies and the manner in which we understand these concepts are influenced by social factors" (p. 6). Understanding health as a social construction allows us to include illness, disability, mental health, but also broader notions of well-being, such as the quality of family relationships, the health of the communities where we live, and even the environment. For sociologists, health is impacted by the spaces where we live our day-to-day lives and the relationships that inform our understanding of who we are. "Health is not understood solely as a biophysical state experienced in the same manner by all people in all times and places, but, rather, as a social constructed experience that varies according to cultural factors" (Segall and Fries 2011, p. 7). Sociologists of health thus consider individual experiences, as well as the broader structure of public and community healthcare services, delivery, and systems. This allows sociologists to consider the impact of policies beyond specifically health related fields. For example, sociologists of health would also examine the health implications of policies within social work and community development because within these fields individuals aim to overcome broader systemic inequalities and as such, impact individual and population health (Gerhardt 1989, 1990; Mikkonen and Raphael 2010; Raphael 2012).

Similar to sociologists of health, sociologists of religion typically adopt a broad understanding of religion. According to Reimer-Kirkham (2009), within health scholarship, religion and spirituality are often understood as opposed. Where, religion "carries transcendent (sacred) and social dimensions, with its practice typically occurring through relatively formal institutions" (p. 407). In contrast, spirituality "...although having to do with the metaphysical, has been interpreted as a less institutionalized and more individual expression of values and beliefs" (p. 407). Reimer-Kirkham argues that we ought to see "religion and spirituality not interchangeably, but as closely related" (p. 407). Similar to Orsi's argument for the study of *lived religion*, this understanding of religion and spirituality allows us to consider context and the ways that individuals construct meaning in daily life. This chapter employs both religion and spirituality throughout depending upon the scholarship, research, or policy in question.

Secular is a term used to refer to the separation between religious institutions and the public functions of the state. In a secular society, it is assumed that the government and all its officials are no longer tied to religion or religious institutions. In Canada, critical scholars of religion point out that while, on the surface, Canada appears to be a "secular" nation, the traces of our Christian past can still be detected.

The most obvious example is the naming of "God" in the preamble to the *Canadian Charter of Rights and Freedoms*. The recognition that Canadian society has historically been characterized by a predominantly Christian worldview, coupled with the reality that this is no longer the case as religious diversity has increased with new waves of immigration, has led to a rising sensitivity to diverse religious traditions and cultural pluralism within pastoral care in hospitals. We will return to this issue later in this chapter.

Compared to other nations, and despite rising evidence of secularism, Canada has a considerable degree of *religious diversity*. For example, there were over 108 different religious groups listed in the 2011 National Household Survey; the list included Buddhist, Catholic, Hindu, Jewish, Muslim, Sikh, and Aboriginal, as well as other religions, including, Baha'i, Jain, and Pagan. A separate grouping allowed individuals to specify "no religious affiliation", with categories ranging from agnostic, atheist, to no religion. The relatively high degree of religious diversity in Canada makes it an interesting site from which to begin a study of health and religion, in part because we are likely to find differences in values and beliefs, as individuals and groups struggle to find space within what was, and in many ways remains, a Christian-dominated settler society.

The *Canadian Charter of Rights and Freedoms* enshrines freedom of conscience and religion. "Ideally, this means that everyone living in Canada is free to believe (or not believe) whatever he or she chooses. It also means that the government is responsible for eliminating barriers for those wishing to practice their religion—even if governmental inconvenience or cost is the result" (Anzovino and Boutilier 2015 p. 106). However, as we will explore in subsequent sections, there have been and continue to be many instances where minority religious groups have struggled to find recognition within Canadian society. This is all the more surprising given that Canada is perceived as a multicultural mecca, where diversity is encouraged and embraced.

2.2 Social Study of Health and Religion

When health intersects with religion and religious diversity, our attention is drawn towards ongoing debates between *structure* and *agency*. Structure refers to the social forces (institutions, politics, social norms and expectations) that shape our experience and limit individual choices. Agency refers to "…our capacity to shape our socially-constructed lives" (Ravelli and Webber 2015). For example, religious institutions have actually played a significant role in shaping the formation of state-delivered health services, like hospitals. Further, within Canadian hospitals we find a multitude of individual experiences of religious believers as they negotiate questions of life and death within constrained circumstances.

Within sociology, the classic example of the social study of health and religion comes from the work of Emile Durkheim (1897), and in particular, his study of suicide. In *Le Suicide*, Durkheim examines the relationship between social integration (as tied to religious affiliation) and rate of suicide. Those individuals with a higher level of social integration (Catholics) were found to be less likely to commit suicide. Whereas, those with lower levels of social integration (Protestants) were found to be more likely to commit suicide. Durkheim's research invites us to explore the relationship between religion and health outcomes in a population. In more recent research, Koenig et al. (2001) found that those who participated in "non-organized spiritual practices" experienced positive health benefits. Further, Dein et al. (2010) note that those who identified with and were actively involved in a religious community experienced even more significant benefits to overall health.

One of the most well-known studies examining the role of prayer in healing was completed by Randolph Byrd, a physician at the San Francisco General Medical Center. Byrd was interested in the impact of prayer on cardiac patients. In a random and controlled experiment, Byrd found that prayer by a group located elsewhere had an impact on his patients (Pargament 1997). Similarly, Levin and Vanderpool (2008) have examined religious factors in physical health and the prevention of illness. They argue that "religion-health connections are a nearly universal feature within the cosmologies of religious traditions and are supported by empirical evidence from various scientific disciplines" (p. 41). The positive health benefits of religion and spirituality have led Miller (2013) to argue that spiritual healthcare should be part of the curriculum for all future doctors and nurses. In line with this, many American medical schools now include a discussion of religion and spirituality in healthcare training, and similar shifts are occurring in Canada. However, factoring religion into discussions of health remains difficult in part because the dominant model of understanding health remains rooted in a biomedical understanding, and reflects the shift to a secular system of healthcare delivery (discussed in the following section).

Beyond a consideration of the benefits of religion and spirituality, the social model of health is helpful for highlighting those factors that contribute to health inequalities or the social determinants of health. Fig. 2 is an infographic produced by the Canadian Medical Association. According to Homeless Hub, we tend to focus healthcare delivery on maintaining physical health from a primarily biological perspective. In fact, characteristics of "your life", including income, disability, education, and race, all play a significant role in determining the health outcomes you experience.

According to the World Health Organization:

> The social determinants of health are the conditions in which people are born, grow, work, live, and age, and the wider set of forces and systems shaping the conditions of daily life. These forces and systems include economic policies and systems, development agendas, social norms, social policies and political systems (WHO 2017).

Canada, like many other Western liberal capitalist states, has embraced this broad definition and includes social determinants of health within policies that determine healthcare delivery and development. For example, the Public Health Agency of Canada (2016), identifies the following as social determinants of health that influence "the health of populations":

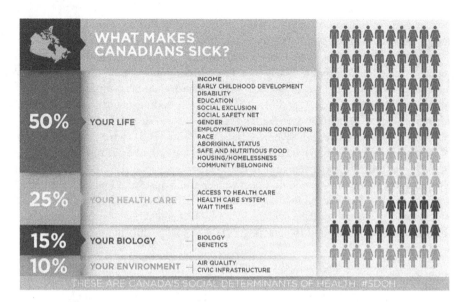

Fig. 2 What makes Canadians sick? (CMA)

...income and social status; social support networks; education; employment/ working conditions; social environments; physical environments; personal health practices and coping
skills; healthy child development; biology and genetic endowment; health services; gender;
and culture.

de Leeux and Greenwood (2011) observe that social determinants of health allow
us to acknowledge the complexity of factors influencing health outcomes for "vulnerable and marginalized populations", such as Indigenous peoples, immigrants,
and refugees. Gender, ethnicity, socio-economic status, sexual orientation, and age
"interact with and affect one another to produce differentially lived social inequalities among people" (p. 55).

For example, researchers commonly cite the "healthy immigrant effect", where
immigrants report better health outcomes when compared to the Canadian-born
population (see Dunn and Dyck 2000; McDonald and Kennedy 2004). Segall and
Fries (2011) point out that in some sense, this is not surprising as "individual health
status is one of the most important criteria used by the Government of Canada to
screen those who attempt to immigrant to this country" (173). However, this reality
does not explain why health outcomes for immigrants become worse over time.
Meaning the more years' immigrants spend in Canada, the poorer health they can
expect (Beiser 2005). Researchers have also found significant differences in health
when occupation and education are taken into account. For example, in a study
examining health status and social capital of recent immigrants in Canada, Zhao
et al. (2010) found that "skilled workers have the largest share of healthy immigrants, followed by family class immigrants and refugees" (p. 10). Further,
"Refugees are more likely to report their health as fair or poor initially because they

often come from areas of conflict with poor public health infrastructure and are more likely to be at risk for malnutrition and infectious diseases" (p. 10).

In a study examining cervical cancer screening amongst women in the Sikh community, Oelke and Vollmann (2007) found that "immigrant women tend not to take advantage of screening" and that "culturally appropriate screening services for immigrant women are few" (p. 174). Their research findings suggest that training for nurses ought to include discussions about how to offer services for particular populations, for example, Sikh women. Beiser and Hou (2001) have examined rates of depression amongst newly arrived immigrants. In their study, a majority of participants expressed experiencing discrimination because of their ethnicity. Symptoms of depression would dissipate when participants were finally able to find work. In both cases, the biomedical model would limit our understanding to the incidence of a particular illness with an identifiable medical response, as opposed to the underlying systemic and societal factors that impact health outcomes and overall well-being.

Further, if we understand health as tied to social processes, we can consider religion, spirituality, and religious diversity as potential factors in the experience of seemingly 'natural' biological processes. Childbirth is a good example of this. Several studies have explored the religious and spiritual dimensions of giving birth for women within conservative religious traditions (see Callister et al. 1999; Semenic et al. 2004). In discussions with Orthodox Jewish-Canadian women, Semenic et al. (2004) identified the following themes tied to the "spiritual/cultural dimensions of the childbirth experience": "(a) birth as a significant life event, (b) birth as a bittersweet paradox, (c) the spiritual dimensions of giving birth, (d) the importance of obedience to rabbinical law, and (e) a sense of support and affirmation" (p. 80). Similar to the more general studies discussed above that examined the connection between religion and health outcomes, the studies summarized here point to the need to factor in religion and spirituality, from both a practical and ethical standpoint, in terms of healthcare delivery. And yet, despite the breadth of research available on religion as a social determinant of health, religion and spirituality are rarely directly listed. This has led to a paucity of available quantitative data that provides an over-arching view of this intersection. Often religion is lumped in with culture, race, and/or ethnicity, leaving researchers to infer what is influencing what. I will return to this challenge later in the chapter.

To wrap up this section, the aim is not to eliminate or discredit the biomedical approach, but rather to add and employ the social model where appropriate. Arguably, drawing on both models has added substantially to the health professions, as reflected in the increasing tendency to include postcolonial critiques, intersectionality, and critical disability studies within consideration for healthcare service delivery. Religious diversity and the challenges it presents should thus be understood as a starting point for dialogue, debate, and discussion that can lead to a more complete reflection of the people who make up Canadian society.

3 Religion, Health, and Healthcare Within Canadian Society

I'm sure that the standard of public morality we've helped build will force government in Canada to approve complete health insurance (Tommy Douglas).

If I were to ask a group of Canadians what defines Canada, chances are many would place universal and free healthcare near the top of the list. Medicare, the system of state-provided "free" healthcare, is perceived by many to be a defining feature of Canadian identity and society. However, I would suspect that not all Canadians know that the founder of modern Canadian healthcare, Tommy Douglas, before turning to politics, was a Baptist minister. Like many of his time, his passion for social justice and equality was deeply inspired by his religious beliefs. Indeed, a brief scan of the history of Canadian healthcare, reveals that Douglas is not alone. A multitude of Jewish, Catholic, and Protestant individuals and groups laid the foundation for hospitals and medical schools in Canada. Furthermore, religious groups continue to play a significant role in shaping healthcare delivery to this day at both the national and international level (Karpf 2007). At the same time, Canadians, like many other individuals living within late-modern capitalist states increasingly understand their lives through a radical lens of individualism (Rose 1996). Many individuals are increasingly understanding religion and spirituality as tied to individual choices, as opposed to affiliation with a particular group or institution. This section offers a somewhat brief overview of the historical relationship between health and religion, before turning to a consideration of the contemporary Canadian landscape.

3.1 Religion and Health: A Brief History

In the past, across Western societies, religion and religious practitioners played a central role in the administration of health and healthcare. As mentioned at the outset of this chapter, most religious traditions consider, in some capacity, questions of life and death, as well as pain and suffering. However, in the past, the separation between religious healthcare and "other" healthcare was minimal. Healthcare was religious care (Weiss and Lonnquist 2009). "Before the development of medical science, quasi-religious views of health and illness were dominant, whereby illness was connected with sin, penance, and evil spirits: the body and soul were conceived as a sacred entity beyond the power of human intervention" (Germov and Hornosty 2017, p. 13). Across most Western societies, science has come to dominate within fields related to medicine, health, and illness. For example, in contemporary Canadian society, the authority of doctors and scientists is typically given more weight than a religious or spiritual leader or practitioner. The shift away from religion as a site through which to understand health problems took place gradually over the past several hundred years and is marked by corresponding changes in other social institutions, as well as changes in broader patterns and social systems of power, truth, and knowledge, as tied to the human body.

In Western Europe, during the Medieval era, the monastery and later, the Church, were responsible for health and illness. We began to see secular doctors near the close of the Medieval era (Weiss and Lonnquist 2009). Speaking specifically about disability, Covey (2005) observes that within early Christianity, disease and illness were understood "…as a punishment for sin or as a test of one's faith and commitment to God. For example, people with disabilities were viewed as sinners or as the offspring of parents who had sinned. This view prevailed until the seventeenth century" (p. 107). The Scientific Revolution reflected a move towards a scientific understanding of "medical knowledge and practice". Weiss and Lonnquist document this change below:

> The Renaissance period marks the beginning of a more scientific approach to medical knowledge and practice. This was a period of significant intellectual growth and discovery; the teachings of the Church were being challenged and Christianity began to lose authority and control to the state. … Medical specialization became more pronounced. Physicians, that is, graduates from a school of medicine, provided diagnosis and treatment to the wealthy. Surgery, however, was practised mostly by barbers and had lower status (2009, p. 21).

By the nineteenth century, new findings in health treatment, along with a rising interest in *public health,* led to a further displacement of religion and religious authority. The findings of John Snow led to an increased awareness of the city landscape and geography in the spread of diseases, such as cholera (Ball 2009). Around this time, hospitals as places to treat illness became more common and widespread (Weiss and Lonnquist 2009). The Canadian state came into being during this transitional period. Thus, while the history of Canadian healthcare institutions reflects religious foundations, this history has been increasingly erased under Canadian secularism.

3.2   The Contemporary Canadian Mosaic and Health

John Murray Gibbon's (1938) classic work, *Canadian Mosaic,* has in part, formed the modern day understanding of Canada as a society where diversity is encouraged and nourished. It is worth mentioning that Canadians are not responsible for the existence of diversity. The first occupants of the land now known as Canada, Aboriginal peoples, have a rich and diverse set of spiritual traditions and beliefs. However, under colonization, Catholics and Protestants became the overwhelming majority (Anzovino & Boutilier 2015). Until very recently, most immigrants came from Christian, specifically, Protestant countries. As of 2011, the National Household Survey reveals that 40.6 per cent of the population is Catholic, 20.3 per cent is Protestant, and 23.9 per cent is not religious; the remainder of the population is Muslim, Jewish, Hindu, Buddhist, or Sikh (Anzovino & Boutilier 2015; Statistics Canada 2003). As discussed in Tomlin's chapter in this volume, one of the groups that is growing incredibly quickly are those who indicate "no religion"—or the religious-nones.

The dramatic drop in religious observers as indicated by statistics and the increasing reality of empty-churches, has led many to pronounce the demise of religion in Canada. However, while some churches are emptying, the situation is quite different for faith groups comprised of certain Christian denominations and newer immigrants. While some churches are empty, mosques, temples, and evangelical Christian churches are full (Anzovino & Boutilier 2015). "Between 1991 and 2001, the population of Muslims in Canada doubled from approximately 250,000 to over 500,000. Muslims went from 1% to 2% of the Canadian population in only 10 years (Statistics Canada 2003). In the present, religious diversity is particularly apparent in urban centres. However, the expectation is that this will gradually extend to rural areas as well. Stephenson (2004) observes,

> When people of different ethnic traditions, holding dissimilar or even contradictory religious beliefs about the meaning of life come together to make decisions about the care and treatment of those who are suffering, the experience may be fraught with difficulties. The contested body may reflect a collision of cultures rather than a helpful consultation over the course of treatment, especially where life is transformed either through renewal, or death. Some systems of religious belief and practice make special use of meditation, chanting, and deprivation (fasting) in order to induce altered states of consciousness as well. This may be understood in many ethnic groups to have beneficial consequences for overall health—of the body as well as the mind. Religious belief and practice can also be brought into question after migration to a new country with different standards of behaviour and cultural norms, so religion is often bound to mental well-being, and to suffering as well (p. 202).

There is no doubt that Canada is being reshaped by the influx of immigrants. Many, though not all newcomers hold religion as a central tenet of their lives.

The Canadian sociologist Reginald Bibby (1993) notes that while traditional religion is on the decline, more individual forms of spirituality are alive and well. Under this new regime of the self, spirituality, understood in a broad sense, is seen as a form of healthcare. The use of yoga as a "catch-all" form of destressing to be added into an overall regimen of "good health" is a good example of this shift. Consider the following passage from a Canadian health publication.

> She considers walking in nature an active spiritual practice, one that gives her comfort and makes her feel less alone in the world. "I believe spirituality is something you have to practise every day," says Green (Best Health 2016).

This article is a good example of what Robert Bellah (1985) calls "Sheila-ism". Increasingly, as Shipley's chapter explores in this volume, Canadians construct their own rules in relation to beliefs and values. Spirituality is often used to reflect this move away from traditional belief systems and towards more fluid understandings of meaning.

This brief account of the religious underpinnings of the contemporary Canadian landscape has hopefully offered some insight into the ways that religion has shaped health and healthcare in Canada. In the following section, we turn to instances of conflict and contention in relation to religion and health. While public discussion and concern is often directed towards new immigrant populations as a source of difference, it is worth noting that many of the cases relating to religious rights and health have actually emerged within Christian communities who are by no means new to Canada.

4   Religion and Health: Conflicts and Possibilities

It's not normal that a public institution such as a hospital … denies women services such as abortions because of the hospital's affiliation with a particular religion," says Dr. Henry Morgentaler, who operates 8 abortion clinics across Canada. "Hospitals should be providing care according to the dictates of the Canadian Medical Association and according to the dictates of good medical practices" (Gagnon 2003, p. 331).

After the birth of my first baby, the women in my small group from the Church of the Highlands showed up each night with meals. I was new at the motherhood game, fumbling, and desperately trying to keep my wailing son happy by never putting him down. We all might have starved to death had it not been for those women. Shortly after that, we moved away for a new job and left the church community. Everything they did for us was done with no expectation of reciprocity, as they all knew about our pending relocation. These are acts of kindness I will never forget (Thomas 2016, p. 112).

Debates over who has the right to shape decisions relating to health and health-care draw us into a wider consideration of power and power relations, not to mention inequality. In the passage above, Dr. Henry Morgentaler defiantly challenges existing power relations, patriarchy, and gender inequality that persist under the guise of justice and fairness, and advocates for the right of a woman to abortion services. This section will delve into the Morgentaler case and other controversial cases, where religion and health have been at the forefront. Like the sociologist Dorothy Smith, Morgentaler sees institutions as reflections of the everyday *relations of ruling* (Smith 1987), whereby the power of the dominant group is maintained and ultimately given legitimacy. Mechanisms like the *Canadian Charter of Rights and Freedoms* can thus be understood as powerful tools for challenging inequality, but with ultimately mixed results. Regardless, the outcome of Charter challenge cases, and the ensuing debates, raise questions about the nature of equality within our society. On the other hand, as we have already discussed, for many people, religion and religious communities can play an important role in fostering more intangible, but equally important factors that influence health, such as social cohesion. This view is expressed by Kate Hendricks Thomas in the quotation above.

4.1   Health and the Individual

"The Pope has simply lost all relevance for me." "I don't really care what he said in the encyclical," she says, "because I've already made up my mind" (CBC 1968).

The above quote comes from a CBC television special that featured young female university students confronting a panel of Catholic priests at the University of Toronto. Like many of the young women who participated in the panel, she is a devout Catholic but takes issue with the pope's stance on birth control. The panel included Monsignor Austin Vaughan, president of the Catholic Theological Society of America, Reverend Edward Sheridan of Regis College, Reverend Walter Principe, and Reverend Robert Crooker of St. Michael's College. At the time of the panel, Pope Paul VI had taken a very firm stance against the birth control pill. In a letter to Catholics entitled, "Of Human Life", the pope made the controversial claim that using the birth control pill was a sin.

The rejection of the organizational structures and dogma of the church, and in particular, the Catholic church, were fundamental to the rise of the Women's Health Movement, which emerged during the latter half of the twentieth century (Tone 2001). Though centered in the United States, similar social transformations and struggles occurred in Canada (McLaren and McLaren 1997) and other parts of the Western world. Among other issues, the movement sought to reshape existing power structures, like patriarchy, that limited health outcomes for women. *Patriarchy* is defined here as the systemic and wide-spread domination of men over women. Given that many of the decisions about healthcare at the time were guided by religious dogma and authority, it is not surprising that the Women's Health Movement targeted and sought to eliminate the influence of religious authority within the delivery of healthcare for women. Within this context, religion and religious authority were understood, rightly so, as a barrier to women's autonomy. In Canada, the legal barriers placed on abortion and access to contraception, both of which were illegal until 1969, were widely supported by the dominant religious authorities of the time, in particular, the Catholic church.

Even after the introduction of the Omnibus bill, access to abortion was permitted only under very limited circumstances. It was not until 1988, in the decision for *R. v. Morgentalar*, that the Supreme Court officially struck down Canada's abortion law on the grounds that it violated Section 7 of the Charter, which protects "security of the person". Dr. Henry Morgantaler, the plaintiff in the case, has become widely known as an advocate for women's right to abortion. He has also argued that all hospitals ought to be free of religion and religious influence (Gagnon 2003, p. 331).

I feel it is useful at this point to offer some insight into the complex ways that religion and spirituality can factor into the politics of reproductive health. Nuance is important here. Not all those against abortion and contraception argue on the basis of religious grounds. For example, some individuals argue for the sanctity of life on secular grounds (drawing on philosophical arguments). Further, many devout religious followers have advocated in favour of women's reproductive rights. For example, John Rock, one the co-creators of the pill, was himself a devout Catholic (Tone 2001). Furthermore, several studies have considered the ways that conservative religious women negotiate birth control within the context of specific life circumstances, as well as other factors, such as relationship status (Amaro 1988; Kaplan et al. 2001; Romo et al. 2003). That said, religion remains a powerful factor in religious beliefs that seek to remove women's access to abortion. It is important to separate institutional power structures from individuals, and sometimes individuals from institutions.

In this case, a nuanced approach remains difficult, particularly where abortion is concerned. Abortion provision remains a swing issue in Canadian politics and gains won by women's movements are tenuous at best. Despite the fact that abortion is legal, access to abortion remains difficult in many locations across Canada (Sethna and Doull 2012). Prince Edward Island only recently opened an abortion clinic and already doctors are protesting on religious grounds (Ross 2016). The protest took place outside the hospital where the clinic is being built and was organized by the PEI Right to Life Association. Although many of the members are motivated by religious beliefs, religion is not mentioned on the organization's website. However, the organization targets abortion and euthanasia as key sites for intervention.

Like abortion, euthanasia and physician-assisted suicide engage with questions of individual autonomy and the right of the state to intervene in individuals' choices. As with abortion, religious values are not the only factor here. However, some of the most outspoken proponents on both sides of these debates come from religious groups. Those interveners who have spoken against the legalization of euthanasia include the Christian Medical and Dental Society (CMDS) and the Canadian Federation of Catholic Physicians' Societies. The Canadian Unitarian Council have often spoken in favour of decriminalization. In the cases of euthanasia and abortion, what is at stake are competing notions of rights within the context of different and contrasting belief systems. Ultimately, these views are not reconcilable. Furthermore, religious views of morality are increasingly seen as out of place. In Canada, like many modern societies, religious authority is seen as irrelevant in determining the moral questions of the day (Giddens 1991). Within this context, religion becomes one of many "competing authorities in the modern world of expertise" (Hornosty and Strazzari 2017 p. 253).

4.2   Spirituality (and Sometimes Religion) Welcome Here...

We call upon those who can effect change within the Canadian health-care system to recognize the value of Aboriginal healing practices and use them in the treatment of Aboriginal patients in collaboration with Aboriginal healers and Elders where requested by Aboriginal patients (Truth and Reconciliation Commission of Canada 2015, p. 3).

In contemporary Canadian society, religion within the context of health is often framed as a problem that generates conflict. Religious groups and believers are often portrayed and perceived as naïve, out of touch with reality or dogmatic traditionalists. In contrast, there is a growing body of scholarship that encourages, promotes, and in some cases, demands the inclusion of spirituality. For example, the above excerpt from the recent Truth and Reconciliation Report makes explicit reference to the inclusion of traditional healing practices within healthcare. The inclusion of traditional Aboriginal spirituality within healthcare is seen by many as key to repairing the damages of colonialism. Similar shifts are taking place in Australia where Indigenous groups are reclaiming traditional spirituality within health treatment as a part of the broader process of decolonization (see Kirmayer et al. 2000, 2003; Tse et al. 2005).

While the importance of spirituality is particularly prevalent and stated in the treatment of mental health and wellness, demands for holistic and culturally-appropriate healthcare are increasingly a general and defining feature of healthcare delivery for Aboriginal peoples in Canada. The recognition of the importance of traditional Aboriginal spirituality within healthcare has led to key changes in policy and practice that have, in part, started with shifting definitions. For example, a recent summary report, produced by Health Canada and the Assembly of First Nations, entitled *First Nations Mental Wellness Continuum Framework*, defines mental wellness as follows:

> Mental wellness is a balance of the mental, physical, spiritual, and emotional. This balance is enriched as individuals have: *purpose* in their daily lives whether it is through education, employment, care giving activities, or cultural ways of being and doing; *hope* for their future and those of their families that is grounded in a sense of identity, unique indigenous values, and having a belief in spirit; a sense of *belonging* and connectedness within their families, to community, and to culture; and finally, a sense of *meaning* and an understanding of how their lives and those of their families and communities are part of creation and a rich history (Health Canada and Assembly of First Nations 2015, p. 1).

Similarly, the Winnipeg Regional Health Authority recently produced a guide entitled *The Culture of Well-Being*. The report employs the following definition of mental health:

> When people of any cultural background are feeling mentally healthy, they can feel good about themselves most the time. Traditionally, the Aboriginal cultural view of mental health and well being is a balance of the body, mind, emotions and spirit which is maintained through good relationships within oneself, with others, with the community and Creation (Winnipeg Regional Health Authority 2014, p. 2).

The boundary between spirituality and culture is not clearly defined in these publications. This disjuncture is worthy of further exploration, however, space does not permit a deep analysis of this issue. For the moment, the inclusion of language that implies and makes reference to spiritual traditions is obvious and evident, particularly within the context of a supposedly "secular" healthcare system.

At least on the surface, medical education in contemporary Canadian society is no longer grounded within religious institutions. Even so, today, several universities across Canada offer programs with the aim of forming hospital chaplains capable of offering pastoral care services. The continued presence of these training programs, reflects in part a link to the religious foundations of healthcare. At the same time, nursing programs and medical education increasingly recognize the value of training around religious diversity and cultural pluralism. In spite of this, it is important to acknowledge the subtle and not so subtle ways that Christianity continues to shape contemporary Canadian society, and inform state institutions, such as hospitals. Nevertheless, contemporary discussions about spiritual caregiving for nurses and doctors has begun to reflect an awareness, and place importance on the reality of increased religious diversity within the patient population.

Today, *spiritual* or *pastoral care* is included in the hopes of improving healthcare delivery and meeting needs that cannot be addressed with biomedical interventions alone. Further, scholars of nursing have "...turned their attention to developing culturally responsive and spiritually sensitive nursing practice" (Reimer-Kirkham et al. 2004, p. 149). Van de Creek and Burton (2001) outline the reason for this renewed interest in spirituality:

> Spirituality demonstrates that persons are not merely physical bodies that require mechanical care. Persons find that their spirituality helps them maintain health, cope with illnesses, traumas, losses, and life transitions by integrating body, mind and spirit. ...Many persons both inside and outside traditional religious structures, report profound experiences of transcendence, wonder, awe, joy, and connection to nature, self, and others, as they strive to make their lives meaningful and to maintain hope when illness strikes (p. 82).

Pastoral care is frequently employed in the treatment of Post-Traumatic Stress Disorder for war veterans (Nieuwsma et al. 2013). Similarly, Buck (2007) observes that "Historically, compassion, comfort measures, and spiritual care for the sick and dying were the cornerstones of hospice care" (p. 115). Buck notes persistent societal bias "...that result[s] in an overemphasis of the value of physicians and medical institutions to society, while overlooking the significance of the role that families, religious groups, and nurses have historically played in community-based care of the dying" (p. 135). At least while when we suffer or all hope is lost, it would seem, spirituality (not religion) is welcome.

To conclude, this section began with a consideration of key sites of conflict over the place of religion in individual choices in relation to health. Throughout Canadian history, religious groups have often acted as special interest groups, and sought to shape the provision of healthcare and health policy. Reproductive health and euthanasia are key examples of this influence. Following this, the reader was introduced to instances where religion, and most often spirituality, are encouraged and even demanded in relation to healthcare and treatment. Key changes in the underlying principles guiding Aboriginal health and health care have led to increased space for spirituality. Other examples of the inclusion of a spirituality and religion relate to the continued importance of pastoral care as part of healthcare delivery. These cases demonstrate that despite the aforementioned conflicts, religion and spirituality remain powerful sites for personal and social transformation.

5   Where *Should* Religion Fit? Hospitals, Healthcare Workers, and Religious Neutrality in Quebec

In this section, I turn to the broader question of religious diversity and health, by presenting a sub-section of results from a qualitative study examining the public hearings for the Quebec Charter of Values (see Beaman and Smith 2016), as well as some brief reflections on Bill 62. Following this, I summarize current research in the field of spiritual caregiving. In the case of the former, religion is a source of contention, while in the latter, spirituality is seen as the answer to the problem.

Fig. 3 Ostentatious
religious symbols.
Source: Gouvernement de
Québec, 2013

However, arguably, both instances have grown out of and can be better understood
in light of the rising pluralism previously noted, as well as a more general awareness
of religious diversity within the delivery of healthcare services. However, as we
shall see, these issues are particularly salient in Quebec, where the place of religion
in the public sphere has been hotly debated.

In Quebec, 2013, in the spring, the government began discussing the Québec
a Charter of Values as a way to finally resolve issues related to reasonable accommodation that had begun with the Bouchard-Taylor Commission. On November 7,
2013, the Charter was presented as Bill 60. The aim of the Charter of Values was to
amend the Québec Charter of Human Rights and Freedoms, establish a standard of
neutrality for all civil service employees, and create a framework for accommodation requests. One of the main aims of the Charter revolved around the banning of
religious symbols or ostentatious religious symbols within public institutions, such
as hospitals (Beaman and Smith 2016). The problematic symbols are depicted in the
pamphlet below—turbans, kippas and head scarves—which was circulated throughout the province of Québec (Fig. 3).

Both individuals and representatives for key social institutions debated the
restrictions on religious dress in the formal hearings, as well as within the media.
Those who were pro-Charter (including both individuals and groups) found the
presence of religious dress in the public sphere unacceptable and evidence of the
continued presence of religion in what should be a secular space. Anti-Charter
individuals and groups were concerned that the restrictions of religious symbols

would pose problems for many individuals working in the public sector. In the case of health, concerns were voiced in relation to nurses, doctors, and other healthcare providers (Beaman and Smith 2016).

Several health-related organizations spoke at the public hearings, including the Federation of Quebec Nurses Union, McGill University Health Centre, the Jewish General Hospital, the Federation of Resident Doctors of Quebec, and the Confederation of Organizations for Handicapped Persons of Quebec. In most submissions, the promotion of laïcité in hospitals and amongst healthcare workers played a secondary role to the bigger questions of education and neutrality of the state. However, within the submissions of health organizations, the everyday working conditions of employees was front and centre.

For example, McGill University Health Centre (CUSM), stated in the brief presented to the hearing, "…the McGill University Health Centre has never officially had an issue where an employee is proselytizing while working with patients or other staff members. We do not foresee this becoming an issue in the future". The position of the CUSM was that the presence of religious symbols had never been an issue, so why should these symbols be banned? Similarly, the Federation of Medical Residents of Quebec were in agreement that the state should be neutral and secular. They did not, however, see the need to extend this requirement to people working in the public sector. In particular, they took objection to the condition that doctors and health professionals cannot wear religious symbols.

> The neutrality of the State is different from the neutrality of individuals. We are strongly opposed to creating two classes of citizens by limiting the fundamental human rights of those who work within the public service sector especially given that these limitations do not exist in the private sector.

In line with this, the Quebec Confederation of Organizations for Handicapped Persons stated, "Fundamental rights are interdependent and should not be placed in opposition to one another; those who need those rights protected are not the majority, but are rather those groups who face discrimination because they are seen to apart from the majority." During the public hearing, many hospitals and health-care institutions across Quebec asked for a permanent exemption from the ban on workers wearing religious symbols. The concern was that the healthcare sector would lose staff members if the Charter actually became a law.

The Federation of Quebec Nurses Union (FIQ) spoke in support of the secular Charter. The results of a telephone survey conducted by the FIQ were reported in the media as follows:

- 60 per cent support the secular charter;
- 97 per cent support the principle of equality between men and women;
- 74 per cent support neutrality of the state;
- 61 per cent support a ban on the wearing of religious symbols for all employees who work in the public sector.

The FIQ maintained that despite the potential for negative repercussions on nurses wearing religious symbols, the pressing need of *laïcité* could not be under-stated. Ultimately, the positions of the various groups that participated in the public discussions can be broken down into pro-Charter or pro-religious diversity versus anti-Charter or anti-religious diversity. However, our research argued that they are ultimately more similar than different, as all groups approach religion as an either/or scenario (Beaman and Smith 2016). In both cases, the presence of religion is over simplified, and there is little to no distinction between religion and spirituality, nor a recognition of the complex ways that religion can inform health and decisions about treatment and illness. According to the FIQ, healthcare delivery ought to be fully *laique*, with no room for a grey zone.

The Quebec Charter debates arguably laid the foundation for Bill 62 which was introduced October 18, 2017. The new Bill prohibits those working in the public service, and those accessing public services, from covering the face. While the government argues the Bill addresses pressing safety and security concerns, critics argue that the restrictions in the Bill clearly target women who wear the burka or niqab. As such, the new Bill excludes workers and clients of public services alike. Further, the Bill amplifies the social exclusion of an already marginalized group in Quebec society, Muslim women. Further, the public nature of these debates has made it difficult to allow for in-depth discussions about the challenges of navigating across differences in belief systems, and tactics for addressing and dismantling systemic and institutional discrimination and racism.

In seeking to articulate an alternative framework, I draw on the scholarship of Sheryl Reimer-Kirkham on nursing and diversity. In her work, Reimer-Kirkham considers diverse themes, such as *spiritual caregiving* (Reimer-Kirkham et al. 2004), ethics and religion (2009) in healthcare delivery (2014), and religious and spiritual plurality in health care (2012). In reference to spiritual caregiving, she explores the "…moral dilemmas faced by nurses and chaplains in intercultural spiritual caregiving, and how these moral dilemmas are shaped by social context" (Reimer-Kirkham et al. 2004, p. 154). She observes that the practice of spiritual caregiving has been complicated by a paucity of literature within nursing about spirituality and care.

> As our societies become increasingly diverse, the nursing profession is faced with new challenges across its practice and scholarship domains. To support nurses in the provision of care across a breadth of ethnic, religious, gender, class, and sexual orientation diversity, significant attention has been directed to the areas of culture and spirituality over the past decade or two (Reimer-Kirkham et al. 2004, p. 149).

It is widely assumed that Canada is a secular society. As such, it is also assumed that religion and spirituality are no longer a part of public institutions, such as hospitals, and public life, such as health. The reality of religious diversity offers a challenge to nurses, but equally an invitation to think carefully about the differences between religion and spirituality, as well as the tendency "…to subsume religion under culture and ethnicity" (Kirkham-Reimer 2004, p. 154). Drawing on Orsi's notion of "lived religion" within the context of healthcare, Reimer-Kirkham observes that "…the negotiation of religious and spiritual plurality" is an ongoing process. Ultimately, Reimer-Kirkham's work is helpful in articulating a path forward without dismissing existing differences and difficulties. Further, she understands religious/spiritual diversity and pluralism as a process, rather than a static and unchanging reality.

6 Current Challenges and Future Opportunities

I would like to draw the reader's attention towards current challenges that indicate opportunities for future research within the field of religion and health. First, in many settings, the secular state is seen as a *fait accompli*. As we have discussed in this chapter, it is true that, when compared to the past, adherence to the Anglican and Catholic churches in Canada has declined significantly. This has not meant that religion and spirituality have disappeared from the public realm, nor that individuals do not continue to identify with or draw on religious and spiritual beliefs. However, the denial of religion and spirituality as important for people makes it difficult to study in the broader context of health and illness. Further, the belief that religion and spirituality no longer matter has meant that available data on religion as it relates to health outcomes is sparse compared to other social determinants of health, such as race, ethnicity, or social class. As such, researchers interested in this area are often left to infer from other factors. More research in this area is needed.

Second, the rising diversity of the population and of religious adherents is definitely a challenge, but ultimately an opportunity for scholars interested in religion and health. There is an ongoing need to bring the education of healthcare professions in line with the shifting religious and spiritual landscape that defines contemporary Canadian society. Further research is needed to provide best practice guidelines in developing training and education for delivering healthcare to a religiously diverse society. And religious diversity should include a consideration of religious-nones. Do they have spiritual care needs? And if yes, what are they? Furthermore, just because someone identifies with a particular religious group does not mean they have spiritual needs. New forms of religion and spirituality particular to the contemporary social landscape challenge previous categories that have been employed to make sense of the relationships between religion and health.

7 Concluding Thoughts

This chapter began with a somewhat simple question: *Is religion still a factor in how Canadians understand and experience health?* It is true that religious adherents are on the decline, and the number of religious-nones is rising. And yet, at the same time, we have seen an incredible increase in the diversity of religious groups in Canada. Given that health and illness are intimately tied to religion and spirituality, we have seen some of the complex, multi-faceted, and interesting ways that conflicts and possibilities emerge out of this contemporary landscape. Through a careful examination, it becomes apparent that the answer is far from simple. To gain a deeper understanding of the relationship between religion, health, and religious diversity, this chapter has examined:

- key terminology and theoretical perspectives in the social study of health, illness, spirituality, and religion;
- the sociological study of medicine, health, and illness, as related to religion, spirituality, and religious diversity;
- the history of health and religion, with a particular focus on the Canadian context;
- key sites of conflict centered on religion and health, but also instances where religion and spirituality are seen as fundamental to health;
- the Quebec Charter of Values, with a focus on hospitals and healthcare workers, within the wider context of discussions about religious diversity and healthcare;
- current challenges and future opportunities in research and scholarship in religion and health.

Today, in Canada, most individuals would consider health to be a fundamental human right. Nevertheless, we do not always consider the variety of ways that our health and well-being can be impacted by factors both beyond and within our control. From the time we take our first breath, to the time we take our last, our experience of health and illness are deeply and profoundly shaped by our unique experiences, cultural background, and the wider social system within which we find ourselves. From this perspective, decisions in relation to religion, spirituality, health, and illness, are far from straightforward.

8 Questions for Critical Thought

1. Do religion or spirituality play a role in how you understand health and illness? If yes, how so? If no, are there particular health circumstances where you would seek out religious or spiritual guidance? Why or why not?
2. The *Canadian Charter of Rights and Freedoms* offers the promise of protection for sincerely held religious beliefs. Do you think healthcare providers should be allowed to refuse services to patients on religious grounds when those beliefs are sincerely held? What arguments can you think of to support the position of a devout healthcare provider? What arguments can you think of to support the rights of the patient?
3. What are some of the challenges of healthcare delivery within the context of an increasingly diverse population? Are these challenges the same or different from other public institutions? For example, education?
4. Should hospitals aim to represent diversity? If yes, what form should this take? Where does religious diversity play a role? Are the issues the same or different from diversity more generally?
5. In a secular pluralist state, should all public institutions be free of religion and religious symbolism? Would you support a ban of religious symbolism in hospitals? Why or why not?

9   Online Resources

1. In this video from the Religion and Diversity Project, Professor Meredith McGuire discusses her research on *lived religion* in the United States, focussing on non-medical approaches to healing:

https://www.youtube.com/watch?v=z36j2D9ndSU

2. In this video from the Religion and Diversity Project, United Church of Canada member Charlotte Campbell discusses her use of walking as a meaningful spiritual practice:

https://www.youtube.com/watch?v=rOc8kIMjxvc

3. This project, lead by Sheryl Reimer-Kirkham, PhD, RN, investigates the role of prayer in healthcare institutions in Canada and Britain:

http://prayerastransgression.com/

10   References for Further Reading

Canadian Hospice Palliative Care Association. (2013, October 31). *How spiritual care practitioners provide care in Canadian hospice palliative care settings: Recommended advanced practice guidelines and commentary.* Ottawa: CHPCA Spiritual Advisors.

In this publication, students can explore guidelines for practice for spiritual care practitioners within Canadian palliative care. In particular, the document explores important definitions, as well as a discussion of the issues currently facing spiritual care practitioners.

Raphael, D. (2016). *Social determinants of health: Canadian perspectives.* Toronto: Canadian Scholars' Press.

Dennis Raphael is a prominent Canadian scholar within the field of Sociology of Health and Illness. This publication can act as a helpful resource for students in articulating the broader field of sociology of health and illness, as related to social determinants.

Reimer-Kirkham, S. (2014). Critical refractions: Nursing research on religion and spirituality through a social justice lens. *Advances in Nursing Science, 37*(3), 249–257.

Dr. Reimer-Kirkham's research is innovative and engaging and delves into pressing issues in relation to religious diversity, cultural pluralism, and nursing. In this article, Reimer-Kirkham applies a social justice lens to the incorporation of religion and spirituality within nursing.

11   Researcher Background

Lisa Smith is an instructor in the Departments of Sociology and Gender, Sexualities, and Women's Studies, at Douglas College, located in New Westminster, British Columbia. Lisa is first and foremost a devoted and passionate educator and is currently teaching a variety of courses within the areas of feminism, diversity, social control, and sociology of the lifecourse. She particularly enjoys collaborative research projects with community actors interested in pursuing social justice, anti-oppression, and social change. Her work has appeared in a variety of peer-reviewed publications including *Studies in the Maternal, Social Compass, Girlhood Studies*, and several edited collections.

References

Amaro, H. (1988). Women in the Mexican-American community (religion, culture, reproductive attitudes and experiences). *Journal of Communication Pyschology, 16*, 6–20.

Anzovino, T., & Boutilier, D. (2015). *Walk a mile: Experiencing and understanding diversity in Canada*. Toronto: Nelson.

Ball, L. (2009). Cholera and the pump on broad street: The life and legacy of John snow. *The History Teacher, 43*(1), 105–119.

Beaman, L., & Smith, L. (2016). "Dans leur propre intérêt": La charte des valeurs québécoises, ou du danger de la religion pour les femmes. *Recherches Sociographiques, 62*(2–3), 475–504.

Beiser, M. (2005). The health of immigrants and refugees in Canada. *Canadian Journal of Public Health, 96*, 30–44.

Beiser, M., & Hou, F. (2001). Language acquisition, unemployment and depressive disorder among southeast Asian refugees: A 10-year study. *Social Science and Medicine, 53*(10), 1321–1334.

Bellah, R. (1985). *Habits of the heart: Individualism and commitment in American life*. Berkeley: University of California Press.

Best Health. (2016). What it means to be spiritual but not religious. *Readers Digest Best Health*. http://www.besthealthmag.ca/best-you/wellness/what-it-means-to-be-spiritual-but-not-religious/. Accessed 5 Dec 2016.

Bibby, R. (1993). *Unknown gods: The ongoing story of religion in Canada*. Toronto: Stoddart Publishers.

Brotman, J., Moore Mensah, F., & Lesko, N. (2010). Exploring identities to deepen understanding of urban high school students' sexual health decision-making. *Journal of Research in Science and Teaching, 47*(6), 742–762.

Brown, R. (2001). Australian indigenous mental health. *Australian and New Zealand Journal of Mental Health Nursing, 10*, 33–41.

Buck, J. (2007). Reweaving a tapestry of care: Religion, nursing, and the meaning of hospice, 1945-1978. *Nursing History Review, 15*, 113–145.

Callister, L., Semenic, S., & Foster, J. (1999). Cultural and spiritual meanings of childbirth: Orthodox Jewish and Mormon women. *Journal of Holistic Nursing, 17*(3), 280–295.

Catholic Health Care Association of Canada. (2000). *Standards of spiritual and religious care for health services in Canada* (pp. 1–24). Ottawa: Catholic Health Association and the Canadian Association for Pastoral Practice and Education.

CBC. (1968, August 18). *The birth control pill sparks religious furor*. CBC. Retrieved from http://www.cbc.ca/archives/entry/the-birth-control-pill-sparks-religious-furor

Covey, H. (2005). Western Christianity's two historical treatments of people with disabilities or mental illness. *The Social Science Journal, 42*(1), 107–114.

Dein, S., Cook, C. C., Powell, A., & Eagger, S. (2010). Religion, spirituality, and mental health. *The Psychiatrist, 34*(2), 63–64.

Dunn, J. R., & Dyck, I. (2000). Social determinants of health in Canada's immigrant population: Results from the National Population Health Survey. *Social Science and Medicine, 51*, 1573–1593.

Durkheim, E. (1897). *Le suicide*. Paris: Felix Alcan.

Gagnon, L. (2003). Morgentaler's call for secular-only hospitals earns tepid response. *Canadian Medical Association Journal, 168*(3), 331.

Gerhardt, U. (1989). *Ideas about illness: An intellectual and political history of medical sociology.* London: Macmillan.

Gerhardt, U. (1990). Qualitative research on chronic illness: The issue and the story. *Social Science and Medicine, 30*, 1149–1159.

Germov, J., & Hornosty, J. (2017). *Second opinion: An introduction to health sociology*. Don Mills: Oxford University Press.

Gibbon, J. M. (1938). *Canadian mosaic: The making of a northern nation*. Toronto: McClelland & Stewart.

Giddens, A. (1991). *Modernity and self-identity: Self and society in the late modern age*. Stanford: Stanford University Press.

Grossman, C. (2010, February 11). Christian churches in Canada fading out: USA next? *Faith and Reason*. Retrieved from http://content.usatoday.com/communities/Religion/post/2010/02/christian-churches-in-canada-fading-out-usa-next/1#.WRH3_9IrJPZ

Health Canada and the Assembly of First Nations. (2015). *First nations mental wellness continuum framework: Summary report*. Health Canada.

Hornosty, J., & Strazzari, M. (2017). Aging, dying, and death in the twenty-first century. In J. Germov & J. Hornosty (Eds.), *Second opinion: An introduction to health sociology* (pp. 234–256). Don Mills: Oxford University Press.

Kaplan, C. P., Erickson, P. I., Stewart, S. L., & Crane, L. A. (2001). Young Latinas and abortion: The role of cultural factors, reproductive behaviour, and alternative roles to motherhood. *Healthcare Women International, 22*, 667–689.

Karpf, T. (2007). Faith-based organizations play a major role in HIV/AIDS care and treatment in sub-Saharan Africa. *World Health Organization: Media Centre*. http://www.who.int/mediacentre/news/notes/2007/np05/en/. Accessed 5 Dec 2016.

Kirmayer, L. J., Brass, G. M., & Tait, C. L. (2000). The mental health of Aboriginal peoples: Transformation of identity and community. *Canadian Journal of Psychiatry, 45*(7), 607–616.

Kirmayer, L., Simpson, C., & Cargo, M. (2003). Healing traditions: Culture, community and mental health promotion with Canadian aboriginal peoples. *Australasian Psychiatry, 11*, 15–23.

Koenig, H. G., McCullough, M. E., & Larson, D. B. (2001). *Handbook of religion and health*. Oxford: Oxford University Press.

Larimore, W. L., Parker, M., & Crowther, M. (2002). Should clinicians incorporate positive spirituality into their practices? What does the evidence say? *Journal of Health Care Chaplaincy, 21*(1), 1–13.

de Leeux, S., & Greenwood, M. (2011). Beyond borders and boundaries: Addressing indigenous health inequities in Canada through theories of social determinants of health and intersectionality. In O. Hankivksy (Ed.), *Health inequities in Canada: Intersectional frameworks and practices* (pp. 53–70). Vancouver: UBC Press.

Levin, J. S., & Vanderpool, H. Y. (2008). Religious factors in physical health and the prevention of illness. *Prevention in Human Services, 9*(2), 41–64.

Masters, K. S. (2005). Research on the healing power of distant intercessory prayer: Disconnect between science and faith. *Journal of Psychology and Theology, 33*(4), 329–338.

Masters, K. S., & Spielmans, G. I. (2007). Prayer and health: Review, meta-analysis, and research agenda. *Journal of Behavioural Medicine, 30*(4), 329–338.

McCullough, M. E. (1995). Prayer and health: Conceptual issues, research review, and research agenda. *Journal of Psychology and Theology, 23*(1), 15–29.

McDonald, L., & Kennedy, S. (2004). Insights into the "healthy immigrant effect": Health status and health services use of immigrants to Canada. *Social Science and Medicine, 59*, 1613–1627.

McLaren, A., & McLaren, A. T. (1997). *The bedroom and the state: The changing practices and politics of contraception and abortion in Canada, 1880–1997.* Don Mills: Oxford University Press.

Mikkonen, J., & Raphael, D. (2010). *Social determinants of health: The Canadian facts.* Toronto: York University of School of Health Policy and Management.

Miller, A. (2013). Incorporating theology into medical education. *CMAJ, 185*(1), 35–37.

Mills, C. W. (1959). *The sociological imagination.* London: Oxford University Press.

Nancarrow Clarke, J. (2016). *Health, illness, and medicine in Canada.* Don Mills: Oxford University Press.

Nieuwsma, J. A., Rhodes, J. E., Jackson, G. L., Cantrell, W. C., Lane, M. E., Bates, M. J., Dekraii, M. B., Bulling, D. J., Ethridge, K., Drescher, K. D., Fitchett, G., Tenhula, W. N., Milstein, G., Bray, R. M., & Meador, K. G. (2013). Chaplaincy and mental health in the Department of Veteran Affairs and Department of defense. *Journal of Health Care Chaplaincy, 19*(1), 3–21.

Oelke, N. D., & Vollmann, A. R. (2007). "Inside and outside": Sikh Women's perspectives on cervical Cancer screening. *CJNR, 39*(1), 174–189.

Orsi, R. (2002). Is the study of lived religion irrelevant to the world we live in? *Journal for the Scientific Study of Religion, 42*(2), 169–174.

Pargament, K. (1997). *The psychology of religion and coping: Theory, research, practice.* New York: The Guilford Press.

Patriquin, M. (2016, October 28). A Jehovah's witness and her deadly devotion. *Macleans.* Retrieved from http://www.macleans.ca/news/a-jehovahs-witness-and-her-deadly-devotion/

Public Health Agency of Canada. (2016). *What makes Canadians healthy or unhealthy.* Retrieved from   http://www.phac-aspc.gc.ca/ph-sp/determinants/determinants-eng.php#unhealthy. Accessed 15 Dec 2016.

Raphael, D. (Ed.). (2012). *Tackling health inequalities: Lessons from international experiences.* Toronto: Canadian Scholars Press.

Ravelli, B., & Webber, M. (2015). *Exploring sociology: A Canadian perspective* (3rd ed.). Toronto: Pearson.

Reimer-Kirkham, S. (2009). Lived religion: Implications for nursing ethics. *Nursing Ethics, 16*(4), 406–417.

Reimer-Kirkham, S. (2014). Nursing research on religion and spirituality through a social justice lens. *Advances in Nursing Science, 37*(3), 249–257.

Reimer-Kirkham, S., Pesut, B., Meyerhoff, H., & Sawatzky, R. (2004). Spiritual caregiving at the juncture of religion, culture, and state. *CJNR, 36*(4), 148–169.

Reimer-Kirkham, S., Sharma, S., Sawatzky, R., Meyerhoff, H., & Cochrane, M. (2012). Sacred spaces in public places: Religious and spiritual plurality in health care. *Nursing Inquiry, 19*(3), 202–212.

Romo, L. F., Berenson, A. B., & Segards, A. (2003). Sociolcultural and religious influences on the normative contraceptive practices of Latino women in the United States. *Contraception, 69*(3), 219–225.

Rose, N. (1996). The death of the social? Refiguring the territory of government. *Economy and Society, 25*(3), 327–356.

Ross, S. (2016, December 3). Abortion services not needed on P.E.I., protesters say. *CBC News.* Retrieved from http://www.cbc.ca/news/canada/prince-edward-island/pei-abortion-prince-county-hospital-1.3880384

Segall, A., & Fries, C. J. (2011). *Pursuing health and wellness: Healthy societies, healthy people.* Don Mills: Oxford University Press.

Seljak, D., Schmidt, A., Benham Rennick, J., Bramadat, P., & Da Silva, K. (2007). *Religion and multiculturalism in Canada: The challenge of religious intolerance and discrimination.*

Waterloo: Strategic Policy, Research and Planning Directorate Multiculturalism and Human Rights Program Department of Canadian Heritage.

Semenic, S. E., Callister, L. C., & Feldman, P. (2004). Giving birth: The voices of Orthodox Jewish women living in Canada. *Journal of Obstetrics, Gynecology, and Neonatal Nursing, 33*(1), 80–87.

Sethna, C., & Doull, M. (2012). Accidental tourists: Canadian women, abortion tourism, and travel. *Women's Studies: An Inter-disciplinary Journal, 41*(4), 457–475.

Smith, D. (1987). *The everyday world as problematic: A feminist sociology*. Milton Keynes: Open University Press.

Smith, M. (2007, April 6). Religion in a secular society. *The Star*. Retrieved from https://www.thestar.com/opinion/2007/04/06/religion_in_a_secular_society.html. Accessed 15 Dec 2016.

Statistics Canada. (2003). *Religions in Canada*. Ottawa: Minister of Industry.

Statistics Canada. (2011). *National household survey: Data tables*.

Stephenson, P. (2004). Health care, religion and ethnic diversity in Canada. In P. Bramadat & D. Seljak (Eds.), *Religion and ethnicity in Canada* (pp. 201–221). Toronto: Nelson.

Thomas, K. H. (2016). Warrior faith: A Marine's lesson in religion, health, and healing. *Social Work & Christianity, 43*(1), 108–123.

Tone, A. (2001). *Devices and desires: A history of contraceptives in America*. New York: Hill and Wang.

Truth and Reconciliation Commission of Canada. (2015). *Truth and reconciliation Commission of Canada: Calls to action*. Winnipeg: Truth and Reconciliation Commission of Canada.

Tse, S., Lloyd, C., Petchkovsky, L., & Manaia, W. (2005). Exploration of Australian and New Zealand indigenous people's spirituality and mental health. *Australian Occupational Therapy Journal, 52*, 181–187.

Van de Creek, L., & Burton, L. (2001). Professional chaplaincy: Its role and importance in health-care. *The Journal of Pastoral Care, 55*(1), 81–97.

Weiss, G., & Lonnquist, L. (2009). *The sociology of health, healing and illness* (6th ed.). Upper Saddle River: Pearson Education.

Winnipeg Regional Health Authority. (2014). *The culture of well-being: Guide to mental health resources for First Nations, Métis & Inuit people in Winnipeg*.

Wolpe, P., Burnett, W., & Idler, E. (2014). Religion's role as a social determinant of twenty-first-century health: Perspectives from the disciplines. In E. Idler (Ed.), *Religion as a social determinant of public health*. New York: Oxford University Press.

World Health Organization. (2017). *Constitution of the World Health Organization: Principles*. http://www.who.int/about/mission/en/. Accessed 25 Nov 2016.

Zhao, J., Xue, L., & Gilkins, T. (2010). Health status and social Capital of Recent Immigrants in Canada: Evidence from the longitudinal survey of immigrants to Canada. *Citizenship and immigration Canada* (pp. 1–29).

Christian Congregational Life in a Changing Social Environment

Steve McMullin

Abstract As Canadian society continues to be transformed by the pervasiveness of digital media, by a more postmodern way of understanding truth, and by new immigration patterns and other effects of globalization, Christian congregations in Canada are experiencing remarkable change. In some cases, those changes are creating new diversities within and among congregations and in other ways change results in new uniformities. The ways that Canadians understand and practice their Christian faith have been profoundly impacted by those changes. The changes represent more than merely an evolution of religious belief and practice or the secularizing impact of rationalism. In this new social environment, many Christian congregations are experimenting with media and with new models that represent paradigmatic shifts in the ways that Christianity is practiced. This chapter focuses on recent sociological research about how Christian congregations in Canada are affected by new media and how congregational life is experienced—often in unexpected and in quite different ways—by men and by women.

Keywords Digital media · Congregations · Technology · Religious leaders · Social connectedness · Mainline protestant · Evangelical protestant · Religious change

1 Introduction

In sociological studies of Christian congregations in the Western world, the issue of secularization has been a central theme for at least a half century. In the mid twentieth century, social theorists like Peter Berger predicted a continuing decline of religion in the West: he predicted that as modern people became more educated and as scientific advances provided godless explanations of natural phenomena, an increasingly scientific and rational understanding of life would lead to the demystification of life and therefore to a continuing decline in religious belief and practice

S. McMullin (✉)
Acadia University, Wolfville, NS, Canada
e-mail: stephen.mcmullin@acadiau.ca

© Springer International Publishing AG, part of Springer Nature 2018   135
C. Holtmann (ed.), *Exploring Religion and Diversity in Canada*,
https://doi.org/10.1007/978-3-319-78232-4_7

(Berger 1967). To some extent, it is obvious that Berger and those with similar views were correct (see Hay 2014 for an application of Berger's theory to the Canadian religious context). There have been great changes in the religious landscape. In Canada, as in other Western countries, previously shared religious beliefs served as robust plausibility structures during such confusing times as the two World Wars and the Great Depression. For many Canadians, Christian doctrines that had been learned by rote during their childhood years served to make sense of a complex world that was often confusing and worrisome. The church was a central institution in every community and it had influence over much more than just religious beliefs. Today, those traditional doctrines are now shared by fewer Canadians and the church's influence in society is not the same. Canada has become a more secular society.

Measures of participation in Canadian congregations have shown steady declines since the 1970s, especially among the most traditional or "mainline" Christian denominations, and especially during the decade between the 1991 and 2001 censuses. Among the largest Protestant denominations in Canada, the 2001 census reported that the number of respondents who identified themselves as Presbyterian had declined by 35.6% during the decade since 1991, while the number who claimed to be United, Anglican, and Lutheran declined by 8.2%, 7%, and 4.7% respectively[1]. Bibby points out that over a 70-year period, the census shows that the number of people who identified with one of the Mainline Protestant denominations (United, Anglican, Presbyterian, Lutheran) declined from 48% to 20% of the Canadian population. During the same period of time, the percentage of people who identify as Roman Catholic or Evangelical Protestant has remained virtually unchanged at 43% and 8% respectively (Bibby 2011, p. 30). Bibby describes the much more dramatic drop in denominational affiliation among United and Anglican youth, and among Roman Catholic youth in Quebec, as "almost breathtaking" (Bibby 2011, pp. 32–33).

Another noticeable change in the overall Canadian population is the recent increase in the number of people who identify as having no religion. Based on the National Household Survey (2011), the Statistics Canada website indicates that among Canada's total 2011 population of 32,852,320, more than two thirds (22,102,745) identified themselves as "Christian." The next largest group (7,850,605 people or 24% of all Canadians) claim to have "no religious affiliation."

The sphere of religious influence in public life has also diminished. Whereas for much of the twentieth century the Christian scriptures would have at least been read regularly, and in many cases taught regularly, in Canadian public school classrooms, and Christian prayers would be included in most public events, such practices would today be considered unacceptable or at least inappropriate by most Canadians (including practicing Christians).

But as Berger himself has pointed out, secularization theory has proven inadequate to explain what is happening to religious life in the Western world (Berger 2005). The incredible modern scientific advances of the twentieth century were unsuccessful in answering humanity's existential questions about life and death

---

[1] Canada census data is available at http://www.statcan.gc.ca/

issues and about suffering and ultimate meaning. In a postmodern environment where disillusionment with rational truth has become increasingly common, even most people who claim to have "no religion" continue to express the importance of religious beliefs and practices (Hout and Fischer 2002).

At the same time, many (though not most) Christian congregations in Canada are changing in dramatic ways, and many of those congregations are experiencing quite rapid growth. While the overall chronic decline of traditional religion in Canada continues, it is clear that a remarkable shift is happening among Christian congregations that are embracing new models of communication and community. Descriptive data from two Canadian congregations—one very traditional and one that has embraced change—will illustrate that shift.

2 Real-Life Stories from Qualitative Research

2.1 Centre City Church

On a typical Sunday morning, about 30–40 aging members of Centre City Church gather for worship in a sanctuary where once there were 300–400 worshippers each Sunday. They open heavy wooden doors to enter a foyer where buckets are in place on the floor to catch rain from the leaking roof. As they enter the ornately decorated sanctuary and make their way to the pew where they usually sit, they are comforted as they hear the familiar sound of classical music being played as a prelude on the pipe organ and as they see the names of long-departed church members etched in the stained glass of the gothic-shaped memorial windows. Although the many rows of long, straight wooden pews are almost empty, the members do not sit in close proximity to one another; they are scattered around the sanctuary in groups of two or three with large empty spaces between them.

The members choose to sit where they have always sat; perhaps some of them are still sitting where they used to sit with their parents and their young siblings 50 or 60 years ago, when the Sunday School rooms were filled with as many as 500 children and it seemed like almost everyone in the neighbourhood attended a church. They watch as four elderly robed choir members—three women and one man—enter the choir loft that was built to seat 30 singers. In a building that seems not to have changed much since they were young, they now reflect on the fact that neither their children nor their grandchildren attend the church with them, and they wonder what will happen to Christianity in Canada.

In a focus group, one woman remarked that there are now a maximum of two children in the church's Sunday School—both of them are children whose parents do not attend but who occasionally attend with their grandparents. A man responded that they need to do something to get more children coming to their church or they will not survive, while another man said glumly that "we've run out of steam." With most members in their retirement years, they see no way to find the number of volunteers that would be necessary to maintain the kinds of programs that might attract the many children in their neighbourhood. They do not recall how long it has been since there was a baptism in their church. Is this the last generation of Christians, they wonder?[2]

2.2   Hope Community Church

On the same Sunday morning, about three miles from Centre City Church, hundreds of members of Hope Community Church are gathering for the second worship service of the morning. In the foyer before the service, at least four languages can be heard as people informally chat with friends. The congregation has doubled in size over the past decade. Even though they just completed construction of their new and much larger building, there already is not enough room for everyone to be able to worship together at one time. The "sanctuary" is actually a full-sized gym that will be used for children's and youth activities later in the week. There is no stained glass, there are no pews, there are no memorial plaques, and there is no pipe organ. As the many young families with children and youth enter along with older life-long church members, they wave to their friends and try to find a row of chairs where there is room for all of them to sit together in the increasingly crowded room. While contemporary Christian music plays through the state-of-the-art sound system, information about church activities appears on the three big projection screens.

When the digital countdown on the projection screens indicates that it is time for the service to begin, the house lights dim and the lighting focuses on the multi-ethnic team of musicians who use electronic keyboards, guitars, drums, and vocals to lead the congregation in an extended time of enthusiastic worship. At the end of that segment of the service, four young adults approach the baptistery. After they tell the congregation about their recent decisions to follow Jesus (two of their accounts are spoken in Mandarin, with an English translation on the projection screen), the pastor baptizes each of them using a traditional formula of Christian baptism. The congregation responds with loud applause after each person is baptized. Then, prompted by a slide on the projection screens, scores of children leave to go to their programs in another part of the building before the pastor begins his sermon.[3]

At Hope Community Church, the weekend worship experience employs a variety of new media, and throughout the week members are encouraged to meet in small groups that are primarily for the building of community so people gain a sense of belonging. Though the Sunday service attracts several hundred people who may know very little about one another and who may not see each other except at church

---

[2] Centre City Church (not its real name) is based on an ethnographic study of a 200-year-old urban Canadian congregation that decided to close after years of chronic decline (see McMullin 2011).

[3] Hope Community Church (not its real name) is based on an actual congregation in the same city as Centre City Church. The congregation participated in a sociological study of the use of digital media.

functions, through the kinds of midweek small groups that now characterize many growing congregations the members are able to get to know a few other people very well and close friendships develop. In one such small group that agreed to serve as a focus group for research purposes, twelve young adults (six married couples) reflected on the role of digital media and the role of a sense of belonging as contributors to the growth at Hope Community Church: When one man said that "Our congregation has been growing quite a bit in the past two years, I would say, and I don't know how much of that is associated with technology but it's hard to believe that some of it wouldn't be just because of technology", a woman responded that "The technology might bring you there in the first place but it's not going to be what keeps you there. It has to be the real personal connections that are going to keep you in the church but the website and things like that certainly help draw people in." A young man agreed: "Because in the end we all want to be part of, and belong to something, right?" While this congregation does make extensive use of media in a variety of ways, it is clear that they understand that media does not replace devout faith and a genuine sense of belonging in community.

Rather than simply seeing media only in terms of how it is employed in the weekly worship services, the senior pastor of Hope Community Church emphasized that social media allows congregations and their leaders to engage meaningfully in conversations that are happening in the surrounding culture:

> I think it allows us to be part of conversations that we wouldn't be a part of. The internet allows you to chime in on something, maybe you have something really relevant to say, but they wouldn't ask you or call you about it because you're the church. I think if churches would embrace that kind of thing, there's all kinds of meaningful conversations going on online about important issues, whether they're about city issues or issues of people's lives.

Hope Community Church represents an increasing number of growing Canadian congregations where hundreds or even thousands of people gather for Christian worship every weekend (Bird 2015). They have not simply evolved from traditional expressions of the Christian Church; they represent intentional and sometimes radical departures from the ways that congregations previously met together and engaged the surrounding culture. Such congregations did not exist before the digital age. In these twenty-first century congregations, the Sunday morning worship service is only part of the social aspect of the church. Small groups invite people to belong before they believe and the congregation uses social media to engage people in dialogue about faith instead of simply providing rote doctrines to accept.

3 Decline and Growth

Because all across Canada there are so many very traditional congregations like Centre City Church in both urban and rural settings, and because of the dramatic decrease in membership and attendance in most mainline Protestant congregations, much recent scholarly literature about Christian congregations in Canada has focused on decline. Quantitative measures such as weekly worship attendance, church membership and denominational identity are all at lower levels in Canada than they were a generation ago (Bibby 2011, 2012; Penner et al. 2011) and that is especially true among specific groups such as the mainline Protestant denominations and Roman Catholics in Quebec (Bibby 2012:5; Bowen 2004). What the literature about decline often fails to understand or consider is that the changes taking place in Canadian religious life are much more profound and complex than just a lack of interest in organized religion or a growing degree of secularization or a rejection of Christian beliefs. Many Canadian congregations are not in decline; some groups and many individual congregations remain quite stable and others are growing (Flatt 2013; Haskell et al. 2016). More and more Canadians are worshipping in what sociologists describe as megachurches—which are defined as congregations where more than 2000 people typically gather for worship each week <http://hirr.hartsem.edu/megachurch/definition.html>.

In the increasingly postmodern conditions of Canadian social life, hallowed institutions and traditions are questioned, community is created and mediated by the use of digital devices, and global diversities are experienced routinely because of new immigration patterns, the ease and frequency of international travel, and internet access that allows the virtual crossing of national borders and ethnic boundaries. In such a society, the kinds of Eurocentric traditions that defined most Canadian congregations during the grave challenges and modern advances of the twentieth century now seem irrelevant or quaint. As a result, Canadian Christian congregations are changing. Many that attempt to maintain the past are slowly dying as the disconnect between their outdated religious traditions and the new Canadian social realities becomes increasingly apparent. At the same time, many congregations are experiencing growth as they experiment with digital media as they communicate in new ways to a postmodern culture, and as they welcome diverse groups of people. The type of traditional religious life that characterized Canada for most of the twentieth century is ending in many ways, and what will take its place is just beginning to become clear.

3.1   The Decline of Denominations

For much of the twentieth century, Canadian religious life reflected a strong European heritage. Immigrants from England and Scotland brought with them their Anglicanism, Methodism, and Presbyterianism, and smaller numbers of northern European immigrants arrived with their Lutheranism or Reformed Church heritage. Those from Ireland, France, and southern Europe were accompanied by their Roman Catholic traditions. Smaller evangelical groups, with backgrounds among English nonconformists or with American revivalist roots, also became an important though smaller part of the Canadian religious landscape. Part of the comfort of Canadian religion in the twentieth century was that worship forms and governance structures in every Presbyterian congregation were quite similar, just as they were in every Baptist congregation and in every Lutheran congregation; that was true among most denominational groups. Denominational hymnbooks and liturgies that were particular to each group helped to make worship styles quite uniform within each Christian tradition, while making each denomination seem distinct from others. There was very little ethnic or doctrinal diversity within denominations; most congregations reflected the common ethnic heritage and the European traditions of the denomination. With few exceptions, children were taught using curricula or catechisms that were common for the whole denomination. Although such national groups often created thick social and liturgical boundaries between themselves and other denominations, there really was not a lot of difference between denominations either. No matter the religious tradition, each week Canadian Christians from coast to coast dressed in their best clothes on Sunday morning and went to church where they received a traditional "church bulletin" as they entered the building, they sang hymns accompanied by a pipe organ, they recited scriptures and prayers, and they listened to a homily or sermon.

Today in Canada, most denominations have lost much of their status, not only in the wider society, but even among the very congregations that comprise those denominations. Especially among growing churches, particular congregations and clergy today are as likely to associate across denominational lines as they are within those traditional boundaries. Those European religious roots that so clearly defined denominations during the twentieth century have lost much of their influence. Most major Canadian Christian denominations have had to decrease the number of staff members and have cut back on programs as their member congregations provide decreasing levels of financial support. At the same time, it is important to realize that informal networks among churches are growing, especially among Canadian evangelical congregations (some of which may identify denominationally as mainline Protestant or Roman Catholic). Additionally, there are important renewal movements within mainline denominations (Flatt 2010) that advocate for change.

Adding to the former strengths of denominational traditions was the close connection between religion and public life in Canada (Van Die 2001). For much of the twentieth century, whether at the local Rotary Club meeting, at political party gatherings, or in the Canadian Parliament, meetings were routinely opened with Christian prayers. A Canadian who, for a lifetime, had rarely if ever attended worship services still was routinely given a Christian funeral. In church buildings large and small across Canada, memorial plaques and stained-glass windows and photos of war veterans were installed to remind people of those young Canadians who had paid the supreme sacrifice for King and country. Using phraseology from the Christian scriptures (John's gospel, Chap. 15), a theology of Jesus' sacrifice for his friends was applied to those young Canadians (whether devoutly religious or not) who gave their lives on the battlefield during two world wars. In the aftermath of wars, the memorial aspects of church buildings took on a community role as they provided a theological lens for understanding suffering and sacrifice.

At the same time, community events, such as the annual cenotaph services on November 11, were tied closely to Christian themes and routinely included the involvement of Christian clergy. Sunday was "The Lord's Day" when stores closed and recreation facilities fell silent (McMullin 2013). In the minds of many people, twentieth-century Canada was a Christian country. That meant that most communities, no matter how rural or how small, usually included one or more small church buildings. In rural Canada, very small congregations typically functioned as important social institutions even if clergy only visited occasionally. In small towns across English Canada, most of the major denominations typically supported a congregation, with clergy often being shared with another congregation in a nearby town in order to survive financially. In Quebec, more so than in any other part of Canada, until the 1960s (the "quiet revolution") the Roman Catholic Church was the primary social institution, with great influence over many essential aspects of public life.

Christian churches today have far less influence or involvement in Canadian public life. Recent immigration has made Canada a more religiously diverse country, and the relationships between church and state are quite different from what they had been. The point is that what has changed is not simply that fewer Canadians now go to church or that Canada is a more secular society. Religion itself has changed in Canada.[4] The role of religion in the lives of Canadians has changed and the relation between religion and public life has also changed—first and most noticeably in Quebec but also throughout the rest of the country (Bowen 2004). Outside of those many traditional congregations like Centre City Church that are slowly dying, many Christians who devoutly practice their faith in Canada today do so in ways that are vastly different from what was the case just a generation ago. In ways that would not have been expected in the twentieth century, many local congregations today regularly and routinely make substantial changes to aspects of their religious and social life. Christian religious practice in Canada today is neither as predictable nor as unlikely to change as it had previously been.

The extent of those changes has been considerable: instead of being characterized by what would once have been seen as essential things such as wooden pews, handcrafted pulpits, stained-glass windows, gothic architecture, organ pipes, a robed choir, a church bell, memorial plaques, denominational hymn books, ornate platform furniture, and decorative crosses, the worship spaces of most growing Canadian congregations today include few if any of those accoutrements. Amid the fears and the uncertainty and the hardship of the twentieth century, such outward and traditional aspects of church life provided comfort and a sense of stability. In the aftermath of the Great Depression, two world wars that took many Canadian lives, and the Cold War with its constant nuclear threat, familiar religious traditions communicated to members that the Christian church in Canada was a place of refuge and stability that connected the generations and would not change.

Today, surrounded by very different social conditions, church has changed. In a society in which people are far more concerned with inner spirituality than they are with the external trappings of religion, what Charles Taylor calls the "ethic of authenticity" (Taylor 2007) has become the essential aspect of how younger

---

[4] For a much fuller discussion about ways that religion in the West is changing, see McMullin, Steve (2010). A New Paradigm for the Study of Religion: A Re-examination. *Implicit Religion* *13*(1), 3–16.

Canadians evaluate and experience religion. Many congregations now focus much more on inward aspects of spirituality than they do on outwardly religious forms and rituals. Certainly, most Canadians do. That means that previous measures of religiosity such as worship attendance and church membership are not as useful or as accurate as they once were for measuring Canadians' spiritual life. Many Canadians who claim to have no religion still see themselves as intensely spiritual. Growing congregations focus much more on members' understanding of who they are in relation to God (their personal sense of identity), their sense of belonging in Christian community (their social connectedness), and their experience of spiritual life and vitality.

Shifting immigration patterns are also having a remarkable impact on Canadian religious life. Although most Canadians still identify themselves as Christian,[5] the number of people affiliated with religious groups other than Christianity or Judaism is growing as a percentage of the Canadian population, and many Christian congregations are becoming much more ethnically diverse. As an increasing number of Christians from the global south and from China arrive in Canada, and when immigrants with different religious backgrounds embrace the Christian faith after their arrival in Canada, they bring with them different perspectives on what it means to be a Christian. As they join existing Canadian congregations they bring change and diversity. Statistics Canada has documented the extent to which the countries of origin for immigrants to Canada have shifted in the past few decades from mostly European to mostly Asian countries.[6]

To an incredible extent, the religious lives of emerging adults in Canadian society are being influenced by globalization and by postmodern understandings. Digital media are changing many aspects of Canadian religious life because they are affecting younger Canadians' understandings of themselves and of their social connectedness with others. Media have also changed people's understandings of God and of spirituality. In some cases, those changes have created new diversities within and among congregations and in other ways change has resulted in new uniformities. Digital media have allowed some Canadian congregations to become so large that they are in the megachurch category (Bird 2015) while an increasing number of Canadian Christians are transitioning from traditional congregations to form "house churches" that are not encumbered with the expense and care of a church building. The proliferation of music on media platforms such as Youtube means that a newly released worship song is likely within days or weeks to be included in worship in Christian congregations of every denomination and in every province. The thousands of Canadian congregations that livestream their worship services every weekend on Youtube or Vimeo or some other media platform means that there are many Canadians who do not physically attend any worship service on a weekend yet consider themselves to have participated in a Christian worship service online.

---

[5] According to the 2011 National Household Survey, more than 22 million Canadians identify themselves as Christian (http://www.statcan.gc.ca/eng/help/bb/info/religion).

[6] See Statistics Canada, *150 Years of Immigration in Canada*. <http://www.statcan.gc.ca/pub/11-630-x/11-630-x2016006-eng.htm> Accessed May 1, 2017.

In order to understand examples of some particular changes that Christian congregations have been encountering, two areas of recent sociological research will be examined: the increasing influence of digital media on Christian congregations, and the changing ways that the roles of women and men in congregations are affected by new social realities.

3.2   Digital Media and Canadian Congregations

As is true in other parts of the world, the quite sudden arrival of digital media in Christian congregations in the 1990s and the subsequent adoption of many aspects of digital media in social life have profoundly altered many aspects of religious life in Canada. At first, congregations began to incorporate digital media in worship services in much the same way that analog media had been used. Local churches across Canada began to explore the advantages of digital media for communication (email), for publicity (websites), and for programming (video). For some more traditional congregations that is still the extent to which digital media have been incorporated into church life, even if congregants' lives are being affected by media in diverse ways outside of church. But in many other churches, new media capabilities have transformed social life; innovative uses of the internet are enabling some congregations to exist in ways never before possible. The growing number of megachurches and multisite congregations in Canada are made possible by the availability of digital technology. Satellite worship sites that are often described as "video venues" can be located in shopping malls, in rented facilities such as schools or cinemas, or even in older church buildings that were about to be abandoned because of chronic decline. Many Canadian churches in both rural and urban settings now exist as multisite congregations; such new forms of congregational structure change the very meaning of what it means to be a "local church."

Digital technology brings change. Worship services, church buildings and facilities, clergy, and worshippers are all affected by digital media. Whether it is the installation of wi-fi capability throughout the building, or the placing of a projection screen in the worship space, or the purchase of digital hardware and software, or the decision to go paperless instead of providing traditional paper newsletters and bulletins for congregants, religious leaders must make decisions that will change the experience of worship and of belonging. For a 20-year-old who cannot imagine a world without digital devices, the decision to go paperless is environmentally and financially wise; for an 80-year-old congregant who is no longer able to attend church regularly, the loss of a church newsletter arriving in the mail may be spiritually and socially devastating.

Technology has financial implications, which means that the annual church budget will need to reflect the new digital realities. Christian churches in Canada typically operate as registered charitable organizations; in many cases the weekly offerings and other income for the congregation are managed locally by a volunteer treasurer and perhaps a finance committee. In more hierarchical church structures, finances may be centrally managed by denominational officials. Traditional hierarchical structures are challenged because digital media tends to democratize the church, which may make such media seem like a threat to those who want to defend those traditional structures. Because of social media, the hierarchy cannot control the church's message or the conversations among members.

Digital media affect power relations in congregations; in particular, media may empower younger and more tech savvy members at the expense of older members. If older clergy and other religious leaders in a congregation are as not skilled in their use of media, it can disempower those traditional leaders and force them to rely on the skills of younger members who may have less religious understanding and more technological ability. Young adults who have grown up in a digital world are much more astute in their ability to use media than are those who grew up in an analog world (Palfrey and Gasser 2008; Prensky 2011; Stahl 1999). In some declining congregations, older members seek to maintain their power by refusing to include sufficient finds for technology in the church budget, or by insisting that they must control the media that are used in the worship services. For example, in research interviews, the leaders of several mainline Protestant congregations told of the unwillingness of older members to permit a projection screen in the traditional worship space.

But most profoundly, digital media affect members' religious lives and experiences (Postman 1993). The kinds of multi-media worship experiences made possible by digital technology may produce a different understanding of God for congregants (see Table 1). The social life of the congregation is changed when it is mediated by technology; media may make younger adults feel more connected, but it may leave older members feeling left out. Digital media also produces new differences between religious groups: overall, it has been more common for evangelical congregations to have embraced digital technology, while many mainline Protestant and Roman Catholic congregations have been more reticent about incorporating such media into church life.

Table 1 Digital technology and perceptions of God

Digital technology has changed the way I think about God (Scale of 1–10):		
Age	Mean	N
25 and younger	4.13	n = 157
26–35 years	3.34	n = 196
36–65 years	2.80	n = 782
66–75 years	2.24	n = 144
Older than 75	2.42	n = 57
Digital technology has had no effect on the way I think about God:		
25 and younger	28.0%	
26–35 years	39.8%	
36–65 years	54.5%	
66–75 years	67.4%	
Older than 75	71.9%	

My recent sociological research among more than 1500 church members in 20 Christian congregations looked at ways that digital media affect congregations and their leaders. Paper surveys that were distributed during regular worship services were completed by 1545 adults. After the surveys had been completed, 82 young adults participated in 11 focus groups, and 27 church leaders (most are ordained clergy) were interviewed. The data demonstrate ways that digital media affect age groups and denominational traditions in quite different ways; it also shows that the changes taking place in Canadian religious life are much more complex than some have previously realized.

An analysis of the data shows that part of the effect of media relates to a lack of critical thought among religious leaders about how congregants and community are changed by digital technologies: many congregations have embraced digital media to the point that the technology is pervasive in all aspects of church life, but the reasons for using such media are often related to convenience or style or personal preferences, or to an attempt to appear more relevant to younger people, with little thought about how the social and religious lives of people will be affected (McMullin 2011).

Many theorists (Ellul 1964; Campbell 2012; Postman 1993; Stahl 1999; Turkle 2011) have argued that media are not morally neutral, but that the very existence of a technology has moral implications. In congregations, using digital media will empower some people while disempowering others. After one church service, a homeless man told me that his lack of a cellphone makes him feel socially isolated in his congregation; at the same church, an elderly woman said that she and her friends were being left out of the church conversations on social media. In some cases, the technologies themselves may be prioritized over people. Yet many congregations seem not to realize any moral dimension with regard to the effect of media on social identity and community. Postman (1985), writing about a pre-digital world, goes even further, arguing that electronic media is inherently secularizing and that it has an agenda; in a later work, he argues that electronic media (referring to television in his day) has the effect of trivializing religion. Postman is not opposed to technology, but he is concerned about the uncritical acceptance of technology: "No medium is excessively dangerous if its users understand what its dangers are. It is not important that those who ask the questions arrive at my answers.... This is an instance in which asking the questions is sufficient. To ask is to break the spell" (p. 161). By asking the critical questions "Has the use of technology made us more impersonal?" or "Do we provide more spiritual resources to those who use digital devices than to those who cannot afford them?" or "Have we become more enamoured with the media itself than with the God we claim to worship?" congregations and their leaders can guard against some of those dangers.

My research in congregations made it clear that few church leaders ask such critical questions. Among those comparatively few Christian leaders who had critically considered the social and religious implications of media use, there is both concern and excitement about ways that new media bring change. The congregations in the study who resisted the incorporation of digital media into the life of the congregation were all dying, but so were some of the congregations that

Table 2 Digital technology and religious faith

Digital technology has affected my own religious faith (scale of 1–10):		
Age	Mean	N
25 and younger	6.13	n = 159
26–35 years	6.29	n = 204
36–65 years	5.68	n = 808
66–75 years	4.06	n = 151
Older than 75	3.41	n = 64
Digital Technology has had no effect on my religious faith:		
25 and younger	5.7%	
26–35 years	6.9%	
36–65 years	11.4%	
66–75 years	22.5%	
Older than 75	40.6%	

had incorporated new media in many ways. It was the congregations that were critically thinking about the ways that digital technology was changing them and their message that were more likely to include younger adults and families and were more likely to be growing.

Quantitative data from the research consistently showed that the effects of media on the lives of congregants were inversely related to age; the older the respondents were, the less likely they were to say that their personal sense of identity, their social connectedness, and their spiritual lives were being affected by digital technology. But all age groups are being affected. Especially noteworthy is the age-related effect of digital media on how respondents perceive that they think about God (Table 1) and about how media affects their religious faith (Table 2). Among even the oldest age group (those older than 75 years), the majority of adult respondents recognize that digital technology has had at least some effect on their religious faith.

The complexity of how media affect Christian faith was expressed by one young woman in a focus group who reflected: "The ideas I see are available on the internet and in some ways I think it's caused me to have a lot more struggles in my faith and a lot more doubts and at the same time helped me to build a stronger faith because I have to discern what I think amidst all of these other ideas that are right in front of me" (female 14:1). While the internet exposes her to new ideas that may potentially threaten her faith, the ways that it forces her to grapple with those threatening ideas in light of her religious beliefs may actually lead to a much more robust faith, because rather than simply accepting what she has been told by others she is thoughtfully determining for herself what she believes.

There are other ways that digital media may threaten traditional religious practices while at the same time forcing believers to be more intentional regarding their Christian faith and practice. A pastor said, "I think it again goes to that always-on thing. I think it is harder to have quiet times and listen for the still small voice of God with technology. It has to be very intentional to do that" (Pastor 1:2). Here again we see the complexity: the constant intrusion of the digital world in our lives may make it less likely that Christians take time as they once did for quiet spiritual meditation and reflection, but on the other hand when they do take time it may be much more deliberate and intentional (and therefore more meaningful). Another young adult commented: "I'm checking Facebook before falling to sleep versus praying which I did as a middle-schooler.... I spend a lot less time in conversation with God than I did as a 10-year-old" (female 14:3). Although she refers to her personal schedule, comments from pastors and other respondents indicated a concern that it is more challenging for members of congregations to maintain a daily spiritual routine than it was in a pre-digital age.

In addition to these two measures of specifically religious effects, the survey responses related to one's sense of personal identity and experience of community demonstrate that the young adults in these congregations are more than three times more likely than seniors to think differently about themselves because of digital technology, and all age groups except seniors believe that digital technology has affected their friendships in positive ways (both the number of friends and the closeness of friendships). The church has traditionally played a strong role in the lives of Christians in determining their sense of personal identity and their social connectedness (Good and Willoughby 2007). Today, the use of social media has become an essential aspect of community in Canadian society and those Christian congregations and their leaders who are attuned to social changes are carefully considering how social media affects religious life.

Christian congregations have traditionally emphasized the importance of belonging. Such an understanding of the congregation as shared community is central to a Christian theological understanding of church. In most traditions, congregants are encouraged to identify themselves as church members, with the understanding that a religious faith that is common among all members allows individuals of very different backgrounds and experiences to belong. Nevertheless, it was the case in many congregations that most members shared a similar socio-economic status or represented a particular ethnic background. By providing opportunities to share life experiences with a broad range of people with different backgrounds, social media platforms have made it more likely that congregations may be socio-economically and ethnically diverse.

Christian congregations in Canada are changing, and digital media are contributing in major ways to those changes. Because of media, people think of themselves differently as worshippers. They think of the church community differently because their connectedness to others is not based as much on gathering together in a building as it once was; for many people, connections on social media platforms in which everyone contributes to the spiritual conversation may even be more religiously meaningful than gathering together in the same building on a Sunday morning to listen to a single voice preach a sermon. The extent to which digital media will affect congregations, and Canadian society as a whole, is not yet clear because the digital technologies are still developing. What is clear is that congregations are being re-shaped in previously unexpected ways by the changes that media are bringing to religious life.

3.3   Roles of Women and Men in Canadian Congregations

The changes taking place in Christian congregations in Canada are affecting religious life in some unexpected ways. For example, the mainline Protestant denominations were among the first to welcome women into all aspects of church leadership both in local congregations and in the life of the denominations and today, increasing numbers of mainline congregations are led by women clergy. What is surprising is that because many mainline Protestant congregations have experienced the most noticeable and dramatic declines in membership and in worship attendance, it is affecting the ways that some people in those congregations view women in leadership. In an atmosphere of congregational decline, the increasing role of women in leadership in mainline Protestant congregations has hit new obstacles in spite of the gains that had previously been made.

At the beginning of the twentieth century, few women held positions of leadership in any aspect of Canadian society, including the church. Women could not even vote in Canadian elections. Gradually, the status of women in Canada began to change and amid those changes most Canadian Protestant denominations decided to ordain women to pastoral ministry and most denominations also elected women to top positions of leadership in their governance structures. These changes were in many ways part of the modernization of the church. Especially among mainline Protestants, church groups recognized that, as women took on new roles in society, it was right that they should also be leaders in the church.

The unexpected new difficulty in the twenty-first century that my recent research has uncovered is that because many mainline congregations are facing serious rates of decline, and many of those congregations now are served by women clergy, the response among some rank-and-file members is to link the women in leadership with that decline. In two separate studies (McMullin 2011, 2015), numerous respondents in mainline congregations (both clergy and congregants, and both women and men) referred to the increased number of women in church leadership as the reason for the decline.

For example, a United Church of Canada minister said in a research interview, "I think that's a difficulty in the [United] church, is that men are not as prevalent or as present as they used to be on the sessions and boards and committees and so on and so forth. We have basically relegated it to women." Having said that, he went on to provide this explanation of why few men attend or provide leadership in his congregation:

> I think that there was the pushing, the bringing in of, entrusting it to the women to [be church leaders]. And they did. And they did a good job. And they're doing a good job. But there is that male presence absent from the church. And they, it almost becomes, if you're going to be involved in the church, it's almost a girlie thing. And it's not the cool thing for guys to do which makes it very difficult—it's, I'll use the terminology, well that's "women's work."

After a decade of service as pastor of a declining urban United Church congregation, a pastor expressed her own sense of frustration about the way her congregation sees her: "As a woman in ministry, I look at some of the stuff that happens and I keep thinking, my gosh, I've been at this for 30 years and we seem to be moving backwards." She emphasized that for her, the ordination of women is about women's rights, and she is frustrated that although the United Church began ordaining women to ministry in 1936, "there are still people stuck on that." But the interview with that pastor and a focus group with members of the congregation made it clear that the big issue for both pastor and people is the dramatic decline in worship attendance. It seemed unlikely that the ordination of women would be an issue in that congregation if it were growing.

Unlike the mainline Protestant denominations that began ordaining women as a matter of equality and social justice, among evangelical Protestant denominations in the twentieth century, the inclusion of women in leadership has been resisted by some on theological grounds, so decisions to ordain women could not be made simply to conform to current social changes. Instead, evangelical advocates for the ordination of women had to argue for change that was based on clearly articulated theological principles. The result is that among the evangelical denominations that have affirmed an equal role for women as ordained leaders, the rationale for the ordination of women has primarily been theological. Once a denomination affirms a Biblical and theological basis for the ordination of women, it is less likely to be open for debate.

The following two quite different stories from ordained Christian ministers (one in a growing Baptist congregation, one in a declining Anglican congregation) illustrate these issues in Canadian churches. First, the Baptist senior pastor in a major Canadian city talked about how her gender affects her role as an ordained pastor and leader:

> At the end of the day, I pray that the gender thing, that they don't see [me as] the woman, but [as] the leader, the pastor, the shepherd, because I have brought them through times and trial and have offered counsel. ... The social scripts assign women, it's all the weak side, you're a follower, you're weak. I have a wardrobe crisis every weekend. I have to make sure I am dressing modestly but I don't want to look like a monk either. What am I presenting, what am I communicating with my clothing? I am really careful. I don't think [a male pastor] stands in front of the mirror and asks, "What am I communicating with this outfit?" In a meeting, if I come out strong on an issue, how are people perceiving me in that moment? Are they perceiving me as a b-i-t-c-h or are they perceiving me as passionate and strong about this issue as a leader? So I've a hard time asserting myself in a room because I don't want to come across as the word I just spelled out and how do I as a woman find my voice? I don't want to be a man; I want to be a woman who is a pastoral leader who has gifts and abilities.

On the other hand, the rector of an aging and mostly female Anglican Church of Canada congregation discussed challenges that are quite different. For example, she says she is always contacted and expected to bake cakes or pies for all church functions—something that she suspects that male clergy would never be expected to do. She says that women in the congregation are more likely to view her as a friend than as the rector, which leads to a lot of phone calls for personal reasons, which she also believes would be rare for male clergy. She thinks male clergy are expected by their congregations to be authoritative, while females are expected to be more relational. Since she was the first woman to be rector of her congregation, she said that it caused a bit of a crisis regarding the mowing of the rectory lawn. The congregation had always expected the previous male rectors to mow the lawn themselves, but in her case they were not sure if it would be proper for them to expect her husband to mow the lawn or if they should hire someone to do it, apparently not considering the possibility that she might mow the lawn herself.

In mid-twentieth-century Canada, it would have been comparatively rare to find an ordained woman serving as the pastor of an evangelical Protestant congregation. Some mainline Protestant denominations, in contrast, have accepted women as ordained leaders in congregations for nearly a century. That may have resulted in a stereotypical (and sometimes accurate) view that theologically conservative denominations were less affirming of women in leadership. The responses of these two pastors are quite different from the stereotypical view of how clergy from mainline and evangelical Protestant congregations would have viewed their roles, but it is an illustration of how Christian congregations are changing. Although both women and men in mainline Protestant congregations expressed their belief that gender roles in congregations are social constructions, some of them went on to express doubts about whether that is actually the case. It was the Baptist pastor quoted above who most strongly argued that the role differences are entirely due to social scripts. Furthermore, when discussing the challenges of being a woman minister, the women clergy in mainline congregations focused either on peripheral aspects of their roles—the expectation of baking cookies or who should mow the lawn—or on their own question about whether men did not attend or participate as often because of the pastor's gender. On the other hand, the Baptist pastor focused much more directly on questions of pastoral leadership and pastoral ministry and ways that she seeks to ensure that social scripts (including her dress on Sunday morning) do not diminish her ability to lead.

The point of these two illustrations—about digital media and about gender roles—is to emphasize that congregations in the twenty-first century are not just evolving or adjusting to social change. Paradigmatic shifts are underway. Socially, the Canadian church is becoming something quite different from what it had previously been. Instead of thinking of congregations only in terms of numerical decline or growth, or with regard to secularization, it is important to see that Christian congregations are adapting and changing in unexpected ways to new and very different social and religious realities. As digital technologies continue to develop and become even more pervasive in society, and as Canada continues to be affected by changing immigration patterns, many congregations will be unable to cope with the changes and will die. But new expressions of congregational life are developing and will develop as Christians consider how to live out their faith in community.

4 Conclusion

Christian congregations in Canada are experiencing change. They find themselves in a very different social environment from just a generation ago. Although most Canadians still identify themselves as Christian, far fewer people attend Christian worship services today. Inner spirituality is more highly valued than religious tradition. New immigration patterns are leading to diverse ethnicities in society and in congregations. Digital media have become pervasive in the social lives of most Canadians and that is reflected in congregational life. In this new and much-changed social environment, it appears that the congregations that resist those social changes are the ones that are in decline and will eventually die. Those that choose to insist on the priority of hallowed traditions that are no longer spiritually meaningful for a new generation will find themselves losing all but their oldest members. Those that try to preserve their European heritage will be seen by their communities as antiquated and irrelevant. Those that are unwilling to wisely adopt digital media will find themselves unable to communicate meaningfully with the surrounding culture or with the next generation in their own families. At the same time, though, many Christian congregations are embracing change and experiencing growth as they realize that the modern ideas of twentieth-century Canada have shifted to an increasingly postmodern outlook. Those growing congregations are focused on authentic spirituality in congregational life, they are embracing the new demographic realities of Canada by sponsoring refugees, by welcoming immigrants, and by celebrating ethnic diversity, and they are carefully embracing the digital world in the ways that they create community and communicate their message.

5 Questions for Critical Thought

1. Why has Christian church attendance decreased so much in the past few decades? Why has that decrease been especially great among the mainline Protestant denominations?
2. How is consumerism affecting Christian congregations? What is the role of digital media in the changes taking place in Christian congregations?
3. Why are some Christian congregations growing, while others are in decline? What are some of the differences between those congregations?
4. How has the role of the Christian church in Canadian society changed? Why have those changes taken place, do you think?

6   Online Teaching and Learning Resources

1. For resources and information about growing Christian congregations in Canada, go to the website of the Flourishing Congregations Institute: http://www.flourishingcongregations.org/resources
2. To see ways that Canadian congregations are facing the new challenges, go to the Religion and Diversity Project website http://religionanddiversity.ca/en/projects-and-tools/projects/linking-classrooms/photo-essays/ and see the two photo essays entitled "Apple Pie Day" and "Bible Study."
3. For insights about a growing evangelical urban congregation that is made up mostly of young adults, go to http://religionanddiversity.ca/en/projects-and-tools/projects/linking-classrooms/religious-leaders-panel-workshop-study-religion-atlantic-canada-/and listen to the video by Allyson Marsh's about Deepwater Church in Halifax
4. Another helpful learning exercise would be to compare and contrast online resources from the three major Christian traditions in Canada: http://www.faithtoday.ca provides insight into the lives of Canadian evangelicals, while http://www.ucobserver.org shows the views of a mainline Protestant denomination and http://www.cccb.ca/site/ provides information from the Canadian Conference of Catholic Bishops.

7   Suggestions for Further Reading

Bibby, R. (2017). *Resilient Gods: Being pro-religious, low religious, or no religious in Canada.* Vancouver: University of British Columbia Press.
Bibby, R. (2012). *A new day: The resilience and restructuring of religion in Canada.* Lethbridge: Project Canada Books.
Bibby, R. (2011). *Beyond the Gods and back: Religion's demise and rise and why it matters.* Lethbridge: Project Canada Books.

Reginald Bibby has published a number of books about religion in Canada; the strength of the books is the excellent quantitative data that he has collected over many years and included in his publications.

Flatt, K. N., Haskell, D. M., & Burgoyne, S. (2017). Secularization and attribution: How mainline protestant clergy and congregants explain church growth and decline. *Sociology of Religion,* srx044.
Haskell, D. M., Flatt, K. N., & Burgoyne, S. (2016). Theology matters: Comparing the traits of growing and declining mainline protestant church attendees and clergy. *Review of Religious Research 58,* 515. doi:https://doi.org/10.1007/s13644-016-0255-4

These well-researched articles by Haskell, Flatt, and Burgoyne provide helpful insights about changes taking place in mainline Protestant congregations in Canada.

Penner, J., Rachael, H., Erika, A., Bruno D., & Rick, H. (2011). *Hemorrhaging faith: Why and when Canadian young adults are leaving, staying and returning to church.* Retrieved from www.hemorrhagingfaith.com

The *Hemorrhaging Faith* study led by James Penner is important for two reasons. It provides a mountain of quantitative data about the religious experiences of Canadian youth and young adults. Even more importantly, though, the report has itself become a part of the ways that many evangelical leaders see and understand the place of religion in Canadian society.

8 Researcher Background

Steve McMullin is the Academic Dean and Sheldon & Marjorie Fountain Associate Professor at Acadia Divinity College. Much of Steve's sociological research has focused on social aspects of congregational life. In addition to his study regarding the social aspects of decline in many Christian congregations, he has been investigating ways that digital media are affecting congregations and their leaders, and the ways that congregations may blame the secularization of society for the new and quite daunting challenges they face in a postmodern culture. He has also been studying ways that women and men may experience congregational life in quite different ways. Steve is an ordained Christian minister who served as a pastor of three growing Canadian congregations over a period of 27 years and continues to be actively involved in congregational life. The "insider knowledge" that those years provided help him to understand the lives of religious leaders and also to see Christian congregations from a *lived religion* point of view.

References

Berger, P. (1967). *The sacred canopy.* New York: Doubleday.
Berger, P. L. (2005). Religion in the west. *The National Interest, 80,* 112–119.
Bibby, R. (2011). *Beyond the Gods and back: Religion's demise and rise and why it matters.* Lethbridge: Project Canada Books.
Bibby, R. (2012). *A new day: The resilience and restructuring of religion in Canada.* Lethbridge: Project Canada Books.
Bird, W. (2015). Large Canadian churches draw an estimated 300,000 worshippers each week: Findings from a National Study. *Leadership Network.* Retrieved from http://leadnet.org/wp-content/uploads/2014/12/Canadian-Large-Church-Report-2015-final.pdf. Accessed 1 May 2017.
Bowen, K. (2004). *Christians in a secular world: The Canadian experience.* Montreal: McGill-Queen's University Press.
Campbell, H. (2012). *Digital religion: Understanding religious practice in new media worlds.* New York: Routledge.
Ellul, J. (1964). *The technological society.* New York: Vintage Books.

Flatt, K. (2010). The loyal opposition: A brief history of the renewal movement in the United Church of Canada, 1966–2010. *Church & Faith Trends, 3*, 3.

Flatt, K. (2013). *After evangelicalism: The sixties and the United Church of Canada.* Montreal: McGill-Queen's University Press.

Good, M., & Willoughby, T. (2007). The identity formation experiences of church-attending rural adolescents. *Journal of Adolescent Research, 22*(4), 387–412.

Haskell, D. M., Flatt, K. N., & Burgoyne, S. (2016). Theology matters: Comparing the traits of growing and declining mainline Protestant church attendees and clergy. *Review of Religious Research, 58*, 515. https://doi.org/10.1007/s13644-016-0255-4.

Hay, D. A. (2014). An investigation into the swiftness and intensity of recent secularization in Canada: Was Berger right? *Sociology of Religion, 75*(1), 136–162.

Hout, M., & Fischer, C. S. (2002). Why more Americans have no religious preference: Politics and generations. *American Sociological Review, 67*, 165–190.

McMullin, S. (2010). A new paradigm for the study of religion: A re-examination. *Implicit Religion, 13*(1), 3–16.

McMullin, S. (2011). *Social aspects of religious decline* (Unpublished Ph.D. Thesis). Fredericton: University of New Brunswick.

McMullin, S. (2013). The secularization of Sunday: Real or perceived competition for churches. *Review of Religious Research, 55*(1), 43–59.

McMullin, S. (2015). Gendered responses to decline in Protestant congregations. *Research in the Social Scientific Study of Religion, 26*, 21–39.

National Household Survey. (2011). Available on the Statistics Canada website: http://www23.statcan.gc.ca/imdb/p2SV.pl?Function=getSurvey&SDDS=5178

Palfrey, J., & Gasser, U. (2008). *Born digital: Understanding the first generation of digital natives.* New York: Basic Books.

Penner, J., Harder, R., Anderson, E., Désorcy, B., & Hiemstra, R. (2011). *Hemorrhaging faith: Why and when Canadian young adults are leaving, staying and re turning to church.* Retrieved from www.hemorrhagingfaith.com

Postman, N. (1985). *Amusing ourselves to death.* New York: Penguin Books.

Postman, N. (1993). *Technopoly.* New York: Vintage Press.

Prensky, M. (2011). Digital natives, digital immigrants. In M. Bauerlein (Ed.), *The digital divide* (pp. 3–11). New York: Penguin Group.

Stahl, W. A. (1999). *God and the chip: Religion and the culture of technology.* Waterloo: Wilfrid Laurier University Press.

Statistics Canada. (n.d.) *150 Years of Immigration in Canada.* Retrieved from http://www.statcan.gc.ca/pub/11-630-x/11-630-x2016006-eng.htm. Accessed 1 May 2017.

Taylor, C. (2007). *A secular age.* Cambridge, MA: Harvard University Press.

Turkle, S. (2011). *Alone together.* New York: Basic Books.

Van Die, M. (Ed.). (2001). *Religion and public life in Canada: Historical and comparative per-spectives.* Toronto: University of Toronto Press.

Canadian Catholic Experience: The New Evangelization and Identity in a Diverse Canada

Paul L. Gareau

Abstract The New Evangelization is a recent development in the Catholic Church that seeks to preserve, restore, and re-invigorate Catholic religious identity in the face of what it perceives to be a dominance of secular values. This proselytization program attempts to instigate emotional religious experiences among adherents in the hopes of forming an evangelical Catholic identity vis-à-vis the institutional Catholic Church. However, little is known of the processes and discourses of Catholic evangelization, especially among young people in Canada. This chapter focuses on an annual summer Catholic youth conference in rural Ontario called *Journey to the Father*. This conference serves as a case study shedding light on the dissemination of Catholic perspectives, the development of a personal and charismatic religious experience, and the instigation of an evangelical impetus in young Catholic participants. The following discussion will explore the New Evangelization (NE) in the Canadian context, outline personal, theoretical, and methodological reflections on studying youth and religion, and provide inquiry for further research on the youth and Catholic identity. This chapter underscores the dynamics of identity formation of Catholic evangelical youth in a diverse Canada.

Keywords Identity formation · Catholics · Youth · Evangelization · Values · Agency · Charismatic catholics · Proselytization

1 General Introduction/Synopsis of the Theme

1.1 The New Evangelization in the Canadian Context

Evangelical Christian values and worldview have taken hold of discourses of socio-political identity in the US and Canada. Ironically, these are two political contexts dominated by discourses of political and ethno-cultural pluralism, and secular values. Nevertheless, you need only to look at the influence of the Christian Right on

P. L. Gareau (✉)
University of Alberta, Edmonton, AB, Canada
e-mail: pgareau@ualberta.ca

© Springer International Publishing AG, part of Springer Nature 2018   157
C. Holtmann (ed.), *Exploring Religion and Diversity in Canada*,
https://doi.org/10.1007/978-3-319-78232-4_8

US politics over the past three or four decades to see how embedded Christian values are, not only in the structures of governance, but in the way people self-identify (Gregg 2013; Kyle 2009; Smith 2014b; Sutton 2014). Though this does not discount the longitudinal impact of Christianity on Western norms and worldview (Beaman 2003), the attitudes and tone of evangelicalism today relates to how people present themselves with the view of being recognized by others for their religious identity. In short, evangelicalism has become an ubiquitous force in the engagement of a politics of identity in a context of social, political, and moral pluralism.

The impact of evangelicalism, however, is a relatively recent phenomenon for the Catholic Church. Evangelicalism is a trans-denominational political movement that operationalizes Protestant theological values of faith through Jesus Christ and through Biblical scripture alone by focusing on personal religious experience, such as religious conversion, as the driver to socio-political identity (Kyle 2009; Noll 2010). Before the mid-20th century, evangelical Christianity was largely the domain of Protestant denominational movements—being somewhat anathema to Catholicism (Bokenkotter 2004; Fay 2002; Hitchcock 2012). The *New Evangelization* (NE), however, developed in the last half of the 20th century as a grassroots response to the call of the contemporary Catholic Church, which had been shaped by the discourses of evangelization from the Second Vatican Council (Faggioli 2012; Paul VI 1975; Second Vatican Council 1964; Wilde 2007). The NE is largely informed by the perspective that secular values dominate Western societies and have permeated the Catholic Church (Dulles 2008, 2009; Portmann 2010). This social and political view perceives secularism as corrosive and hegemonic, which in turn must be challenged and overturned in order to regain the lost ground of the Church.

This understanding of "lost ground" is based on a perceived decline in Catholic adherence in Canada over the past few decades (Clarke and Macdonald 2017). However, according to the last reliable dataset on religion in Canada from 2001 (Government of Canada 2005), denominational adherence was rather stable for the Catholic Church. In Canada, there were 12,936,905 Catholics out of a population of 29 million representing nearly 41% of the Canadian population, down from 45% in 1991. Note that the current population in Canada is 35.5 million; a difference of 6.5 million over 13 years will have generated change in the number of Catholics in Canada (Government of Canada 2014). Nevertheless, according to the 2001 data, it is obvious that Catholicism remains the largest religious denomination in Canada and the data tells a peculiar story. Between 1991 and 2001, the number of Catholics increased 4.8% (Government of Canada 2001). In provinces like Quebec, Catholics make up an overwhelming majority at 83%, whereas in Ontario, Catholics account for 34% in close parity with Protestant denominations at 35%. In both of these provinces, there is a trend of denominational decline among Protestant denominations, but Catholics have remained stable if not increasing through this period—e.g., Ontario shows a 10% rise of Catholics from 1991 to 2001 (Government of Canada 2001). Though there was a slight growth in the 1990s, there was nevertheless an overall downward trend in terms religious participation.

According to the General Social Survey (GSS) data, church attendance (i.e., measure of active participation) has fallen dramatically over 15 years. In 1986, 28% of individuals over the age of 15 noted they did not attend church service, while

43% (4 in 10 adults) reported non-attendance in 2001. This 15% jump in non-participation contrasted by the seemingly constant number of denominational affiliation has an effect on how the Catholic Church sees itself and its membership. What this says to the NE is that there is large population of Catholics who adhere to Catholicism but do not participate or are seemingly inactive. Therefore, this perspective justifies the NE approach to "internal" proselytization rather than external; meaning Catholics need to evangelize Catholics rather than non-Catholics. The *modus operandi* of the NE is to tap into this largely "disaffected" denominational affiliation to the Catholic Church with the enticements of a personal, evangelical religiosity. Therefore, the main purpose of the NE is to engage Catholics in personal relationship with Jesus Christ, which reflects a turn towards the institutional Church. This Catholic type of evangelism is the marriage of personal religious conviction with institutional authority.

The NE is a broad proselytization programme for the Catholic Church reaching all sectors of the Church; from the Magisterium to the laity (Synod of Catholic Bishops 2012a, b). Truly a widespread initiative, there are various NE activities in every Catholic diocese and church across Canada. There has been, moreover, an intense focus on young people, specifically adolescents and young adults. Currently, there are many Catholic youth organizations that serve to assert and disseminate the NE program. Two important organizations in Canada that operate on a national scale are Catholic Christian Outreach (CCO) (Catholic Christian Outreach 2013) and National Evangelization Team (NET) Ministries (NET Ministries of Canada 2016). Both of these proselytization programs seek to engage young Catholics in the values of the institutional Church through personal, charismatic religious experiences. The goal of this engagement is to instigate in Catholic youth an evangelical orientation to their socio-political identities.

Due to the fact that the NE is a recent movement in the Catholic Church, there is a lack of academic research on the impact of evangelization on young people in Canada and around the globe (Norman 2011; Smith 2014a). The presence of the NE and religiously active, evangelical Catholic youth within the political landscape in Canada raises questions about the dynamics and contours of Canadian diversity, and the role of religion in shaping modern identity: *How are young people engaging and interpreting modes of religious and socio-political identity, and integrating or negotiating this worldview in a diverse Canadian society?*

This chapter focuses on my recent doctoral research of an annual summer Catholic youth conference called *Journey to the Father* that serves as a case study on the production of personal and charismatic religious experiences, and the instigation of an evangelical impetus in Catholic youth. More importantly, this research examines the process and formulation of a "minority" identity politics in these young people. Identity politics is typically reserved for socially and politically marginalized individuals, groups, communities, or cultures based in liberal socio-political values of freedom, equality, and choice (Kelly 2005). However, *Journey to the Father* serves to help young Catholics assert their right to be to be recognized for their "outed" (i.e., *openly evangelical in a secular world*) religious identities, which necessitates a language of minority identification. The message is: *it is okay to be Catholic—it is okay to be different.* My doctoral research looks into the dissemination and appropriation of concepts of contemporary socio-political identity formation among young people. This chapter, however, will review the process and structure, and theoretical and methodological approaches for this research, look at the challenges and opportunities for future research endeavors, and note important literature on this topic. Though not confined to the topic of Catholic identity, this chapter serves as a general exposition and guide on doing research among religious youth at the intersection of liberal values and conservative religious discourses in a diverse Canadian society.

1.2 Researching Faith and Socio-Political Identity: The New Evangelization at Journey to the Father

The confluence of evangelical and secular values within Canadian society became the starting point for my research on the engagement of youth by Catholic socio-political discourse. My thesis entitled "Journeying to the Father: Researching faith and identity in a contemporary Catholic youth movement in Canada" centred on a specific location of religious evangelization—the *Journey to the Father* youth conference in rural North-Eastern Ontario. This annual three-day conference was designed to instigate emotional and charismatic religious experiences with young people with the hopes of encouraging them into becoming more religiously active in their lives. Though I will expand on the details of my research below, this research describes the culture generated by the adult organizers as well as the lived experience and socio-political perspectives of the young participants.

Overall, the research centres around the dynamics of socio-political identity. Identity has become central hub for how an individual can be understood in the analysis of different social systems and competing messages about how to form the *self* and how to engage the *other(s)* (Akhtar 2011; Parekh 2008; Taylor 1989; Winter 2011). This research is informed by the idea that Catholic youth are more likely to invest themselves in the Catholic evangelization program by way of highly affective and emotional experiences akin to the activities at *Journey to the Father*. It is through such experiences that youth are able to generate a directed (or constructed) sense of Catholic identity that both drives their participation in the Catholic Church, and helps them understand and negotiate the social and political pluralism of the world in which they live. But this hypothesis is tempered by the nuances of how the adults in these programs promote evangelical Catholic values, and how the young participants at *Journey to the Father* encountered and appropriated or negated these messages and values. From this discourse, three main themes emerge: 1) crisis of faith; 2) regime of liberal values; and 3) youth "between two worlds."

The first theme speaks to the intersections of political values and concepts regarding narratives of the perceived ubiquity of secularism in contemporary society. This perception and attitude is core to the NE and the organizers of *Journey to the Father*, and justified a deployment of a minority identity politics while imploring the need for religious identity. This socio-political engagement in identity politics points to the second theme regarding underlying liberal values of freedom, choice, and agency that undergird contemporary Western societies. This work delves into the ideas of authenticity and recognition inherent to the discussion on identity and how the NE has operationalized it to assert evangelical values and worldview among Catholic youth. This leads to the third theme regarding how young people negotiate the competing values of religious evangelization and secular society. The title *Journeying to the Father* refers to the young Catholics in this study as they negotiate different and yet intersecting socio-political values on their own terms in the process of identity formation. Their thoughts and actions point to an experiential and relational agency that is indeed a matter of *journeying in the direction of* an evangelical Catholic identity within a diverse Canada. Meaning, these young Catholics are exercising resistance while embracing evangelical values in an overall negotiation of their place in the social, political, and moral pluralism that is Canadian society.

Overall, this research provides an insight into a nascent conservative, Christian phenomenon of evangelization in the Catholic Church, which is largely unobserved and understudied. It also comments on the convergence of competing socio-political values within the frame of a more fluid identity formation among young people. This analysis serves as the lynchpin for the abovementioned idea that "it's ok to be different," which inherently reflects the idea that identity is formed in comparison and contrast to others as well as through a consolidated understanding of the self. Though this does not represent a universal understanding of identity formation, within the confines of this research young people at *Journey to the Father* claim a minority identity against the perceived hegemonic force of secular society in order to access a socio-political recognition within a diverse Canada.

2   A Real-Life Story from Qualitative Research

2.1   Case Study Approach: Journey to the Father

In order to examine the deployment of Catholic evangelical discourse and its impact on identity formation in youth, I centred my research on a single case study; the Catholic youth conference called *Journey to the Father*. This was an annual, three-day conference that took place in a tiny village called Saint Raphael's, located 30 minutes outside of Cornwall, Ontario. *Journey to the Father* ran for 15 years between 1999 and 2013, except in 2002 (World Youth Day in Toronto). It was modeled after the Steubenville Catholic Conferences, which still operate at the Franciscan University of Steubenville in Steubenville, Ohio, US. The Steubenville conferences are big events with up to 2000 young people participating at each conference. There are now 18 regional conferences across the US and two Canadian events. One is called Steubenville Atlantic (Canada) that takes place in Halifax, NS (Steubenville Conferences—Atlantic n.d.) and in Toronto, which was recently initiated in 2014 ('Steubenville Conferences—Toronto n.d.). *Journey to the Father* was relatively small, hosting an average of 300 students annually, with 500 at its peak in the mid to late 2000s.

Journey to the Father was operated by a core group of roughly 200 volunteers from the Alexandria/Cornwall Catholic diocese (i.e., senior's groups, Knights of Columbus, individual young people, etc.) and attracted young participants between 13 and 18 years old from across Southern and North-Eastern Ontario, and Western Quebec. Following the same structure each year, the weekend activities presented the possibilities of an engaged Catholic identity through skits, sessions, and music (plus a talent show), a highly affective charismatic experience of the Catholic sacraments through Eucharistic Adoration followed by Reconciliation (confession). These experiences were then consolidated with an open-mic session and Altar Call on the final day. These activities were all conducted in the hope of instilling an evangelical impetus in young participants.

In 2013, after 15 years, *Journey to the Father* came to a close due to decreasing participation, the fatigue of organizers and volunteers (many of whom had been volunteering for the full 15-year run of the conference), and the inauguration of Steubenville in nearby Toronto. At this point, in 2018, there is no longer any online presence for *Journey to the Father*, and the organizational team have turned their attention elsewhere; to youth ministry in their parishes and diocese, Alexandria-Cornwall. The termination of the conference does raise questions about the stability and effectiveness of *Journey to the Father* as a venture as well as the efficiency of the NE program in general. Nevertheless, *Journey to the Father* offers insight into the intersections of religious discourse, religious experience, and the formation of evangelical Catholic identity among young people.

Journey to the Father as a case study helps us to understand the dynamics of Catholic evangelization as it centres on a specific location of religious revivalism and socialization, outlining a description of the culture and worldview that it embodies. The basic premise for the NE in terms of evangelical values and perspectives in the Catholic Church is: (1) a personal relationship with Jesus Christ, and (2) moderated through the moral and ritual prerogative of the institutional Catholic Church. *Journey to the Father* was a platform in which young Catholics could encounter NE values and perspectives as well as affective and charismatic religious experiences. *Journey to the Father* serves as a means to capture the multilayered messages of evangelization from the adult organizers, as well as providing a platform for young people to spell out their reflections on religion and society, experience and agency. Therefore, this case study provides two related reflections on the inculcation of evangelical identity: (1) the perception and promotion of evangelical Catholic identity by the adult organizers; and (2) how young participants embodied and operationalized these values in forming their socio-political identities.

2.2   Ethnographic Research: Experiencing the Experiences

As a case study, *Journey to the Father* helps illuminate the process of Catholic evangelization over its three days of activities. On Friday night and Saturday throughout the day, the conference introduced young people to the idea of religious engagement. Saturday evening allowed the opportunity for charismatic and emotional religious engagement and experience. Finally, Sunday morning aimed to provide the means to apply these lessons and experiences to real life. This structure offers much in terms of how the adult organizers wish to disseminate the message of Catholic evangelization, and the various ways in which young people interpret this message.

In studying *Journey to the Father*, participant observation was an important step in understanding how people behaved and reacted. My participant observation spanned three years, from 2011 to 2013. I was present to observe and take note of the activities before and during the conference. I attended many organizational meetings in Cornwall where decisions were made regarding fundraising, organizing food and drinks, directing volunteers into their different functions, etc. These were great opportunities to network, ask questions, and build trust with the organizing team. As well, before the conference at Saint Raphael's each year, I would spend 1 to 2 days with the youth leaders—known as *Disciples*—as they prepared for their special roles. Activities consisted of team-building exercises, spiritual and religious development, organizing theatre plays, and learning how to help the young participants maximize their experience. Finally, I volunteered my time during the conference, helping out when I was needed. This included pegging tarps into the ground for the sleeping tents, placing chairs, raising tent shelters, moving picnic tables, and even, one year, working a graveyard shift as security. This was very fulfilling work that allowed me access to the experience behind the scenes.

During the *Journey to the Father* conference, I participated in all of the scheduled activities. I wrote field notes on a flip notepad describing the different themes of each event, the tone and performance of each session, my sense of the feelings of the participants, and my own emotional and analytical reflections. When I had free time, I strolled through the grounds, reflecting on my own preconceived notions, personal biases, and expectations. I did not seek to interview any of the young participants or adult organizers during the conference. My goal was to participate, to observe, and to build trust with the organizers and leaders so that I could interview the participants at a later date with written parental consent. Ultimately, being a participant observer allowed me a deeper insight into how *Journey to the Father* was organized and how it affected people. These experiences informed my interview questions, which make up a large part of the data for this research project.

Journey to the Father offered a different experience from what young people are used to at church, at home, and at school. The young interviewees highlighted challenges in understanding their own religious identities, as well as communicating their views to the people around them. The common theme was that religious identity is difficult for individuals to understand, and then to integrate into their private and public lives. And this is the reason why *Journey to the Father* existed: to transport young people into a social geography where being religious was normal and they would not be scorned or scrutinized. From the bursts of energy from the raucous band to the charismatic outpouring of Adoration, *Journey to the Father* provided a highly affective religious experience that could shift those who felt undecided in their religious identities towards being more "openly" Catholic.

2.3   Semi-Structured Interviews: Adult Organizers and Youth Participants

Over the span of two years, from 2012 to 2014, I conducted a total of 50 semi-structured, face-to-face interviews to ensure that the different types of participants involved in *Journey to the Father* had voices in my research. This enabled me to better analyze the different perspectives as well as the larger picture of *Journey to the Father*. These interviews were split between the adult organizers (over 18) and the young participants (ages 13 to 17).

I conducted 25 individual interviews with adult organizers. I interviewed the main organizers, most of whom had volunteered for the entire 15 years. I also interviewed conference keynote speakers and session leaders as well as the bishops of Alexandria/Cornwall and Gatineau. The second part of this first block of interviews was conducted with the Disciple leaders, aged between 18 and 25. Being close in age, the Disciples provided a mentorship role for the young participants throughout their *Journey to the Father* experience. Each of the adult organizers was asked to reflect on their role in organizing the conference, their views on religion in Canadian society, and their future goals for engaging youth through Catholic evangelization. Finally, I conducted 25 interviews with young participants from *Journey to the Father*. Because these interviewees were minors (below the age of 18), I received written, informed consent from each individual as well as from their parents or guardians.

Having had limited success with post-conference interview recruiting through techniques such as email and phone calls, I sought the help of youth group leaders who had participated in *Journey to the Father*. I was able to organize interview sessions with four different youth groups, each having between 4 and 8 young interviewees who had participated in *Journey to the Father* during the time of this research (2011–2013). Like the adult organizers, the young participants were asked to share their experiences of the conference, their outlook on religion in society, and their daily religious practices.

My overall experience of the face-to-face interviews was that the interviewees were generous, candid, thoughtful, and enthusiastic in speaking about their religious identities, their forms of religious engagement, and their socio-political views. These interviews were among the most rewarding aspects of this research. Following a semi-structured format with an interview guide, the questions were intended to explore and help understand Catholic identity through the experiences of *Journey to the Father*.

This qualitative research served to ground me and my research in the lives and experiences of my participants. From here, I was able to challenge my pre-conceived notions of conservative, Christian perspectives as well as inquire on the dynamics of socio-political engagement regarding identity formation. These attitudes emerge from my own childhood and the recent blooming political hegemony of evangelization in the US and in Canada. However, *Journey to the Father* as a research space offered me the opportunity to ask different questions about what it was like negotiating evangelical, Catholic values in a secular and pluralistic Canada. *Journey to the Father* was definitely something that I had never experienced before.

3   Key Concepts

3.1   *Major Themes from this Work: Lived Religion, Identity Formation, and Youth Perspectives*

Sourced in my research questions and my lived experience of Catholic identity formation, I sought broad theoretical and methodological approaches to help contextualize my research. *Journey to the Father* as a case study necessitates a theoretical framework that explicates the dynamics of the social formation of identity, the subjective experience of religion, and a methodological view of the agency of young people. I therefore settled on three key theoretical concepts that helped explain the dynamics of *Journey to the Father* as an alternative social geography for the inculcation and formation of Catholic identity in young people. These concepts are: 1) lived religion and the importance of religious action; 2) identity formation that engages notions of authenticity and recognition; and 3) youth perspectives, which reflects on a methodology of young people's agency that helps mitigate adult interference, misrepresentations, and distortions of young people's perspectives and experiences. Each discussion will be linked to the research on *Journey to the Father*.

3.1.1   Lived Religion: Experiential Meaning

Framed and popularized by Meredith McGuire and Robert Orsi, lived religion allows a place for the nuance of an individual's personal engagement with religion against deterministic perspectives of the impact of institutions on religious identity. *In Lived Religion: Faith and Practice in Everyday Life*, Meredith McGuire (2008) presents a compelling and critical look at the study of religion. Concerned with the dominance of institutional models of religion in the social sciences, she argues that the traditional conceptualization of religion based on confessional affiliation is a historical continuation of discourses of authority and power sourced in what she calls the "Long-Reformation," which involves a dichotomous valuing of religious belief over practice. She writes, "Definitional boundaries are the outcomes of *contested meanings*; that is, people have actively exerted their power to affect the outcome and to resist others' efforts to gain control" (2008, p. 22). McGuire argues that the exertion of power in defining social normativity, which is historically apparent in Christian Europe, is perpetuated in contemporary scholarly perspectives, assumptions, and analyses. Instead, McGuire draws attention to the ways in which individuals define religion, as opposed to focusing strictly on how it is defined by institutions.

In *Between Heaven and Earth* (2005), Robert Orsi complements McGuire's perspective by presenting a radically personal approach to the social scientific study of religion. Through sets of personal narratives, Orsi explores the intersections between social construction and subjective interpretation—between imposed and negotiated meaning—occurring within the lives and lived experiences of religious people. On a theoretical level, he advocates for the notion that lived experiences cannot be easily abstracted and compartmentalized into epistemologically normative categories. He attempts to admonish and destabilize the illusion of scholarly objectivity, and the imposition of the values of the researcher upon the subject, by advocating for an interpretive subjectivity that includes both the perspectives of researcher and research subject, in turn affecting the overall analysis.

Lived religion provides the space to hear untold narratives—experiences or feelings—of people negotiating the different facets of religion in their everyday lives. These stories came out through the interview questions revolving around my participants' experiences of religion in the parish, at home, at school, and at *Journey to the Father*. In my ethnographic work, I integrated the voices of both adult organizers and young participants in order to add context and colour to how they live their Catholic identity. With that said, their perspectives were not homogenous, but highly varied. Adults and young people were often critical of the state of Catholicism in and around their private and public lives, while speaking highly of the religious experiences of the *Journey to the Father* event. On the surface, you could easily construe these perspectives as an apologetic assertion of the value of evangelization in combatting a lethargic and hostile culture of secularism within Catholicism. However, the young participants provided particularly varied and nuanced experiences of this narrative of religious identity that helped mitigate assumptions.

Many youth participants spoke of the challenges of being *religious* at school or with friends. Upon returning from *Journey to the Father*, some found it difficult to talk about their experiences with friends. Erika, aged 16, took a defensive and assertive stance toward her participation in *Journey to the Father*: "I don't find it that big of a deal, like I don't get why people have to make fun of you for it. So even if everyone did I'd be like, 'Yah I go to church big deal, and then go to Jesus Camp in the summer, what's the big deal?!'" Many explained that the charisma and religious zeal they had felt at *Journey to the Father* quickly dissipated due to either being confronted and ridiculed for participating in a religious camp, or just forgetting about the details and feelings of the experience.

Counter to this feeling of marginalization for asserting a religious identity are the ambivalent experiences of *Journey to the Father*. When asked about the different events, Vanessa, aged 16, candidly stated, "Yah, not anything that was like [*makes the blotchy sound of "mind blown"*] or anything, but they were good." Mark, 14 years old, noted that he couldn't remember the content, but, "I don't know, I just like listening to people talk." And Erika, who above defended her experience of "Jesus Camp," spoke candidly of her mixed experience of *Adoration*: "It was pretty emotional and then everyone was like, 'Did you feel God's presence?' And I was like, 'Yah but didn't really have the Jesus moment.'" She was disappointed by her perceived failure to attain the common experience of those around her. But this did not dissuade Erika from seeking out her "Jesus moment" by continuing her annual participation in *Journey to the Father*, nor did it reduce its significant impact on her understanding of her religious identity.

The textured and emotional experiences of my participants, trying to live religion at school and musing on failed religious experience, are examples of their asserting or negotiating the role of religion in their sense of identity. Lived religion theory shifts our focus away from the imposition of dominant discourses towards the significance of individuals' lived experience in shaping their own social, political, and symbolic worlds. With respect to my work, this allows us to move beyond a deterministic view of the institution of the Catholic Church, and appreciate the varied perspectives and experiences of individuals who participated in *Journey to the Father*. Accompanying this approach, however, is the need for a more complex discussion on how identity is structured and informed.

3.1.2   Identity Formation: Authenticity and Recognition

The concept of identity has become increasingly relevant in the social scientific study of religion. Lived religion theory draws substance from the subjective experiences of my participants, which necessitates a deeper understanding of how the individual is engaged and impacted by multiple forces of meaning. Identity becomes the form for the substance of religious experience with which the individual can negotiate the different forces of social formation and power relations. Though there are multiple approaches in the study of identity, the concept of identity in this research focuses on social theories of *self* and *other* mainly through a discussion of authenticity and recognition, as well as by reviewing theories on the capacity for individual action through agency.

Charles Taylor (1989, 1991) has done much to establish the view that modern identity is formed and informed as a *dialogical* engagement between self and other, i.e., through an emphasis on social, cultural, and personal interchange between different people. Countering what he sees as the alienation of the self through the modern *subjective turn*, Taylor advocates the importance of common *horizons of significance* (i.e., universal, relational commonalities) as a means of establishing a society of reciprocal relations wherein people can live together responsibly. Taylor argues that in order for people to begin to relate to one another in a dialogical framework, they must first explore conceptions of self through *authenticity*, so as to nourish relations between self and other by being "understood" through *recognition*.

For Taylor, authenticity is a philosophical idea that denotes a "genuine" being within the modern identity complex—a personal drive towards greater or better forms of "true" selfhood. It revolves around the question: *how does an individual engage her/his "full potential"*? The dependent variable for Taylor is that modern individualism has a "dark side" in which the self becomes the moral centre around which the world is measured and understood. He argues that this social malaise undermines a more genuine sense of authenticity, a result of the move towards an ambivalent moral relativism, self-centeredness brought on by instrumental reason where our interactions are based on the logic of individual gain, and the devastating effects of technology and industry on social and environmental wellbeing. Taylor believes that there are "inescapable horizons" or universal truths that must be acknowledged in order to rectify these social malaises and re-establish a sense of authenticity within modern identity. The most important thing for Taylor is that the individual is uncompromisingly important in qualifying authenticity, but subjectivity is not hegemonic, for she/he is constantly shaped in connection with others.

In plural social and political settings, recognition becomes the foundation upon which identity is negotiated and built from the place of an authentic self in relation with others. Taylor, however, sees a misappropriation of recognition in modern, individualistic identity. As with his critique of authenticity, recognition under these terms is self-absorbed and narcissistic, always asking to be recognized for one's sovereign individuality. His understanding of common horizons of meaning does not mean erasing the other's distinctiveness, but rather allowing difference to define identity. It is about recognizing in the other *who they are, what they do, and what they need*. For Taylor, respect and recognition are fundamental elements in any deliberation process where recognition is not tied to relative individual capacities, but takes place in dialogical and reciprocal relations with diverse others. This reciprocal process of mutual recognition is teleological—that is, holding the promise of mutual benefit and betterment with every cycle of engagement between self and other, between authenticity and recognition. The key distinction in Taylor's reckoning, however, is that the constructive action of recognition always has the other in mind, rather than being driven by the inductive reasoning of a selfish individual. The ethos of authentic engagement then results in an identity based on recognition.

Taylor provides important elaborations on the theoretical framework of identity formation by seeing identity formation as largely relational, with a strong emphasis on dialogical engagement. His language of loss and recovery through authenticity, and of recognition in terms of both being recognized and recognizing others, has much to add to our understanding of how identity was understood and formed at *Journey to the Father*. We can see in this instance of identity formation an attempt to retrieve an authentic identity in evangelical Catholicism, and to gain recognition for one's socio-religious identity. This was a strong theme throughout the interviews with the adult organizers of *Journey to the Father* involving a sense of fear or trepidation regarding a "crisis of faith" at the heart of the contemporary Catholic Church, and in society at large. This fear is linked to a historical antagonism between religious institutions and secularism as a prevalent force shaping modern identity. This perspective justified *Journey to the Father* as a means of countering the prominence of secularization by reaching young Catholics with the messages and experiences of evangelization.

This was illustrated by André, one of the important leaders of *Journey to the Father*, who stated, "The Church has spent too much time being on the defense. [...] We should be proposing the faith on the offence. [...] [Young people] need to understand their missionary identity." For André, the search for identity outside of Catholic tradition had led to a sense of loss, which affirmed the need for recovery through the authenticity of Catholic identity through an evangelical lens. He reflected the feeling of alienation that many adult organizers expressed throughout these interviews—that the draw of secular society and how it is made manifest in the Church could no longer stand. André's idea of missionary identity seeks to assert evangelization as a way to normalize and define religious identity within the Catholic worldview. André's missionary identity focuses on the *self*, establishing an "authentic" Catholicism in order to go out into the world and proselytize to the *other* (i.e., other non-evangelized Catholics). And this vision was echoed among the adult organizers and some of the young participants.

Though the perspective of the organizers of *Journey to the Father* matches the underlying message of Taylor's identity formation, there remains a nuance to his overall structure regarding the tacit formation of the *self* through experience. This is a valuable elucidation regarding theories of social formation and power that hinge upon the individual. Taylor's view that identity is dialogical allows for the interplay between authenticity and recognition to be a matter of the *self* relating to the *other*, with the *other* informing the *self* within a *common horizon* (i.e., areas of common values and perspectives). More importantly, Taylor's view assures that the individual is not alienated from her/his social relations. The challenge of authenticity is to negotiate a pluralism of values and perspectives in a deliberate *reciprocal* process. However, the view of what constitutes authentic Catholic identity is somewhat different among adults and young people—i.e., different in tone more than content. Where the adult organizers of *Journey to the Father* stated that an engaged, evangelical Catholicism—related to the benefits of a personal relationship with Jesus Christ—is the best option for happiness in an alienated secular world, the young participants agreed but conveyed a more nuanced engagement with the world outside the directed structure of evangelical identity. This is a case of adults and young people agreeing on the terms of evangelization, but having different perspectives on its execution.

What emerged from my research was that young people were largely keen on the adult discourse of proselytization, but at the same time, had little to no problem negotiating the ambiguities of modern life. Though the young participants had many different thoughts and experiences regarding their negotiation of a "missionary identity," gender serves as an effective optic for understanding socio-political worldview, underscoring their tacit acceptance of ambiguity in their everyday lives as they negotiated the conservative values of the NE against the different values of normative society. In this research, one of my key questions was "what does it mean to be a Catholic woman or a Catholic man?" My male participants spoke mostly on the temptations of secular society regarding unfettered materialism, pre-marital sex, and the sexual objectification of women. They pointed to a personal experience with Jesus as the mitigating factor in their daily struggles.

My female participants also spoke of challenges regarding the idealized representations of women's bodies in popular culture and how this negatively impacts body image, as well as issues around premarital sex and the values regarding chastity. But they also went a step further. Many raised the idea that women should not be defined by their relationships with men—instead, women should realize their capabilities on their own. Lisa, aged 15, with a curious attitude and a sharp wit, said, "I think a lot of people don't see themselves, they're just so desperate for boyfriends and need someone [...] I think I'm totally fine on my own. I'm going to be totally honest [...] in the future I do want someone. I think God really made me feel that I don't need someone right now, but it's his plan that someday it will happen." This statement raised a sense of female empowerment—that Lisa, with the help of Jesus, did not need to be defined by men in order to exercise her individual agency and make choices.

In line with this idea of agency (which is further discussed in the next section), when asked about the challenges Catholic women face, Carry, who at 18 reflected much on the next stage of her life, said, "Well there's the obvious gender discrimination, we can't become priests, we can be nuns. It's the same but it's different. I don't know, I think in today's society we're getting more equality, and everyone is meeting the same challenges keeping the faith to begin with." Carry's concern was not with changing the structure of the Church but with the challenges of keeping faith, which she saw as relevant to Catholic men and women equally. Carry was able to challenge the inherent gender inequalities in the Catholic Church without detracting from her Catholic identity.

Throughout this discussion, it is surprising to hear these Catholic evangelical perspectives on gender equality that are moderately progressive/liberal. The subtext to this notion of equality is that, though there are gendered differences, there is no *moral* difference between Catholic women and men. But the perspective is nevertheless evangelical in that Catholic men and Catholic women have the capacity to overcome gender disparities by putting God at the center of their lives. Estelle, aged 17, put it this way: "It's not really about equality between man and female, but just females respecting themselves." Again, this was an important piece of the puzzle of Catholic evangelical agency in that faith affords young people a certain capacity or power to attain freedom from the conventions of secular society and reflect on their own identities.

3.1.3   Youth Perspectives: Reflecting on a Methodological Approach to the Agency of Young People

Youth have become an important subject in the multidisciplinary study of religion around the world, with a proliferation of theories and methods for researching young people's engagement with religion in terms of belief, practice, and experience in the formation and maintenance of their identities. Some of the more germane literature covers a general approach on how best to think about youth and how to engage youth in the context of studying religion (cf. Collins-Mayo and Dandelion 2010; Giordan 2010; Madge et al. 2014). The theoretical discussions of this research necessitate an understanding of how young people are studied and their relative agency with regard to identity formation.

Agency, as mentioned above, speaks directly to the underlying elements of autonomy and freedom that allow an individual to act within systems of social formation, power, and identity. The traditional conception of agency relates to the individual's capacity to act in the way that she or he chooses. There are, however, significant critiques of the idealization of freedom and choice that underscore agency. Saba Mahmood, for example, critiques the Western ideal of autonomy attached to agency, describing it as an "imaginary freedom" based on the view that "an individual is considered free on the condition that she act autonomously: that her actions be the result of her own choice and free will, rather than of custom, tradition, transcendent will, or social coercion" (2005, p. 148). This perspective serves to question the very idea that people have the agency to make independent choices. Agency therefore is tempered by different realities of coercion. Though sometimes coercive forces can be restrictive or hegemonic, Mahmood assuages this interpretation by asserting the importance of different relations for the individual, stating that the terms of engagement for agency must remain sensitive to multiple layers of subjectivity and reciprocal relationships, as individuals reflect on *who they are* in relation to others.

Peter Hemming and Nicola Madge (2012) delineate a clear methodological approach stressing that research in the area of youth, religion, and identity should focus on the agency of young people. They make four interrelated points. The first is that religious identity is complex, and one must remain sensitive to *what people are* as well as *what they are not*. Secondly, they define religious identity by four elements, "(1) affiliation and belonging; (2) behaviours and practices; (3) beliefs and values; and (4) religious and spiritual experiences" (2012, pp. 39–40). Thirdly, they assert that agency is exercised among young people, to the possible contradiction of adult misperceptions and/or misconceptions, and that youth may develop religious identities that challenge "dominant representations and discourses" (2012, p. 45). And finally, they examine the methodological implications of research on youth, religion, and identity, which include the notion that social spaces are complex, fluid, and in flux, which necessitates using mixed-methods in order to generate comprehensive research.

Peter Beyer and Rubina Ramji in *Growing Up Canadian: Muslims, Hindus, Buddhists* (2013) provide an example of the study of young people and religion within a Canadian context that relates directly to this discussion operationalizing this methodology of young people's agency. Beyer and Ramji provide a qualitative and quantitative analysis of the religious identity of 1.5 and 2nd generation Canadian youth between the ages of 21 and 22 of Muslim, Hindu, and Buddhist backgrounds. In summary, their findings are that young people have a belief in gender equality, but even more in *complementarity* (i.e., the genders are equal but different), accept multiculturalism and celebrate religious diversity, have no favourable view of religious politicization, and that their religious identities are based on socialization but are also tempered by individual engagement. This suggests that identity is in flux, presenting an image of minority young people engaging with dominant sociopolitical values in a Western context. Beyer and Ramji write,

> There was a consistent expectation that beliefs and practices had to make sense, to fit into a larger context of meaning, to have a reason other than that this was simply the way things were done. At the same time, it was up to the individual to discover this meaning from whatever sources each found authoritative or trustworthy, whether that be family, religious leaders, books, friends, the Internet, school, or other media. (2013, p. 11).

The authors speak of a level of cultural and social negotiation on the part of young 1.5 or 2nd generation immigrant youth in the process of forming identity, pointing to an underlying premise of agency. This supports the view that young people are always negotiating religious tradition and socialization as active agents and not as passive recipients of inherited tradition.

In summary, Beyer and Ramji provide us with a substantive insight into the theoretical models of Hemming and Madge by focusing on youth agency in the negotiation of different, and often competing, discourses of religious identity formation. However, Kylie Valentine warns, "A critical account of agency requires that the concept do more work than establishing that children are capable of willed action and are competent in specific situations" (2011, p. 356). With regards to my research, it is imperative for research on Catholic evangelization and *Journey to the Father* to emphasize how young people actively engage the different elements of identity formation, and not to relegate their agency to the purview of adult organizers.

The adult organizers of *Journey to the Father* believed that young people need to make a choice in order to fully embrace a conversion to the Catholic evangelical worldview away from the dominance of secular values in Canadian society. There was a conviction that young people cannot be coerced into doing things they do not want to do. *Journey to the Father* offered youth the opportunity to experience charismatic forms of religiosity bracketed by ecclesiastical support and religious/moral teaching, which would ultimately serve to shape Catholic identity. The adult organizers believed that, if treated with care and respect, young people can absorb and expound these values and experiences to the point of paradigmatic religious conversion; i.e., from *living with* Catholicism to *living their* Catholicism. To be clear, though the adult organizers spoke of the choices that young people were free to make, their rhetoric was morally unilateral. The implication was that to choose not to embrace an authentic Catholic identity would leave one spiraling deeper into the confines of the secular world. Though this was understood by the young participants, what became apparent was that young people were exercising the choices presented by the adult organizers, but maybe not in the same direction or aspirations of the organizers.

The young people of *Journey to the Father* expressed a religiosity that combines a lived and engaged commitment to Catholicism, but with less of the urgent tone projected by the adult organizers. This is not to say that the young participants were not engaging in or are disinterested in the Catholic evangelical project of identity formation. The reality is that the young participants at *Journey to the Father* were synthesizing religious experiences and secular values in their everyday lives. Case in point would be Jimmy, aged 17, who reflected with me on the idea that there may not be a God. He talked of how "everyone seems to prefer the idea that there is none, no God, no nothing. Um, yeah. So occasionally, I'll get the feeling that maybe we're wrong. Just occasionally. I don't like that feeling. [...] But then, immediately after, I'll snap myself out of it. Like, 'why are you even thinking this?'" In this piece of introspection, Jimmy reflected on the importance of doubt and how it reflects a social reality that does not entirely fit with his own values and view of the world. Ultimately, Jimmy had no regrets, and the choice he had made and continues to make in developing his own religious identity had led him down what he felt was the right path. But, importantly, that did not stop him from musing on the impact conventional social mores had on his life, and his view of doubt as a factor that seeks to undermine his faith.

Like the participants in Beyer and Ramji's study, the youth of *Journey to the Father* reflect an implicit acceptance of socio-political diversity and moral pluralism while attending to their religious identities. The reality is that the message of secular, liberal tolerance is married to a rather conservative socio-religious identity formation. In the case of this research, it was clear how liberal values were being deployed in order to furnish the conservative moral and social purview of the NE, especially regarding evangelical proselytization. At *Journey to the Father* and throughout the interviews, the common theme was that *evangelization is not something you talk about, it is something you do*. In other words, to evangelize others in the Catholic context is a somewhat indirect action—*to lead by example*, and not through direct proselytization. But, what is important to note in the analysis is that people do things differently. Within this same evangelical paradigm, the young participants' thoughts and actions point to an experiential and relational agency that is indeed a matter of *journeying* towards an evangelical Catholic identity within a diverse Canadian society.

4 Current Challenges and Future Opportunities

4.1 The Challenges of Studying Young Evangelicals Effectively

In the study of identity formation among evangelical Catholic youth, the greatest challenges are simply a matter of gaining access and insightfully representing their agency. It is a matter of respecting young people and their diverse perspectives. As academics, we tend towards understanding conservative socio-religious movements as being recalcitrant and endemically oppositional. This perspective is not surprising given the link between political conservatism and religion among the Christian Right in the US and Canada. In this context, there is a sense of a desperate need to assert one's socio-political values no matter the cost. This urgency can still be seen through the work of the adult organizers at *Journey to the Father*.

Echoing Taylor's notions of authenticity as a response to the social malaise of loss in the modern world, and recognition as facilitating dialogue with others, the adult organizers of *Journey to the Father* built an identity framework that effectively promoted evangelical Catholicism to young Canadians. The contours of this evangelical Catholic identity structure are: (1) a person endowed with the recovery of an *authentic self* through a personal relationship with Jesus Christ (2) can enter into a mutually beneficial *process of recognition* with others (non-evangelicals) due to the defining quality of a Catholic evangelical collective identity and (3) brought on by the *marginalization of religious identity* by secularist forces, even from within the Catholic Church. Ventures like *Journey to the Father* help assert the right of Catholic youth to be recognized for their "outed" (i.e. *openly evangelical in a secular world*) religious identities, which necessitates a political language and minority identification. As mentioned above, the message that is therefore justified and becomes increasingly clear is that *it is okay to be Catholic—it is okay to be different*. Ultimately, this further justifies the implicit rapprochement rather than the separation of evangelical Catholic discourse present at *Journey to the Father* from the socio-political purview of the diversity framework that characterizes normative Canadian society.

To elaborate what was mentioned in the previous section, it is clear that the young people who participated in *Journey to the Father* encountered a complex and enticing discursive structure deployed by the adult organizers that represented the socio-political elements of the norm and the margins in a campaign to instigate an evangelical Catholic identity. With regard to the regime of secularism, the Catholics of this study were offered an applicable framework in which to engage in a politics of recognition relevant to the Canadian socio-political context. The adherence to the political liberal values of freedom, agency, and choice intertwine with the institutional conservatism of the Catholic Church as a moral authority against the moral antagonisms of conventional, secular society. Though there were participants who critiqued the Catholic evangelization movement for its overemphasis on individualism over the corporate moral structure of the Catholic Church, the majority of young participants spoke of their experiences in terms of living without much cognitive dissonance regarding their evangelical identities. As will be discussed below, delineating this approach to identity as embedded in normative socio-political structures helps explain much of the "moderate tone" of the young participants at *Journey to the Father*.

In this research, I have come to the realization that young people were exercising the choice that the adult organizers had promoted throughout *Journey to the Father*. That is, an evangelical, charismatic engagement of Catholic religious tradition and institution through a personal relationship with Christ. The young people in this study engaged in this Catholic evangelical praxis, but not to the exclusion of secular values and worldview. They expressed a religiosity that involves a lived and engaged commitment to Catholicism without reifying the urgent tone projected by the adult organizers. The reality is that the young participants were synthesizing secular values in their regular lives, reflecting an implicit acceptance of socio-political diversity, while remaining dedicated to a conservative, charismatic Catholic religious praxis. It is unclear if this acceptance of pluralism contradicted the expectation and purview of the adult organizers. But, overall, these young evangelical Catholics have a strong case for asserting their religious identities that speaks of being unique (i.e., the power of being different), but without any debilitating or dissonant social marginalization (i.e., the grace of being normal).

When I entered into this research, I did not anticipate the complex ways in which the young participants of *Journey to the Father* would exercise agency or the manner in which they would navigate the complexities of modern life and construct their religious identities alongside commitments to values that might be construed as belonging to liberal secularism. I was expecting an expression of politically conservative, hard-line proselytization of evangelical Christian social and political identity. In other words, I was expecting a polemical *culture war* between the political and moral values of conventional society and those of the evangelical Catholics. The case study of *Journey to the Father* has helped unpack the situation, offering insight into the proximity and interaction between what are commonly defined as liberal and conservative value systems through which young people engage as social agents, determining and shaping their own religious identities.

4.2   Ethno-Nationalism and Catholic Identity: New Avenues of Research

This research on *Journey to the Father* bore fruit in terms of shifting preconceived notions on religious conservatism in evangelical culture as well as effectively recognizing the social agency of young people as they negotiate their different relations in forming their socio-political and religious identity. There is room, however, for additional research on Catholic youth and the ways in which they form their identities in a diverse society. Questions related to ethnic and cultural identification to Catholicism have not been examined: *how does ethnic Catholic identity negotiate socio-political liberalism, moral pluralism, and Catholic evangelization culture?* This question seeks a deeper reflection on the impact of ethno-cultural religious identity engaging liberal secularism and the NE. It also speaks to the importance of studying social and political contexts that negotiate secular liberalism within a homogenous Catholic national identity. Ethnic identity and religious identification would be areas of further research for understanding the negotiations of socio-political identity among Catholics in Canada today.

The management of religious diversity has become a major concern in liberal democracies around the globe due to intensifying pluralism. An example of this in Canada is evidenced in the recent debates about reasonable accommodation in Quebec. What is key to this example is the underlying importance of Catholicism to Quebecois (French-Canadian) identity as part of a historical national identity reflecting the dominance of the Catholic Church and a subsequent secularization (Baril and Lamonde 2013; Stevenson 2006). Underlying these issues of "accommodation" is the separation of Church and State (or *laïcité* in France and Quebec), which relegates religion to the private sphere for the sake of political neutrality in the public sphere (Arneson 2014; Beaman 2014; Westmoreland 2011). This vision of political neutrality is based on core liberal values of tolerance and equality, and has given rise to secularization as its main operational factor. In Quebec, *interculturalism* is the ethno-cultural, nationalist ethos that puts into practice a secular worldview in the management of religious and ethno-cultural diversity while still asserting the importance of religious heritage in safeguarding the host society's communal values (Bouchard 2012; Cantle 2012). Against this backdrop of secular values and religious heritage, religion remains relevant in the recognition of identity in the public sphere.

As we have discussed at the outset of this chapter, evangelical Christianity has become a strong political force throughout the world, and is primarily invested in gaining recognition for their religious identities in the public sphere. Though evangelicalism has historically been the domain of Protestant Christianity, the NE has done much to shape the form and substance of the Catholic Church today. Catholic proselytization organizations like CCO and NET Ministries have grown out of the NE mandate to generate an evangelical impetus through charismatic and personal religiosity with its members. NET Ministries in fact is attempting inroads into Quebec (NET Ministries of Canada 2016). Quebec presents an enticing proselytization opportunity for groups like NET for the rather homogenous population that still asserts a Catholic identity (Government of Canada 2005). However, it is unclear what effect secularism has on the process of evangelizing nominal or *cultural Catholics*, especially in formally secular societies like Quebec. This leaves unanswered the question: *how is Catholicism influencing Quebecois identity on the ground?* Though there is little academic research on the NE and cultural Catholics (Martel-Reny 2008; Inglis 2014; Lefebvre 2011; Seljak 1997; Stevenson 2006), their encounters represent negotiations between liberal/secular and religious values in the struggle to gain precedence in shaping public and national identity.

A research program based on the above theoretical discussion on lived religion, identity formation, and the agency of young people would be applicable to the question: how do Quebecois youth actually interpret Catholicism within secular worldviews in the construction of ethno-cultural identity? This research could focus on the tensions between liberal/secular values and evangelical Catholic values and revolve around three components: (1) an analysis of the impact of secularism and Catholicism in defining national identity in Quebec; (2) a focus on the encounter between evangelical Catholics and cultural Catholics, and how they define national identity between religious and secular ideals; and (3) an empirical focus on young people negotiating these different power relations. This research would fill the gaps of knowledge regarding how Catholicism operates within formally secular societies in generating ethno-national identity.

5   Questions for Critical Thought

Questions for critical thought are drawn from each section of this chapter.

1. **The New Evangelization in the Canadian context:** When you think about the term "evangelization" what is the first thing that comes to mind? Televangelists? The evangelical Protestant church in your neighbourhood? Maybe you know someone who is evangelical. Does an evangelical Catholic identity seem familiar or foreign to you?
2. **Methodological reflections (case studies; youth agency; participant observation and interviews):** If you were to do research on young people and religion, what would be the best way to capture their thoughts and feelings? Would it be through interviews? Would it be best to visit spaces imagined and understood as religious? Or is it best to think of different creative or arts-based ways of finding answers?
3. **Subjectivity and self-reflexivity (challenging empirical objectivity):** What do you consider as religion or religious? Does religion look like a person sitting in a church or crouched over in prayerful supplication? Do you have a set definition? Can you think of alternative definitions?
4. **Youth:** Why do you think it is difficult to understand young people's perspectives in social science research? Do you think adults have the capacity to understand young people's thoughts and feelings on the topic of religion? Why is it important to make those connections and understand young people's perspectives?
5. **Socio-political impact of religion:** Have you ever heard someone say, *never talk of religion or politics at the dinner table.* Why is that? Why are the topics taboo? Should we focus on politics when we talk about religion or should things remain separate?

6 Online Teaching and Learning Resources

The following websites provide a sample of materials regarding the study of religion and youth germane to the discussion of this chapter:

1. *National Study of Youth and Religion*, Christian Smith and Lisa Pearce: http://youthandreligion.nd.edu/

This website brings together a massive research output in qualitative and quantitative research on the religious lives of different Christian young people in the United States.

2. *Religion, Gender and Sexuality Among Youth in Canada (RGSY)*, Pamela Dicky Young and Heather Shipley: http://www.queensu.ca/religion/faculty-and-research/faculty-research/pamela-dickey-young-rgsy

This website outlines the research on young adults in Canada ages 18–25 on questions of religiosity and gender and sexuality. Using an extensive survey methodology, the RGSY looks to underscore how young people in Canada form and manage their sexual and gendered identities.

3. *The Project Teen Canada Youth Surveys,* Reginald W. Bibby: http://www.reginaldbibby.com/projectcanadaprogram.html

Reginald Bibby has been collecting data on the topic of religion and youth since 1984. This has produced a rare longitudinal data-set on how young people in Canada negotiate their religious identities. This website offers a good platform to delve into the material representing relevant research outcomes.

4. *National Evangelization Team (NET Canada)*: https://www.netcanada.ca/en/ | *Catholic Christian Outreach (CCO)*: https://cco.ca/

NET Ministries and CCO are Catholic evangelization programmes that seek to engage youth in Canada with the message of the Catholic New Evangelization regarding a personal and charismatic religiosity as well as a moral orientation to the Roman Catholic Church. NET Ministries has proselytization programmes in the US, the UK, and Australia where young people evangelize to young people through retreats, music, drama, and religious practice. CCO is a Canadian student organization present in 14 universities across Canada. The main goal of both organizations is to evangelize young Catholics and non-Catholics through peer witnessing and emulation (i.e., leading by example).

7   References for Further Reading

This section below provides some basic literature reflective of the major themes covered in this chapter.

1. Catholic Identity and Evangelization:

Grogan, P., & Kirsteen, K. (Eds.). (2015). *The new evangelization: Faith, people, context and practice*. London/New York: Bloomsbury Publishing.
Grogan and Kirsteen (2015) discuss the theological and historical development of the New Evangelization. They provide a Catholic institutional perspective key to understanding the tone and values of this contemporary Catholic proselytizing movement.

2. Identity Formation:

Parekh, B. (2008). *A new politics of identity: Political principles for an interdependent world*. Basingstoke/New York: Palgrave Macmillan.
Post-colonial political theorist Bhikhu Parekh (2008) elaborates a theoretical model of identity formation that is both approachable and useful. Providing key terms and concepts of identity, this reading outlines an effective structure that helps explain the dynamics of modern identity.

3. Lived Religion:

Ammerman, N. T. (2007). *Everyday religion: Observing modern religious lives*. Oxford/New York: Oxford University Press.
Lived religion is a dynamic and engaging theory in Religious Studies. Ammerman's edited volume effectively showcases lived religion's theoretical and methodological reflections on the definitions of religion, the fluidity of *place* with regards to religious actions, and the production of religious meaning and meaningful religious action.

4. Youth and Religion:

Collins-Mayo, S., & Dandelion, P. (Eds.). (2010). *Religion and youth*. Farnham/Burlington: Ashgate Publishing.
There is varied literature on the topic of youth and religion underscoring the importance of focusing on youth in the study of religion. Collins-Mayo and Dandelion have produced a relevant resource for anyone considering studying the religious lives and experiences of young people.

8   Researcher Background and Connection to the Topic

Dr. Paul Gareau is Métis and French-Canadian from the village of Bellevue near Batoche, Saskatchewan. He is Assistant Professor in the Faculty of Native Studies and Research Fellow for the Rupertsland Centre for Métis Research at the University of Alberta. His research is grounded in critical theory and methodology relating to the social and cultural impacts of religion on identity formation. This chapter reflects the idea that the actions and worldview of people are equally important to those disseminated or deployed by dominant institutions (i.e. the Church, government, civil society, race-based identity structures, etc.). His academic publications and community research projects explore the influence of Catholicism on early and late modern identity, the legacy of colonial discourses on Indigenous and ethno-cultural minorities, and the experiences of rural spaces. Critically reflecting on the dynamics of power informing religious identity has allowed Gareau to delve deeper into his personal Métis identity by looking for the untold stories of Métis experiences of religion. This exploration reflects a next phase in his program of research, looking into the relationship between the civilizational project of Catholic institutional structures and the resistance of Métis kinship/religious practices and worldview. Overall, his research focuses on the Métis, Indigenous religiosity, youth, gender, *la francophonie*, and rural Canada.

References

Akhtar, S. (2011). Liberal recognition for identity? Only for particularized ones. *Politics, Philosophy & Economics, 10*(1), 66–87.

Ammerman, N. T. (2007). *Everyday religion observing modern religious lives*. Oxford/New York: Oxford University Press.

Arneson, R. J. (2014). Neutrality and political liberalism. In R. Merrill & D. Weinstock (Eds.), *Political neutrality* (pp. 25–43). Basingstoke/New York: Palgrave Macmillan.

Baril, D., & Lamonde, Y. (Eds.). (2013). *Pour une reconnaissance de la laïcité au Québec: Enjeux philosophiques, politiques et juridiques*. Québec: Presses de l'Université Laval.

Beaman, L. G. (2003). The myth of pluralism, diversity, and vigor: The constitutional privilege of Protestantism in the United States and Canada. *Journal for the Scientific Study of Religion, 42*(3), 311–325. https://doi.org/10.1111/1468-5906.00183.

Beaman, L. G. (2014). Between the public and the private: Governing religious expression. In S. Lefebvre & L. G. Beaman (Eds.), *Religion in the public sphere: Canadian case studies* (pp. 44–65). Toronto: University of Toronto Press.

Beyer, P., & Ramji, R. (Eds.). (2013). *Growing up Canadian: Muslims, Hindus, Buddhists*. Montreal: McGill-Queen's University Press.

Bokenkotter, T. S. (2004). *A concise history of the Catholic Church*. New York/Toronto: Doubleday.

Bouchard, G. (2012). *L'interculturalisme: Un point de vue québécois*. Montréal: Boréal.

Cantle, T. (2012). *Interculturalism: The new era of cohesion and diversity*. Basingstoke/New York: Palgrave Macmillan.

Catholic Christian Outreach. (2013). *CCO*. http://cco.ca/. Accessed 13 Sept 2016.

Clarke, B. P., & Macdonald, S. (2017). *Leaving Christianity: Changing allegiances in Canada since 1945*. Montreal: McGill-Queen's Press.

Collins-Mayo, S., & Dandelion, P. (Eds.). (2010). *Religion and youth*. Burlington/Farnham: Ashgate Publishing.

Dulles, A. R. (2008). Current theological obstacles to evangelization. In S. C. Boguslawski & R. Martin (Eds.), *The new evangelization: Overcoming the obstacles* (pp. 13–25). New York: Paulist Press.

Dulles, A. R. (2009). *Evangelization for the third millennium*. New York: Paulist Press.

Faggioli, M. (2012). *Vatican II: The battle for meaning*. New York: Paulist Press.

Fay, T. J. (2002). *History of Canadian Catholics: Gallicanism, Romanism, and Canadianism*. Montreal: McGill-Queen's University Press.

Giordan, G. (Ed.). (2010). *Youth and religion*. Leiden: Brill.

Government of Canada. (2001). *Religions in Canada*. http://www12.statcan.gc.ca/english/census01/Products/Analytic/companion/rel/qc.cfm. Accessed 4 Apr 2017.

Government of Canada, S. C. (2005, January 25). *Population by religion, by province and territory (2001 Census)*. http://www.statcan.gc.ca/tables-tableaux/sum-som/l01/cst01/demo30a-eng.htm. Accessed 11 Sept 2015.

Government of Canada, S. C. (2014, September 26). *Population by year, by province and territory*. http://www.statcan.gc.ca/tables-tableaux/sum-som/l01/cst01/demo02a-eng.htm. Accessed 12 Sept 2015.

Gregg, S. (2013). *Tea Party Catholic: The Catholic case for limited government, a free economy, and human flourishing*. New York: The Crossroad Publishing Company.

Grogan, P., & Kirsteen, K. (Eds.). (2015). *The new evangelization: Faith, people, context and practice*. London/New York: Bloomsbury Publishing.

Hemming, P., & Madge, N. (2012). Researching children, youth and religion: Identity, complexity and agency. *Childhood, 19*(1), 38–51.

Hitchcock, J. (2012). *History of the Catholic Church: From the apostolic age to the third millennium*. San Francisco: Ignatius Press.

Inglis, T. (2014). *Meanings of life in contemporary Ireland webs of significance*. Basingstoke/New York: Palgrave Macmillan.

Kelly, P. (2005). *Liberalism*. Cambridge/Malden: Polity Press.

Kyle, R. G. (2009). *Evangelicalism: An Americanized Christianity*. New Brunswick: Transaction Publishers.

Lefebvre, S. (2011). Disestablishment of the church and voluntary culture: The case of francophone Roman Catholics in Canada. *Quebec Studies, 52*, 33.

Madge, N., Hemming, P., & Stenson, K. (2014). *Youth on religion: The development, negotiation and impact of faith and non-faith identity*. New York: Routledge.

Mahmood, S. (2005). *Politics of piety: The Islamic revival and the feminist subject*. Princeton: Princeton University Press.

McGuire, M. B. (2008). *Lived religion: Faith and practice in everyday life*. New York: Oxford University Press.

Martel-Reny, M. P. (2008). Religion et spiritualité chez les adolescents québécois: Et eux, qu'en pensent-ils?' In F. Gauthier, J-P. Perreault, & L. Voyé (Eds), *Jeunes et Religion au Québec* (61–71). Québec: Presses de l'Université Laval.

NET Ministries of Canada. (2016). http://www.netcanada.ca/en/. Accessed 13 Sept 2016.

Noll, M. A. (2010). *The rise of evangelicalism: The age of Edwards, Whitefield and the Wesleys*. Downers Grove: InterVarsity Press.

Norman, A. (2011). World youth day: The creation of a modern pilgrimage event for evangelical intent. *Journal of Contemporary Religion, 26*(3), 371–385.

Orsi, R. A. (2005). *Between heaven and earth: The religious worlds people make and the scholars who study them*. Princeton: Princeton University Press.

Parekh, B. (2008). *A new politics of identity: Political principles for an interdependent world*. Basingstoke/New York: Palgrave Macmillan.

Paul VI. (1975, December 8). *Evangelii nuntiandi* [Apostolic exhortation to the episcopate, to the clergy and to all the faithful of the entire world]. http://w2.vatican.va/content/paul-vi/en/

apost_exhortations/documents/hf_p-vi_exh_19751208_evangelii-nuntiandi.html. Accessed 2 Feb 2015.

Portmann, J. (2010). *Catholic culture in the USA: In and out of church*. London/New York: Continuum International Publishing.

Second Vatican Council. (1964, November 21). *Lumen gentium* [Dogmatic constitution on the Church]. http://www.vatican.va/archive/hist_councils/ii_vatican_council/documents/vat-ii_const_19641121_lumen-gentium_en.html. Accessed 14 Nov 2014.

Seljak, D. (1997). Catholicism without the Church: Despite low church attendance, Catholicism is still at the heart of Quebec's civil society. *Compass: A Jesuit Journal, 14*(6), 6–8.

Smith, C. (2014a). *Young Catholic America: Emerging adults in, out of, and gone from the church*. Oxford/New York: Oxford University Press.

Smith, C. (2014b). *American Evangelicalism: Embattled and thriving*. Chicago: University of Chicago Press.

Steubenville Conferences—Atlantic (Canada). (n.d.) *Steubenville conferences*. https://steubenvilleconferences.com/youth/atc/. Accessed 23 Jan 2018.

Steubenville Conferences—Toronto (Canada). (n.d.). *Steubenville conferences*. https://steubenvilleconferences.com/youth/tor/. Accessed 23 Jan 2018.

Stevenson, G. (2006). *Parallel paths the development of nationalism in Ireland and Quebec*. Montreal: McGill-Queen's University Press.

Sutton, M. A. (2014). *American Apocalypse: A history of modern evangelicalism*. Cambridge, MA: Harvard University Press.

Synod of Catholic Bishops. (2012a). *The new evangelization for the transmission of the Christian Faith - Instrumentum laboris*. http://www.vatican.va/roman_curia/synod/documents/rc_synod_doc_20120619_instrumentum-xiii_en.html. Accessed 3 Ap 2016.

Synod of Catholic Bishops. (2012b). *Instrumentum laboris* [The New Evangelization for the transmission of the Christian Faith]. http://www.vatican.va/roman_curia/synod/documents/rc_synod_doc_20120619_instrumentum-xiii_en.html. Accessed 17 Apr 2016.

Taylor, C. (1989). *Sources of the self: The making of the modern identity*. Cambridge, MA/London: Harvard University Press.

Taylor, C. (1991). *The ethics of authenticity*. Cambridge/London: Harvard University Press.

Valentine, K. (2011). Accounting for agency. *Children & Society, 25*(5), 347–358. https://doi.org/10.1111/j.1099-0860.2009.00279.x.

Westmoreland, R. (2011). Realizing 'Political' neutrality. *Law and Philosophy, 30*(5), 541–573. https://doi.org/10.1007/s10982-011-9102-5.

Wilde, M. J. (2007). *Vatican II: A sociological analysis of religious change*. Princeton: Princeton University Press.

Winter, E. (2011). *Us, them and others pluralism and national identities in diverse societies*. Toronto: University of Toronto Press.

Reasonable Accommodation

Amélie Barras

Abstract This chapter starts by discussing the legal concept of reasonable accommodation, focusing on how it has been used in religious freedom decisions at the Supreme Court of Canada (SCC). It then moves to describing how the concept has, over the past decade, broken away from law and entered public discourse. This shift is illustrated by briefly discussing how the Bouchard-Taylor Commission (2008) in the province of Quebec has referred to and used the notion of reasonable accommodation in its proceedings. In so doing, the chapter highlights some of the power-dynamics lodged within that notion and the conundrums they present for thinking about the complexity of religious lives in contemporary Canada. In the last section, the chapter explores potential alternative frameworks to reasonable accommodation better equipped to capture the richness and intricacies of everyday lived religion.

Keywords Reasonable accommodation · Sincerity of belief · Religious minorities · Bouchard-Taylor Commission · Navigation · Negotiation · Supreme Court of Canada · Lived religion

1 General Introduction

When and why is the concept of Reasonable Accommodation (RA) used in Canadian law? How is it related to religious freedom? Does its legal understanding differ from the ways it is being used in public discourse? What are the power asymmetries lodged within that framework? These are a few important questions this chapter tackles. This chapter starts by discussing key concepts related to RA through the study of two well-known religious freedom cases at the Supreme Court of Canada. Second, it explores how the concept of RA has made its way in the past decade from law to public discourse, and surveys some of the conundrums of this new usage. This chapter refers to the Quebec Bouchard-Taylor commission (2008) to illustrate

A. Barras (✉)
Department of Social Science, York University, Toronto, ON, Canada
e-mail: abarras@yorku.ca

© Springer International Publishing AG, part of Springer Nature 2018
C. Holtmann (ed.), *Exploring Religion and Diversity in Canada*,
https://doi.org/10.1007/978-3-319-78232-4_9

these conundrums, including the power asymmetries lodge within the framework of RA. Finally, this piece draws on recent qualitative research with self-identified Muslims in Canada to suggest possible alternative frameworks to RA that may be better equipped to capture the complexity of religious lives in Canada.

2 Reasonable Accommodations: Real Life Stories

2.1 Ontario Human Rights Commission and Teresa O'Malley vs Simpson Sears [1985] 2 S.C.R. 536

In 1971 Ms. O'Malley starts working for Simpson Sears in Quebec as a salesperson. She continues to work for the same company when she moves in 1975 to Kingston, Ontario. At the time she is hired, O'Malley is informed that all full-time employees are required to work on a rotating basis on Friday evenings, and two Saturdays out of three every month, as these are the busiest times for the store. O'Malley works this schedule until 1978, when she converts to the Seventh-Day Adventist Church. Because one of the tenets of her new faith requires that she not work from Friday sundown to Saturday sundown, O'Malley informs her manager that she will not be available anymore during that period. This schedule is problematic as it contravenes the policy that requires all full-time sales clerks to work on these busy days. The manager offers her part-time employment, which is intended to meet her need of a more flexible schedule. He also mentions that the store will keep her informed of any full-time job openings that do not have this schedule requirement. She accepts this solution, but sees her monthly income shrink substantively. As a result, O'Malley decides to file a complaint in court alleging discrimination on the basis of religion. O'Malley's case reaches the Supreme Court of Canada (SCC) in 1985, that rules in a unanimous decision that Simpson Sears has discriminated against her.

2.2 Multani vs Commission Scolaire Marguerite-Bourgeoys [2006] 1 S.C.R. 256, 2006 SCC 6

Gurbaj Singh Multani, a public school student in Montreal, is an orthodox Sikh who believes that his faith requires him to wear a kirpan (a Sikh ceremonial dagger) made of metal under his clothes. In 2001, Gurbaj, who is 12 years old at the time, unintentionally drops his kirpan in the playground of his school. As a result, the school board sends a letter to his parents suggesting a "reasonable accommodation," whereby Gurbaj would be allowed to continue wearing his kirpan provided that it is well sealed inside his clothing. The family accepts this solution. Nonetheless, the district school board refuses to endorse the arrangement. For them, it infringes on the code of conduct of the school that prohibits weapons in schools. As an alternative, the district school board explains that it could allow Gurbaj to wear a symbolic kirpan that would take the form of a pendant, or that would be made of another risk-free material like plastic. Gurbaj is unable to accept these solutions. They go against his belief that he needs to wear a kirpan made of metal at all times. As a result, Gurbaj changes schools and attends a private institution. Moreover, he and his father decide to contest the decision of the governing board in court, on the ground that it violates Gurbaj's freedom of religion and belief. They ask that the original arrangement proposed by the school board, which allowed him to wear his kirpan as long as it was sealed under his clothes, prevail. In 2006, after a series of appeals, their case reaches the SCC, which decides in a majority decision that the district school board did violate Gurbaj's religious freedom and should have made greater efforts to accommodate his need.

While more than 20 years apart, both the O'Malley and Multani cases are important as they help us flesh-out the contours of RA in the Canadian legal context. In the following section, I draw on these two cases to explore the parameters developed by Canadian courts to evaluate whether particular claims fall within the framework of RA. In so doing, I also highlight some of the tensions lodged within this concept. This chapter then moves on to trace the evolution of the notion of RA over the past decade, emphasizing the fact that it has travelled outside the court system and into public discourse, and exploring some effects and conundrums of this displacement. In the last section, I discuss an alternative model to RA—a negotiation/navigation model—that is perhaps better equipped to capture the lived and contextual dimensions of religion, and whose structure is less conducive to (re) producing asymmetrical power relations.

3   Delimiting the Contours of Reasonable Accommodations: Key Concepts

Neutrality of the Norm—moving beyond formal equality?

While the notion of RA is referenced in both the Multani and O'Malley cases to address the grounds of religious discrimination, at the outset it is noteworthy to underline that Canadian courts draw on this notion in cases involving a range of other discriminations prohibited under the Canadian Charter of Human Rights and Freedoms, including discriminations based on age, sex, pregnancy, age, and disability (see also Bosset 2005: 3).

To get a better sense of what RA entails, it is relevant to understand in what context and why this notion is used. One of the underlining ideas structuring the notion of RA is that while a rule, norm, or law might appear neutral, as its aim is to affect everyone equally and not discriminate against a particular group, when it gets applied it may nevertheless discriminate against particular individuals. In other words, even if the intention and objective of the rule is precisely not to discriminate, by applying the same treatment to everyone, it may still discriminate against individuals who do not, because of their age, religion, health, etc., correspond to the average individual for whom the rule was designed.

To better understand these distinctions, it is important to differentiate between two sets of related concepts: formal and substantial equality, and direct discrimination and adverse effect discrimination. Both O'Malley and Multani found themselves in environments where institutions had developed rules that were intended to apply to all employees or students. In O'Malley's case the SCC explains that the policy requiring full-time sales clerks to work on Friday evenings and Saturdays was: "adopted for sound business reasons and not as the result of any intent to discriminate against the complainant, or members of her faith" (Ontario Human Rights Commission (O'Malley) v. Simpsons-Sears 1985, para 3). Likewise for Multani, the rule in the school code of conduct prohibiting weapons in schools was not meant to discriminate against particular students, but was meant to: "ensure a reasonable level of safety at the school" (Multani v. Commission scolaire 2006, para 48). In other words, in neither case is the institution's intention to directly discriminate. This clarification is well articulated by Judge McIntyre, who wrote the O'Malley decision, and underlines that the rule adopted by Simpsons-Sears does not: "on its face discriminate on prohibited grounds. For example: No Catholics or no women or no blacks employed here" (Ontario Human Rights Commission (O'Malley) v. Simpsons-Sears 1985, para 17). And yet the SCC's decisions highlight how these rules had adverse effects for both O'Malley and Multani by infringing on their religious freedom. In so doing, the SCC embraces a substantive reading of equality, one which requires adapting "apparently neutral rules and policies" (Ryder 2008, p. 88) that actually infringe on the religious practice and/or belief of individuals to limit adverse effects.

To put it simply, this understanding of equality foresees the possibility that an apparently neutral ruling can result in putting particular individuals, like O'Malley and Multani, in front of an impossible dilemma (e.g. choosing between accessing full-time employment or attending public school, and practicing their religion the way they wish to) and requires that reasonable measures be taken to mitigate this situation. This is grounded in the idea, as Ryder sensibly explains, that: "True equality requires that religious differences be accommodated and that coercive pressures of neutral rules on religious observance be avoided" (Ryder 2008, p. 88). To be clear, in cases of RAs, like O'Malley's and Multani's, the apparently neutral rule will not be stricken down. This is because the rule does not directly discriminate against particular individuals, nor is that its intent. On the contrary, it is conceived as applying to everyone, and it is actually this general application that leads to adverse effects. It is a rule based on a formal reading of equality. The duty of RA requires, on the other hand, that institutions take reasonable steps to adapt the rule for individuals whose rights it infringes.

3.1   Religious Sincerity

Another important question that courts have to evaluate when deciding whether institutions have a duty to reasonably accommodate an individual's religious request is the extent to which this request falls in the category of freedom of religion or belief. In other words, the courts must evaluate the sincerity of belief of the claimant, and draw the difficult line between: "subjective preferences and meaning-giving beliefs" (Maclure 2011, p. 271). It is important to note here that according to the SCC this 'sincere belief' does not need to necessarily be related to the teachings of established religions, nor to those followed by the majority of believers (Bosset 2005). Neither does the claimant, in principle, have to follow past practices. This explains why in the Multani decision, the SCC makes it clear that the fact that other Sikhs agree to wear a replica of the kirpan not made of metal, is irrelevant (Multani v. Commission scolaire 2006, para 39). What *is* relevant is that Gurbaj sincerely believes that he has to follow this requirement. In so doing, the SCC seeks to embrace a subjective understanding of freedom of religion precisely to account for the variability of beliefs and practices between believers as well as during the life course of an individual (see Amselem v. Syndicat Northcrest 2004, p. 554). In other words, claimants have to prove the sincerity of their beliefs, but are not required to show that this belief is related to: "some sort of objective religious obligation, requirement or precept" (Amselem v. Syndicat Northcrest 2004, p. 554). Courts are required to assess this sincerity, which means determining the honesty of belief that should not be "fictitious nor capricious" (Amselem v. Syndicat Northcrest 2004, p. 554), but they are not in a position to evaluate the "content of subjective understanding of a religious requirement" (Amselem v. Syndicat Northcrest 2004, p. 554). To do so, they can analyze "the credibility of a claimant's testimony, as well as [...] whether the alleged belief is consistent with his or her other current religious practices" (Amselem v. Syndicat Northcrest 2004, p. 554). A contextual and case-by-case analysis is therefore required here since only this type of analysis will allow courts to get a sense of the subjective practice of a particular individual, and to account for variability of practices (see Lepinard 2016, p. 71). This sincerity test is important as it is the sincerity of belief that triggers the duty of RA.

Several scholars have highlighted the difficulty of this test, especially when it comes to refraining from evaluating the content of particular faiths and, therefore, from relying on an objective reading of religion. In her analysis of the Multani decision, Lori Beaman (2008), for instance, notes that despite the SCC emphasis on the fact that a religious practice need not be required by the tenets of a religion to be protected, the Court's language still indicates a reliance on the "essence" of that particular faith. She explains:

> The Court begins with "in the case at bar, Gurbaj Singh must show that he sincerely believes that his faith requires him at all times to wear a kirpan made of metal." The words "require", "must comply", "strict disciplinary code requiring," and so on reinforce the notion that there is a direct link between Singh's religious practice/belief and an ideological orthodoxy connected to a specific faith tradition. Were the link non-existent or tenuous, or more

possibly subjective, it is difficult to imagine that the Court would have been so decisively supportive (p. 203).

Likewise, Woehrling provides us with insights on this tension. He notes that it is much easier for Canadian courts to rely on the idea of subjectivity to assess sincerity of beliefs when they are faced with a precept that is clearly part of the teachings of a known religion (1998, p. 389). This insight can shed light on why assessing the sincerity of the beliefs of both O'Malley and Multani was not a central question with which courts struggled. In O'Malley's case the SCC clearly notes that observing Shabat (i.e. not working from sundown Friday to sundown Saturday) is a tenet that: "must be strictly kept" by members of the Adventist Church (Ontario Human Rights Commission (O'Malley) v. Simpsons-Sears 1985, para 3). As discussed, similar language weaves through Multani. Woehrling notes that in fact tensions around sincerity of beliefs are visible when the claimant is the only one believing in this particular belief or practice and/or if he does not belong to a "known" religion. He stresses that in this context it is harder for the believer to prove that her beliefs/practices are more than "simple opinions" (p. 391, my translation). One could add that this "suspicion" ends up affecting members of not "well-known" religions, who often tend to also be members of religious minorities (Beaman 2008).

In sum, courts in Canada have opted to ground part of their evaluation of whether a religious request should be warranted accommodation on the sincerity of belief of the claimant. In this process, judges should avoid evaluating whether a particular request fits within the known content of a religion, but rather base their judgment on the subjective understanding of religion of the claimant. This is partly to account for the variability and flexibility of religious beliefs and practices. Yet, as seen, this approach comes with its own share of conundrums. In fact, it has been difficult for judges in their decisions not to refer to, nor try to extract the essence of particular religions, making the sincerity test easier for believers like Multani or O'Malley whose practices are in tune with well-known tenets of their faith.

3.2   Undue Hardship

Besides establishing the sincerity of belief of the claimant, courts are also responsible for evaluating arguments of undue hardship provided by institutions that consider they cannot accommodate a request. In other words, the duty of accommodation does not mean that all sincere religious requests should be accepted. It is limited by the notion of undue hardship, which entails that an institution is not required to accommodate a particular request if it leads to excessive interference (Bosset 2005). According to the SCC, undue hardship can be triggered by three factors. The first two were fleshed out in labor law decisions (e.g. Ontario Human Rights Commission (O'Malley) v. Simpsons-Sears 1985): (1) undue expenses to a business (i.e. granting the accommodation request costs too much to a business) and (2) undue hindrance to the ways a business functions (i.e. granting the accommodation would significantly interfere in how a business/institution works). The last and third (3) one was developed later and is related to infringement on the rights of others, including other employees.

The SCC explains that institutions claiming that an accommodation request would cause undue hardship need to provide clear facts that this would be the case based on the specificities of their institutions. In other words, context is again highly important, as proof of undue hardship will vary in relation to a number of things, including the type of organization (e.g. schools, private businesses, courtrooms, for profit or non-profit organizations), its size, budget, mission, the broader economic and/or political climate, and so on. Likewise, the employer is advised not to ground his/her arguments on speculations:

> When the employer refuses to grant the leave request of an employee for religious reasons because he/she says that they worry that this will trigger an avalanche of similar demands, he/she has to prove that this "snowball" effect effectively happened and cannot limit himself to affirming that this could eventually happen (Woehrling 1998, p. 346, my translation).

It is useful to return to the O'Malley and Multani decisions to think through the specificities of this notion of undue hardship and how it is applied in practice. O'Malley is interesting as it is a good example of how this notion was used to mitigate employer –employee relations. The SCC in O'Malley clearly establishes that it is up to the institution — in this case Simpson-Sears — to prove that the accommodation would lead to undue hardship for its business. Judge McIntyre explains: "it seems evident to me that in this kind of case the onus should [...] rest on the employer, for it is the employer who will be in possession of the necessary information to show undue hardship" (Ontario Human Rights Commission (O'Malley) v. Simpsons-Sears 1985, para 28). O'Malley's employer tried to accommodate her needs by offering her part-time employment. However, the decision notes that it never produced evidence that rearranging O'Malley's work schedule so that she could continue working full-time would lead to undue expenses or interferences in the functioning of the company:

> There was no evidence adduced regarding the problems which could have arisen as a result of further steps by the respondent, or of what expense would have been incurred in rearranging working periods for her benefit, or of what other problems could have arisen if further steps were taken towards her accommodation (Ontario Human Rights Commission (O'Malley) v. Simpsons-Sears 1985, para 29).

As described in the vignette, while O'Malley accepted the part-time offer, she did not consider this accommodation 'reasonable', as it affected her ability to earn a decent living quite substantively. It is precisely the absence of evidence of undue hardship that leads the Court to rule that Simpsons-Sears did discriminate against O'Malley (Ontario Human Rights Commission (O'Malley) v. Simpsons-Sears 1985, para 29). Context is therefore key in informing this decision. Indeed, if the company had provided solid proof of undue interference, one could imagine that the outcome of the case could have been quite different.

The Multani case provides us with even more information on the importance of context to evaluate the level of hardship. One of the arguments put forth against allowing Gurbaj to keep his kirpan is that doing so would lead the school to: "reduce its safety standards", which would result in undue hardship for that institution (Multani v. Commission scolaire 2006, para 12):

> According to the CSMB [*Commission Scolaire Marguerite Bourgeoys* (district school board)], to allow the kirpan to be worn in school entails the risks that it could be used for violent purposes by the person wearing it or by another student who takes it away from him [from Gurbaj], that it could lead to a proliferation of weapons at the school, and that its presence could have a negative impact on the school environment (Multani v. Commission scolaire 2006, para 55).

In other words, not only would the wearing of the kirpan produce undue hindrance in the functioning of the school, but it would also disproportionally affect the rights of other students by putting their safety at risk. To buttress these points, the school district governing board posits that the kirpan is a weapon that symbolises violence (Multani v. Commission scolaire 2006, para 55). In its close examination of these arguments, the SCC contextualises them. This is an exercise that requires evaluating their accuracy when juxtaposed with Gurbaj's reality. In its assessment of whether the kirpan infringes on the safety of Gurbaj's school, the Court first notes that there is no evidence that Gurbaj has "behavioural problems", or that he has had a violent behaviour in school (Multani v. Commission scolaire 2006, para 57). In fact, there has never been one reported violent event related to the wearing the kirpan in Canadian schools (Multani v. Commission scolaire 2006, para 59). The decision also highlights that the risk that other students would use his kirpan violently is minimal. This is especially true given the initial arrangement with the school board after the incident in the school playground, which required Gurbaj to wear his kirpan sealed and inside his clothes. This solution substantially limited the ability of other students to take the kirpan or chances that the kirpan would fall. Judge Charron, who authored the majority, decision notes that there are numerous objects more accessible on school grounds that could be used for violent purposes, such as scissors, compasses, or pencils (Multani v. Commission scolaire 2006, para 46 and 58). As Lépinard underlines, in her analysis of this decision, these comparisons are part and parcel of a contextual analysis that allows the SCC to conduct a concrete evaluation of the arguments put forth to prohibit the kirpan on the ground of undue hardship in a school setting (2016).

Delving into the particularities of school settings also allows Judge Charron to respond to the district school board arguments that schools are similar environments to airplanes and courts, in which courts' decisions confirmed the prohibition of the kirpan (Multani v. Commission scolaire 2006). While Judge Charron notes that safety is important in these different spaces, she also stresses the importance of not forgetting to account for the specificities of these different environments. Schools are unique spaces in the sense that they are "living communities" that are conducive to developing meaningful relationships between staff and students: "These relationships make it possible to better control the different types of situations that arise in schools" (Multani v. Commission scolaire 2006, para 65). This is not the case for airports and planes, where in the first space "groups of strangers are brought together" (2006, para 63), and where the second is an adversarial setting. Moreover, students are required to attend school on a daily basis, whereas the presence in courts and airplane is "temporary" (Multani v. Commission scolaire, para 65). In other words, the prejudicial effects of forbidding the kirpan are quite different, as its prohibition in schools would potentially affect years in the life of a student. To put it simply, it is through this careful consideration of context, including through these comparisons with other settings and objects, that the SCC is able to assess the respondent's claim that allowing the wearing of the kirpan would result in undue hardship. Here again, the lack of concrete evidence related to this particular case leads the Court to reject this claim: "Justice Charron found that an absolute prohibition was not justified. The minimal risk to school safety posed by the wearing of kirpans could be managed in the school environment by the imposition of conditions on the wearing of kirpans" (Ryder 2008, p. 103).

4 Reasonable Accommodations: A Few Statistics

It is interesting to note that the Quebec Human Rights Commission (*Commission des droits de la personne et des droits de la jeunesse* (CDPDJ)) underscores that between 2009 and 2013, out of the 3583 complaints regarding accommodation requests it received only 0.7% that were related to religion, and that complaints on the ground of disability were 13 times more frequent (CDPDJ 2013). In another study that focuses more specifically on cases of religious RAs filed with the CDPDJ, Paul Eid concludes that one request for RA out of two is filed by Christian plaintiffs (2007). These statistics are relevant if only because it puts in perspective the fact that while public discourse has, over the last decade, focused on religious RAs, and more particularly on those filed by Muslim plaintiffs, the range and types of complaints that are filed in Canadian courts and/or with provincial Human Rights Commissions offer a much more complex picture.

This recent discursive importance given to religious RA is discussed in detail in the Bouchard-Taylor report. In its study of RA in the province of Quebec, the Bouchard-Taylor report underscores that from 1985 to 2006, 25 cases were covered by the media, the majority of which were related to court decisions on these cases. In contrast, from March 2006 to June 2007, approximately 40 cases were reported in the media (2008). The commissioners note that this considerable rise in media coverage of religious RAs does not necessarily reflect a rise in the number of accommodations, but rather is representative of a shift in public discourse where the language of accommodation limited until that point to the legal realm starts to become part and parcel of public parlance, and thus central to the journalistic gaze (this shift, including some if its consequences, is discussed at greater length in Sect. 5). This also means that cases making the headlines cease to be limited to those that reach courts, but extend to those understood as being related to the "integration of immigrant population and minorities" (2008, p. 53). In that process, RA becomes a broader and more ambiguous notion not restricted to its legal definition.

5 Reasonable Accommodations: Current Challenges and Future Opportunities

5.1 Reasonable Accommodations: Recent Evolutions

The Multani decision is particularly important in understanding the recent evolutions of RA. Not only is it identified as the first decision that uses the concept outside employment law, but it also marks the beginning of animated debates outside the legal arena around the "limits" that should be put on religious RAs. Reactions to the decision were particularly strong in the province of Quebec, where "much of it [the reaction] [was] negative, and much of it focused on the idea that there was simply 'too much' accommodation happening" (Beaman 2012a, p. 3). To put it simply, with the Multani decision, the notion of RA acquired a life of its own outside of the legal arena (Beaman 2012a; Barras 2016). It is noteworthy that while

Fig. 1 Courtesy of Frederic Serre/Concordia University Magazine

discussions around this topic seem to have been the most virulent in Quebec, the RA framework as a means to deal with religious requests has been an important topic of debates elsewhere in Canada: "the debate over accommodation is nationwide and its resolution has profound implications for the entire country" (Beaman and Beyer 2008, p. 4) (Fig. 1).

Accordingly, following the Multani decision, a number of concerns around the RA framework have started to circulate in the Canadian public imagination, including the following: (1) that RAs are used almost exclusively by religious individuals to get their religious needs accommodated, and that these requests are increasing; (2) that religious RAs are unfair and unreasonable because religious practices, unlike race, age, or other forms of discrimination, can easily be changed to meet the rules of particular institutions (on this see Maclure 2011, p. 266); (3) that a great number of requests for religious RAs are incompatible with Canadian "values", especially gender equality (see Moon 2008, p. 12); and (4) that non-Christian religious minorities, especially Muslims, are the ones that use the notion of RA most frequently because they tend to be more orthodox and rigid in their approach to religion, which explains why they are less inclined to adapt their faith (Eid 2007).

While most of these concerns have been challenged by academic research, they have nonetheless delimited the parameters of discussions on RA. This is clearly visible in Quebec, including in the successive responses of Quebecois policymakers and politicians to these debates. For example, in 2007, in the aftermath of the release of the Multani decision, the provincial government headed by the Liberal Party established the Bouchard-Taylor Commission to conduct provincial consultations on accommodation practices: "in response to public discontent concerning reasonable accommodation" (Bouchard and Taylor 2008, p. 17). In so doing, the Commission instigated "a public discussion" and produced "a public response" to address a perceived crisis (Beaman 2012a, b, p. 3), whereby the values of the province were believed to be under threat by an increase in "unreasonable" accommodation requests, and whereby this situation required an urgent need to develop a clear framework governing these requests (Bouchard and Taylor 2008, p. 18). Although the mandate of the Commission was to analyze "Accommodation Practices Related to Cultural Differences", public debates delimited the specifics of this focus. As a consequence, stories that came up during public consultations and examples used in the Commission's report were almost exclusively related to religious requests by minorities, in particular Muslims (on this see Barras 2016; Bender and Klassen 2010: 4; and Mahrouse 2010). In other words, while the Bouchard-Taylor Commission tried to debunk several of the above-mentioned concerns by giving them space in public debate, it participated, at the same time, in delimiting the terms of discussion, and set a precedent for other policy-making initiatives. As such, Bill 94, tabled in 2011 by the Liberal Party at the Quebec National Assembly, aimed to provide a framework to regulate accommodation requests. Likewise, this idea of developing a clear framework was picked up by Bill 60, tabled in 2013 by the Party Quebecois, whose advocates saw it as a way to limit "unreasonable" religious requests, and again by Bill 62, tabled by the Liberal Party in 2015.

Numerous scholars have criticized debates around the notion of RA, in particular because they have facilitated the (re) production of an unequal "us" (majority) versus "them" (minority) framework. Beyer, for instance, considers that (re) producing this dichotomy is particularly problematic since in practice the boundaries between minorities and majorities are increasingly blurred and fluid (Beyer 2012). While this dichotomy is already visible in the legal use of RA (see Berger 2010, p. 100 on this), it seems to become magnified in public debate. In fact, scholars argue that this framework is inherent to how the notion of RA is structured. Beaman notes that like the notion of tolerance, the notion of accommodation conveys the idea that: "there is a part of Canadian society that is entitled to accommodate and tolerate and a portion that is asking to be tolerated and accommodated" (2012b, p. 212). It thus produces and sustains unequal relationships and categories between a majority "entitled to accommodate", and a minority vulnerable to "majoritarian desires and fears" (Beaman 2012b, p. 212).

The narratives around which the Bouchard-Taylor report is structured are a good illustration of these mechanisms. As argued elsewhere (Barras 2016), religious minorities in the report are identified as requesters that are asking Canadian institutions to accommodate their religious needs. They are, in this process, differentiated from institutional managers who are described as the ones responsible for evaluating the validity, reasonableness, and compatibility of these requests with the good functioning of their organization, and if necessary, suggest compromises to requesters. Managers, on the one hand, come out as thoughtful actors capable of flexibility and innovation. Requesters, on the other hand, appear as quite passive and inflexible in this framework. While the Bouchard-Taylor report offers a description of the process that managers go through in evaluating requests (2008, p. 171), there is no such discussion when it comes to requesters. In other words, this leaves very little space to consider: "the process that brought them [the requesters] to make a request and to their willingness or unwillingness to compromise (or to propose a compromise)" (Barras 2016, p. 63), as well as to capture the variability and subjectivity of religious practices. These same dynamics are visible in the consultation processes on RA conducted by the Bouchard-Taylor Commission in different cities across the province of Quebec (see Mahrouse 2010; Côté 2008). For instance, Mahrouse argues the majority of participants to these forums were French Canadians who identified themselves as such, and who dictated the terms of the conversation:

> By and large, testimonies in the citizens' forums followed a pattern: French-Canadian Quebecers lamented the loss of the mythical days when Quebec identity was untainted by the threat of "cultural differences"; in response, members of immigrant and minority communities were expected to soothe such fears (2010, p. 89).

Even if one of the aims of these consultations was to question 'racial hierarchies' (Mahrouse 2010, p. 88), it ended-up (re) producing them. In other words, while the SCC has had limited success in giving some place to the voices and thought process of claimants, including by trying to rely on a subjective understanding of religion (remember the place given to Gurbaj's understanding of his religion), examples of this thought process and subjective approach to religion remain limited in the

Bouchard-Taylor report, and are quasi-absent in public debates. To put it simply, because the focus of public debates has been on how institutions should deal with, evaluate, and limit requests for accommodations, requesters are almost obliged to adopt a defensive position where they have to justify their religious needs and how these are compatible with Canadian values (on this see Barras 2016 and Mahrouse 2010). In this process, their religious identity tends to be framed as an all-encompassing one that defines them, and that they have to be willing to refer to in order to have a voice in those debates. This raises a number of concerns, including the fact that it gives prevalence to the voices and perspectives of individuals who feel comfortable working with this framework (Barras et al. 2016, p. 107–108). It also leaves little space to consider the fact that it is often difficult to detangle religious needs from other life circumstances, and that the ways individuals will carve a space for these needs will depend greatly on the individual herself and her context (Selby et al. 2018). Finally, the fact that the language of RA is frequently associated in public discourse with problems, tensions, conflicts, and refusals, limits our ability to consider and hear 'positive' stories related to religious diversity in Canada (on this see Beaman 2014). While the Bouchard-Taylor report tries to provide some glimpses of these stories, this is nonetheless difficult given that is it written as a response to public debates largely framed along these negative terms. This negative undertone is well conveyed by Samaa Elibyari of the Canadian Council for Muslim Women interviewed by Sharify-Funk, and who was asked in the aftermath of the Bouchard-Taylor Commission to react to the notion of RA: "I don't like the word accommodation because it seems like we're [Muslims] a pain in the neck—they have to accommodate us, they have to live with us. I'm rather pessimistic" (2010, p. 546).

5.2   Thinking of Alternatives to Reasonable Accommodation: Future Possibilities

The legal notion of RA was developed to provide a mechanism to adjust a rule that seemed on its face to be neutral, but that actually had discriminatory adverse effects for particular individuals. It is, in other words, inspired by a substantive understanding of equality. Yet, as discussed, it comes with its own share of conundrums. The most significant one, perhaps, is that it is structured around a minority versus majority dichotomy, which (re) produces power asymmetries. With regards to requests for RA around religion, this structure also requires an evaluation of the religious requests, and in so doing, of the sincerity of the believer. As seen in our discussion of SCC decisions this is not an easy task. It often, even if only inadvertently, requires judges to delimit the "essence" of religion. In so doing, it fails to do justice to the variability of religious practices. These power asymmetries and essentializing dynamics are magnified when the notion of RA is used in public discourse and policy debates. Rather than being approached as "a legal instrument to redress a

discriminatory situation between citizens", RA becomes associated in public imaginary with a "privilege granted" to religious minorities —as we saw in the previous
section with Sharify-Funk citing a representative of a Muslim association based in
Montreal (2010, p. 546).

Given this situation, it is worth asking ourselves if we can do better than RA, and
if there are alternatives to the RA framework where minorities are not left in a "'less
than' position" (Beaman 2012b, p. 212). As a starting point for thinking about what
these alternatives could look like, some scholars have suggested that we shift languages and approaches. For instance, Beaman (2014) and Selby et al. (2018) have
taken as their point of departure for their reflection one of the observations made in
the Bouchard-Taylor report. The report highlights that citizens generally work out
their differences without great fuss, or without resorting to filing formal requests for
RA (Bouchard and Taylor 2008, p. 19). Consequently, rather than focusing on cases
of RA that make the headlines or/and that are settled in courts, Selby, Barras, and
Beaman suggest that there is value to exploring how citizens in their everyday life
actually negotiate religious differences. While analyzing court decisions is important to think about notions of equality and discrimination, this exploration remains
nonetheless partial, limited by the adversarial processes that structure the act of filing a claim in court. Focusing on these everyday interactions can provide new
insights on the intricacies of religious diversity in Canada.

In order to map these on-the-ground dynamics, Beaman explains that a: "shift of
focus (not a dismissal or ignoring of them) from negative experiences to those positive ways in which people work through difference" (2012b, p. 221) is needed.
Selby, Barras, and Beaman (2018) also suggest using a negotiation/navigation
framework, which they see as better suited to capture these dynamics than the notion
of RA. This framework conveys the idea that working out differences is a dialogical
process. This, of course, does not mean that this process is not marked by power-
asymmetries — it most certainly is. But it does convey a sense of flexibility and
dialogue with oneself and/or others that is often eluded by the RA framework. This
negotiation/navigation framework also leaves space to consider that working out
difference does not always or necessarily happen with others, but that it can be
something that an individual does with oneself. The term "navigation" is used in
this framework purposely to capture the internal arithmetic religious practitioners
are often required to do in their everyday lives to juggle their religious priorities
with other important parameters (e.g. job security, health, parenting, friendship,
education). Navigation often acts as a first step in an external negotiation with others. The concept of negotiation is thus used to think about the process of working
out differences with others.

In short, for these scholars, shifting our focus to the everyday and moving away
from using the RA framework can help capture different and overlooked facets of
how religion gets woven into Canadian fabric. It can also help us theorize more
inclusive understandings of equality and respect — on this see Beaman's work on
deep equality (2014) and Selby et al. discussion of respect (2018). This does not
mean that the concept of RA becomes irrelevant, but it does highlight the importance of not approaching it as an end goal. In other words, it does signal that we can

hope for more and do better than RA; that a shift in focus has the potential to initiate a move away from the language of problems, conflicts, and assessment of (un) reasonability currently dominating public conversations, to one where recognition, respect, and equality are given a more prominent place.

To get a better sense of the dynamics that shape mundane accounts, let us finish this section by turning to the experience of Sonia, who participated in the research conducted by Selby, Barras, and Beaman on how self-identified Muslims in Canada negotiate their religion in daily life. Sonia, a 40 year-old researcher living in Montreal who self-identifies as Muslim, describes how she crafted a place for her religious needs at parties organized by her Quebecois friends and colleagues:

> S: And then I, I remember they invited me, I don't remember the first time but I remember the first couple of times they invited me to their place for a late night party. And I said sure I would. So I went there with my samosas [laughs]. They love it so I brought that and they made some *poutine* [Quebecois traditional dish] and there was a *pâté chinois* [sheppard's pie]. All the Quebecois things. And then they asked me, because they knew about Muslims but they didn't know anybody personally […] So they asked me like 'what do you eat'. And I said 'What do you have, tell me the ingredients'.
>
> I: They asked you before or at the party?
>
> S: At the party […]. They asked me because they're aware. It's not like 'go eat'. They were aware that I'm from India, that I'm Muslim. And then drinks they knew. I brought my own diet coke but it was a great party. Great party. I mean I don't mind smoking a couple of puffs of a cigarette but so I was a part of the party but at the same time I kept my religion.

Sonia goes on to explain that one of her friends had baked a cake for the party, and had asked what ingredients she should avoid when baking it:

> S: So I'm like gelatin is something that I don't eat. So: 'what else should not be on the package'? I'm like nothing, just gelatin or if there's animal product. That's easier because they're all scientists [her friends]. Even if there is something that's not obvious that it comes from an animal but they know that. This time when she cooked it and I was there and I started you know just to pick it up and she was like 'no no let me check the package'. She checked the package and she's like 'you can't eat it, it has gelatin in it'. I'm like 'thank you'. That's so sweet. Like get yourself something else, you know, fruits or something. So that's respect you know. I'm really touched by it.

Analyzing Sonia's experience through a navigation/negotiation framework directs our gaze to important subtleties. First, it allows us to pay particular attention to her mental arithmetic. It becomes clear that she has already thought through what she would be comfortable with and what she would not at this event. She does not want to miss the party and chooses to bring her own non-alcoholic beverage to mitigate the presence of alcohol. She chooses to address the presence of alcohol by crafting her own arrangement with herself. It seems that for her, not drinking alcohol, eating *halal* food, but also partaking in parties and socializing with colleagues and friends are important, and perhaps, one could say, almost non-negotiable elements at this moment in her life. She finds a way to assemble these different elements. She gives herself more leeway with other aspects, such as smoking cigarettes. Her account offers us a snapshot of the navigation that she does before negotiating other aspects with her hosts. In fact, it is equally interesting to note that she does not initiate the negotiation. Actually, one could imagine that she might just have navigated her way through the party without sharing details about her religion or negotiating with others a space for her dietary requirements, simply, for example, by avoiding food items that she cannot eat, or eating the dishes that she had brought. Yet, she ends up sharing her dietary restrictions with her hosts when they ask her what she can and cannot eat. By asking this question, her friends acknowledge power-asymmetries while at the same time not judging her or/and trying to change her (on this see Beaman 2014, p. 98). This, according to James Tully, is an essential step in the process of recognition (see Tully 2000, p. 476, 1995, p. 128).

If we zoom in on the exchange between Sonia and her friends we also see how it is marked by a generosity on both sides, which requires not being afraid to put oneself in an awkward or/and vulnerable position. Indeed, they ask her questions that enable this exchange: "what do you eat?", "what ingredients should I avoid?" These queries are essential for these friends to share a moment together, but they also carry the risk of making incorrect assumptions or/and putting Sonia in an uncomfortable position, where she has to share details of her religious practice when she does not want to. Yet, for Sonia, like for several other participants that Selby, Barras, and Beaman interviewed, these moments are typically lived as a sign of respect, a gesture of care that validates their identity. Sonia, by choosing to partake in an event where there is alcohol and mitigating this by bringing her own beverage, is also putting herself in a vulnerable position. Bringing her 'diet coke' (and her samosas) might be her way to avoid putting her hosts in an uncomfortable position, protecting herself as well as her friends from harm, but it could equally be interpreted by her hosts as overstepping hospitality codes. And yet, it seems that her gestures, not unlike her friends' questions, are understood as being conducive to allowing them to fully experience the party together. Unlike the RA framework, a navigation/negotiation lens helps us consider the possibility that crafting a place for religious difference is not necessarily an end in and of itself, but that it is part and parcel of a process where the goal is sharing a moment together, living *well* together. In other words, this lens is process oriented rather than outcome based, and allows us to capture the dialogical and flexible dimension of exchanges rather than focusing on how a majority can accommodate a minority. To put it simply, while these everyday moments and exchanges have generally been the focus of little attention in scholarly and public discussions around religious governance in Canada, they are nonetheless extremely rich. They can help us think beyond and outside the boundaries of the notion of RA, to develop new and more comprehensive understandings of equality, respect, and generosity.

6 Concluding Thoughts

This chapter started with a discussion of the legal notion of RA. This notion has been developed to account for the fact that rules that may appear neutral can actually have adverse discriminatory effects for particular individuals in particular contexts. In other words, one of the sensible impetuses behind the RA framework is to move beyond formal equality and enable a substantive reading of equality. As discussed, a contextual analysis has therefore been essential for courts to evaluate whether a request warrants an accommodation. While the RA framework can be used to ask for redress for any types of discrimination prohibited under the Charter, when it comes to evaluating religious requests, courts are required to evaluate the sincerity of belief of requesters. They are required to do so, while at the same time refraining from assessing whether a specific practice is actually essential to a particular religion. This is an arduous task, and for some observers almost an impossible one. Indeed, in reviewing decisions where courts evaluate the sincerity of belief of claimants, scholars note that the sincerity of believers of "known" faiths, especially those who follow "known" tenets of these faiths, like Multani and O'Malley, tend to be subject to less scrutiny than the sincerity of believers whose practices are not well-known. This reliance on the essence of religion is problematic since it does limit the ability of the RA framework to account for the variability and flexibility of religious practices woven through everyday life.

As discussed, the Multani decision (2006) seems to mark a turning point in the history of RA. Not only is it the first time that this legal notion has been used outside of employment law, but it is also identified as the moment when the notion of RA broke away from law and entered public discourse. It is noteworthy that while the SCC, after the Multani decision, has moved away from formally using this legal standard in other religious freedom rulings outside of employment law, such as R v. N.S. (2012) or Mouvement laïque québécois v. Saguenay (2015), the notion of RA continues to be used in the background of those decisions, such as in the summaries of the arguments made by applicants and respondents (Selby, Barras, Beaman, 2018). Likewise, RA has become prevalent in Canadian media coverage, policy discussions and reports, and more generally, in popular discourse on how to manage religious diversity. As noted through our brief discussion of this phenomenon in the province of Quebec, tensions that are already present when RA is used as a legal standard seem to become magnified when it is used outside the legal realm. The fact that the RA framework is structured around two parties in which one party finds itself in a position of authority responsible for evaluating and assessing the reasonableness of a request, and in which the other party is left in a vulnerable position waiting on the outcome of this assessment is particularly problematic. It reproduces structural power-asymmetries easily conflated with a majority/minority dichotomy. At the same time, it facilitates a situation where the party responsible for assessing the request becomes a theological arbitrator: encouraged to determine whether the request falls within the "common" practices of a particular religion, and therefore for fleshing out the contour of what is "common" and what is not. Again, this process eludes, even inadvertently, the subjective, flexible, and textured dimension of lived religion.

In response to some of those conundrums, and, in particular, to try to do justice to how religion is lived and negotiated in quotidian life, the last part of this chapter proposes to shift our gaze away from the RA framework. As an example of that shift, it suggests adopting a navigation/negotiation framework that seems better equipped to capture the organic and textured ways individuals manage their religious differences in their everyday lives. Thinking beyond the RA framework is important, especially since it carries the possibility of providing a more accurate picture of religious diversity in Canada, or at least an alternative and complementary picture that has, until now, been obscured by the dynamics structuring the RA framework. It is equally relevant on a theoretical level, as thinking through mundane experiences like Sonia's, in which individuals describe how they work out their differences with friends, neighbors, colleagues, and even strangers, can help to flesh out more comprehensive understandings of equality and respect (on this see Beaman 2014, and Selby et al. 2018). While this does not mean that we should disregard the notion of RA altogether, this shift of focus seems to be an important and necessary first step towards changing and widening the dominant terms of the conversation around religious diversity in Canada.

7 Reasonable Accommodations: Questions for Critical Thought

1. To which extent has the notion of RA been used to delimit the boundaries of 'Canadianness' and 'Canadian values'? What does this tells us about 'Canadian values', and the power-relations lodged in how these values are delimited? Can you think of other discursive frameworks that are also used to delimit these values?
2. Can you think of cases, besides the ones mentioned in this chapter, where the notion of RA has been used? In your university, neighborhood, city? Have they succeeded in enabling a substantive understanding of equality? If so, in which ways? If not, why? Was the notion of RA used formally or informally in those cases? Does this, in your opinion, make a difference in the ability to account for lived religion in the resolution of those cases? If so, how?

8 Online Teaching and Learning Resources

Religion and Diversity Project: Linking classrooms videos: http://religionanddiversity.ca/projects-and-tools/projects/linking-classrooms/linking-classrooms-videos/(in particular, Meredith McGuire's video on lived religion).

This resource will allow students to learn about recent trends in the study of religion in and beyond Canada by listening directly to scholars of religion, religious leaders, and religious practioners.

Canadian Court Cases Involving Religion Database: http://religionanddiversity.ca/media/uploads/canadian_court_cases_involving_religion_november_2016_web.pdf

This list of Canadian court cases on religion is useful especially for students interested in further exploring legal decisions on religion.

Forces of Law Bibliography: http://religionanddiversity.ca/media/uploads/projects_and_results/biblio_and_case_law/force_of_laws_bibliography.pdf

This is a relevant resource as it is a non-exhaustive list of scholarly literature on religion and law. This will be helpful for students who want to further research the connection between religion and law.

Ontario Human Rights Commission Research: Negotiating Differences http://religionanddiversity.ca/media/uploads/memo--methodology_themes_and_trends.pdf

This study is interesting, as it provides information on why parties decide to bring cases to the Ontario Human Rights Tribunal to resolve religious differences.

Commission Des Droits de la Personne et Des Droits de la Jeunesse (CDPDJ) (Quebec): Reasonable Accommodation: http://www.cdpdj.qc.ca/en/droits-de-la-personne/responsabilites-employeurs/Pages/accommodement.aspx

This resource developed by the CDPDJ will help students get a better sense of the material available to employers to assess the reasonability of a request for accommodation.

Reasonable Accommodation Requests (statistics): http://www.cdpdj.qc.ca/en/droits-de-la-personne/droits-pour-tous/Pages/accommodement_demandes.aspx

This resource provides statistics related to RA requests processed by the CDPDJ from 2009 to 2013.

Ontario Human Rights Commission (OHRC) (Ontario): OHRC and the Human Resources Professionals Association (HRPA) webinar on preventing discrimination based on creed:

http://www.ohrc.on.ca/en/ohrc-and-hrpa-webinar-preventing-discrimination-based-creed

This resource developed by the OHRC will provide students with information on the ways employers can prevent, recognize and address discrimination based on creeds.

Policy on Preventing Discrimination Based on Creed: http://www.ohrc.on.ca/en/policy-preventing-discrimination-based-creed

This is a policy developed by the OHRC to prevent discrimination based on creed. One interesting element about this resource is that it provides a definition of creed.

On religious accommodation and discrimination in the experience of Jewish communities in Ontario: http://www.ohrc.on.ca/ko/node/8750

Students will find this study relevant as it looks at the current experience of Jewish communities in Ontario with RA, including new tensions around accommodation practices that were granted in the past.

Documentaries: Nitoslawski, S. 2010. *Liberté, égalité, accommmodements.* Cinéfête. http://www.cinefete.ca/fr/site/products/74686#.WAo6qNBRfww

This documentary provides students with a background on the events that led to the Bouchard Taylor Commission and on the proceedings of the Commission.

9   Further Reading

Brown, W. (2008). *Regulating aversion: Tolerance in the age of identity and empire.* Princeton: Princeton University Press.

In this book, Brown takes a critical look at the notion of tolerance. Given that several of her criticisms are also valid for RA, this resource should help students better understand the scope of those criticisms.

Dabby, D. (2017, February 1). Opinion: Quebec should stop trying to legislate on religion. *Montreal Gazette.* Retrieved from http://montrealgazette.com/opinion/columnists/opinion-quebec-should-stop-trying-to-legislate-on-religion

This opinion piece discusses the most recent attempt in Quebec to legislate on religious accommodation. Given that Bill 62, was voted into law in November 2017, students will find this piece of particular relevance.

Policy Options. (2007). *Reasonable accommodation, 28*(8). Retrieved from http://policyoptions.irpp.org/magazines/reasonable-accommodation/

This resource will provide students with a range of different views on RA by academics and practitioners in and outside Quebec.

Jézéquel, M. (Ed.) (2007). *Les accommodements raisonnables: quoi, comment, jusqu'où? Des outils pour tous.* Cowansville: Editions Yvon Blais.

This edited collection provides a valuable analysis of RA in the employment, education and health sectors.

10 Researcher Background

Amélie Barras' interest in how states regulate and delimit religion and the right to religious freedom started during her doctoral research which she completed at the London School of Economics in the Department of Government. In *Refashioning Secularisms in France and Turkey* (Barras 2014), she looks at how the French and Turkish states are using the concept of secularism to regulate the bodies of Muslim women wearing headscarves, and the impact this had on the right to religious freedom. She became drawn to a similar set of questions when she came to Canada in 2012 to do a post-doctoral fellowship with the Religion and Diversity Project headed by Professor Lori Beaman. One of her areas of research since then has been to explore the power of the concept of reasonable accommodation both in law and in public discourse to demarcate the boundaries of what is religiously acceptable and what is not in the Canadian public imaginary. She has equally been interested in thinking about the extent to which this concept is used by and is useful for religiously practicing individuals in their everyday life. Barras is currently Assistant Professor in the Department of Social Science at York University.

References

Amselem v. Syndicat Northcrest. (2004). Supreme Court of Canada. *SCR, 2*.

Barras, A. (2014). *Refashioning secularisms in France and turkey: The case of the headscarf ban*. London: Routledge.

Barras, A. (2016). Exploring the intricacies and dissonances of religious governance: The case of Quebec and the discourse of request. *Critical Research on Religion, 4*(1), 57–71.

Barras, A., Selby, J., & Beaman, L. G. (2016). In/visible religion in public institutions: Canadian Muslim public servants. In B. Berger & R. Moon (Eds.), *Religion and the exercise of public authority* (pp. 95–110). London: Hart Publishing.

Beaman, L. G. (2008). Defining religion: The promise and the peril of legal interpretation. In R. J. Moon (Ed.), *Law and society: Law and religious pluralism in Canada* (pp. 192–216). Vancouver: UBC Press.

Beaman, L. G., & Beyer, P. (2008). Introduction: Religion and diversity in Canada. In L. G. Beaman & P. Beyer (Eds.), *Religion and diiversity in Canada* (pp. 1–9). Brill: Leiden.

Beaman, L. G. (2012a). Introduction: Exploring reasonable accommodation. In L. G. Beaman (Ed.), *Reasonable accommodation: Managing religious diversity* (pp. 1–12). Vancouver: UBC Press.

Beaman, L. G. (2012b). Conclusion: Alternatives to reasonable accommodation. In L. G. Beaman (Ed.), *Reasonable accommodation: Managing religious diversity* (pp. 208–224). Vancouver/Toronto: UBC Press.

Beaman, L. G. (2014). Deep equality as an alternative to accommodation and tolerance. *Nordic Journal of Religion and Society, 27*(2), 89–111.

Bender, C., & Klassen, P. (2010). *After pluralism: Reimagining religious engagement*. New York: Columbia University Press.

Berger, B. (2010). The cultural limits of legal tolerance. In C. Bender & P. Klassen (Eds.), *After pluralism: Reimagining religious engagement* (pp. 98–127). New York: Columbia University Press.

Beyer, P. (2012). Religion and immigration in a changing Canada: The reasonable accommodation of 'reasonable accommodation'? In L. G. Beaman (Ed.), *Reasonable accommodation: Managing religious diversity* (pp. 13–32). Vancouver: UBC Press.

Bill n °62. (2015). *An act to foster adherence to State religious neutrality and, in particular, to provide a framework for religious accommodation requests in certain bodies.* Quebec National Assembly, Canada. http://www.assnat.qc.ca/en/travaux-parlementaires/projets-loi/projet-loi-62-41-1.html. Accessed 11 Apr 2017.

Bill n°60. (2013, November 7). *Charter affirming the values of state secularism and religious neutrality and of equality between women and men, and providing a framework for accommodation requests.* Quebec National Assembly, Canada. Available at: http://www.assnat.qc.ca/en/travaux-parlementaires/projets-loi/projet-loi-60-40-1.html. Accessed 11 Apr 2017.

Bill no94. (2011, February 24). *An act to establish guidelines governing accommodation requests within the administration and certain institutions.* Quebec National Assembly, Canada. Available at: www.assnat.qc.ca/en/travaux-parlementaires/projets-loi/projet-loi-94-39-1.html. Accessed 11 Apr 2017.

Bosset, P. (2005). *Reflections on the scope and limits of the duty of reasonable accommodation in the field of religion.* Commission des droits de la personne et des droits de la jeunesse. Retrieved from: http://www.cdpdj.qc.ca/publications/religion_accommodation_opinion.pdf. Accessed 11 April 2017.

Bouchard, G., & Taylor, C. (2008). *Building the future: A time for reconciliation.* Report, Gouvernement du Québec.

Commission des droits de la personne et des droits de la jeunesse Québec. (2013). *Comments on the government policy paper.* http://www.cdpdj.qc.ca/Publications/commentaires_orientations_valeurs_En.pdf. Accessed 11 Apr 2017.

Côté, P. (2008). Québec and reasonable accommodation: Uses and Misues of public consultation. In L. G. Beaman & P. Beyer (Eds.), *Religion and diversity in Canada* (pp. 41–65). Boston: Brill.

Davison, J. (2014, August 9). How much government accommodation can you expect because of religion or a disability? *CBC News.* http://www.cbc.ca/news/canada/how-much-government-accommodation-can-you-expect-because-of-religion-or-a-disability-1.2731312. Accessed 11 Apr 2017.

Eid, P. (2007). *La Ferveur Religieuse et les Demandes d'Accommodement Religieux: Une Comparaison Intergroupe.* Commission des droits de la personne et des droit de la jeunesse Québec. http://www.cdpdj.qc.ca/publications/ferveur_religieuse_etude.pdf. Accessed 11 Apr 2017.

Sharify-Funk, M. (2010). Muslims and the politics of "reasonable accommodation": Analyzing the Bouchard-Taylor report and its impact on the Canadian province of Québec. *Journal of Muslim Minority Affairs, 30*(4), 535–553.

Lepinard, E. (2016). Juger/inclure/imaginer les minorités religieuses: la prise en compte de la subjectivité minoritaire dans l'exercice du jugement au Canada et en France. In A. Barras, F. Dermange, & S. Nicolet (Eds.), *Réguler le religieux dans les societies liberals: les nouveaux défis* (pp. 63–82). Genève: Labor et Fides.

Maclure, J. (2011). Reasonable accommodation and the subjective conception of freedom of conscience and religion. In A. Eisenberg & W. Kymlicka (Eds.), *Ethnicity and democratic governance series: Identity politics in the public realm: Bringing institutions back in* (pp. 260–280). Vancouver: UBC Press.

Mahrouse, G. (2010). 'Reasonable accommodation' in Québec : The limits of participation and dialogue. *Race Class, 52*(1), 85–96.

Moon, R. (2008). Introduction: Law and religious pluralism in Canada. In R. J. Moon (Ed.), *Law and society: Law and religious pluralism in Canada* (pp. 1–20). Vancouver: UBC Press.

Mouvement laïque québécois v. Saguenay. (2015, April 15). Supreme Court of Canada. 2 SCR, 3.

Multani v. Commission scolaire. (2006, March 2). Supreme Court of Canada. *SCR, 256.*

Ontario Human Rights Commission (O'Malley) v. Simpsons-Sears. (1985). *SCR, 536.*

R. v. N.S. (2012, December 20). Supreme Court of Canada. *SCR, 726.*

Ryder, B. (2008). The Canadian conception of equal religious citizenship. In R. J. Moon (Ed.), *Law and society: Law and religious pluralism in Canada* (pp. 87–109). Vancouver: UBC Press.

Selby, J., Barras, A., & Beaman, L. G. (2018). *Beyond accommodation: Everyday narratives of Muslim Canadians.* Vancouver: UBC Press.

Tully, J. (2000). Struggles over recognition and distribution. *Constellations, 7*(4), 469–482.

Woehrling, J. (1998). L'obligation d'accommodement raisonnable et l'adaptation de la société à la diversité religieuse. *McGill L.J, 45*, 325–401.

Muslim Canadians

Jennifer A. Selby

Abstract This chapter centres on "Dina," a twenty-one-year-old Sunni engineering student of Ethiopian-origin, who lives in St. John's, Newfoundland and Labrador, Canada. Taking what some scholars call a "lived religion" approach, the chapter introduces primary tenets and practices shared by many Muslim Canadians, often known as the "five pillars," with attention to Dina's account of *salat*. It then overviews statistical data to map historical trends and considers significant political moments that have impacted Muslim migration to Canada. 9/11 is a turning point for Canadian Muslims in that its legal and societal implications continue to shape the contexts in which Dina and other Muslim Canadians live. The chapter concludes with consideration of the burdens of representation inferred on Muslim Canadians like Dina amidst contemporary neo-Orientalisms and neo-colonialisms.

Keywords Muslims · Islamic law · Islamophobia · Newfoundland, Canada · Lived religion · Negotiating religious difference · Multiculturalism

1 Introduction

> I'm a smiley person. I go around, I smile. I say hi [...] Especially because I'm in Engineering, I have, you know, a lot of boys in my classes. I do communicate with them and everything. You know, there's a boundary, but I don't pass that boundary [...] It just makes you pretty aware of different cultures. I am definitely more culturally aware [now, since living in Canada].

J. A. Selby (✉)
Department of Religious Studies, Memorial University of Newfoundland,
St. John's, NL, Canada
e-mail: jselby@mun.ca

This chapter centres on "Dina," a twenty-one-year-old Sunni[1] engineering student of Ethiopian-origin, who lives in St. John's, Newfoundland and Labrador.[2] In this excerpt from a 2012 interview in the busy food court of Memorial University of Newfoundland (MUN)'s student centre, she describes how she navigates her everyday interactions among an ethnically diverse and mostly masculine student body in the Faculty of Engineering.[3] Dina is studious and outgoing, and, as we will see, her religious beliefs and practices play a significant role in her life. Focusing on her experiences as a religiously practicing person in St. John's gives us a window into some of the commonalities among many Muslims in Canada: she is a first-generation immigrant, and she is highly educated and racialized. Indeed, many of her experiences resonate with recent social scientific findings that outline a concurrent climate of "tolerance," multiculturalism, and Islamophobia. Dina wears hijab, a hair-covering headscarf, in a small Canadian city that is not as diverse as the country's bigger cities—namely, the Greater Toronto Area, Montreal, Vancouver, Ottawa, Calgary and Edmonton[4]—where most Muslims live.[5] This chapter describes Muslims as a group, but, of course, religiosity often varies over the course of an individual's lifetime, let alone among members of the same family or community. Moreover, Muslims are Canada's most ethnically, linguistically, and socio-economically diverse religionists. Thus, while this chapter focuses on Dina, when grouped together, Muslim Canadians encompass a multitude of perspectives and experiences that, for our purposes here, will be similarly grouped.

Taking what some scholars call a "lived religion" approach, I begin by introducing some of the primary tenets and practices among many Muslim Canadians, often known as the "five pillars." From there, I consider Dina's account of *salat*. The chapter then overviews broader quantitative data to map historical trends and considers the significant political moments that have impacted Muslim migration to Canada. 9/11 is a turning point for Muslims and non-Muslims, bringing legal and societal shifts that shape the Canadian context in which Dina and other Muslim Canadians live.

---

[1] The central sectarian divide in Islam—between Sunnis and Shi'ias—resulted primarily from a dispute regarding succession and leadership following the death of the Prophet Muhammad in 632 CE.

[2] Dina is a participant in a qualitative study conducted in this easterly city in 2012–2013 as part of a project co-directed with Lori G. Beaman examining religious diversity and negotiation among Muslim Canadians. I gratefully acknowledge the participation of our anonymized interlocutors, the support of the Social Sciences and Humanities Research Council, and the research assistance of Caitlin Downie and Jennifer Williams. Beaman and I later collaborated with Amélie Barras, who conducted similar interviews in Montréal. I also thank Cory Funk for his able bibliographical assistance.

[3] This qualitative study involved semi-directed interviews with 55 self-described Muslims (including so-called mainstream, conservative, cultural and non-practicing Muslims) in St. John's.

[4] Several qualitative research projects examine aspects of Muslim life in the Greater Toronto Area (Zine 2008a, b), Montreal (Eid 2007; Mossière 2013; Barras 2016), the Vancouver area (Dossa 1994, 2002, 2009, 2014) and the Edmonton region (Waugh and Wannas 2003; Waugh 2012).

[5] According to 2011 Household Survey data, the Greater Toronto Area, Muslims make up 3.2% of the population; in St. John's 0.5% (Statistics Canada 2011).

2 Key Concepts

Most descriptions of Islam begin by outlining the "five pillars." The five pillars refer to the *shahadah* (the declaration of faith[6]), *salat* (rituals and beliefs involving daily prayer, usually five times daily), *zakat* (almsgiving), *Ramadan* (a month-long fast) and the *hajj* (pilgrimage to Mecca, Saudi Arabia). Their usefulness as a proxy to understand Islam has been critiqued,[7] but the pillars are a practical snapshot of what most Muslims believe and practice. At twenty-one, Dina has not yet had the oppor-tunity to go on *hajj*, the world's largest annual pilgrimage to Mecca, the birthplace of Islam, which many Muslims believe they should attend in their lifetime if they are financially and physically able, but she intends to. Her account of her daily prac-tice references these pillars and others related to "living halal,[8]" to cite her. For Dina, "living halal" means incorporating modesty,[9] a way of being that encourages her hijab and modest dress and shapes how she interacts with others. Dina has a bright and contagious smile. She says "hi" easily. At the same time, in a context in which she is a religious minority, she is careful to remain modest in her interactions, particularly with members of the opposite sex.

Given some of these realities, engaging with these pillars in contemporary Canada can be a challenge. Let us briefly consider the lived realities of *salat* in St. John's. For as long as she can remember, Dina's days have been punctuated by prayer five times per day. Their timing depends on geography and the situation of the sun, but typically take place close to dawn, near noon, in the afternoon, at sunset, and in the evening. As a student living in a private room on her university's campus,

---

[6] The *shahada* is a creedal statement affirming absolute monotheism and Muhammad as the final prophet: *ā 'ilāha 'illā-llāh, muḥammadur-rasūlu-llāh* or "There is no god but God. Muhammad is the messenger of God." In Shi'a Islam, the *shahada* includes a third phrase that affirms Ali as *wali* or friend of God.

[7] The utility of the pillars can be critiqued from a theoretical perspective insofar as understanding the traditions of Islam through standardized categories necessarily collapses heterogeneity. Robert Hefner (1998: 92) describes this collapse as "world-religions-based" approach that is a response to "demands for a unitary profession of faith." The pillars reflect a tendency in the study of religion to favour visual and ritual components of religiosity, perhaps because there is little doubt they reflect "religion."

[8] *Halal* generally denotes that which is permissible, according to Islamic law, itself a centuries-old and varied complex system of interpretation of the tradition's central revealed text, the Qur'an, and the *hadith*, a collection of the sayings and actions attributed to the Prophet Muhammad. Generally, conceptualizations of *halal* refer to food and drink (alcohol and pork being the commonly served products which are avoided), as well as matters of daily life (for more on contemporary interpreta-tions, see Fisher 2010).

[9] For Dina, "living modestly" (*haya*) encompasses 'inner' and 'outer' realms and includes her attire, her disposition, her speech, and so on. Jouili's (2015) ethnography on second-generation Muslim women in urban France and Germany is a helpful companion to Mahmood's (2005) semi-nal fieldwork on female piety in Cairo. Jouili relays the pressures laden in her interlocutors' ethical commitments and practices, namely in balancing their professional and personal lives by delaying marriage, motherhood or both and in wearing visibly Muslim-identified dress in Western "secular" contexts.

Dina has privacy and space to pray in the early morning and evening. During the school week, she often prays in a passkey entry room in the Engineering Building. It is usually busy, but she likes that she can slip in and out easily. Because the city's one mosque[10] is not easily accessible without a vehicle, she attends *jumu'ah* (congregational prayer) on Fridays in the campus' repurposed chapel.[11] Students temporarily move the pews to lay out prayer mats. Women pray behind the men, reflecting the group's mores around sexual segregation.[12] These gatherings are organized by the Muslim Students' Association, with which Dina is a member, and which is the university's largest and the most active student group. Of course, not all Muslim Canadians pray regularly or communally. A number of the university students we interviewed at MUN preferred to pray quietly by themselves or to find alternative private spaces like in the stairwell of the library or in an office, using their smartphones to determine the *qibla*, or the direction of prayer. Some participants describe these daily prayers as a "check-in with God" or a way of training the mind and body to be in sync with Allah (c.f. Mahmood 2001). Despite its visibility and frequency, generally speaking, the Muslim students we interviewed at MUN negotiate *salat* with relative ease. But off-campus, it can be more complicated to negotiate. Dina explains how she was able to pray in an oil and gas company where she recently completed a cooperative work term:

> In my work terms [as part of her cooperative learning program in Engineering] I've asked my supervisors, I'm like, "I need a place where I can pray." Cuz I, especially in the winter, there's two prayers [during the work day] so I'm going to miss all of them. So I've been lucky that they've had, you know, a little storage room or whatever and that's enough space for what I need really. And I take my stuff and I take five minutes and go pray [.. .] If it's a work term I'll first scope a place out and see where I can, if there's a prospective place that I can so I won't be like "oh yeah, find me a place." But I'll then be like, "oh I've seen this room is empty or you know someone is not there so can I do it there." So that kind of thing. So, you know, if you give them, you know, ideas [.. .] that helps.

Dina takes an *ad hoc* approach to finding places to pray when she works, like an out-of-the-way storage room in this private company. Before negotiating this space, Dina surveyed the office layout to get a sense of the possibilities so to offer her supervisor a specific suggestion, akin to what Selby et al. (2018) call "navigation". Dina recognizes the power relations at play: she makes a request to her workplace superior in a temporary job and does not feel she is in a position to be demanding. In general, her aim is to live her religious life and find suitable options in the variety of environments in which she finds herself. To be clear, not all of our participants in Montreal and St. John's approached prayer in this way or were able to approach their bosses. Some did not want prayer space for reasons that include that they did not pray, or preferred to physically leave their office to separate their religiosity

---

[10] Newfoundland and Labrador's only mosque was built in 1990.

[11] In our larger dataset of 90 participants in St. John's and Montreal a number of our participants relied upon "repurposed" Christian chapels in hospitals and at universities (see Barras et al. 2016).

[12] Zarqa Nawaz's National Film Board documentary *Me and the Mosque* (2005) captures changing beliefs and debates in mosques across Canada (see "Online teaching and learning resources").

from the workplace, or prayed with Muslim colleagues (see Barras et al. 2016 for examples among Muslim Canadian public servants).

One way of conceptualizing these differences in practice is to map individual approaches of engagement with *fiqh*, or Islamic jurisprudence. Scholars have pointed to noteworthy findings in how individual Muslims engage with religious law in contemporary Canada. Julie Macfarlane's (2012a, b) work on Islamic legal interpretations among Muslims in southern Ontario, for one, found that, at the time of divorce, differences in Sunni schools of law were not significant. Traditionally, there are four schools of jurisprudence in Sunnism, which draw differently on primary sources of law: the Qur'an (the revealed text of the tradition) and the *hadith* (the sayings of the Prophet) are central, and, in order of significance, are followed by interpretation that draws upon *qiyās* (analogy), consensus among the *ulama* (religious scholars) and *ijtihad* (independent reasoning). The different schools differ geographically and accord differing weight to these methods. For instance, Dina identifies as Sunni. Based on her Ethiopian origins, we might guess she identifies with the Shafi' legal school.[13] However, at least at this stage in her life, *fiqh* and these schools of legal interpretation are not points of reference. So too, Macfarlane finds that rather than affinity with specific legal traditions based on one's country of origin, at the time of religious divorce, Muslims in Ontario most often seek out expeditious religious rulings, a situation she and other scholars on Islamic law in Canada call "imam shopping" (Macfarlane 2012b; see also Bunting and Mokhtari 2007; Saris and Potvin 2010), referring to how individuals seek efficiency more than Islamic legal specificity. A much smaller study I conducted (Selby 2016) among Sunni young women in the Greater Toronto Area at the time of their *mahr* (dowry) negotiation similarly found that while engaging with *fiqh* was important for them, they made little distinction between schools of Islamic law and relied on friends, family and a handful of websites to negotiate *mahr*-related concerns. Together these studies suggest that Muslim Ontarians are not concerned with the particularities of Sunni jurisprudence, but simply want to "get on with it" in an Islamic way. Also notable is Dina's insistence that she wants to live Islamically according to "Canadian life," a viewpoint some scholars call a "*fiqh* for minorities" (*fiqh al-aqalliyyat al-muslima*) or the interpretation of Islamic jurisprudence with a minority context in mind.[14] In sum, living as religious minorities and alongside Muslims of different backgrounds appears to encourage a context in which sectarian interpretations of Islamic law have less resonance.

---

[13] The Shafi' legal school, founded by Muhammad ibn Idris al-Shafi'i (d. 204 AH/820 CE), is considered by many as the most influential and sophisticated legal scholar in Islamic history. His writings emphasize the Qur'an's relationship with the *Sunnah* (the life and deeds of the Prophet Muhammad), followed by community consensus and analogy. In contrast, *ijtihad* (private reasoning) is largely absent in the Hanafi school.

[14] Members of the Canadian Council of Imams, established in 1990, meet every month to discuss issues that affect Muslim Canadians. In keeping with the notion of *fiqh* for minorities, the council writes *fatwā* (legally nonbinding edicts) with this context in mind and engages in advocacy work (see Canadian Council of Imams 2012).

3 Statistical Data

Dina has lived in St. John's for three years, moving directly from Addis Ababa, Ethiopia, but Muslims have lived in Canada since before its Confederation in 1867. The first Canadian census in 1871 documented eight Muslims who lived in Northern Alberta and worked primarily as merchants and fur traders. There were surely more than eight; Canadian Muslim minorities have long had reason to not be counted. Ali Abu Shehadi or Ali Abou Shehade (the latter according to his great-grand-nephew, undertaking a PhD in St. John's), for one, who arrived in Lac La Biche, Alberta from Lebanon with the Klondike as his destination, changed his name to Alexander Hamilton. Historians suggest that an immigration officer who struggled to pronounce his name made the switch (Hamdani 2015, p. 3; Waugh 1980, p. 125).[15]

Muslims have a long history of settlement and political participation in the Canadian prairies, despite evidence of political and climate-related challenges. Fatima Shaben, for example, describes her voyage from what is now Lebanon to Montreal by boat and then to Edmonton by train in her journal. She notes a "1907 blizzard [that] drove the mercury down to 48 degrees below zero" (cited in Lorenz 1998, p. 29). Fatima migrated to Alberta following her marriage to Samuel Shaben in Lebanon in 1907. "Big Sam", as he was known, had migrated with his brother through Ellis Island four years earlier to flee military service. Fatima and Samuel began farming in the Brooks, Alberta region, where a number of Lebanese families had settled. Reflecting this growing population in northern Alberta, Canada's first official mosque was built in 1938 in nearby Edmonton; its Orthodox-style domes evidence the original contractor's Ukrainian heritage.[16] Early settlers lived in Edmonton, but also as traders and farmers in Lac la Biche, a town with a long history of Muslim settlement that, today, still boasts the highest number of Muslims per capita in Canada. The Shaben family shifted their business from farming to a general store, which the couple's son Albert renamed "The Endiang Trading Company". Albert's son and Fatima's grandson Larry Shaben (1935–2008) went on to serve as a Conservative Cabinet minister and Member of Alberta's Legislative Assembly (MLA) for 14 years. This broader trajectory from early prairie settlers to political success reflects this family's long settlement in Alberta and mirrors the successes of many immigrant families over generations of settlement.[17]

The census data on the country's Muslim population must be read critically. Some, like Ali/Alex Hamilton, were likely reluctant to be counted. The country's immigration policies have not often been welcoming to religious minorities.

---

[15] Pressure to change one's name occurs contemporarily, as well. Another student participant in St. John's was encouraged by a mentor to "Africanize" his name—from "Mahmoud" to "Mamadou"—so that it would not sound as "Arab Muslim" (see Selby et al. 2018). These name changes have also been called "resumé whitening" (see Kang et al. 2016).

[16] This early community quickly outgrew the Al Rashid mosque. It was later restored and moved to an historical park in 1991 (Lorenz 1998). The new Al Rashid Mosque is one of six mosques in present-day Edmonton that serve more than 20,000 Muslims (A New Life in a New Land 2015).

[17] For more on this family's settlement story in northern Alberta, please see Selby et al. 2018.

Policies aimed at curtailing religious minorities were tabled concurrently with the two World Wars. In 1914 and again in 1939, the Canadian federal government invoked the War Measures Act, which meant that certain groups—including Muslims—were closely monitored. More than 8000 so-called enemy aliens were interned as prisoners of war in remote camps across the country. In this heightened climate of securitization and incarceration, a number of Turkish Muslims returned to Turkey, as did other Muslims to their countries of origin. Immigration policies further cemented these exclusionary practices. Until 1952, Canada stated a clear preference for British Protestant immigrants. Beginning in 1967, in part in response to shame following the refusal of Jews and other refugees throughout the Second World War, the "points system" removed language detailing ethnic and religious profile preferences for immigrants. As a consequence, more non-British Protestants began to settle, including many highly educated English and French-speaking Muslim professionals.

By 1971, the Canadian Census counted over 33,000 Muslim Canadians—a substantial growth from eight, one hundred years earlier. Still, this figure reflects only 0.0015% of the total Canadian population at that time. The category "Muslim" was listed as a check box under the census' question of religious affiliation only in 1981, when Muslims numbered approximately 100,000, again a substantial leap from a decade earlier (Bryant 2001). Arguably, the introduction of the Muslim tick box on the census questionnaire may have granted the category some social legitimacy and may have encouraged Muslim Canadians to self-identity. Like today, most of the Muslim Canadian population in this decade lived in the provinces of Ontario, Quebec, and Alberta (Abu-Laban 1983).

Increased immigration and greater diversity in the backgrounds of Canadian Muslims in these decades were also bolstered by a federal government policy of "multiculturalism" that was followed by the Multiculturalism Act. In theory, the 1971 policy and 1988 Act were intended to foster commonality while nurturing cultural group differences.[18] Also significant in setting a new tone toward immigration and religious minorities was the introduction of the Charter of Rights and Freedoms in 1982. Again, in theory, the Charter aimed to promote diversity and the protection of religious minorities. At the same time, on a whole, the socio-political climate in Canada in this period was largely indifferent to visible Muslimness. McDonough and Hoodfar (2009, p. 133) note that "before the 1980s, Muslims in Canada lived in a society that was largely ignorant of Islam, but generally hospitable." At the same time, scholarly work on Muslims in Canada similarly focused on the group's ethnic and national backgrounds rather than religion per se.[19] This apa-

---

[18] A number of scholars have critiqued these initiatives, noting the policy's silence related to Canada's colonialist roots and Indigenous worldviews, so that they promote racism and exclusion (see Bannerji 2000; Yegenoglu 2003; Bissoondath 2011; Haque 2012).

[19] Kashmeri's (1991) book examines the impact of the 1990–1991 Gulf War on Canadian Arabs; Hennebry and Momani's (2013) edited volume further examines the stigmatized experiences of Arab Canadians. Buckridan (1994) investigates Muslims from Trinidad. Dossa (1994) offers a case study of elderly Ismaili Canadians. McLaren (1999) turns to Indonesian Muslims in Canada. Berns McGown (1999) considers the transnational lives of Somalis in London and Toronto. Eid (2003,

Table 1 Muslims as a proportion of Canada's total population, by year

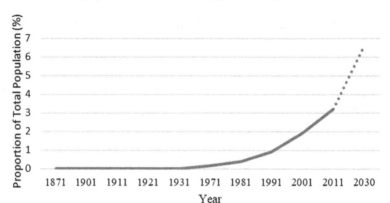

thy toward Muslimness shifted with the Iranian Revolution in 1979. Scholarship and political attention accorded to Muslims changed. Indeed, if in the 1960s and 1970s immigrant communities in Canada were studied through the lenses of race and ethnicity, with the Iranian Revolution (and later, 9/11), attention was aimed at these same individuals' expressions of religiosity. Muslim Canadian women of different origins have since received the greatest amount of scholarly and political attention.[20]

As evidenced by Table 1,[21] many Muslims immigrated to Canada in the 1990s. A 130% population increase between 1991 and 2001 (Statistics Canada 2001) is often cited in historical chronologies. In general, arrivals in this decade held more diverse economic backgrounds and attained higher levels of education.[22] In his study of

2009) focuses on the multiple identities of second-generation Arab Canadians in Montreal. Hirji (2010) looks to South Asian youth in British Columbia. Based on qualitative data, Brahimi (2011) compares the economic integration of Algerians, Moroccans and Tunisians in Quebec.

[20] For instance, Gibb and Rothenberg (2000) compare the diasporic experiences of Harari and Palestinian women in Toronto drawing on in-depth interviews. Dossa (2002) analyzes the mental health experiences of immigrant Iranian women. Dossa (2009) also studies the migration narratives of Afghan women, and later (2014) analyzes their transnational post-war lives at home and in the Vancouver area by considering their domestic lives and cooking practices. Akter (2011) interviews Bangladeshi Muslim women on the East Coast. Hameed (2015) interviews 1.5 and 2nd generation Muslims living in Winnipeg of a variety of backgrounds. Holtmann (2016) turns to Christian and Muslim women of a variety of ethnocultural backgrounds to consider their experiences of domestic abuse.

[21] This graph includes data compiled from a number of sources: (1) baseline national population data (Statistics Canada 2011); (2) Muslim population statistics drawn from Hamdani 1999; (3) 2001 Muslim population and total population statistics (Statistics Canada 2001); (4) 2011 Muslim population and total population statistics (Statistics Canada 2011); and (5) 2030 projection statistics (PEW Research Center 2011).

[22] Along with immigrants from Syria, Lebanon, Pakistan, Bangladesh and India, a greater number of Arab Muslims immigrated during this period, particularly to Ontario and Quebec following the Iran-Iraq War (1980–1988) and the Gulf War (1990–1991) (Kaba 2002; Hussain and Scott 2012).

Muslims in the early 1990s in the nation's capital, Ahmad F. Yousif (1993) outlines five factors that drew Muslims to Ottawa (in descending order): economic advantages; educational opportunities; political alienation from native countries; family sponsorship; and notions of a freedom of faith and expression guaranteed in Canadian law. Also significant in this decade was the 1991 Canada-Quebec Accord that granted Quebec responsibility in its selection of immigrants (Hachimi Alaoui 1997, 2001). This accord meant that, concurrent with political upheaval in Lebanon and Algeria, a great deal more Muslims of Francophone origin migrated to Quebec (McAndrew 2010), largely of Maghrebian origin (Fortin et al. 2008). Between 2007 and 2011, Algerians constituted the province's highest number of migrants (Brahimi 2011). Algerians in Quebec hold the highest level of family regroupment immigration but also the highest unemployment rate (13.7% in 2006) (Brahimi 2011; Grenier and Nadeau 2011; Hachimi Alaoui 2006; Lekhal 2010; Rousseau et al. 2013).

Steady population growth of Muslim Canadians in the 1990s translated into greater institutionalization of Muslim organizations.[23] McDonough and Hoodfar (2009) note a general shift from mosque construction to the creation of "voluntary associations," which they see as reflecting the vitality and social commitments of Canadian Muslim groups. Hussain and Scott (2012) count more than 250 Islamic organizations in the Greater Toronto Area. One notable example is the volunteer-based Canadian Council of Muslim Women (CCMW), inaugurated by Lila Fahlman—politician, PhD, and recipient of the Order of Canada—in Winnipeg, Manitoba in 1982, that continues to advocate for and stimulate Islamic thinking and action across Canada.

These population demographics on Muslims in Canada do not distinguish different branches of the traditions of Islam. Historically and contemporarily, most of the Canadian population has been and remains Sunni. Shi'is have also been present in Canada since the early part of the twentieth century. Based on worldwide percentages, we can imagine they make up between 10–15% of the Muslim Canadian population. The Shi'i population grew in the 1970s with migration from troubled areas (Mamodaly and Fakirani 2012; McDonough and Hoodfar 2009),[24] as

---

Other groups fleeing persecution who arrived in Canada include refugees from Ethiopia, Eritrea, Somalia, Sudan, Albania, Kosovo, and Bosnia.

[23] Numerous Muslim organizations operate within Canada including: the Muslim Association of Canada (established in 1997), Muslim Students' Associations on university campuses (established in 1963), the Canadian Islamic Congress (founded in 1994), the Muslim Canadian Congress (established in 2001), the Canadian Council of Muslim Women (established in 1982), the Islamic Society of North America (established in 1982), and the Canadian Council on American-Islamic Relations (established in 2000), which became the National Council of Canadian Muslims in 2013. Most Muslim community organizations in Canada are located in the Greater Toronto Area, which is home to more than 60 ethno-cultural groups (Toronto Muslims 2015).

[24] The Shi'i Imami Ismai'ili community grew in 1972, when, following a Ugandan expulsion order, leader Aga Khan contacted then-Prime Minister Trudeau to negotiate the acceptance of approximately 6000 Ismai'ili refugees. An influx of Ismai'ili immigration from Kenya, Zaire, Madagascar and South Asia continued throughout the 1970s, largely to Ontario. The number of Shi'is also grew

did a smaller number of Ahmadiyyas, who, as minorities within Islam, continue to face persecution.[25] Ismai'ilis have garnered a reputation in Canada for their social activism and involvement in politics.[26] The Canadian Muslim population includes converts (Mossière 2012, 2013) who are difficult to count given how conversion is often private (i.e. not subject to the involvement of religious authorities), and due to the high numbers who are "unmosqued," or do not attend prayers in these settings (see Flower and Birkett 2014). Greater visibility of Islam in Canada has led to a higher rate of conversion, even if, as Flower and Birkett (2014) note, the contemporary era of securitization has meant that converts have been increasingly scrutinized in the media in relation to so-called radicalization. For Dina, converts, who she calls "the Canadians," referring to Canadian-born youths of mostly Christian background, serve as important "bridgers" in the local community:

> We [in the St. John's Muslim community] have some Canadians that have, like, converted. So having them around too is very good, you know. It gets the conversation going with the Muslim society and with others, as well so it's like, you know, positive.

The number of Canadian Sufis is more challenging to determine, largely because of a tendency to also attract the unmosqued, non-Muslims (who may be drawn to some orders' music, art and spirituality) and because of its at-times contested location within Islam. Some Sufi centres are associated with Turkish, South Asian and Iranian ethnic communities (see Sharify-Funk and Dickson 2013, p. 192).

Pairing Dina's narrative of daily life in St. John's, NL with this quantitative statistical data elucidates trends in Muslim migration and settlement until 2001. Dina's arrival in Canada as a student, post-1990s, with hope to settle permanently following her studies, is also emblematic.

4 Current Challenges and Future Opportunities

Islamophobia, or the irrational fear and hatred of Islam and Muslims (and those perceived as Muslim) that translates into individual, ideological (including racisms and xenophobia) and systemic forms of oppression, existed long before the 2001

---

with some fleeing Iran in the 1970s (see Khan 2008), and Iraq and Afghanistan beginning in the 1980s (Hussain and Scott 2012). Approximately 90,000 Ismai'ilis live in Canada, the majority in Quebec and Ontario, with an estimated 20,000 in Alberta (see Clive 2001).

[25] Maclean (2010) estimates there are 25,000 Ahmadis in Canada, most of whom settled as refugees after 1974 when they were declared non-Muslims in Pakistan (owing primarily to their belief in the Messianism of their founder). Canada's largest mosque, the Baitun Nur Mosque, is Ahmadi and opened in Calgary in 2008.

[26] The Global Centre for Pluralism, inaugurated by the group's spiritual leader, Aga Khan and Canada's then-Governor General Adrienne Clarkson in 2005, is located along prestigious Sussex Drive in Ottawa, Ontario. The Aga Khan Canadian Foundation is active in national political and humanitarian projects (see Aga Khan Foundation of Canada 2015).

attacks in the United States. Still, reported incidents escalated with pejorative characterizations of Islam post 9/11, as did academic writing on its impacts on Muslim life in Canada. Indeed, a growing population and public presence of Muslims in Canada coupled with world events influenced a significant (and proven) rise in Islamophobia that has continued to impact Muslim Canadians.[27] Academic interest also grew in this moment, and has been especially attentive to women's experiences,[28] related to the meanings of religious signs and interpretations of Muslim family law, including marriage and divorce.[29] Jasmin Zine's qualitative-based work (2001, 2006, 2007, 2008a, b) with attention to young hijabi women's experiences in schools signals this shift in the literature, and is an important scholarly contribution to a topic that, until then, had been rarely analyzed (with the exception of Alvi et al. 2003).

If, since 2001, Muslim women and their head-coverings have been emphasized—by scholars, in policy, and by media—Muslim men have been pejoratively scrutinized in relation to issues of securitization.[30] Peter Beyer's (2014) study of Muslim Canadian male youth draws on interviews with 35 second-generation young Muslim men to inquire about their experiences with terrorism and securitization. Beyer finds that, despite their uniform non-engagement with radicalism, that "none" is already "too much." In other words, as racialized young men, they cannot escape prejudicial and racist pigeonholing no matter what they do. A small number of cases, namely that of Canadian Omar Khadr (born 1986), held at the Guantanamo Bay detention camp for ten years,[31] and the radicalization of a group of young Muslim men in the Greater Toronto Area, who, following the largest anti-terror bust to date in Canada in 2006 (bolstered by legislation introduced post-9/11) whose

---

[27] In the wake of this heightened climate of fear and prejudice, scholars also focused their attention on the impacts of 9/11 for Muslim Canadians. For more general reflections on this impact, see: Khalema and Wannas-Jones 2003; Helly 2004a, b; Sheridan 2006; LeBlanc et al. 2008; Bakht ed. 2009; Nagra 2011a, b; and Jamil and Rousseau 2012. Razack's book, *Casting Out: The Eviction of Muslims from Western Law and Politics* (2008) considers this moment from a feminist critical race perspective.

[28] On this point, significant literature was published, including Dossa 1999, 2002; Kurd 1999; Gibb and Rothenberg 2000; Hussain 2002; Khan 2002; Lamoureux Scholes 2002; Zine 2002; Reitmanova and Gustafson 2008.

[29] See Hadj-Moussa 2004; Ruby 2004; Haddad 2005; Jafri 2005; Atasoy 2006; and al-Fartousi 2015. On de-veiling, see Kullab 2012; on marriage, including the *mahr*, forced marriage, polygamy, and Muslim divorce, see Razack 2004; Fournier 2004, 2006, 2010; Milot 2008; Korteweg 2013; Selby 2016.

[30] On the impacts of securitization on Muslims more generally, see Razack 2007; Hanniman 2008; Haggerty and Gazso 2005; Caidi and MacDonald 2008; Leuprecht and Winn 2011; Gazso and Haggerty 2009; Flatt 2012; Caidi and MacDonald 2008; Patel 2012; Jamil and Rousseau 2012; and Bramadat and Dawson (Eds.) 2014.

[31] Khadr's young age, interrogation methods, his guilty plea related to war crimes, his Canadian citizenship and a later civil suit against the Canadian government for conspiring with the U.S. in abusing his rights have been the subject to a great deal of academic study and debate (see Dore 2008; Shephard 2008; Grover 2009; Jiwani 2011, Mendes 2009; Macklin 2010; McGregor 2009, 2010; Roach 2010; Rangaviz 2011; Smith 2011; Williamson 2012).

suspects became known as the "Toronto 18," have come under media and academic spotlights (see Dawson 2014).[32] Anti-terror legislation has placed significant surveillance on Muslim and perceived-to-be Muslim Canadian men.[33]

Other public controversies that followed 9/11 have disproportionally targeted Muslim Canadians. So-called "Sharia Courts" in Ontario from 2004–2006 and a 2007 unanimously voted town charter in Hérouxville, Quebec that aligned new residents with barbaric cultural practices, elucidate these tensions. These cases—the "Sharia Debate[34]" and the "Reasonable Accommodation" commission[35]—spurred commissions, reports, and produced formal policy recommendations. In the first case, debate centred upon the availability of faith-based legally binding private family arbitration with faith leaders relying on theological arguments as arbiters. This option was made possible in that province in 1991 by a Conservative government that sought to privatize a number of programs in a cost-reducing endeavour. Faith-based arbitration (FBA) remained under the radar until 2003 when the leader of the Islamic Institute of Civil Justice (IICJ) held a press conference to announce it would hold "Sharia Courts" for "good Muslims" (Reda 2012; Selby and Korteweg 2012). As though Sharia or Islamic law were a uniform instrument, this phrasing falsely raised a spectre of the stoning of women and capital punishment. The IICJ's invocation that "Good Muslims" should use their services further cast piety in these violent shades. In response to the debate, former attorney general Marion Boyd presented a 192-page report, "Protecting Choice, Promoting Inclusion" in December

---

[32] The "Toronto 18" refers to eleven men and four youths arrested on 2 June 2006 (two others were arrested who were already serving prison terms, another was arrested two months later), accused of participating in plots to attack Parliament Hill among other locations. That these were the first arrests after the 9/11-related anti-terrorist legislation and that these threats to Canada were "home-grown" raised the spectre of radicalization.

[33] On June 20, 2014, Bill C-24 became law in Canada, allowing citizenship to be rescinded for those with dual citizenship for reasons other than fraud and without a live hearing or the right to appeal (see Adams et al. 2014). In June 2015, Bill C-51 received royal assent to become Canada's Anti-Terrorism Act. It amends the Canadian Criminal Code and broadens the mandate of the Canadian Security Intelligence Service in ways that some have argued curtails civil liberties. CSIS may now physically disrupt "acts of terrorism" and has policing power (see Forcese and Roach 2015).

[34] Much of the scholarly writing on the 2003–2005 Sharia Debate in Ontario (Khan 2005; Thornback 2005; Bakht 2006, 2007; Razack 2007; Korteweg 2008; Sharify-Funk 2009; Brown 2010, 2012; Reda 2012; Korteweg and Selby eds. 2012; Zine 2012; Razavy 2013; Selby 2013) examines the ways Muslims were represented. Potvin and Saris (2009) and Helly et al. (2011) have also examined private arbitration practices among Muslims in Montreal, and Saris and Potvin (2013) in Canada, more generally. Others have considered the impact of MPP Fatima Houda-Pepin's quickly passed motion before the Quebec provincial government to ban "sharia courts" in that province (Ibnouzahir 2015, p. 122). Most compellingly, interviews conducted with Muslims and imams in Ontario by Julie Macfarlane (2012a, b) and Christopher Cutting (2012) show that the debate's premise was erroneous: religiously based family law arbitration was not something that Canadian Muslims engaged in or that Muslim Arbitration Boards conducted.

[35] The 2007 Bouchard-Taylor commission in Quebec has also been the subject of excellent critical analysis (Brodeur 2008; Mahrouse 2010; Sharify-Funk 2010; Lefebvre and Beaman 2012; Barras 2016).

2004. The "Boyd Report" solicited positions from a number of actors, both for and against faith-based arbitration. In considering the limits of the Family Law Act, the Canadian Charter of Rights and Freedoms and the Multiculturalism Act, Boyd concluded that faith-based family law arbitration should be legally sanctioned, with some caveats. Yet, despite Boyd's careful balancing of interests, and despite studies that show imams' involvement in mediation and not arbitration (Macfarlane 2012b), in their promotion of their *Darul-Qada* (Islamic Court of Justice), the IICJ negatively monopolized the pro-side of the debate in the media.[36] Boyd's reasoning to maintain FBA in Ontario fell on deaf ears as subsequent international protests at Canadian embassies against "Sharia Courts" in September 2005 referenced patriarchal violence and human rights atrocities. With mounting international pressure, on 11 September 2005 (a Sunday, not typically reserved for government press releases), then-Ontario provincial Premier Dalton McGuinty announced: "There will be no Shariah law in Ontario. There will be no religious arbitration in Ontario. There will be one law for all Ontarians", thus barring FBA for all religious groups. The frightening image of Sharia was thus silenced and solidified. The legislature passed the family statute law amendment act in February 2006, banning FBA in Ontario. While faith-based arbitration was the central question, the debate centred upon Muslim Canadians.

In the second case, the incident in Hérouxville, a small town north of Montreal, which in part inspired the Bouchard-Taylor commission and its discussion on "reasonable accommodation," was followed by Bill 94, proposed in 2010 by the provincial Liberal Party to restrict full-face veils, a 2013 Parti Québécois-proposed Bill 60 or the "Charter of Secularism" followed (see chapter 9 by Barras for more on these proposals). This latter bill, titled "Charter affirming the values of State secularism and religious neutrality and the equality between women and men, and providing a framework for accommodation requests," proposed to limit "conspicuous" religious signs for all government personnel and made an uncovered face mandatory in providing or receiving government services. Official parliamentary debate was suspended when the Liberal Party defeated the PQ in provincial elections in April 2014, but some members of the National Assembly have pushed forward and debate remains. Notably, Charles Taylor, co-convener and co-author of the Bouchard Taylor Report (2008) that outlined recommendations in Quebec to "reasonably accommodate" religious minorities, announced, following the devastating mass shooting of six Muslim Canadian men at the end of evening prayers on 29 January 2017 at the Islamic Cultural Centre of Quebec City, that he rescinded his recommendation in the Bouchard-Taylor report that government officials like judges and crown attorneys not wear visible religious signs on the job (Hébert 2017). Proposed by the provincial Liberal Party in Quebec, Bill 62, "An Act to foster adherence to State religious neutrality and, in particular, to provide a framework for religious accommodation requests in certain bodies," was instituted in October 2017.

---

[36] Prior to this period, faith-based family law arbitration had taken place in Ontario for 14 years with no public fanfare, largely among Orthodox Jews but also among some Christian groups as well as Shi'ite Ismailis (see Boyd 2004).

The ban prohibits anyone whose face is covered (read: wearing a full-face veil) from the delivery or reception of public services and, more generally, claims it provides a more stringent framework to address religious accommodation requests in Quebec. Following a challenge launched by the National Council of Canadian Muslims and the Canadian Civil Liberties Association, on 1 December 2017, the law was suspended by Quebec Justice Babak Barin (Peritz 2017). At the time of writing, it is not yet clear whether a full constitutional challenge of the law will be heard. More generally, these legislative efforts evidence how government interest in and surveillance of publicly visible signs of Muslim religiosity have grown considerably in Quebec and in the rest of Canada in the past fifteen years.

Niqabs, face-covering garments which leave the eyes visible and with disputed links to Islamic practice and belief (i.e. some Muslims do not see them as a prescription in the tradition), have received a disproportionate amount of political and media attention in these efforts. A few flashpoints include the 2012 N.S. (an acronym to protect the claimant's identity) case regarding whether a woman could wear her niqab while testifying in a sexual assault trial,[37] and controversy around prohibiting women to wear the niqab during citizenship ceremonies and in public when dispensing or receiving government services. More specifically, the acceptability of the garment became a divisive topic of discussion during the 2015 Canadian federal election in response to the presence of Ms. Zunera Ishaq's niqab in a citizenship oath ceremony. Ishaq successfully challenged the government's 2011 policy that banned her garment in a fast-tracked decision (see *Ishaq v. Canada (Citizenship and Immigration)* 2015 FC 156; CBC News 2015). The then Canadian Prime Minister Stephen Harper voiced his opposition, saying at one point: "Why would Canadians, contrary to our own values, embrace a practice at that time that is not transparent, that is not open and frankly is rooted in a culture that is anti-women" (Chase 2015). During the same election season, the former Prime Minister also proposed the creation of a "barbaric practices" hotline to respond to violence of all kinds, presumably related to Muslims. The additional scrutiny meant that all Muslim Canadians experienced an increased gaze and, for many, discrimination and prejudice. For example, in response to this proposed phone line, *Globe and Mail* columnist Sheema Khan wrote that, "Never in 50 years have I felt so vulnerable. For the first time, I wonder if my children will have the opportunity to thrive as I did" (Khan 2015). Moreover, contrary to Harper's characterization of the putative silence of niqabi women, Ishaq spoke a great deal to the press, as did Naima Ahmed who was expelled from a government-sponsored French language class in Montreal for her face-covering garment (see Selby 2014). Lynda Clarke's (2013, p. iv) qualitative study of 81 niqab-wearing women who live primarily in Ottawa and Toronto, Ontario finds that a typical Canadian niqabi is:

[37] In a 4–2–1 split decision, the Supreme Court of Canada ruled that the courts should make determinations on the niqab on a case-by-case basis, considering the sincerity of the religious belief, trial fairness and alternative accommodations available (see Beaman 2011; Leckey 2013; Rochelle 2013; and Chambers and Roth 2014; R. v. N.S. 2012).

a married foreign-born citizen in her late twenties to early thirties who adopted the practice after arriving in Canada. Most of the women possessed a high level of education having attended university, graduate school, community college, or some form of vocational education.

In sum, most Canadian women who wear niqab are married, highly educated new immigrants who, as evidenced by Ishaq and Ahmed, are often neither quiet nor submissive.

In addition to these high-profile cases, Muslim Canadians have also received attention internationally thanks to the worldwide syndication of the Canadian Broadcasting Corporation's *Little Mosque on the Prairie* produced between 2007–2012 (examined by Anderson and Greifenhagen 2013; Dakroury 2012; Khan 2009). More generally, however, scholarly data on the Canadian media's treatment of Muslims demonstrates more negative characterizations. Karim H. Karim (2003, 2009) chronicles discrimination in media portrayals of Muslim Canadians; others have similarly pointed to misrepresentation in the country's primary media outlets (see also Zehiri 2009; Antonius 2013).

Evidence shows that Islamophobia, affects the everyday lives of Muslim Canadians. For instance, from 2000–2004, the Canadian Islamic Congress (n.d.) conducted media research reports examining anti-Islamic content in the country's eight largest daily newspapers, and noted the widespread use of terms like "Muslim extremist" and "Islamic militant" in reporting on conflicts in Muslim-majority countries. A 2002 study from the CCMW similarly demonstrates the pejorative effects of 11 September 2001 for Muslim Canadian women.[38] A 2004 CAIR.CAN (The Council on American-Islamic Relations - Canada, later the National Council of Canadian Muslims) study found that 43% of its participants knew of someone questioned by the Royal Canadian Mounted Police, the Canadian Security Intelligence Service, or local police, of whom most were of Arab origin and male.[39] These reports chart depictions in the mainstream media of Muslims as extremists, and how hijabis have received unwarranted pejorative attention and discrimination, problems at airports, and heightened securitization more generally.

Dina has had discriminatory experiences in her three years in Canada to date, whether based on racism, sexism, Islamophobia or xenophobia, as a black immigrant young woman who wears a visibly Muslim religious sign. Here she describes one "everyday" encounter with Islamophobia:

> I haven't had any moments where people have been like attacking me personally or like, you know, the religion or anything like that. But just comments that come in, and after you think about it, you're just like "Woah." (laughs) [.. .] This lady, she was like. .. I was asking for a lot of vinegar or something at the [university] dining hall for a project that we were doing in the house for a [n engineering] competition. Anyways, so she's like, "Oh what are

---

[38] Fourteen nationwide focus groups revealed a sense of horror at the terrorist attacks as well as significant distress about unfair negative stereotyping of Muslims and difficulties in travel (McDonough and Hoodfar 2009; see also Hamdani 2005)

[39] A 2002 study by the same organization also found that 56% of respondents reported anti-Muslim incident(s) in the year following September 11, 2001. 61% of respondents also reported kindness or support from friends and colleagues of other faiths in the post-9/11 period (CAIR-CAN 2004).

you gonna do with all that? Are you gonna make a bomb out of it or something?" And I really just laughed at it and left. But my friend was like, she was mad. She's like, "We're going to report her" and all that. And I don't think about things that, you know, in that way or whatever. That was just a comment and I left it. But the, she was like, "Did you hear what she said to you?' [.. .] I guess they don't realize what they are saying or sometimes they do and they're just doing it.

In this instance, Dina preferred to not engage with this cafeteria employee, but the slur was clear and angered her non-Muslim friend. Unlike a few of the other Muslims we interviewed in St. John's, Dina has not experienced an overt instance of hatred, but has encountered these kinds of micro-aggressions, in this case, when a woman working in the dining hall made a "joke" in which she implied that Dina is a terrorist. Shahzad's (2014) study of Canadian university students similarly demonstrates the multitudinous ways the "War on Terror" and its discourse of fear—which she describes as "racism, Islamophobia, and social control" (p. 467)—affect Canadian university students, no matter their religious background. Some of this hatred surfaced most recently with the January 2017 murder of six innocent Muslim men at evening prayers at the *Centre Culturel Islamique de Québec* in Quebec City. Jasmin Zine (2017) notes how a number of recent political moments, as I have sought to detail in this section, have contributed to a climate of hatred that may have motivated this violence:

> The Barbaric Cultural Practices Act and proposal for a corresponding "tip line" by Conservative MP Kellie Leitch, Bill C-51 /Anti-Terrorism Act, Security Certificates, as well as Bill 94 which sought to ban the niqab in Quebec and is now enforced through the Quebec Charter of Values (Bill 60) are among the policies that have cast Muslims as potential threats to national security and as illiberal and antithetical to "Canadian values."

Even in the most benign situations, Muslims in and of Canada are more often required to negotiate their religious difference (see Barras 2016; Jamil and Rousseau 2012).

This discrimination appears in unemployment statistics. According to 2001 Canada Census data, besides the small percentage of those who adhere to the Salvation Army (their unemployment rate is 15.7%), per capita, Muslims in Canada represent the highest unemployment rate in the country at 14.4%. On average they experience two months of unemployment every year and make $20,000 less than non-Muslim Canadians (see Kazemipur 2014). 2007 PEW data examining poverty rates in six countries (the US, France, Germany, Spain, Britain, and Canada) found the largest gap between Muslim and non-Muslim poverty rates to be in Canada (cited in Kazemipur 2014). 2016 Environics survey data confirm that, although Muslims are on average better educated than Canadian-born citizens, their rates of unemployment and underemployment are higher. The Environics study also found that more than half of its participants were very or somewhat worried about unemployment in Canada.

Two recent responses to this rise in discrimination are worth considering. First, Liberal MP Iqra Khalid tabled Motion 103 in December 2016 that sought to formally condemn Islamophobia and religious discrimination in Canada. Following debate regarding whether the private member's motion would limit free speech or single out Islam for special protection, much of it on Twitter (as Funk 2017 shows), the motion passed in March 2017. Khalid's motion calls for the condemnation of all forms of systemic racism and religious discrimination but also compels the Commons' heritage committee to develop a wide-reaching approach to address systemic racism and religious discrimination, including Islamophobia, (CBC News 2017). Second, in an attempt to show their support of mosque-attending Muslims following the Quebec City shootings, non-Muslims across Canada organized "human shields" around mosques at the Friday congregation prayers the same week. In St. John's, between 1000–2000 people surrounded the Masjid-an-Noor, and several hundred circled the on-campus chapel where students like Dina pray on Fridays (Brake 2017).

Since the shift in Canada's immigration policy in 1967, Muslim Canadians are increasingly a part of Canada's national fabric. Yet, as numerous studies and Dina's experience show, and as an inquiry that is part of 2017's Motion 103 will attempt to address, discrimination based on religiosity (real and perceived) exists in Canada. This discrimination is multifaceted. Orientalism (Said 1978), racisms, xenophobia and Islamophobia frame Muslims in Western contexts as "foreigners, subversives, and terrorists" (Beydoun Forthcoming, p.18). Suspicion or discrimination must be disproven, diminished, or disavowed by many Muslim Canadians. Even if she is not knowingly the target of overt surveillance, the disproportionate targeting of Muslim Canadians has pervasive reverberations. As Dina explains in this passage, this burden of representation or, what she calls, being forced to be an "ambassador," can weigh heavily:

> Let's say on a work term when they hire international students and you, if you're lazy they're not going to hire another international student [...] I'd be like "oh these people", you know, "they don't work." So it's the same thing with your religion or with…if you're, you know, if you're nasty to people and everything and the first thing that they think of, I dunno, let's say when they think of Dina the first thing think is that "oh this is a grumpy girl" or you know? And things like that. Then when they think of Islam, they equate it to that.

Dina insightfully captures the additional scrutiny she experiences as an "ambassador" of Islam and as a racialized international student. She explains how if she fails to be a pleasant, hard worker (i.e. if she is "lazy" and "nasty"), her presence may have pejorative effects on Muslims and/or minority students who seek similar jobs in the future. Dina's visibility thus engenders tremendous pressure. This burden of representation is rarely discussed in scholarly literature, but impacts young Canadian Muslims like Dina in immeasurable ways. Beydoun (forthcoming) outlines ways in which Muslim Americans have responded to President Trump's early mandate against Muslims, noting four forms of "Acting Muslim": confirming affiliation, conforming to a "Moderate" Muslim approach, covering up their beliefs, or outright concealing them. In her everyday life in St. John's, NL, Dina is pressured to be a "good Muslim" (Mamdani 2002) and conform to an accepted performance of a moderate Islam. A clear hurdle for the future for Muslim Canadian youths like Dina involves responding to and challenging this burden.

5 Conclusion

Much has changed for Muslim Canadians since Ali/Alex Hamilton's nineteenth-century migration to Northern Alberta from Lebanon. In 2011, Muslims made up about 3.2 percent of the Canadian population, a figure that is expected to more than double by 2030. In considering this trajectory, this chapter has sought to consider Muslim communities in Canada from a socio-historical perspective, drawing on 21-year-old Dina's narrative as a practicing Sunni Muslim of Somali origin living as an international student in St. John's. The chapter has outlined common elements of Muslim practice and belief, known as the "five pillars," how immigration and other policies and laws continue to shape the contours of religious life in Canada, with heightened impacts for racialized minority traditions.

6 Questions for Critical Thought

1. How has Canadian immigration policy shaped the Canadian Muslim population?
2. What elements of Canadian public life impede and/or encourage expressions of the five pillars of Islam?
3. Does the Canadian context impact Muslim theology? Consider the notions of *fiqh* (Islamic jurisprudence) for minorities and "imam shopping" in Ontario.
4. How has knowledge production (or, the stuff written from an academic perspective) on Muslim Canadians shifted alongside geopolitical events?
5. Imagine yourself in Dina's position as racialized religious minority and as a foreign student in a university cafeteria. How would you respond to the cafeteria worker's question, "Are you gonna make a bomb out of it or something?" Should there be in/formal implications for individuals who employ this kind of language?

7 Online Teaching and Learning Resources

Canada's oldest mosque (http://alrashidmosque.ca) has transformed since it was first inaugurated in 1938. This website includes interactive information and documentary footage about the Alberta community's history as well as links to its offered services in education, counselling, banquet and funerary services, among others.

Carleton University's Centre for the Study of Islam (https://carleton.ca/islam-studies/), the University of Toronto's Institute for Islamic Studies (http://iis.utoronto.ca), and McGill's Institute for Islamic Studies (http://www.mcgill.ca/islamicstudies/) are three examples of Canadian academic centres that focus on the study of Islam.

Formerly known as CAIR-CAN (The Council on American-Islamic Relations - Canada) until 2013, the National Council of Canadian Muslims (https://www.nccm. ca) is a Muslim civil liberties activist organization. Its website features some of its publications, as well as its ongoing work in human rights and media advocacy.

The Canadian Anti-Islamophobia Collective (*Collectif Canadien Anti-Islamophobie, CCAI*) is a Quebec-based non-governmental non-for-profit organization that aims to combat Islamophobia in all its forms (http://www. islamophobiequebec.org).

The Canadian Council of Muslim Women's website (http://ccmw.com) offers a number of resources and documents related to Islam and Muslims in Canada. As a non-profit organization, more generally, the CCMW aims to promote Muslim women's identities and rights in Canada.

Me and the Mosque (NFB 2005) is a Canadian documentary by Zarqa Nawaz, who also created *Little Mosque on the Prairie* for the Canadian Broadcast Corporation, that examines sexual segregation in Canadian mosques (https://www. nfb.ca/film/me_and_mosque/).

8   Suggestions for Further Reading

Dossa, P. A. (2009). *Racialized bodies, disabling worlds: storied lives of immigrant Muslim women.* Toronto: University of Toronto Press.

With consideration of the narratives of four South Asian and Iranian immigrant women with disabilities who live in metropolitan Vancouver, Dossa's ethnographic-based book examines South Asian and Iranian Muslim life in B.C., while also bridging dis-ability studies and antiracist feminist methodologies.

Kazemipur, A. (2014). *The Muslim question in Canada: A story of segmented integration.* Vancouver: University of British Columbia Press.

The Muslim Question in Canada draws primarily on large-scale survey data to map the experiences of Muslim Canadians since before Confederation. Kazemipur introduces a four-part framework—institutional, media, economic, and social/communal—to show differences in the integration of Muslims in Canada in comparison with Europe and the United States. Kazemipur convincingly demonstrates the centrality of economic discrimination in Canada.

Korteweg, A. C., & Selby J. A. (Eds.). (2012). *Debating Sharia: Islam, gender politics, and family law arbitration.* Toronto: University of Toronto Press.

This edited volume examines the international debate that followed the Islamic Institute of Civil Justice's 2004 announcement that it would open "Sharia Courts" in Ontario. The volume sets out the context for this debate and its contributors approach it from a range of methodological and disciplinary vantage points.

Macfarlane, J. (2012). *Islamic divorce in North America: A Shari'a path in a secular society.* New York: Oxford University Press.

Legal scholar Macfarlane's book examines divorce among self-defined Muslims in contemporary North America. Almost 90% of her informants (including 212 Muslim men and women in southern Ontario and a few US cities) seek out *nikahs* (Islamic marriage contracts), no matter their broader religious engagement, which explains the significance and importance of Islamic divorce. Macfarlane's book is filled with compelling narratives and practical legal suggestions.

Mossière, G. (2013). *Converties à l'islam: Parcours de femmes au Québec et en France.* Montreal: Presses de l'Université de Montréal.

Anthropologist Mossière compares Muslim female converts in contemporary Quebec and France, which includes 44 *Québécoise* converts. Nearly all of her respondents came from Catholic family backgrounds and married men who were born into Islam. Mossière convincingly situates these women's conversion experiences within a renewed, alternative model of feminism in QC, while they reconcile what they see as two worlds: the religious and the secular.

Razack, S. (2008). *Casting out: The eviction of Muslims from western law and politics.* Toronto: University of Toronto Press.

Casting Out is a compilation of essays that examine representations of Abu Ghraib, the so-called Sharia Debate, and other socio-legal instances of Islamophobia and exclusion. Razack demonstrates a constructed and exploited climate of fear and the othering of racialized communities in particular, namely through the surveillance, incarceration, and discrimination of Muslim Canadians (or those perceived to be).

Zine, J. (2008). *Canadian Islamic schools: Unraveling the politics of faith, gender, knowledge and identity.* Toronto: University of Toronto Press.

Sociologist Zine is one of the foremost scholars on Muslims in Canada. *Canadian Islamic Schools* is her first book and, based on qualitative data, focuses on her participants' ability to express their religiosity in public and Islamic schools, with attention to young hijabi women's experiences in the Greater Toronto Area.

9   Researcher Background and Connection to the Topic

Jennifer A. Selby is Associate Professor of Religious Studies and affiliate member of Gender Studies at Memorial University of Newfoundland. Her research considers Islam in contemporary France and Canada, focusing on secularization theory and taking a Muslim Studies approach. She is the author of over 20 articles and book chapters, as well as *Questioning French Secularism: Gender Politics and Islam in a Parisian Suburb* (Palgrave MacMillan, 2012), and co-editor of *Debating*

Sharia (with A. Korteweg, University of Toronto Press, 2012). Data from this chapter is drawn from research conducted with Amélie Barras and Lori G. Beaman in *Beyond Accommodation: Everyday Narratives of Muslim Canadians* (forthcoming in 2018 with the University of British Columbia Press).

References

A New Life in a New Land. (2015). *A new life in a new land: Documentary series*. Retrieved from http://www.anewlife.ca/documentary

Abu-Laban, B. (1983). The Muslim Canadian Community: The Need for the New Survival Strategy. In E. H. Waugh, B. Abu-Laban, & R. B. Qureshi (Eds.), *The Muslim Community in North America* (pp. 75–93). Edmonton: University of Alberta Press.

Aga Khan Foundation of Canada. (2015). *Aga Khan Foundation of Canada*. Retrieved from http://www.akfc.ca/en/

Akter, N. (2011). *The Religious Lives of Immigrant Muslim Women in Canada: The Case of Bangladeshi Women in St. John's*. St. John's: Lambert Academic Publishing.

Al-Fartousi, M. (2015). Enhancing contextualized curriculum: Integrated identity in young Shi'i Muslim Arabic-Canadian students' social worlds. *Journal of Curriculum Studies, 48*(2), 1–33.

Alvi, S. S., Hoodfar, H., & McDonough, S. (Eds.). (2003). *The Muslim veil in North America: Issues and debates*. Toronto: Canadian Women's Press.

Anderson, B., & Greifenhagen, F. V. (2013). Covering up on the Prairies: Gender, Muslim identity and security perception in Canada. In E. Tarlo & A. Moores (Eds.), *Islamic fashion and anti-fashion in Europe and North America* (pp. 55–72). London: Bloomsbury Publishing.

Antonius, R. (2013). L'islam intégriste, l'hostilité à l'immigration, et la droite nationaliste : quels rapports? In R. Antonius, P. Toussaint, & M. Labelle (Eds.), *Les nationalismes québécois face à la diversité ethnoculturelle* (pp. 107–123). Montreal: Éditions de l'IEIM.

Atasoy, Y. (2006). Governing women's morality: A study of Islamic veiling in Canada. *European Journal of Cultural Studies, 9*(2), 203–221.

Bakht, N. (2006). Were Muslim barbarians really knocking on the gates of Ontario?: The religious arbitration controversy: Another perspective. *Ottawa Law Review 40th Anniversary Edition, 40*, 67–82.

Bakht, N. (2007). Religious arbitration in Canada: Protecting women by protecting them from religion. *Canadian Journal of Women and the Law, 19*(1), 119–144.

Bakht, N. (Ed.). (2009). *Belonging and banishment: Being Muslim in Canada*. Toronto: TSAR Publications.

Bannerji, H. (2000). *The dark side of the nation: Essays on multiculturalism, nationalism, and gender*. Toronto: Canadian Scholars' Press.

Barras, A. (2016). Exploring the intricacies and dissonances of religious governance: The case of Quebec and the discourse of request. *Critical Research on Religion, 4*(1), 57–71.

Barras, A., Selby, J., & Beaman, L. G. (2016). Religion as visible and invisible in public institutions: Canadian Muslim public servants. In B. L. Berger & R. Moon (Eds.), *Religion and the exercise of public authority* (pp. 95–110). Oxford: Hart Publishing.

Beaman, L. G. (2011). "It was all slightly unreal": What's wrong with tolerance and accommodation in the adjudication of religious freedom? *Canadian Journal of Women and Law, 23*(2), 442–463.

Berns McGown, R. (1999). *Muslims in the diaspora: The Somali communities of London and Toronto*. Toronto: University of Toronto Press.

Beydoun, K. A. (n.d.). "Acting Muslim." *Harvard Civil Rights – Civil Liberties Law Review*. (Forthcoming).

Beyer, P. (2014). Securitization and young Muslim males: Is none too many? In P. Bramadat & L. Dawson (Eds.), *Religious radicalization and securitization in Canada and beyond* (pp. 121–144). Toronto: University of Toronto Press.

Bissoondath, N. (2011). *Digging up the mountains*. Toronto: McClelland and Stewart.

Boyd, M. (2004). *Dispute resolution in family law: Protecting choice, promoting inclusion*. Office of the Attorney General of Ontario. Retrieved from https://www.attorneygeneral.jus.gov.on.ca/english/about/pubs/boyd/

Brahimi, L. (2011). *L'intégration Économique des Immigrants Maghrébins du Québec: Le cas des Algériens, Marocains et Tunisiens* (Master's Thesis). Montréal: Université de Québec.

Brake, J. (2017, February 3). People form "human shield" around St. John's Mosque. *The Independent*. Retrieved from http://theindependent.ca/2017/02/03/people-form-human-shield-around-st-johns-mosque/

Bramadat, P., & Dawson, L. (Eds.). (2014). *Religious radicalization and securitization in Canada and beyond*. Toronto: University of Toronto Press.

Brodeur, P. (2008). La commission Bouchard-Taylor et la perception des rapports entre "Québécois" et "musulmans" au Québec. *Cahiers de recherche sociologique, 46*, 95–107.

Brown, A. (2010). Constructions of Islam in the context of religious arbitration: A consideration of the "Shari'ah Debate" in Ontario, Canada. *Journal of Muslim Minority Affairs, 30*(3), 343–356.

Brown, A. (2012). Managing the mosaic: The work of form in "Dispute resolution in family law: Protecting choice, promoting inclusion". In A. C. Korteweg & J. A. Selby (Eds.), *Debating sharia: Islam, gender politics and family law arbitration* (pp. 329–350). Toronto: University of Toronto Press.

Bryant, D. M. (2001). *Religion in a new key*. Kitchener: Pandora Press.

Buckridan, R. (1994). *Trinidad Muslims in Canada: A community in transition* (Master's Thesis). University of Ottawa.

Bunting, A., & Mokhtari, S. (2007). Migrant Muslim women's interests and the case of "Sharia Tribunals" in Ontario. In V. Agnew (Ed.), *Racialized migrant women in Canada: Essays on health, violence, and equity* (pp. 233–264). Toronto: Toronto University Press.

Caidi, N., & MacDonald, S. (2008). Information practices of Canadian Muslims post-9/11. *Ceris Policy Matters, 34*, 1–15.

Canadian Council of Imams. (2012). *Canadian Council of Imams*. Retrieved from http://www.canadiancouncilofimams.com/

Canadian Islamic Congress. (n.d.). *CIC media research reports 2001–2004*. Retrieved from: http://www.canadianislamiccongress.com/rr/rr_index.php

CBC News. (2015, October 9). Zunera Ishaq, who challenged ban on niqab, takes citizenship oath wearing it. *CBC News*. Retrieved from http://www.cbc.ca/news/politics/zunera-ishaq-niqab-ban-citizenship-oath-1.3257762

CBC News. (2017, March 23). House of commons passes anti-Islamophobia motion. *CBC News*. Retrieved from http://www.cbc.ca/news/politics/m-103-islamophobia-motion-vote-1.4038016

Chambers, L., & Roth, J. (2014). Prejudice unveiled: The niqab in court. *Canadian Journal of Law and Society, 29*(3), 381–395.

Chase, S. (2015, March 11). "Niqabs rooted in a culture that is anti-women" Harper says. *The Globe and Mail*. Retrieved from http://www.theglobeandmail.com/news/politics/niqabs-rooted-in-a-culture-that-is-anti-women-harper-says/article23395242/

Clarke, L. (2013). *Women in niqab speak: A study of the niqab in Canada*. Canadian Council of Muslim Women. Retrieved from Canadian Council of Muslim Women. http://ccmw.com/wpcontent/uploads/2013/10/WEB_EN_WiNiqab_FINAL.pdf

Council on American-Islamic Relations Canada (CAIR-CAN). (2004). *Presumption of guilt: A national survey on security visitations of Canadian Muslims*. (No longer available online).

Cutting, C. (2012). Faith-based arbitration or religious divorce: What was the issue? In A. C. Korteweg & J. A. Selby (Eds.), *Debating Sharia: Islam, gender politics and family law arbitration* (pp. 66–87). Toronto: Toronto University Press.

Dakroury, A. (2012). Towards media reconstruction of the Muslim imaginary in Canada: The case of the Canadian broadcasting Corporation's sitcom Little Mosque on the prairie. In J. Zine (Ed.), *Islam in the hinterlands: A Canadian Muslim studies anthology* (pp. 1–18). Vancouver: University of British Columbia Press.

Dawson, L. (2014). Trying to make sense of home-grown terrorist radicalization: The case of the Toronto 18. In P. Bramadat & L. Dawson (Eds.), *Religious radicalization and securitization in Canada and beyond* (pp. 64–91). Toronto: University of Toronto Press.

Dore, C. L. (2008). What to do with Omar Khadr—Putting a child soldier on trial: Questions of international law, juvenile justice, and moral culpability. *The John Marshall Law Review, 41*(4), 1281–1320.

Dossa, P. A. (1994). Critical anthropology and life stories: Case study of elderly Ismaili Canadians. *Journal of Cross-Cultural Gerontology, 9*(3), 335–354.

Dossa, P. A. (1999). (Re)imagining aging lives: Ethnographic narratives of Muslim women in diaspora. *Journal of Cross-Cultural Gerontology, 14*(3), 245–272.

Dossa, P. A. (2002). Narrative mediation of conventional and new "Mental Health" paradigms: Reading the stories of immigrant Iranian women. *Medical Anthropology Quarterly, 16*(3), 341–359.

Dossa, P. A. (2009). *Racialized bodies, disabling worlds: Storied lives of immigrant Muslim women.* Toronto: University of Toronto Press.

Dossa, P. A. (2014). *Afghanistan remembers: Gendered narrations of violence and culinary practices.* Toronto: University of Toronto Press.

Eid, P. (2003). The interplay between ethnicity, religion, and gender among second-generation Christian and Muslim Arabs in Montreal. *Canadian Ethnic Studies, 35*(2), 30–61.

Eid, P. (2007). *Being Arab: Ethnic and religious identity building among second generation youth in Montreal.* Montreal/Kingston: McGill-Queens University Press.

Eid, P. (2009). La ferveur religieuse et les demandes d'accommodement religieux. Une comparaison intergroupe. In *Appartenances religieuses, appartenance citoyenne. Un équilibre en tension* (pp. 283–323). Québec: Les Presses de l'Université Laval.

Environics Institute. (2016, April). *Survey of Muslims in Canada 2016.* Retrieved from http://www.environicsinstitute.org/uploads/instituteprojects/survey%20of%20muslims%20in%20canada%202016%20-%20final%20report.pdf

Fischer, J. (2011). *The Halal frontier: Muslim consumers in a globalized market.* New York: Palgrave Macmillan.

Flatt, J. (2012). The security certificate exception: A Media Analysis of Human Rights and Security Discourses in Canada's Globe and Mail and National Post. In J. Zine (Ed.), *Islam in the Hinterlands: Muslim Cultural Politics in Canada* (pp. 239–271). Vancouver: UBC Press.

Flower, S. & Birkett, D. (2014). *(Mis) understanding Muslim converts in Canada: A critical discussion of Muslim converts in the contexts of security and society.* Canadian Network for Research on Terrorism, Security, and Society: Working Paper Series, 14(06).

Forcese, C., & Kent, R. (2015). Legislating in fearful and politicized times: The limits of bill C-51's disruption powers in making us safer. In M. I. Edward & J. T. Stephen (Eds.), *After the Paris attacks: Responses in Canada, Europe, and Around the Globe,* (pp. 141–58). Toronto: University of Toronto Press.

Fortin, S., LeBlanc, M. N., & Le Gall, J. (2008). Entre la oumma, l'ethnicité et la culture: le rapport à l'islam chez les musulmans francophones de Montréal. *Diversité urbaine, 8*(2), 99–134.

Fournier, P. (2004). The reception of Muslim family law in western liberal states. *The Canadian Council of Muslim Women.* Retrieved from http://archive.ccmw.com/documents/PositionPapers/pascale_paper.pdf

Fournier, P. (2006). In the (Canadian) shadow of Islamic law: Translating Mahr as a bargaining endowment. *Osgoode Hall Law Journal, 44*(4), 649–677.

Fournier, P. (2010). *Muslim marriage in western courts: Lost in transplantation.* Farnham: Ashgate.

Funk, C. (2017). The 50 most tweeted words in #M103 tell a story about contemporary Islamophobia in Canada. *Tessellate Institute*. Retrieved from http://tessellateinstitute.com/wp-content/uploads/2017/03/Article-M103-Cory-Funk-5.pdf

Gazso, A., & Haggerty, K. (2009). Public Opinion about Surveillance in Post 9/11 Alberta: Trading Privacy for Security? In S. Rollings- Magnusson (Ed.), *Anti-Terrorism, Security, and Insecurity after 9/11*, (pp. 141–59). Halifax: Fernwood Publishing.

Gibb, C., & Rothenberg, C. (2000). Believing women: Harari and Palestinian women at home and in the Canadian diaspora. *Journal of Muslim Minority Affairs, 20*(2), 243–259.

Grenier, G., & Nadeau, S. (2011). Immigrant access to work in Montreal and Toronto. *Canadian Journal of Regional Science/Revue canadienne des sciences régionales, 1*(1), 19–33.

Grover, S. (2009). Canada's refusal to repatriate a Canadian citizen from Guantanamo Bay as a violation of the humanitarian values underlying the principle of non-refoulement: A reanalysis of Omar Ahmed Khadr v the Prime Minister of Canada. *High Court Quarterly Review, 5*(2), 42–48.

Hachimi Alaoui, M. (1997). L'exil des Algériens au Québec. *Revue Européenne des Migrations Internationales, 13*(2), 197–215.

Hachimi Alaoui, M. (2001). "Exilés" ou "Immigrés"? Regards croisés sur les Algériens en France et au Québec. *Confluences Méditerranée, 39*, 167–178.

Hachimi Alaoui, M. (2006). Carrière brisée, carrière de l'immigrant. L'expérience montréalaise. *Diversité urbaine, 1*(5), 111–123.

Haddad, Y. (2005). The study of women in Islam and the west: A select bibliography. *Hawwa, 3*(1), 111–157.

Hadj-Moussa, R. (2004). Femmes musulmanes au Canada: altérité, paroles et politique de l'action. *Revue Canadienne de Sociologie, 41*(4), 397–418.

Haggerty, K., & Gazso, A. (2005). Seeing beyond the ruins: Surveillance as a response to terrorist threats. *Canadian Journal of Sociology, 30*(2), 169–187.

Hamdani, D. (1999). Canadian Muslims on the eve of the twenty-first century. *Muslim Minority Affairs, 19*(2), 197–209.

Hamdani, D. (2005, March). Triple jeopardy: Muslim women's experience of discrimination. *Canadian Council of Muslim Women*. Retrieved from http://archive.ccmw.com/publications/triple_jeopardy.pdf

Hamdani, D. (2015, March 29). Canadian Muslims: A statistical review. *The Canadian Dawn Foundation*. Retrieved from http://youthblast.ca/wp-content/uploads/2015/06/Canadian-Muslims-A-Statistical-Review-Final.pdf

Hameed, Q. (2015). *Grassroots Canadian Muslim identity in the Prairie City of Winnipeg: A case study of 2nd and 1.5 Generation Canadian Muslims*. Master's Thesis, University of Ottawa.

Hanniman, W. (2008). Canadian Muslims, islamophobia and national security. *International Journal of Law Crime and Justice, 36*(4), 271–285.

Haque, E. (2012). *Multiculturalism within a bilingual framework: Language, race, and belonging in Canada*. Toronto: University of Toronto Press.

Hébert, C. (2017, February 16). What took Charles Taylor so long to reverse his position on Quebec's religious restrictions? *The Toronto Star*. Retrieved from https://www.thestar.com/news/canada/2017/02/16/what-took-charles-taylor-so-long-to-reverse-his-position-on-quebecs-religious-restrictions-hbert.html

Hefner, R. W. (1998). Multiple modernities: Christianity, Islam, and Hinduism in a globalizing age. *Annual Review of Anthropology, 27*(1998), 83–104.

Helly, D. (2004a). Le traitement de l'islam au Canada. Tendances actuelles. *Revue Européenne des Migrations Internationales, 20*(1), 47–71.

Helly, D. (2004b). Flux migratoires des pays musulmans et discrimination de la communauté islamique au Canada. In U. Manço (Ed.), *L'islam entre discrimination et reconnaissance. La présence des musulmans en Europe occidentale et en Amérique du Nord* (pp. 257–288). Paris: L'Hamattan.

Helly, D., Scott, V., Hardy-Dussault, M., & Ranger, J. (2011). Droit familial et parties "musul-manes": des cas de kafalah au Québec, 1997–2009. *McGill Law Journal, 56*(4), 1057–1112.

Hennebry, J., & Momani, B. (Eds.). (2013). *Targeted transnationals: The state, the media, and Arab Canadians*. Vancouver: University of British Columbia Press.

Hirji, F. (2010). *Dreaming in Canadian: South Asian youth, Bollywood, and belonging*. Vancouver: University of British Columbia Press.

Holtmann, C. (2016). Christian and Muslim immigrant women in the Canadian Maritimes: Considering their strengths and vulnerabilities in responding to domestic violence. *Studies in Religion Sciences Religieuses, 45*(3), 397–414.

Hussain, S. (2002). Voices of Muslim women: A community research project. *Canadian Council of Muslim Women*. Retrieved from http://ccmw.com/wp-content/uploads/2014/04/Voices-of-Muslim-Women.pdf

Hussain, A., & Scott, J. S. (2012). Muslims. In J. S. Scott (Ed.), *The religions of Canadians* (pp. 167–218). Toronto: Toronto University Press.

Ibnouzahir, A. (2015). *Chroniques d'une musulmane indignée*. Montreal: Éditions Fides.

Ishaq v. Canada (Citizenship and Immigration). (2015). No. T-75-14, FC 156. Retrieved from https://www.canlii.org/en/ca/fct/doc/2015/2015fc156/2015fc156.html

Jafri, I. (2005). Muslim women's equality rights in the justice system: Gender, religion and plural-ism. *The Canadian Council of Muslim Women*. Retrieved from http://ccmw.com/wp-content/uploads/2014/04/Public-Policy-Workshop-Report.pdf

Jamil, U., & Rousseau, C. (2012). Subject positioning, fear, and insecurity in south Asian Muslim communities in the war on terror context. *Canadian Review of Sociology, 49*(4), 370–388.

Jiwani, Y. (2011). Race, gender, and the "War on Terror". *Global Media Journal: Canadian Edition, 4*(2), 13–31.

Jouili, J. S. (2015). *Pious practice and secular constraints: Women in the Islamic revival in Europe*. Stanford: Stanford University Press.

Kaba, L. (2002). Americans discover Islam through the Black Muslim experience. In J. A. Melton & M. A. Kőszegi (Eds.), *Islam in North America: A sourcebook* (pp. 25–33). New York: Garland Publishing.

Kang, S. K., DeCelles, K. A., Tilcsik, A., & Jun, S. (2016). Whitened résumés. *Administrative Science Quarterly, 61*(3), 469–502.

Karim, K. H. (2003). *Islamic peril: Media and global violence*. Montreal: Black Rose Books.

Karim, K. H. (2009, February 26). *Changing perceptions of Islamic authority among Muslims in Canada, the United States and the United Kingdom*. Institute for Research on Public Policy. Retrieved from http://irpp.org/research-studies/choices-vol15-no2/

Kashmeri, Z. (1991). *The Gulf within: Canadian Arabs, racism and the Gulf War*. Toronto: James Lorimer & Company Ltd.

Kazemipur, A. (2014). *The Muslim question in Canada: A story of segmented integration*. Vancouver: University of British Columbia Press.

Khalema, N. E., & Wannas-Jones, J. (2003). Under the prism of suspicion: Minority voices in Canada post September 11. *Journal of Muslim Minority Affairs, 23*(11), 25–39.

Khan, S. (2002). *Aversion and desire: Negotiating Muslim female identity in the diaspora*. Toronto: Women's Press.

Khan, A. (2005). Interaction between Shariah and international law in arbitration. *Chicago Journal of International Law, 6*(2), 791–802.

Khan, A. (2008). *Where hope takes root: Democracy and pluralism in an interdependent world*. Toronto: Douglas and McIntyre.

Khan, S. (2009). *Of hockey and hijab: Reflections of a Canadian Muslim woman*. Toronto: Mawenzi House Publishers.

Khan, S. (2015, October 7). Fifty years in Canada and now I feel like a second class citi-zen. *The Globe and Mail*. Retrieved from http://www.theglobeandmail.com/opinion/fifty-years-in-canada-and-now-i-feel-like-a-second-class-citizen/article26691065/

Korteweg, A. C. (2008). The Sharia Debate in Ontario: Gender, Islam, and representations of Muslim women's agency. *Gender & Society, 22*(4), 434–454.

Korteweg, A. C. (2013). The Dutch "Headrag Tax" proposal: The symbolic and material consequences of impossible laws. *Social Identities, 19*(6), 759–774.

Korteweg, A., & Selby, J. (Eds.). (2012). *Debating Sharia: Islam, gender politics, and family law arbitration*. Toronto: University of Toronto Press.

Kullab, S. (2012). The politics of deveiling: Manal Hamzeh and the hijab cycle. *Women in Theatre, 1*(3). Retrieved from http://jps.library.utoronto.ca/index.php/wit/article/view/19175/15920

Kurd, R. (1999). *Reading rights: A woman's guide to the law in Canada*. Retrieved from http://ccmw.com/get-resources/ccmw-publications/

Labelle, M., & Rocher, F. (2009). Immigration, integration and citizenship policies in Canada and Quebec: Tug of war between competing societal projects. In R. Zapata-Barrero (Ed.), *Immigration and self-government of minority nations* (pp. 57–85). Bruxelles: Peter Lang.

Lamoureux Scholes, L. (2002). The Canadian Council of Muslim Women. *Journal of Muslim Minority Affairs, 22*(2), 413–425.

LeBlanc, M. N., Le Gall, J., & Fortin, S. (2008). Être musulman en Occident après le 11 septembre : Présentation. *Diversité urbaine, 8*(2), 5–11.

Leckey, R. (2013). Family law and the Charter's first 30 years: An impact delayed, deep, and declining but lasting. *Canadian Family Law Quarterly, 32*(1), 21–52.

Lefebvre, S., & Beaman, L. G. (2012). Protecting gender relations: The Bouchard-Taylor comission and the equality of women. *Canadian Journal for Social Research, 2*(1), 95–104.

Lekhal, K. (2010, May 16). *L'immigration maghrébine de Montréal: Au regard de la dette*. Lyon: Université Lumière Lyon II.

Leuprecht, C., & Winn C. (2011). What do Muslim Canadians want? The clash of interpretations and opinions. In *True North in public policy*. https://www.macdonaldlaurier.ca/files/pdf/What-Do-Muslim-Canadians-Want-November-1-2011.pdf

Lorenz, A. W. (1998). Canada's pioneer mosque. *Aramco World, 49*(4), 28–31.

Macfarlane, J. (2012a). *Islamic divorce in North America: A Shari'a path in a secular society*. New York: Oxford University Press.

Macfarlane, J. (2012b). *Understanding trends in American Muslim divorce and marriage: A discussion guide for families and communities*. Institute for Social Policy and Understanding. Retrieved from http://ispu.org/pdfs/ISPU%20Report_Marriage%20II_MacfarlaneWEB.pdf

Macklin, A. (2010). Comment on Canada (Prime Minister) v. Khadr (2010). *Supreme Court Law Review, 51*, 295–331.

Maclean, D. (2010). Religion, ethnicity, and the double diaspora of Asian Muslims. In L. DeVries, D. Baker, & D. Overmyer (Eds.), *Asian religions in British Columbia* (pp. 64–84). Vancouver: University of British Columbia Press.

Mahmood, S. (2001). Rehearsed spontaneity and the conventionality of ritual: Disciplines of *salāt*. *American Ethnologist, 28*(4), 827–853.

Mahmood, S. (2005). *The politics of piety: The Islamic revival and the feminist subject*. Princeton: Princeton University Press.

Mahrouse, G. (2010). "Reasonable accommodation" in Québec: The limits of participation and dialogue. *Race and Class, 52*(1), 85–96.

Mamdani, M. (2002). Good Muslim, bad Muslim: A political perspective on culture and terrorism. *American Anthropologist, 104*(3), 766–775.

Mamodaly, A., & Fakirani, A. (2012). Voices from Shia Imami Ismaili Nizari Muslim women: Reflections from Canada on past and present gendered roles in Islam. In T. Lovat (Ed.), *Women in Islam: Reflections on historical and contemporary research* (pp. 213–236). New York: Springer.

McAndrew, M. (2010). The Muslim community and education in Quebec: Controversies and mutual adaptation. The education of Muslim minority students: Comparative perspective, *Journal of International Migration and Integration*, special edition, *11*(1), 41–58.

McDonough, S., & Hoodfar, H. (2009). Muslims in Canada: From ethnic groups to religious community. In P. Bramadat & D. Seljak (Eds.), *Religion and ethnicity in Canada* (pp. 133–153). Toronto: University of Toronto Press.

McGregor, L. (2010). Are declaratory orders appropriate for continuing human rights violations? The case of Khadr v Canada. *Human Rights Law Review*, 1–17.

McLaren, K. (1999). *Indonesian Muslims in Canada: Religion, ethnicity and identity* (Master's Thesis). Ottawa: University of Ottawa.

Mendes, E. P. (2009). Dismantling the clash between the prerogative power to conduct foreign affairs and the Charter in Prime Minister of Canada et al v. Omar Khadr. *National journal of constitutional law/Revue nationale de droit constitutionnel, 26*(1), 67–83.

Milot, J.-R. (2008). La polygamie au nom de la religion au Canada: L'islam est-il en cause? *Cahiers de recherche sociologique, 46*, 123–133.

Mossière, G. (2012). Religion in Québec and otherness at home: New wine in old bottles? *Quebec Studies, 52*, 95–110.

Mossière, G. (2013). *Converties à l'islam: Parcours de femmes au Québec et en France*. Montreal: Presses de l'Université de Montréal.

Nagra, B. (2011a). *Unequal citizenship: Being Muslim and Canadian in the post 9/11 era* (PhD Thesis). University of Toronto.

Nagra, B. (2011b). "Our faith was also hijacked by those people": Reclaiming Muslim identity in Canada in a post-9/11 era. *Journal of Ethnic and Migration Studies, 37*(3), 425–441.

Patel, S. (2012). The anti-terrorism act and national security: Safeguarding the nation against uncivilized Muslims. In J. Zine (Ed.), *Islam in the hinterlands: Muslim cultural politics in Canada* (pp. 272–298). Vancouver: UBC Press.

Peritz, I. (2017, December 1). Quebec judge stays controversial face-cover law bill 62. *The Globe and Mail*. Retrieved from https://www.theglobeandmail.com/news/politics/quebec-judge-stays-controversial-face-cover-law-bill-62/article37169426/

PEW Research Center. (2011). *The future of the global Muslim population*. Washington, DC: Pew Research Center.

Potvin, J.-M., & Saris A. (2009). La résolution de conflits familiaux chez les Canadiennes musulmanes à Montréal: un système de justice parallèle? *Diversité urbaine, 9*,(1), 119–37.

R. v. N.S. (2012). No. 33989. Supreme Court of Canada. FC 156. Retrieved from https://scc-csc.lexum.com/scc-csc/scc-csc/en/item/12779/index.do

Rangaviz, D. (2011). Dangerous deference: The supreme court of Canada in Canada v. Khadr. *Harvard Civil Rights-Civil Liberties Law Review, 46*(2011), 253–269.

Razack, S. (2004). Imperilled Muslim women, dangerous Muslim men and civilised Europeans: Legal and social responses to forced marriages. *Feminist Legal Studies, 12*(2), 129–174.

Razack, S. (2007). "Your client has a profile": Race and national security in Canada after 9/11. *Studies in Law Politics and Society, 40*, 3–40.

Razack, S. (2008). *Casting out: The eviction of Muslims from western law and politics*. Toronto: University of Toronto Press.

Razavy, M. (2013). Canadian responses to Islamic law: The faith based arbitration debates. *Religious Studies and Theology, 32*(1), 101–117.

Reda, N. (2012). The "good" Muslim, "bad" Muslim puzzle?: The assertion of Muslim women's Islamic identity in the Sharia Debates in Canada. In A. Korteweg & J. A. Selby (Eds.), *Debating Sharia: Islam, gender politics and religious law arbitration* (pp. 231–256). Toronto: University of Toronto Press.

Reitmanova, S., & Gustafson, D. L. (2008). "They can't understand it": Maternity health and care needs of immigrant Muslim women in St. John's, Newfoundland. *Maternal Child Health Journal, 12*, 101–111.

Roach, K. (2010). "The Supreme Court at the bar of politics": The Afghan detainee and Omar Khadr cases. *National journal of constitutional law/Revue nationale de droit constitutionnel, 28*(1), 116–155.

Rochelle, S. (2013). *Whether angel or devil: Law's knowing and unknowing of veiled Muslim women in the case of R v. N.S.* (Master's Thesis). Ottawa: Carleton University. Retrieved from https://curve.carleton.ca/system/files/etd/e7d845d7-1bf2-4541-8778-8e1466591433/etd_pdf/1 53933f3fb58d595922bbe93b5deec53/rochelle-whetherangelordevillawsknowingandunknowing.pdf

Rousseau, C., Ferradji, T., Mekki-Berrada, A., & Jamil, U. (2013). North African Muslim immigrant families in Canada giving meaning to and coping with the war on terror. *Journal of Immigrant & Refugee Studies, 11*(2), 136–156.

Ruby, T. (2004). *Immigrant Muslim women and the hijab.* Community-University Institute for Social. Retrieved from https://www.usask.ca/cuisr/sites/default/files/Ruby.pdf

Saris, A., & Potvin, J. M. (2010). Canadian Muslim women and resolution of family conflicts: An empirical qualitative study (2005–2007). In S. Ferrari & R. Cristofori (Eds.), *Law and religion in the 21st century: Relations between states and religious communities* (pp. 339–347). Farnham: Ashgate.

Selby, J. A. (2013). Promoting the everyday: Pro-Sharia advocacy and public relations in Ontario, Canada's "Sharia-Debate". *Religions, 4*, 423–442.

Selby, J. A. (2014). Un/veiling women's bodies: Secularism and sexuality in full-face veil prohibitions in France and Québec. *Studies in Religion/Sciences Religieuses, 43*(3), 439–466.

Selby, J. A. (2016). "The diamond ring now is the thing": Young Muslim Torontonian women negotiating mahr on the web. In A. Masquelier & B. F. Soares (Eds.), *Muslim youth and the 9/11 generation* (pp. 189–212). Albuquerque: University of New Mexico Press.

Selby, J. A., & Korteweg, A. C. (2012). Introduction: Situating the debate in Ontario. In J. A. Selby & A. C. Korteweg (Eds.), *Debating Sharia: Islam, gender politics and family law arbitration* (pp. 12–34). Toronto: University of Toronto Press.

Selby, J. A., Barras, A., & Beaman, L. G. (2018). *Beyond accommodation: Everyday narratives of Canadian Muslims.* Vancouver: University of British Columbia Press. forthcoming.

Shahzad, F. (2014). The discourse of fear: The effects of the war on terror on Canadian university students. *American Review of Canadian Studies, 44*(4), 476–482.

Sharify-Funk, M. (2009). Representing Canadian Muslims: Media, Muslim advocacy, Organizations, and gender in the Ontario Shari'ah debate. *Global Media Journal–Canadian Edition 2*(2), 73–89.

Sharify-Funk, M. (2010). Muslims and the politics of "reasonable accommodation": Analyzing the Bouchard-Taylor report and its impact on the Canadian province of Quebec. *Journal of Muslim Minority Affairs, 30*(4), 535–553.

Sharify-Funk, M., & Dickson, W. R. (2013). Islam. In D. B. Jakobsh (Ed.), *World religions: Canadian perspectives – Western traditions* (pp. 150–200). Toronto: Nelson.

Shephard, M. (2008). *Guantanamo's child: The untold story of Omar Khadr.* New York: John Wiley & Sons.

Sheridan, L. P. (2006). Islamophobia pre- and post-September 11, 2001. *Journal of Interpersonal Violence, 21*(3), 317–336.

Smith, R. (2011). *The company one keeps: The Khadr II litigation in its international and comparative legal context* (Master's thesis). University of Toronto. Retrieved from https://tspace.library.utoronto.ca/handle/1807/31453

Statistics Canada. (2001). *Population by religion.* Retrieved from: http://www.statcan.gc.ca/tables-tableaux/sum-som/l01/cst01/demo30a-eng.htm

Statistics Canada. (2011). *2011 National Household Survey: Data table- Religion.* Retrieved from http://www12.statcan.gc.ca/nhs-enm/2011/dp-pd/dt-td/Rp-eng.cfm?LANG=E&APATH=3&DETAIL=0&DIM=0&FL=A&FREE=0&GC=0&GID=0&GK=0&GRP=0&PID=105399&PRID=0&PTYPE=105277&S=0&SHOWALL=0&SUB=0&Temporal=2013&THEME=95&VID=0

Thornback, J. (2005). The portrayal of Sharia in Ontario. *Appeal: Review of Current Law and Law Reform, 10*, 1–12.

Toronto Muslims. (2015). *Mosques. torontomuslims.com*. Retrieved from http://www.torontomuslims.com/listingcategory/mosques/

Waugh, E. (1980). The Imam in the new world: Models and modifications. In F. E. Reynolds & T. M. Ludwig (Eds.), *Transitions and transformations in the history of religions: Essays in honour of Joseph M. Kitagawa* (pp. 124–149). Brill: Leiden.

Waugh, E. (2012). Canadian Muslim perspectives on a good death in hospice and end-of-life care. In H. Coward & K. Strudjar (Eds.), *A good death in religious perspective* (pp. 77–98). New York: SUNY.

Waugh, E., & Wannas, J. (2003). The rise of a womanist movement among Muslim women in Alberta. *Studies in Contemporary Islam, 1*, 1–15.

Waugh, E., Abu-Laban, B., & Qureshi, R. (1983). *The Muslim community in North America*. Edmonton: University of Alberta Press.

Williamson, J. (Ed.). (2012). *Omar Khadr, Oh Canada*. Kingston: McGill-Queen's Press.

Yegenoglu, M. (2003). Veiled fantasies: Cultural and sexual difference in the discourse of orientalism. In R. Lewis & S. Mills (Eds.), *Feminist postcolonial theory* (pp. 542–566.) New York Routledge.

Yousif, A. F. (1993). *Muslims in Canada: A question of identity*. New York: LEGAS.

Zehiri, M. (2009). Le débat sur l'implantation de tribunaux islamiques tel que reflété par les journaux québécois La Presse et Le Devoir (2003–2005). *Laval théologique et philosophique, 65*(1), 45–54.

Zine, J. (2001). Muslim youth in Canadian schools: Education and the politics of religious identity. *Anthropology Education Quarterly, 32*(4), 399–423.

Zine, J. (2002). Muslim women and the politics of representation. *American Journal of Islamic Social Sciences, 19*(4), 1–22.

Zine, J. (2006). Unveiled sentiments: Gendered Islamophobia and experiences of veiling among Muslim girls in a Canadian Islamic school. *Equity & Excellence in Education, 39*(3), 239–252.

Zine, J. (2007). Safe havens or religious "ghettos?": Narratives of Islamic schooling in Canada. *Race, Ethnicity and Education, 10*(1), 71–92.

Zine, J. (2008a). *Canadian Islamic schools: Unravelling the politics of faith, gender, knowledge and identity*. Toronto: University of Toronto Press.

Zine, J. (2008b). Honour and identity: An ethnographic account of Muslim girls in a Canadian Islamic school. *Topia: Canadian Journal of Cultural Studies, 19*(39), 39–67.

Zine, J. (2012). Unsettling the nation: Gender, race, and Muslim cultural politics in Canada. In J. Zine (Ed.), *Islam in the hinterlands: Muslim cultural politics in Canada* (pp. 41–60). Vancouver: UBC Press.

Zine, J. (2017, February 12). The Quebec massacre, "home grown" Islamophobia & white supremacist nationalism in the "Great White North". *IRDProject*. Retrieved from https://irdproject.com/quebec-massacre-home-grown-islamophobia-white-supremacist-nationalism-great-white-north/

Atheism and Religious Nones: An Introduction to the Study of Nonreligion in Canada

Steven Tomlins

Abstract Atheism is, arguably, as old as theism, yet the sociological study of atheism is relatively new, coinciding with an increase of those who report not having a religion. The study of atheism and "religious nones" is particularly new in Canada, of which religious nones are considered the fastest growing "religion", according to Statistics Canada. This chapter presents an introduction to the study of atheism and "religious nones" in Canada. It provides context by using two historical cases (the use of blasphemy law in 1901; an immigration case from 1965) as a means of deducing popular opinion about atheists, before shifting to the contemporary with an example of ethnographic research in this area. This is followed by a discussion of key concepts, statistics, questions for reflection, current challenges, future avenues for research, and a list of online resources and references for further reading.

Keywords Atheists · Atheism · Nonreligion · Religious freedom · Supreme court of Canada · Science · Freedom of expression

1 Introduction: Narrating Nonreligion in Canada

Atheism is a term derived from the Ancient Greek word *atheos*: *a* refers to "without" or "not," and *theos* refers to "god." *Atheist* entered the English language in the sixteenth century as an accusatory term. However, today the term, in a Canadian context, usually refers to those who self-identify as not believing in the existence of god, gods, or goddesses.

Today atheists may simply call themselves "atheists" or they may go by a number of related terms that reflect nuances of their individual personalities, or emphasize a particular aspect of their identities. In fact, many atheists go by more than one of these terms. These terms include, but are certainly not limited to: agnostic, agnostic-atheist, anti-theist, apathetic, freethinker, humanist, irreligious, rationalist,

S. Tomlins (✉)
University of Ottawa, Ottawa, CA, Canada
e-mail: stoml031@uottawa.ca

© Springer International Publishing AG, part of Springer Nature 2018
C. Holtmann (ed.), *Exploring Religion and Diversity in Canada*,
https://doi.org/10.1007/978-3-319-78232-4_11

237

sceptic, and secularist. In addition, some atheists opt not to self-identify with the term atheist, due to either its negative historical connotations, or because they deem a word for something one does not believe in to be unnecessary. "Religious nones" refer to those who report on surveys that they do not have a religion.

Atheism and religious nones are the fastest growing "religion" categories in Canada, making up 23.9% of the population in 2011, according to Statistics Canada (Statistics Canada 2013). Perhaps because of this growth, scholars have been taking an increasing interest in nonreligion. Yet the history of atheism in Canada is still somewhat elusive. This chapter begins with two case studies that demonstrate how atheists were treated in the past, before moving on to an example of contemporary ethnography in this area, featuring key concepts, statistics, questions, challenges, future avenues for research, online resources, and references for further reading.

1.1   Case #1: Prosecution for Blasphemous Libel, 1901

In 1892, Canada adopted a law prohibiting blasphemous libel, essentially banning "indecent" rhetoric critical of Christianity. Although it had not been enforced since 1936, it was not until 2017 that the Federal Government took steps to remove it from the Criminal Code of Canada, where it read, "Every one who publishes a blasphemous libel is guilty of an indictable offence and liable to imprisonment for a term not exceeding two years" (*Criminal Code 1985*).

Between 1901 and 1936 there were five recorded prosecutions for blasphemous libel in Canada (*R. v. Pelletier*; *R. v. Kinler*; *R. v. Sherry*; *R. v. St. Martin*; *R. v. Rahard*), and four resulted in convictions (*R. v. Pelletier*; *R. v. Sherry*; *R. v. St. Martin*; *R. v. Rahard*). It is important to note that these cases do not necessarily involve atheist or nonreligious defendants; at least two defendants, for instance, criticized some forms of Christianity but were nonetheless Christian themselves. The use of this law does, however, point to how common atheist opinions on matters such as biblical criticism and organized religion were dealt with before the law between 1892 and 1936: simply put, the public expression of atheistic opinions was criminal. In *R. v. Pelletier* (1901), for example, the defendants pled guilty in Montreal for publishing an article that consisted of "a conversation between the author and a servant on the alleged schism between the apostles Saint Peter and Saint Paul at the beginning of Christianity, regarding the baptism of Christians" (Patrick 2008, p. 220) The judge summarized the contents of the article in harsh, but telling, terms:

> Things most sacred have been turned into jokes; sarcasm appears in every sentence in a most impious form, and, I would add, most obscene [...] It is, one feels, the creation of a libertine mind and of a spoiled heart...these expressions can be understood only as the writing of a heathen espousing evil (Patrick 2008, p. 220).

The judge believed the defendants who argued that they neither wrote nor read the article before publication, "I believe that without difficulty, for I do not believe a Canadian pen to be capable of producing such obscenities... A foreign pen must have committed this horror," (Patrick 2008, p. 221) and sentenced them in 1901 to a $100 fine. While the punishment was less severe than jail time, this case offers an example of how the Judge viewed atheism as un-Canadian, inferring that an article criticizing Christianity, by that logic, could not have been authored by a Canadian. Six decades later, however, we see a change of perception toward atheism—by judges, politicians, and the citizenry.

1.2 Case #2: Citizenship Ceremony, 1965

A suitable introduction to the case of atheist immigrants Ernest and Cornelia Bergsma and their legal battle(s) for Canadian citizenship comes from the pages of the *Ottawa Citizen*, in an article dated April 2, 1965:

> Ernest and Cornelia Bergsma live on a small southern Ontario farm. They are quiet, industrious and honest folk such as many would regard as ideal citizens.
> But they are neither citizens nor, as the law now stands, are they ideally suited to be. Mr. and Mrs. Bergsma, of Caledonia, 14 miles south of here, are atheists and because of this the law says they cannot become naturalized Canadians.
> They don't relish the controversy that now centres on them but they want to be Canadian citizens and in this they have the federal government as an ally. It has promised to aid their fight in the courts and alter the law if necessary (Ottawa Citizen, 1965).

On April 3, 1963, the Bergsmas, immigrants from the Netherlands who had been living in Canada for eight years, were informed that their applications for citizenship were denied because their open acknowledgment of being atheists demonstrated that they were not of good character, and they could not honestly comply with the oath of allegiance (Bain 1964a).

The judge found the Bergsmas' lack of faith and religion problematic. Due to the publicity this case garnered, it was subsequently reported that in previous cases judges permitted atheist citizenship applicants to omit the reference to God while making their affirmation, and Judge Leach's denial of citizenship to the Bergsmas came as a surprise to many, if not most, politicians and citizens. Like many articles from other newspapers, the *Ottawa Citizen* was supportive in tone when discussing the couple, and mentioned how they had political support, support from religious leaders, and from the public (95% of letter writers supported the couple) (Ottawa Citizen 1965).

Letters of support were not only written to newspapers, but many were also received by the Department of Citizenship and Immigration, some of which were penned by concerned non-Christian or non-believing citizenship applicants, while others came from "persons already holding Canadian citizenship, some of them born here, who have said that they do not believe in God" (Bain 1964b).

It is clear from his statements to the media and comments in the House of Commons that the head of the department surrounding this controversy, Liberal MP John Nicholson, had no intention of calling into question the suitability of atheists for citizenship, but rather, he seems to have found the Bergsmas' case at times ridiculous and frustrating, and provided public funding for their defence in the Ontario Court of Appeal.

On March 30, 1965, Nicholson addressed this matter directly in the House of Commons, announcing the government's support of the couple:

> It seems less than reasonable that Mr. and Mrs. Bergsma should be required to bear the legal costs of contesting a decision on an aspect of the legislation with which the Government is not in agreement and which, if sustained, we intend to ask parliament to change. I am sure, therefore, that hon. members will be pleased to learn that the Crown intends to pay the reasonable costs to Mr. and Mrs. Bergsma of pursuing this matter in the courts; and their legal advisor [...] is being or has been advised accordingly (*House of Commons Debates* 1965).

Tommy Douglas, Leader of the New Democratic Party and a Baptist minister, spoke after Nicholson, applauding the government's support of the Bergsmas:

> I think the country generally will applaud the minister's decision to meet the necessary costs that the Bergsmas may incur if this case is finally decided in the highest court of the land. It seems to me if we are going to have a country in which there is religious freedom, that religious freedom should extend to people who may have views which differ from those of the majority of Canadians. I think the minister has followed a very wise course, and I offer him my heartiest commendation (*House of Commons Debates* 1965).

On July 22, 1965, the Ontario Court of Appeal—in a unanimous decision — ruled that "lack of religious belief alone is not a ground upon which a citizenship court should decide against an application for citizenship," and that Mr. and Mrs. Bergsma should be deemed "desirable persons" who can take the oath of citizenship with an affirmation of allegiance rather than swearing an oath to God. (Adams 1965a). They became citizens on October 4, 1965 (Adams 1965b).

What is most noteworthy about this case is the extent of public support for atheist immigrants who wanted to become Canadian citizens. They received moral support from letter-writing citizens of both the religious and the nonreligious variety as well as newspaper editorialists, and they received moral, legal, and monetary support from the federal government.

1.3 Contemporary

Since then, some atheists have actively been involved in court cases pertaining to the removal of prayer in public schools and the removal of religious symbols from city council and court, with various degrees of success. Those cases have confirmed, however, that freedom of religion includes the freedom to not be religious; atheism is protected under law, at least in theory. Some cases, such as the Atheist Bus Campaign, which was accepted in Calgary, Toronto, and Montreal, but was banned

Fig. 1 The Atheist Bus Campaign in Ottawa

in Halifax, Vancouver, and Ottawa (the latter of which was later overturned), call that theory into question Fig. 1.

Socially, today atheists may feel equal in multicultural Canada, they may not consider their nonreligion to be an important identity trait, or they may feel misunderstood or judged negatively by the religious people in their lives. Likewise, atheists are increasingly adding their voice to news media discussions on religion and issues pertaining to religion, yet there are still the occasional headlines such as, "Dear atheists: most of us don't care what you think" (Lewis 2010), or "Could atheists please stop complaining" (Enright 2013), which would hardly be socially acceptable if the subject was a *religious* minority group.

The sociological study of atheism and religious nones is relatively new; more so the study of atheism in Canada, which presents many opportunities for future research avenues. In recent years there has been growth in atheist and nonreligious communities across the country, and there has been an increased atheist profile, from coverage of the so-called "New Atheists", court cases, and advertisement campaigns. This increased profile correlates with a statistical increase of those who report having no religion: the religious nones category of Statistics Canada doubled from 2001 to 2011.

This chapter now turns to a story based on qualitative research.

2 Living Ethnography Part I: Atheists in Church, a Story Based on the Author's Qualitative Research

Tony (a pseudonym), the President of the Atheist Community of the University of Ottawa (ACUO), was not shy about participating when the Pentecostal minister invited all church attendees who suffered from physical ailments to join him at the front to be healed. The three of us watched as Tony stood in line until it was his turn, and he complained of his sore shoulder and a knee injury. The minister said some words, blew on Tony's injured areas, and Tony raised his arms in a motion that told the crowd that it was a success: that he had just been miraculously healed! Tony strutted back to the rest of us, basking dramatically in the applause and sharing smiles and nods with all he passed!

Perhaps I should backtrack and provide some context.

I had been conducting participant-observation with the ACUO for over a year, and, although they were very cynical toward religion, they also wanted to engage with religious communities. To that extent, they participated in public "inter-faith" debates with Muslims, Christians, and Jews. They tried to organize an overnight white-water rafting trip with a Christian student group, but declined when the latter announced that it would have to be a male-only event, which the ACUO interpreted as sexist. On the other hand, the ACUO also publicly criticized religion. A stick-figure drawing on a computer of Mohammad sat on one of their club tables, which was reported on—negatively—in the university newspaper. On Reason Week (a weeklong event whereby they set up a public display in a student area in promotion of rationality and logic) they made posters and played videos mocking Christianity and Islam (these latter two incidents are described in more detail in the next section). There seemed to be two sides to the club, they (or some members) wanted to have a friendly rapport with the university community, religious people included, yet they (or some members) wanted to highlight the absurdities, and the dangers, of religious adherence. These were not necessarily contradictions, but they did point to a splintering of agenda.

During Reason Week, the ACUO held a fundraiser for the charity Doctors without Borders. If a student left their name and contact information, and that student made the highest donation, members of the ACUO would join him or her at their place of worship. Since they only received one donation, twenty dollars from a member of a local Pentecostal church, that student won.

That following Sunday I, along with four other students, one being Tony, met the Pentecostal student, an undergraduate in his early-twenties. He was a rather quiet fellow—perhaps he was nervous about bringing atheists to his church service—but everyone was friendly and polite. He was openly hoping that his guests would be inspired by God and the Holy Spirit; in reply his guests were polite and expressed that they were of open minds to experience and/or evidence, although skeptical by default. On a personal note, I was excited to visit a Pentecostal Church since I'd never been, and since I was doing ethnography with the ACUO I felt like it added another dimension to my ethnography: I was conducting participant-observation with the ACUO, who, in an unofficial (but no less valid) way, were conducting participant-observation with Pentecostal Christians!

The Pentecostal service at All Nations Church consisted mostly of worship, including speaking in tongues, urging the audience to take hold of the microphone when they felt compelled to do so by the Holy Spirit, and an apparent irregularity for that specific community: worship, or possession, through laughter. The latter was led by a minister who had a revelation about the spiritual benefit of "free-style automatic laughter". He told the congregation that he had recently been in a hot tub with some of his friends and they all started to laugh uncontrollably for some reason, until the neighbors complained. He urged the crowd to follow his lead and laugh, and since laughter is contagious we all joined in.

The event was well attended. I stood against a wall at the back by the door with the ACUO members alongside regular attendees in a darkly-lit and packed elementary school gymnasium. From the perspective of the ACUO members it was all good fun: a bit ridiculous and absurd, perhaps, but entertaining and amusing—certainly not dangerous.

The President of the ACUO was having such a good time that he voluntarily participated in the "healing" part of the service, which I summarized above. I later asked him if he was healed—he explained that he was not, but he did not want to be rude and argue with the minister; he just felt like participating ironically, and he was clearly enjoying the moment. The service ended with a communal eating of bread and drinking of grape juice.

When it was over we led our host to a bar for beer and conversation. A few other ACUO members joined us, and our host became the centre of a ton of critical questions about religion that were meant to get him to see the error of his ways, but he seemed to be about as convinced by the ACUO's "intellectual" facts as the ACUO members were by his "spiritual" rebuttals.

Overall the visit to the Pentecostal church and the bar were both quite cordial and made for a rather unique day. They also serve to highlight three important points to consider regarding the study of atheism(s):

1. If you only catch a snippet of the story, like the first paragraph, you'd have a misleading understanding of Tony, and by extension the ACUO. With any ethnography there are multiple facets to be uncovered, and the points you leave out can sometimes be just as important to the overall picture as the ones you emphasize. The chore of the ethnographer is to portray those who are studied as accurately as possible, and that often means discussing exceptions to the basic narrative.
2. This story shows a difference between Canadian and American atheism, at least in how it is reported. I have yet to read any academic articles from the United States about atheist communities politely attending a Christian church service (in this case for charity).
3. Thus, atheism is contextual. Atheism in Canada is not necessarily the same as atheism in The Kingdom of Saudi Arabia, nor is atheism in Canada necessarily the same as atheism in The United States of America. Atheism is a response, or

reaction, to theism, or theisms, and since theisms are different around the globe so too are atheisms.

3 Living Ethnography Part II: How the Author Came to Conduct Participant-Observation with an Atheist Community, and Some Insights Into that Community's Identity

As an undergraduate student I took a Religious Studies course entitled, "Interactions between Science and Religion." Whereas previously my interest in Religious Studies was directed toward gaining a better understanding of other cultures, this course sparked in me an interest in the Western philosophy of religion, as well as issues pertaining to the relationship between science and religion, such as the ongoing debate in American public schools about creationism (or Intelligent Design) and evolution. My interest in the interactions between science and religion coincided shortly thereafter with the release of new books written by self-proclaimed atheists, (principally Richard Dawkins, Daniel Dennett, Sam Harris and Christopher Hitchens), whom the media dubbed the 'New Atheists'. Reading through their works on religion I could understand why they generated such heated public interest and debate, and I became interested in their similarities and differences of opinion on matters such as secularization.

I spent two years reading books on, by, and about atheists, for my Master's thesis, which was a discourse analysis of New Atheist literature. Near the end of writing that thesis, which compared the New Atheists' arguments with each other, I started to wonder how much New Atheists had in common with 'average' Canadian atheists, or even Canadian atheist communities, for that matter. Plus, I felt that I had said just about all that I could say about New Atheism. In fact, after graduating I summarized my thesis on New Atheism into the format of a nutrition label and it was published in an American journal; see Fig. 2.

I was still interested in the topic of atheism and religious nones, but a bit dismayed that the narrative on atheism in media and academia was principally derived from authoritative figures as opposed to those without a soapbox. I wanted to know what Canadian atheists thought, or felt, about religion and atheism. For my PhD I wanted to build upon my research in contemporary atheism by venturing into how atheism played out on the 'ground' level by studying how contemporary local atheists who join atheist groups actually 'live' their atheism in a localized setting.

During my first month as a PhD student, as I took a stroll through the recruitment tables set up as part of the University of Ottawa's orientation week, I came across a table display by the newly formed Atheist Community of the University of Ottawa (ACUO). According to the President of the club (one of two people hosting the table), they had approximately a dozen members signed up.

Fig. 2 Atheism on the Shelf, first published as Steven Tomlins, 2011, "Atheism on the Shelf," Chiron Review, 96: 26, Autumn

Nutrition Facts Valeur nutritive Per 250 ml / par 250 ml	
Amount Teneur	% Daily Value % valeur quotidienne
Reason / Raison 140	
Faith / Foi 2 g	3 %
Purpose / But 1.5 g	
+ Religious / Religieux 0 g	7 %
Utopia / Utopie 5 mg	
Agnosticism / Agnosticisme 480 mg	20 %
Secularization / Sécularisation 600 mg	17%
Disrespect / Irrévérence	
Urgency / Urgence 3 g	14%
Progress / Progrès 15 g	
Science / La Science	140 %
Belief / Croyance	2 %
Pluralism / Pluralisme	6 %
Spirituality / Spiritualité	8 %

The club's president seemed welcoming and supportive when I asked him his opinion of me doing participant-observation and, eventually, soliciting interviews with club members. To me it seemed like perfect timing: I was right there at the beginning, and with permission from the group and its president, I could watch as an atheist club grew organically. With his permission orally granted, I immediately decided to focus my PhD research on the ACUO. I secured Research Ethics Board approval and performed participant-observation with them, in addition to interviews with the most active members.

Participant-observation with the ACUO proved to be quite fruitful, and I found interesting similarities and differences with accounts of other atheist clubs: particularly those south of the border. Indeed, unlike some of the American atheist organizations studied (see Smith 2013, and Cimino & Smith 2015), the ACUO was not collectively (nor, to my knowledge, individually) interested in the replication, or the replacement of religious holidays and life transition rituals or practices. However, similar to American organizations, the ACUO constructed their collective identity through public discourse, which often included criticism of religion. The club was quite active in public debates and university tabling, but internal disagreement on its identity following a few controversies with the public seems to have led to its eventual demise.

The first controversy surrounded the depiction of Mohammad. During an event called "Club Day" the ACUO had a relatively sparse table advertising its club, with the notable exception of a rather crudely drawn but otherwise unassuming or 'child-like' stick-man figure under the name "Muhammad" on a laptop. I noticed it when I stopped by, and I was told that it was a statement in support of freedom of expression in the hope that it would entice some like-minded people to join the club. This did not seem like a radical proposition since the inability to depict Muhammad visually without repercussions had by then become a freedom of speech/expression issue, particularly with the adult cartoon South Park having (at the time) recently been censored, and with the Danish Muhammad cartoon controversy still in recent memory. In covering the club tables, a reporter for the university newspaper picked up on the stick figure drawing and subsequently interviewed the president of the ACUO for an article that was published a few days later.

Members of the ACUO did not appreciate the tone of the article, which was entitled, "Athiest [sic] instigators: Muhammad makes appearance on campus," and lines like "We cannot allow the shrillest and most offensive voices to drown out a reasoned and respectful discussion" (Formosa 2011), were seen as an attack on the club. There seemed to be agreement from those discussing the topic on the ACUO Facebook page that the article needed to be rebutted, but the question was how. Some members were concerned with presentation, wishing to show the club as inclusive, while others argued for a blunt or polemical rebuttal. No members wrote anything that can be considered a criticism of the initial drawing of the stick figure itself.

Following the initial article and the flurry of online comments it received, the president of the ACUO was asked by newspaper's executive director to respond with a letter to the editor and he accepted, defending the drawing as a message about free expression:

> Freedom of speech doesn't just involve one's right to speak their mind; it also involves one's right to be exposed to the opinions of others. The moment one wishes to constrain the free expression of other people, either by implying that it may be in bad taste or by enforcing blasphemy laws [...] they are doing a disservice to themselves. (Keith 2011).

While the controversy was limited to public discussion and fizzled shortly thereafter, the incident became a focal point which informed the club's sense of shared identity, and it opened up the door to an internal questioning of their public persona.

The second controversy occurred during Reason Week, a weeklong atheism outreach and awareness event held by the ACUO. While its purpose was ostensibly to engage in dialogue and get their messages across to those who were curious (as well as gain more members), the signs the club displayed during the actual event were quite polemic, and the club's subsequent discussion of Reason Week revealed a difference of opinions in how they would like to present themselves. During Reason Week the community set up tables in a main foyer on campus, played YouTube videos (primarily of popular atheists, comedians, and science educators) on a stage that was within close proximity, and some members wore stickers that read, "Atheist (Ask Away!)". Baked goods such as dinosaur-shaped cookies were sold, and pamphlets about secularism were distributed. The club also held a "de-baptism ceremony" featuring a hair drier, and the previously discussed charity drive that gave the donor an opportunity to "bring an atheist" to his or her church, synagogue, or mosque.

As with most university clubs who have been granted permission to express their concerns or beliefs, or self-promote, through tabling, the ACUO had created some signs. Some of the signs mocked Christianity by selectively quoting the Bible ("Let the woman learn in silence with all subjection but I suffer not a woman to teach, nor to usurp authority over the man, but to be in silence! – 1 Timothy 2: 11-12. LOL u mad feminists?") and some mocked Islam ("Did the Prophet Muhammad Suffer From Schizophrenia When He Heard Voices From God? Share Your Thoughts With Us"). It was the latter sign that sparked controversy.

A Muslim student was offended by the sign questioning her Prophet's sanity, ran behind the table, and tore it down. Soon after that incident a security guard came over and told the ACUO that they had to remove all signs and cease playing videos because they had not previously been reviewed and approved by university Protection Services. The ACUO members were not happy about this, considering it an affront to freedom of expression, but they nevertheless complied and took down the signs, opting instead to hold them for the remaining hour of the event. Following Reason Week, some members wanted to remain publicly critical of religion while others preferred fostering a more tolerant public image by focusing on educating people about atheism. Others preferred that the club focus on its socialization aspects (such as meeting at a bar) over public engagement. Without unanimous agreement and with dwindling passion for future public events, the "socialization" side seemed to have won out, and without having public projects to collectively work on and bond over, members simply began meeting as friends without the need for the ACUO to act as facilitator.

During my interviews I asked members of the ACUO why they decided to join an atheist community. Unlike findings from American cases, no interviewees from the ACUO mentioned being overly concerned with the status of atheism in their country, nor did they express a desire to develop more positive atheist identities through a club. Members instead stressed the social aspects of the club; most inter-viewees simply wanted to meet like-minded people in a safe-place where they could engage freely in conversations about controversial issues pertaining to religion and scepticism without causing offense to others. That to me seemed like a quintessen-tially Canadian answer—that one would want to join an atheist club so as not to cause offense—and it serves as an example of one of the main differences between that Canadian atheist community and American atheist communities. That it did cause some offense, and that many of its members were sensitive to that also speaks to the Canadian experience, as does the fact that others felt that causing offense was justified in the name of free expression and questioning religious beliefs (which they considered "ideologies" that can be debated). Overall, that the group discussed their public persona, and individuals held different opinions of what that should be, calls attention to the importance of not painting all atheists, even those within the same community, with the same brush.

4 Key Concepts

Agnostic: "Agnosticism" (from the Greek: *a* referring to "without" or "not" and *gnostic* referring to "knowledge") was coined by a contemporary of Charles Darwin, Thomas Henry (T.H.) Huxley, in the nineteenth century. While Huxley believed that science provided humans with knowledge, he did not believe that science could tell us anything about God. Today those who self-identify as agnostic are usually identifying with the notion that it is not possible for humans to know if there is a god or not: the answer is beyond human capabilities of understanding. Agnostics are often referred to, however, as those who "sit on a fence" between theism and atheism because they "can't make up their minds." This caricature misses the point that most self-identified agnostics believe that neither side of "the fence" has access to evidence pertaining to God's existence.

Anti-theist: An anti-theist is an atheist who is antagonistic toward religion. Far from apathetic or welcoming to religion, anti-theists tend to view religion as a cause of social ill. The most famous anti-theist is arguably the late Christopher Hitchens. There is presently a lacuna of research on anti-theism as a subset of atheism, in Canada and elsewhere.

Atheism: Atheism is a term derived from the Ancient Greek word *atheos*: *a* refers to "without" or "not," and *theos* refers to "god." *Atheist* entered the English language in the sixteenth century as an accusatory term. Today the term, in a Canadian context, usually refers to those who self-identify as not believing in the existence of god, gods, or goddesses.

Atheist Bus Campaign: The Atheist Bus Campaign was a global phenomenon that originated in the United Kingdom in 2008 as a response to Evangelical bus advertisements, which urged viewers to visit a website that threatened non-believers with an eternity in Hell. The slogan "There's Probably No God. Now Stop Worrying and Enjoy Your Life" ran across the UK and influenced atheist advertisement campaigns in at least fifteen countries, from Brazil to New Zealand.

Humanist: Humanitarianism, as a movement, began in the nineteenth century by English Christian Unitarians and Universalists. In the twentieth century, liberal Humanitarianism as a movement began questioning theism and advocating secularism. "Humanism" is derived from that movement, and today it is largely affiliated with atheism and agnosticism. It commonly refers to a secular philosophy that advocates compassion for other humans, and it is associated with a lack of traditional religiosity, although in some instances humanists embrace social elements that have religious connotations but are not necessarily religious, such as rites of passage.

New Atheism: New Atheism is a neologism that was born from media interest in bestselling books about religion by atheist authors (which arrived on the scene at roughly the same time) and from the willingness of the authors to maintain a united front in order to increase public space for atheism. The most cited New Atheists, along with their books about religion, are: *The End of Faith: Religion, Terror, and the Future of Rea*son (2004) and *Letter to a Christian Nation* (2006) by Sam Harris;

The God Delusion (2006) by Richard Dawkins; *God is not Great: How Religion Poisons Everything* (2007) by Christopher Hitchens; and *Breaking the Spell: Religion as a Natural Phenomenon* (2006) by Daniel Dennett.

Nonreligion: "Non-religion" or "nonreligion" is a term that denotes anything which is primarily defined by a relationship of difference to religion, which is a definition authored by Lois Lee (2012) and commonly used in Religious Studies and related fields.

Religious Nones: "Religious nones" is a statistical category in Canada which denotes those who profess no religion on censuses. This category includes atheists, agnostics, humanists, the other related terms, as well as those who—for a multitude of reasons—do not want to share their religious persuasion on surveys. Religious nones is an umbrella term that includes self-identified atheists and other people who do not belong to a religion, as well as those who wish to shelter their religiosities from others.

Secularization/Secularism/Secular: Secularization theory has its origin in an Enlightenment-era assumption of the inevitable decline of religion, and it has been debated, dismissed, rewritten, and embraced by numerous social scientists. Colloquially, secularism generally refers to social spaces, such as governmental institutions, being free from overt religious influence. Being "secular" also refers to individuals who are not religious. On one extreme, secularization, secularism, and secular can refer to lack of individual religiosity. On the other, it refers to religion as a private practice, rather than a public practice. Atheists, such as the New Atheists, commonly refer to the "secular" as diametrically opposed to the "religious".

5   Statistics

According to Statistics Canada, in 2011 23.9% of Canadians reported having "no religion" when asked to identify their religion. This is an increase from 12% in 1991 and 16% in 2001: 0.1% short of doubling in ten years. The 2004 Statistics Canada General Social Survey found that Canadians between 15–29 years of age were the largest age category to identify as having no religious affiliation, at 23%. It is important to note that Statistics Canada does not document how many Canadians self-identify in more than one category, such as Jewish atheists, or "culturally Catholic" agnostics, for example, so these statistics, while useful for showing basic trends, do not in and of themselves tell the whole story. Figure 3 below shows relevant statistics by region.

	% of population who report having no religion	% of population who report having no belief in God	% of population who report never attending a religious service	% of population who report never praying or meditating
Canada	33.9	17.7	43.1	34.8
Atlantic	15.8	11.2	35.7	31.5
British Columbia	44.1	23.2	55.1	42.3
Ontario	23.1	16.6	38.3	31.3
Prairies	29.3	14.6	41.7	32.1
Quebec	12.1	20.5	47.2	39.2
Territories	31.4	N/A	N/A	N/A

Fig. 3 Indicators of Non-Religion in Canada: Percentage of Canadians who report having no religion, having no belief in God, never attend a religious service, and never pray or meditate, 2011. The findings that were used to create this table were generated by Dr. Sarah Wilkins-Laflamme using data from the 2011 National Household Survey (Statistics Canada), the 2011 General Social Survey (Statistics Canada), the 2006 CROP 3SC survey on religious beliefs (CROP), and the 1971 and 1991 Censuses (Statistics Canada) (Wilkins-Laflamme 2014)

6 Current Challenges and Future Opportunities

There is a challenge in thinking of novel sources for uncovering the history of atheism in Canada, but this also provides an opportunity for future research. Newspapers, case law, church attendance statistics, memoirs, and interviews with elders are some potential avenues that could raise our understanding of atheists in the past. Likewise, when it comes to studying contemporary atheists, gaining access to the opinions of those who are apathetic to religion and who do not belong to any atheist community may be challenging. One solution is snowball sampling, in which interviewees are recruited by former interviewees through word of mouth. A drawback to snowball sampling is that the interviewees may speak to a "type" of atheist that is not representative of other atheists. Similarly, interviewing members of an atheist community is a practical way to find potential interviewees, but they may speak to a small, unrepresentative, segment of atheists.

A related opportunity is the need for more regional, provincial, and local studies of atheists and atheist communities, but a challenge is in not portraying all atheists and religious nones as the same based on the few studies that have been published. Findings may suggest similarities within a local group, but care should be given to avoiding associating those results with the experience and opinions of atheists in other locations.

Given that minorities (religious/ethnic) and religious groups are often viewed as "potential customers" by politicians looking for votes, the steady growth of religious nones means there is a possibility that politicians will start catering to religious nones. This would present a new avenue of research: interactions between atheism and governance. The Centre for Inquiry, for example, has invited politicians to speak at some events, and they have been engaged with the federal government's (now defunct) Office of Religious Freedom, arguing on behalf of persecuted atheists in other countries. In terms of political affiliations, atheists, like Christians, do not belong to one party, but research suggests that active, or communal, atheists tend to be liberal on many social issues but critical of regulating free speech. On the other hand, there has been division in some atheist communities pertaining to the embrace—or rejection—of feminism, as well as the criticism of Islam, both issues point to the difficulty of ascribing to "freethinkers" a collective ideology.

7 Questions for Critical Thought

1. How can we unearth a history of atheism in Canada? What sources can we use?
2. Since it is increasing, and is now at just shy of a quarter of the population, does the "religious nones" category really constitute a minority group in Canada?
3. If the sociological academic study of atheism in Western countries is at its infancy, where does the academic study of atheism in non-Western countries place? Why should this be—or not be—of interest to Canadian scholars of religion and sociology?

8 Online Educational Resources

A Debate: Sam Harris, Christopher Hitchens, & Daniel Dennett vs. Dinesh D'Souza, Nassim Taleb, Robert Wright, & Rabbi Shmuley Boteach: https://www.youtube.com/watch?v=HAmdbBWluYE

The YouTube title is *Epic Debate: Hitchens, Harris & Dennett vs Boteach, D'Souza, & more #religiondebate #newatheists*. The original title of this debate, which took place in Puebla, Mexico, November 8, 2008, is *Ciudad de las Ideas*. There are plenty of debates on religion and atheism, and between religious spokespeople and atheist spokespeople, on YouTube. This one features three new atheists (Christopher Hitchens, Sam Harris, and Daniel Dennett) arguing that God does not exist and four theists (Shmuley Boteach, Dinesh D'Souza, Robert Wright, and Nassim Taleb) arguing that God exists.

Atheist Research Collaborative: http://atheistresearch.org/

The Atheist Research Collaborative is an organization that provides nonreligious individuals a platform for contributing academic research on topics pertaining to the sociology and psychology of atheism and nonreligion.

Institute for the Study of Secularism in Society and Culture (ISSSC):

http://www.trincoll.edu/Academics/centers/isssc/Pages/default.aspx

The Institute for the Study of Secularism in Society and Culture (ISSSC) is a multidisciplinary institute that conducts original research, hosts lectures, conferences, and seminars, and sponsors curriculum development on the topic of contemporary societal and cultural secularization.

Nonreligion and Secularity Research Network (NSRN): https://nsrn.net/

The Nonreligion and Secularity Research Network (NSRN) is an international network of researchers on the topic of nonreligion and secularity. It features interviews, blogs, and conference summaries.

Secularism and Nonreligion: http://www.secularismandnonreligion.org/

Secularism and Nonreligion is an interdisciplinary, open access, peer-reviewed journal dedicated to secularism and nonreligion.

9 Further Reading

Beaman, L. G. and Tomlins, S. (2015). *Atheist identities: Spaces and social contexts*. Cham: Springer International.

This academic volume is the first to focus on atheism and identity. Based on a trans-Atlantic workshop, it features chapters from American, Canadian, and British scholars about varies ways atheists express their nonreligious identities in the United States, Canada, and the United Kingdom. Topics include self-identity and descriptors, collective atheism, legal rulings, and post-Enlightenment era historiography.

LeDrew, S. (2015). *The evolution of atheism: The politics of a modern movement*. New York: Oxford University Press.

Based on extensive research, including interviews with Canadians, for his PhD thesis, this book explains the history of two types of atheism that are prevalent today: scientific atheism (such as the New Atheists), which emphasizes individualism and the authority of science, and humanist atheism, which emphasizes ethics and social justice.

Lightman, B. (1987). *The origins of agnosticism: Victorian unbelief and the limits of knowledge*. Baltimore: The Johns Hopkins University Press.

This book is a well-researched history of agnosticism as a social alternative to religion following debates about evolution in Victorian England. Besides documenting an interesting period where the interactions between science and religion were widely debated, it offers nuance to the term agnosticism and what it meant for those who identified as agnostics in the nineteenth century.

Martin, M. (2007). *The Cambridge companion to atheism.* Cambridge: Cambridge University Press.

This is a solid collection of essays about atheism that provides a good general introduction to many scholarly sub-topics and disciplines, including the ancient and modern history of atheism, terminology, statistical analysis, feminism, philosophy, sociology, theology, and psychology.

Thiessen, J. (2015). *The meaning of Sunday: The practice of belief in a secular age.* Montreal: McGill-Queen's University Press.

This book is based on interviews with three groups of Canadians: weekly attendees of religious services, those who attend religious services primarily only for holidays and rites of passage, and those never attend religious services. It explores the meanings and motivations behind beliefs and practices, and postulates what a waning demand for religion means for Canadian society.

Wilkins-Laflamme, S. (2015). How unreligious are the religious 'Nones'? Religious dynamics of the unaffiliated in Canada. *Canadian Journal of Sociology*, 40 (4), 477–500.

This journal article utilizes statistical analysis to paint a contemporary picture of Religious Nones in Canada. It weaves together data from various sources and offers nuance to the irreligious views and behaviors of a large segment of Canadians and offers provincial and territorial comparisons.

10   Researcher Background

Steven Tomlins obtained his Bachelor of Arts at the University of Prince Edward Island with a major in Religious Studies and a double minor in Political Studies and Art History, graduating with the highest academic standing in the final year of his program. In 2016, he obtained his Doctorate degree in Religious Studies from the University of Ottawa with his thesis, "Navigating Atheist Identities: An Analysis of Nonreligious Perceptions and Experiences in the Religiously Diverse Canadian City of Ottawa." He has also studied multiculturalism, secularism, religion and the media, and the intersections between religious expression and Canadian law, and he is currently interested in the historical use of Commonwealth blasphemy laws. He is co-editor of two international academic volumes pertaining to atheist identities and nonreligious expression: *Atheist Identities: Spaces and Social Contexts*, with Lori G. Beaman, (Switzerland: Springer International, 2015), and *The Atheist Bus Campaign: Global Manifestations and Responses*, with Spencer C. Bullivant (The Netherlands: Brill, 2016). He presently works at the Institute on Governance, a nonprofit think tank where he contributes research and policy options related to evolving governance models in the twenty-first Century context in areas such as governing in a digital age; the evolving characteristics of nation-to-nation (Indigenous/Crown) relations in Canada and models of multilevel/inter-jurisdictional governance.

References

Adams, F. (1965a, July 23). Clapping Bergsmas hail news they can become Canadians. The Globe and Mail, p 1.

Adams, F. (1965b, October 5). Award Dutch family citizenship papers without taking oath. The Globe and Mail, p 35.

Bain, G. (1964a, September 21) Freedom of religion? *The Globe and Mail*, p 7.

Bain, G. (1964b, October 8) The supremacy of god? *The Globe and Mail*, p 7.

Cimino, R., & Smith, C. (2015). Secularist rituals in the US: Solidarity and legitimization. In L. G. Beaman & S. Tomlins (Eds.), *Atheist identities: Spaces and social contexts* (pp. 87–100). Cham: Springer International.

Criminal Code, R.S., 1985, c. C-46.

Enright, M. (2013, September 29) Michael's essay: Could atheists please stop complaining? *CBC Radio*. Retrieved from: http://www.cbc.ca/thesundayedition/essays/2013/09/29/atheists-stop-whining/

Formosa, K. "Athiest [sic] instigators: Muhammad makes appearance on campus." *The Fulcrum*. http://thefulcrum.ca/2011/10/athiest-instigators/. October 12, 2011.

House of Commons Debates. (1965). 26th Parliament, 2nd Session: Vol. 12, 12935–12936.

Keith, S. (2011). "In defense of U of O atheists." *The Fulcrum. Letters. Print edition. November*, 2.

Lee, L. (2012). Research note: Talking about a revolution: Terminology for the new field of non-religion studies. *Journal of Contemporary Religion, January*, 27(1), 129–139.

Lewis, C. (2010, December 5). Dear atheists: Most of us don't care what you think *National Post*. Retrieved from: http://life.nationalpost.com/2010/12/05/dear-atheists-most-of-us-dont-care-what-you-think/#ixzz17MpnptOq

Ottawa Citizen (1965, April 2). Couple's Plea: Has Canada no room for atheist citizens? *Ottawa Citizen*. p 7.

Patrick, J. (2008). Not dead just sleeping: Canada's prohibition on blasphemous libel as a case study in obsolete legislation. *U.B.C Law Review, 41*(2), 193–248.

Smith, J. M. (2013). Creating a godless community: The collective identity work of contemporary American atheists. *Journal for the Scientific Study of Religion, 52*(1), 80–99.

Statistics Canada (2013). *The Daily: National Household Survey: Immigration, place of birth, citizenship, ethnic origin, visible minorities, language and religion*. Retrieved from: http://www.statcan.gc.ca/daily-quotidien/130508/dq130508b-eng.htm. Accessed 4 June, 2013

Wilkins-Laflamme, S. (December 2014) Report: Religion in Canada, *Centre d'études ethniques des universités montréalaises* (CEETUM).

Conclusion: The Changing Shape of Religious Diversity

Lori G. Beaman

Keywords Religious diversity · Religion and Diversity Project · Religious identity · Management of diversity · Complexity · Nonreligious

Diversity is a key buzzword in the lexicon of academics, governments and publics. It seeks to capture the range of human possibilities, but is also subject to regulation and management. This edited collection has captured a wide range of the key discussion points in conversations that have taken place within the Religion and Diversity Project, which I directed for 7 years (2010–2017) and with which many of the authors in this volume were involved.

Now in its final stages, the Religion and Diversity Project involved 37 researchers at 24 universities in five countries (Canada, France, Australia, England and the United States). Situated at the intersection of sociology, political science, religious studies, and law, this programme of research addressed the following central question: *What are the contours of religious diversity in Canada and how can we best respond to the opportunities and challenges presented by religious diversity in ways that promote a just and peaceful society?* Our approach combined multiple methods, reflecting the many disciplines we represented as a team. We used surveys, qualitative methods, video narratives, and discourse analysis, and we disseminated our results in many ways, including on our website <www.religionanddiversity.ca>.

L. G. Beaman (✉)
Department of Classics and Religious Studies, University of Ottawa, Ottawa, ON, Canada
e-mail: lbeaman@uottawa.ca

© Springer International Publishing AG, part of Springer Nature 2018
C. Holtmann (ed.), *Exploring Religion and Diversity in Canada*,
https://doi.org/10.1007/978-3-319-78232-4_12

The Religion and Diversity Project was organized around four thematic strands: 1. religious identity; 2. defining and delimiting religion in law; 3. gender and sexuality as flashpoint issues; and 4. alternative strategies in the management of religious diversity. The discursive and practical uses that are made of ideas of "religious diversity" were at the centre of this research. Its two main aims were (a) to understand how these ideas are constructed, deployed and criticized in private and public contexts that include social scientific data and research, political and legal debates, and policy making, and (b) to consider how best to respond to the opportunities and challenges presented by the variety of meanings attributed to religious diversity in ways that promote a just and peaceful society. The project's main contribution was to identify in detail the contours of religious diversity in Canada and the potential benefits of approaches to diversity that promote deep equality and move beyond tolerance and accommodation. This comparative research thus placed Canada in the context of other western democracies and explored global patterns in responses to religious diversity. The project provided new data and theoretical articulations concerning religious diversity, which it framed as a resource, and proposed strategies for equality that advance knowledge and enhance public policy decision-making.

One of the key questions of the project related to the so-called management of diversity. From a critical scholarship perspective, management is very often equated with control and perhaps all too often associated with the preservation of existing power relations.

Approaching diversity as something to be managed also implies that it is a problem to be dealt with. We tried to modestly reshape the language around this by suggesting, for example, that increased religious diversity presents both challenges and opportunities.

It was impossible to anticipate all of the issues that would emerge in such a large project at the design phase, and one of our goals was to remain flexible in order to respond to issues as they emerged. For instance, 8 years ago we could not have foreseen that an important emerging area within the study of religious diversity is actually nonreligion and its impact on the broader project of living well together. This, together with increased immigration and the magnification of diversity, makes for a dynamic and exciting field of study. As Cathy Holtmann mentions in Chap. 1, technology, globalization, uncertainty, and inequality are all part of this picture.

Although we divided our work as a research team into 4 thematic strands, these areas clearly relate to each other and thus are not completely separable. In fact, our goal as the project progressed was to weave the strands together such that we might be able to tell a coherent story about religion and diversity in Canada. All of the chapters in this volume consider more than one of the core themes we identified as we mapped the direction for our project. Our themes, however, provide a salient beginning point from which to think about the myriad issues that circulate within the framework of the broader project.

The identity theme focused on the social and cultural context in which people, institutions, and narratives conceptualize and construct religious identities. It critically assessed how religion is understood, shaped, and deployed as a category of identity within various contexts such as the media, education, scientific research environments, and religious groups themselves. Simply put, we considered how people engage with religion in everyday life, and also how their experiences are shaped by social institutions such as the media and law. In turn, we also thought about religious identities' impact on social institutions. In Chap. 7, Steve McMullin considers both directions of this relationship in his discussion of church use of digital media, which is prompted by social pressures to be 'relevant', but in turn shapes the media. As McMullin points out, religion's place in society is changing, but so too is the way people practice their religion. This of course means that those who study religion need to revise their tools too.

Religious institutions themselves impact on religious expression, a fact that is poignantly illustrated by Nancy Nason-Clark's portrayal in Chap. 3 of an abused Christian woman who seeks help within her church. As Nason-Clark's discussion makes clear, religious institutions have the potential to effectively address serious social problems like violence against women, though they do not always competently marshal that potential.

Identity diversity within religious groups and organizations also played a role in our project. For example, Paul Gareau's research in Chap. 8 highlights the various ways Catholic youth construct their identities within the context of the new evangelism and, specifically, the impact of *Journey to the Father*. As Gareau observes, one of the biggest surprises for him in conducting this research was the complexity of youth identities: where he expected conservative, hardline approaches, he found an amalgam of commitment to religion and to secular values with no apparent dissonance for his participants. His research found a wide range of interpretations of Catholicism within that broader identity descriptor.

Further, lived religion asks us to consider the variable ways that people practice their religion, but also the contexts within which they do so. In Chap. 10, Jennifer Selby makes this point vividly through the voice of Dina, one of her interviewees in her research in Newfoundland. Selby's discussion reminds us that histories, current events, and day to day interactions shape our ability to be who we are religiously. Selby also reminds us that race is frequently an intersectional companion to religion, complicating singular identity labels and our own identity constructions. A number of chapters in this book press us to ask what are the social consequences and implications when one cannot fully express one's identity—whether religious or nonreligious. However, at the same time, we are also reminded that as carriers of multiple identities it is important not to essentialize people through one identity. Finally, identities are dynamic: people change throughout the life course and, thus, their own self-descriptors do too.

Although identity is important, as Heather Shipley makes clear in Chap. 4, a singular focus on one identity can occlude others which are equally as, and indeed perhaps more, important in everyday life. Moreover, the intersection of identities, like religion and sexuality, have a profound impact on the daily organization of life. The Religion, Gender, Sexuality and Youth project, the results of which Shipley reports, brings alive the complexity of studying identity, which is fluid and multifaceted. It also addresses what we called important flashpoints for issues of religious diversity in Canada. In this thematic area (gender and sexuality) we were especially interested in the ways in which gender and religion intersect in a manner that attracts public, legal and policy attention. Drawing on interviews done under the RGSY initiative, Shipley reveals the complexity of sexuality as it is expressed by religious, spiritual but not religious and nonreligious youth. Shipley also found that both religious and secular spaces can be unwelcoming spaces for youth when it comes to sexuality.

Gender also continues to be an important site of study within religious diversity and within religion itself. McMullin's discussion in Chap. 7 of female clergy and the continuing discrimination they face illustrates the salience of gender in discussions of religion and diversity. Though religion is often singled out as being especially patriarchal, one need only look to the boardrooms of corporations or our government to see that women are still, even in 2018, in the minority. From this vantage point patriarchy clearly knows no bounds.

In Chap. 2, Cathy Holtmann also emphasizes the importance of gender, but from a different angle: the way that Muslim women practice their religion is different from that of men. Once again, we also see the importance of intersectionality in Holtmann's discussion: the experience of being an immigrant adds another dimension to a religious identity. Holtmann uses the term ethno-religious diversity to capture some of complexity of the intersections she observed in her research. Holtmann's chapter prompts another important question about internal diversity, especially given the influx of Syrian refugees, some of whom are observant Muslim, some Orthodox Christian, but many who do not have a religious identity at all. This is part of the new diversity that Canada is experiencing and that requires a response that respects religious identities without assuming them.

Another major theme in the Religion and Diversity Project considered the ways that religion is defined and delimited in the context of law and public policy. Our aim was to trace the relation between the ideals associated with freedom of religion and state neutrality and the practical expression of these ideals in social, political and legal practices. Though this theme has a heavy emphasis on law, Leo Van Arragon's research, in Chap. 5, illustrates the ways in which religion is regulated, often through law, within education. Again, we see the importance of social institutions in thinking about religious diversity. Van Arragon's chapter also illustrates the links between ideas about good citizenship and appropriate religious expression. Religious minorities have been especially burdened with breaking down narrow conceptualizations of citizenship—the fight for Sikhs to wear their turbans as members of the RCMP and, more recently, Zunera Ishaq's fight to wear a niqab while swearing her oath of Canadian citizenship are two examples. As Van Arragon points out, education is a key site for the propagation of 'Canadian values' which may or may not regulate or control particular religious groups. Moreover, it is important to be aware of historical patterns related to religion's place in the education system: the historical conceptualization of Canada as a Christian country has present day implications.

In Chap. 6, Lisa Smith considers the role of religion in healthcare, noting the historical role religious groups played in establishing and maintaining the healthcare system in Canada and the pertinence of life and death to both healthcare and religion. Occasionally religious commitment and healthcare collide, sometimes in ways that are difficult to resolve. One such conflict is whether physicians have a duty to inform their female patients of reproductive health options such as abortion and birth control. Assisted death is also currently a topic of great interest within the religion-healthcare dynamic, with some religious groups supporting Canada's move toward the possibility of physician assisted death and others opposed—both on religious grounds. These issues raise the challenges of living in a country with diverse groups and diversity within groups.

The idea of moving beyond tolerance and accommodation as strategies for the 'management' of diversity has informed our conversation and has proven to be an intriguing point of difference with some of our European counterparts. Our fourth theme considers the ways social, political and legal discourse have tended to rely on the maintenance of an "other" and explores how it might be possible to move to models based on inclusion. As Amélie Barras notes in Chap. 9, reasonable accommodation has shifted from being a rather tightly bound legal concept to one which has much broader application. One criticism of accommodation is that it reifies majorities and minorities such that minorities become the "other". Barras' innovative work on this identifies a major problem with the process involved: minorities are therefore always positioned as "requesting" accommodation. In her words: "Managers, on the one hand, come out as thoughtful actors capable of flexibility and innovation. Requesters, on the other hand, appear as quite passive and inflexible in this framework." Hierarchies are thus reproduced rather than broken down. In my own work, I have proposed the use of a robust, grounded conceptualization of equality to frame the negotiation of difference, a process and concept I've named *deep equality*. In this research, together with Jennifer Selby, we've explored the ways in which Muslims navigate and negotiate everyday life, focusing on dialogue and respect between actors. Though institutional protections such as those offered by law are important, often overlooked are these everyday interactions that can offer insight into modes of difference negotiation that displace rather than reinforce hierarchies of difference.

A key component of our project was that of changing landscapes, by which we meant both geographic and less spatially confined areas, such as shifts in technology within organized religion and its place in the larger society, the Syrian refugee crisis, and the religious dimensions of populism to name just a few changes. The researchers whose work is included in this volume each must contend with these continuously shifting grounds in their own research. As I write this we are conducting a project in Montreal that maps geographic sites of change—former churches that have become condominiums or community facilities that are not religious; two different religious groups sharing common worship space; a business location that is now a mosque, and so on. We also have developed a survey on religious identity that is attempting to capture the dimensions of nonreligion and to meet the challenge of asking people what nonreligion or being not religious looks like in day to day life. Both of these projects respond to the rapidly shifting ground of religious diversity.

As our Religion and Diversity Project comes to an end we find ourselves on yet another edge of diversity: when we began the project we were primarily interested in religious diversity and its management. However, as we worked through a wide range of issues, some of which are included in this volume, the next major issue on the horizon, in addition to continuing to consider the contours of religious diversity and its impact on society, is the significant portion of people in many countries who describe themselves as nonreligious. Steven Tomlins documents the rather broad parameters of this group in Chap. 11, where he explores atheism in Canada. This emerging category has unclear boundaries and issues of identity, practice and beliefs are as yet still understudied by scholars. But, despite this growth in nones and the non-affiliated, religion is highly unlikely to disappear. Rather, this unfolding chapter in diversity highlights a new challenge—how do those who are religiously committed live well with those who have no religious affiliation, including atheists, agnostics, humanists, or the indifferent? The challenges associated with studying the nonreligious make this a particularly daunting task. However, by focusing on areas of shared interest, rather than religion or nonreligion per se, it is possible to uncover some of the complexities of this new diversity. In my own research with volunteers who work on sea turtle conservation I have discovered that such world repairing work is an important site of collaboration both for people who self-describe as religious and those who identify as nonreligious. A shared focus on the well-being of sea turtles becomes the defining point of similarity across difference for the volunteers (see Beaman 2017). Nason-Clark, in Chap. 3, offers a further example of what is at stake: violence against women and intimate partner violence cannot be adequately addressed without cooperation and collaboration from service providers across all sectors. This is the case for any number of pressing social issues, from poverty to climate change. Thus, while studying religious diversity remains important, the focus on diversity must be expanded to meet this new social reality.

Acknowledgement I would like to acknowledge the support of the Religion and Diversity Project in the preparation of this chapter as well as the ongoing financial support of my research through my Canada Research Chair in Religious Diversity and Social Change.

Reference

Beaman, L. G. (2017). Living well together in a (non)religious future: Contributions from the sociology of religion. *Sociology of Religion, 78*(1), 9–32.

Index

© Springer International Publishing AG, part of Springer Nature 2018
C. Holtmann (ed.), *Exploring Religion and Diversity in Canada*,
https://doi.org/10.1007/978-3-319-78232-4

CPSIA information can be obtained
at www.ICGtesting.com
Printed in the USA
LVHW02*0212280618
582163LV00007B/72/P